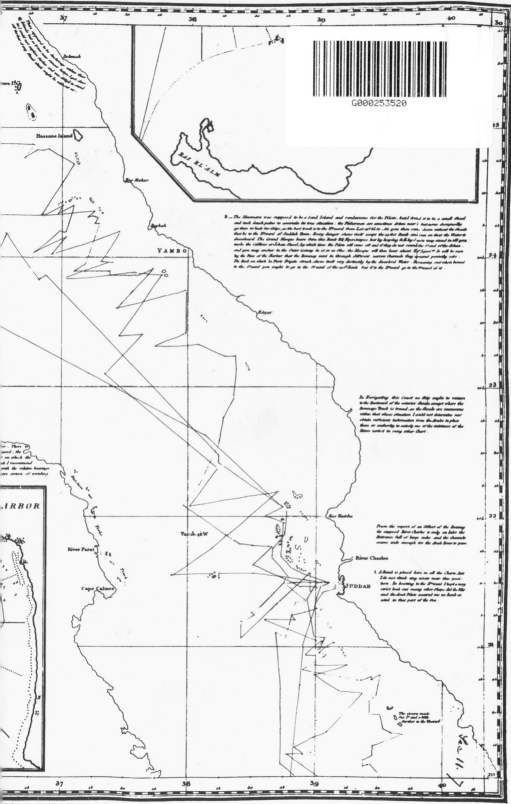
G000253520

A DAMNED CUNNING FELLOW

With the author's compliments &
best wishes -
Christmas '91.

Hugh Popham

A DAMNED
CUNNING FELLOW

—•◦•—

The Eventful Life of
Rear-Admiral Sir Home Popham
KCB, KCH, KM, FRS
1762-1820

Foreword by
John Keegan

Copyright © Hugh Popham and Mary Popham 1991

This book is copyright under the Berne Convention.
No reproduction without permission. All rights reserved.

First published in Great Britain in 1991 by
The Old Ferry Press, 53 Vicarage Road, Tywardreath, Cornwall PL24 2PH

British Library Cataloguing in Publication Data

Popham, Hugh 1920-
"A damned cunning fellow": the eventful life of Rear-Admiral Sir Home
Popham, KCB, KCH, KM, FRS (1762-1820)
1. Great Britain. Royal Navy
I. Title
359.331092

ISBN 0-9516758-0-X

Set and printed in 10 on 11½ Point Times by Blackfords of Cornwall,
Holmbush Industrial Estate, St Austell, Cornwall PL25 3JL
Designed by Clive Tunnicliffe Associates

For Peter by request
with love

By the same author

Poetry
Against the Lightning
The Journey and the Dream
To the Unborn—Greetings

Prose
Beyond the Eagle's Rage
Sea Flight
Cape of Storms
Monsters and Marlinspikes
The Sea Beggars
The Shores of Violence
The House at Cane Garden
The Somerset Light Infantry
The Dorset Regiment
Into Wind: a History of British Naval Flying
Gentlemen Peasants
A Thirst for the Sea: the Sailing Adventures of Erskine Childers
F.A.N.Y.—The Story of the Women's Transport Service, 1904-1984

Contents

Illustrations

Frontispiece

Captain Sir Home Riggs Popham, KM, FRS, by Mather Brown, c.1806. *(By courtesy of Mr Walter Impert, Los Angeles.)*

Plates *(between pages 128 & 129)*

Home Riggs Popham as a lieutenant, c.1793. Formerly attributed to Mather Brown, now regarded as being by an unknown artist. *(National Portrait Gallery, London.)*

Edward Thompson, Popham's first captain. *(Reproduced by Courtesy of the Trustrees of the British Museum.)*

Sketch by Thomas Boulden Thompson, initialled TBT, of the *Padrao* erected at Angra Pequena—the modern Luderitz—in 1486 by Bartolomeo Diaz. *(From Narrative of a Voyage performed in HMS Nautilus . . . By Courtesy of Quentin Keynes, Esq.)*

Sketches of natives of Namibia, also by Thompson.

Chart of South Channel, Prince of Wales Island (Penang) by Home Popham, 1791. *(By Courtesy of the Hydrographic Office, Ministry of Defence.)*

Political cartoon by Jekyll, 23 June 1798, satirising the conflicting accounts of Popham's attack on the Saas Lock, Ostend. *(Reproduced by Courtesy of the Trustees of the British Museum.)*

Paul I, Tsar of Russia. *(Hulton-Deutsch Collection)*

Engraved portrait of Popham by Hastings. *(Reproduced by Courtesy of the Trustees of the British Museum.)*

Silver tea-kettle presented to Popham by the East India Company. *(Photo by Courtesy of Boris Reford, Esq. Montreal.)*

The landing at Lospard's Bay, Cape Colony, January 1806. *(This, the following three engravings, and that of the Scheldt, are from Robert Fernyhough's Military Memoirs of Four Brothers.)*

The landing of the Sea Battalion at Cape Town.

Landing at Quilmes, River Plate, June 1806.

Buenos Ayres, from *Narcissus.*

Sir Home Popham, KM, FRS. An engraving derived from Mather Brown's portrait. *(Reproduced by Courtesy of the Trustees of the British Museum).*

Seals of Popham's Arms, and combined with those of Prince, his wife. *(From, respectively, the Cultural History Museum, Cape Town, and the Africana Museum.)*

Passage of the Western Scheldt forced, August 1809.

King Christophe of Haiti by Richard Evans *(Hulton-Deutsch Collection.)*

Two versions of Portsmouth Signal Station, c.1822. *(By Courtesy of the National Maritime Museum, Greenwich.)*

Home Popham's memorial at Sunninghill, with two details from the plinth. *(Photo, P. Mason.)*

In the text

Endpapers

Front: Detail from Home Popham's chart of the Red Sea. *(Reproduced by Courtesy of the Trustees of the British Museum.)*

Back: 'England expects . . . ' Nelson's signal before Trafalgar using Popham's code.

Operating mechanism of Popham's *Land Telegraph,* as submitted to the RSA. *(Reproduced with their permission.)*

Foreword
by John Keegan

IT IS a great mystery why no life of Admiral Sir Home Popham has previously appeared. He was the inventor of the first practicable system of visual signalling between ships, and one which remains in use to this day. It was with his flags that the most famous of all naval messages, 'England expects . . . ' was made at Trafalgar; and before that, Nelson had depended on his 'chain of frigates', transmitting news of their sightings through the Popham codebook, to maintain his blockade of the French fleet in Toulon.

Many previous attempts had been made to devise a system of signalling with flags that would transmit unambiguous messages rapidly and concisely. None had proved satisfactory. Popham's achievement compares with that of Roget in the compilation of the first thesaurus. He analysed how language was used and perceived a means of tabulating its elements and then encoding the results in the smallest practicable compass. It was an extraordinary intellectual feat, brought off single-handed, and in an astonishingly short time; and it remained in use, virtually unmodified, until this century.

Popham, however, was not only a naval intellectual. He was also a dashing sea warrior and an adventurer on His Majesty's Service in the troubled distant waters of the world during the Royal Navy's epic years in the French wars, from the American Revolution to Napoleon. C. S. Forester—who was fascinated by Popham's system, and did much to propagate knowledge of it among the lay reading public—may not have used the admiral as a model for Hornblower, but he cannot have failed to incorporate elements of his character and personality in his hero. Hornblower's interest in the improvement of naval science undoubtedly owes much to what Forester knew of Popham.

It is particularly appropriate that the admiral's life should now be written by someone who is related to him, if only distantly, and who is an experienced author. Another writer might have been content merely to represent his subject as a naval inventor, and to play down the ingredients of action and adventure in his career. Hugh Popham has written a colourful and exciting biography, which is an important contribution to the history of the Royal Navy in its golden age. It will be read with enjoyment by anyone interested in naval history—and with self-reproach by some professional naval historians, who may well wonder why such a significant British sea officer has had to wait so long for a full-scale biography.

CHAPTER I

The Moroccan Consul's Son 1762-78

1

THE INFANT who would one day become Rear-Admiral Sir Home Riggs Popham, Knight Commander of the Bath, Knight Commander of the Royal Guelphic Order, Knight of Malta, and a Fellow of the Royal Society, was born in Gibraltar in October 1762. His mother, Mary, died either giving him birth or very soon afterwards: there are alternative versions. Her death 'if we are accurately informed', the *Naval Chronicle* wrote in a biographical sketch of her son in 1806, 'was occasioned by the circumstances of Admiral Gell's firing a salute at a period when the enemy were expected. The consequence was that she died before Sir Home was in the world.' However, the family bible, in which his birth and that of his elder brother—though not of his sisters—is recorded, suggests a less melodramatic start in life.

'My son Home Riggs', his father Joseph noted 'was born 12 October 1762 on Sunday at 2 o'clock in Gibraltar; his mother departed this life in about one hour after.' Of the two, this sounds the more authentic; but the fact that there should be two differing accounts of the circumstances of his birth is entirely appropriate. There were alternative versions of almost all the important events in his life.

Joseph Popham is described as 'of the City of Corke, linnen draper', and was descended from a branch of the family which had settled in Somerset but which having supported Cromwell during the Civil War, appears to have found it prudent to move to Ireland at the Restoration. Further back in time, their ancestry included Queen Elizabeth's Lord Chief Justice, Sir John Popham, master of Littlecote, and the man to whom the Queen had given the job of establishing a Protestant plantation in the South of Ireland in the years before the Armada. The family was thus a part of the Protestant Ascendancy centred on Cork and the neighbouring town of Bandon; and their life during the second half of the seventeenth century was distinctly unhappy, for they formed an intrusive enclave in a hostile and ruined land. Bandon's churchyard is well-populated with Pophams, including the first of the settlers, John Popham, Cromwell's Colonel of Horse.

From Somerset they brought their interest in textiles, for they were all either haberdashers, silk and cotton manufacturers, or followers of related trades. 'The Dowdens and Wheelers and Pophams a score', ran an uncomplimentary little couplet of the time, 'All weavers and dyers—a terrible bore...' Perhaps stung by this, Joseph made his escape, it is believed to India and into the service of the East India Company. Certainly the Company had interests near Bandon, and their ships docked downstream from the town.

This is conjectural. What is not is that on 25 October 1758 Joseph Popham was appointed by George II 'our Consul General to the Emperor of Morocco', and directed to proceed, at the Emperor's wish, to Salée on the north western corner of Africa, facing the Atlantic and close to Rabat. Of it a slightly earlier British resident had written: 'The chief Riches of this Place Consist in its Piracies, the *Salée Rovers* being the most expert and daring of any of the *Barbary* Coast.' Their depredations were to provide Joseph with many of his worst moments.

How he had come to enter the consular service in the first place is not known[1], but three years after his appointment he received a new commission as Consul General in Tetuan, a far more important posting and the place where most of the consuls were stationed; and here he remained, officially, for the next nine years.

To take up his original appointment he arrived in Gibraltar early in 1759; and he stayed there for the next twelve months. The reason for the delay was that Britain was attempting to arrange a treaty with the Emperor, Prince Sidi Mohamet Ben Abdallah, who was holding 350 British subjects captive and using them as pawns in the diplomatic game. It was no moment to join them. The treaty, by which the prisoners were released on payment of a hefty ransom, was not finally agreed until March 1760; and in December, after he had made his number at the Court, Joseph wrote to Pitt, then Minister for War and Foreign Affairs, '...I propose going to Tetuan with my family in a few days'.

From then on he shuttles back and forth from Gibraltar to Africa—ten times in 1763—so there was nothing unusual about Mary being in Gibraltar when her last son was born, nor that Joseph was in Tetuan only a week before. The baby was christened Home Riggs. Riggs was his mother's maiden name, but why he was called Home is uncertain. F. W. Popham says that 'there is little doubt that the name derived from that of a naval officer who probably stood god-parent at his baptism', but provides no supporting evidence for what sounds very like a guess. He may be right; but it is worth noting that the Governor of Gibraltar for the first two years of Joseph's consulship—when he was largely there and not in Morocco—was Lord Home [2]. He had died in April 1761, eighteen months before the boy was born, but Joseph had been in close touch with him and wrote appreciatively of his help; so there seems to be as strong a likelihood that for reasons of friendship, deference or snobbery the child was named after him, as after some unidentified naval officer. Whichever is correct, the name does not appear in the family before that time, but recurs frequently thereafter.*

2

Unfortunately we have no details of the family life of His Majesty's Consul General in Tetuan, either there or on his frequent visits to Gibraltar, though we do know that he lived in the Emperor's Palace in the former, for which he paid a rent of

---

* Including the present author

£150 a year, and also that his second wife Catherine Lamb, whom he married within nine months of Mary's death, bore him three children there. As Joseph had no home leave throughout the eleven years of his consulship, they must have been with him; and towards the end of his time he was writing of 'the very large family in my charge'. When Home was born, his eldest brother William was twenty-two, his youngest Joseph fifteen; and there were almost certainly several younger sisters born in the 1750s, for Joseph is reputed to have had the formidable total of twenty-one children by his two wives, fifteen by Mary and six by Catherine.

Whatever their life was like in that city of narrow streets and secret gardens, of wax and leather merchants, of pirates and Christian slaves, Joseph's was a continuous series of crises.[3] For one thing, the Emperor was arbitrary, autocratic and avaricious. It was his way to send for the Consul General at least once a year, and such royal attendances had to be accompanied by lavish presents for which Joseph's stipend of £400 a year was totally inadequate. In addition to the 'crimson velvet, Barcelona handkerchiefs and brocade' he was expected to bring 'as the other Consuls do', there was the hire of a ship, the payment of an armed escort, and the cost of the barrels of gunpowder which were levied as harbour dues. Within a couple of years at Tetuan he was £1000 in debt, and writing with increasing desperation to the Foreign Secretary. He must have money, he pleads, in order 'to maintain His Majesty's Service in a becoming manner with those Worst of Human Race with whom I have to do'. A few years later his debts had risen to £1500, and a gracious Monarch sent him £300.

Then there was the matter of the Emperor's coach, sent to Gibraltar for repair and delayed by lack of materials. If he did not get it back by May, he wrote to Joseph, 'you are not further to be called English Consul ... I will turn you out of my country.'

And there was the Piracy. In September 1763, to cite just one case, a small British trading vessel, the *Charming Kitty,* was captured by a xebeque from Salée, her cargo plundered, the crew enslaved, and the captain 'bastinadoed almost to death.' The Consul's job was to secure the crew's release and extract compensation—both of which Joseph succeeded in doing, as Ben Abdallah happened to be in one of his pro-British moods. Whereupon, once more, he was summoned to Court, but 'I have neither money to bear my expenses, nor a suitable Present'. Small wonder that when he heard that the post of Consul in Cadiz was vacant, he applied for it—in vain.

Year after year the tale of pillage and murder continues: in 1764 a fishing boat driven to the coast by stress of weather has three of her crew killed and the other three enslaved; in 1765 the *Snow Dove* of Hastings is wrecked. Three of her crew survive, to be stripped, beaten, and put on bread and water: another problem for the Consul General, who makes the usual protest and is packed off to Gibraltar 'by order of the Emperor'. So 'unsteady' is the Emperor's behaviour that most of the English merchants have left in despair, and one of the few who remained, a Mr. Hosier, 'locked himself in his room at Mogador ... and cut his throat, of which he died.'

Joseph could not leave, and did not cut his throat, but the strains of the job come through in his letters to the Secretary of State. In February 1768: 'Thank God no Shipwrecks on the Coast this Winter, nor a Subject captive in the Country...'; and in the following month he asked for six months leave 'for the recovery of my Health which of late has been impaired... I have the Honor of being near ten years in a Country whose Sovereign and People are very difficult to be pleased.' The request was granted, in principle, but a year later he was still there and forced to ask again.

By then, however, he had become *persona non grata*. The year had started well enough, for the Emperor, Joseph wrote, 'had been exceedingly good' in releasing the crew of the *Earl of Sandwich;* but in February a crisis blew up over a ship from Alexandria which had been taken by her Moorish passengers, arrived at Tetuan, and was refused entry. The Emperor ordered the Master to be sent to him, and when Joseph refused to hand him over, or pay the 'one thousand Mexicoes' demanded by the Governor of Tetuan, he was arrested. He was soon released; but this insult to His Majesty's Consul General could not be tolerated, and he was allowed to retire to Gibraltar.

Unfairly as it seems, the incident was taken to reflect badly on him. In June he wrote to Lord Weymouth that he was worried about 'the Emperor's objection to me' and hoped that this would not be a cause for his removal. 'I am well assured by several persons of credit who were then at Morocco that the Emperor never made a point of my being removed as has been given out.' The Government at home thought differently. A report from the Governor of Gibraltar had suggested that he was 'an improper person to serve His Majesty in that capacity, though they consider Mr Popham as an honest, well meaning man, who has attempted to discharge his duty with good intention, though with little success...' And the Secretary of State considered that 'among many reasons which have been alledged as the cause of the Emperor's Disinclination to us at present [is] His Majesty's declared aversion to Mr Popham...'

So in November 1769 Joseph was made the scapegoat for the Government's inability to reach a reasonable relationship with the extremely difficult and unpredictable Emperor Ben Abdallah, was recalled, and a 'Person of more Firmness and Activity' appointed. He returned to England with his family, was granted a pension of £200 a year, and seems to have spent at least some time in Chichester, for his third son Joseph Lamb was born there in 1770. His last two children, both daughters, were born in Guernsey, however, and it is assumed that the family settled there. He died—a disappointed man, one feels—in 1774.

3

Home was then twelve, and had already been a pupil at Westminster School [4] in common with two of his brothers though long after them—for two years. His childhood had been unusual and anything but settled: brought up by a stepmother, and a father constantly beset by money worries, ferried to and fro from Morocco to Gibraltar, brought to an England he had never seen at the age of eight, packed off to school two years later. Only imagination can fill in the details of those early years; and for the succeeding ones, until he joined the navy at sixteen there is only the reference in the *Naval Chronicle*. According to this, the captain of the ship he joined in 1778, Edward Thompson, had 'acted the part of father, of instructor, and of protector, to his boyish years'; and again, 'he was brought up with Sir Thomas Boulden Thompson, the present Controller of the Navy and Thompson's nephew'.

There are good reasons for believing this, for Ned Thompson—'Poet Thompson', as he was nicknamed—was a remarkable man. He had been born in Hull about 1730, had joined the East India Company, but was impressed into the Navy, and promoted Post Captain in 1772. At the same time he wrote poetry, satires and plays, and was a friend of David Garrick and John Wilkes. He was married with a son and daughter, and was one of those men who go out of their way to help and encourage the young. There are mentions of other lads he took under his wing in his journal; but whether Home Popham was one of them, and how this could have come about if so, are unknown. Possibly the East India Company could have provided the link with Joseph. Set against this, the *Naval Chronicle* stated that he was indebted to his brother Stephen for his education.[5]

Home was at Westminster for only three years, for on 23 January 1776, aged thirteen, he was *admitted* to Trinity College, Cambridge, as a Pensioner, 'on account of the extraordinary progress which he had made in his studies', according to the *Naval Chronicle*. But was he ever at Cambridge at all?

To be admitted merely meant that he was offered a place at the college, not that he actually attended it. Trinity College archivist Alan Kucia writes;[6] 'He did not matriculate as a member of the University, and it is doubtful if he ever resided here; he certainly did not take a degree. In this period it was fairly common for boys (particularly from Westminster School, which had close ties with Trinity) to be admitted to the College but not come into residence.'

What he may have done, Mr. Kucia suggests, is to have gone to private tutors, but there is no record of this. If, on the other hand, he did attend lectures, one of his tutors would have been George Atwood, a distinguished mathematician. This would fit with Home's later career in the Navy, but cannot be substantiated. Did his mother die before he was born, or an hour after? Did he attend Trinity College, Cambridge, or did he not? Did Stephen pay for his education, or did Thompson? As so often, there are alternative versions; and at this stage of his life insufficient evidence to suggest which of them is the truth.[7]

4

In 1778 ambiguity recedes a little if not yet completely, for if the *Naval Chronicle* was right and Captain Edward Thompson truly acted as young Home's father, instructor and protector, what could be more natural than for the boy to have entered the Navy in his sixteenth year in Thompson's ship the *Hyaena?* Indeed, according to the same source, Home had made one or two short trips to sea before joining the Service. But whether he was under the guardianship of Ned Thompson or not during 'his boyish years', he was lucky with his first ship and her captain. Thompson's 'nautical abilities and general knowledge', the *Chronicle* reported, 'rendered it a most desirable object with young men beginning their naval career, to obtain an appointment on the *Hyaena's* quarterdeck'; and in 1778 Home Popham was one of those young men.

To sum up his adolescent years, then, what evidence there is suggests that he spent at least part of them—perhaps from the time his father died, or when he first went to Westminster—in the care of this delightful, talented, rather melancholy naval officer cum man about town; and that when he joined the Navy, he went to sea technically as an able seaman, but in practice as a probationary midshipman, known as a Captain's Servant, and indeed almost as a son serving under his father.

NOTES ON CHAPTER I

1. The appointment of Consuls was fairly random. The office dated from the 15th century, with 'Conservators...with the jurisdiction to do justice between merchant and merchant beyond the seas.' Sometimes they were merchants themselves, or, as happened in Joseph's time, naval officers. Not until 1825 did Britain follow French practice and include Consuls in the Civil Service.
2. William Home, 8th Earl of Home (c.1710-61): commissioned into the 2nd Dragoons 1735, fought in the '45, reached the rank of Lt-General, and was Governor of Gibraltar from 1757 until his death. I believe the name was pronounced as written, not Hume.
3. Unlike the other states along the North African coast, Morocco was independent of the Sublime Porte, but shared their faith—and their piratical propensities.
4. According to the *History of Parliament*, he first attended Brentford School.
5. Stephen Popham (1745-95) went bankrupt, according to one account, then in 1777 went to India as secretary to Sir John Day. He was killed falling out of his curricle and left a fortune.
6. In a letter to the author, 25 March 1987. 'Matriculate', i.e. his name was not enrolled on the college register.
7. For much of the information in this chapter I am indebted to *A West Country Family: the Pophams since 1150,* by FW Popham.

CHAPTER II

Convoys, Battles, Capture 1778-83

1

IN APRIL 1778 Edward Thompson was busy rounding up a crew for HMS *Hyaena*, a new 24-gun frigate just launched from Fisher's Yard in Liverpool; and on the 25th he wrote to the Admiralty from Gainsborough giving a 'List of such seaman able and ordinary as have been entered for the *Hyaena*, between 2 February and 24 April.' On the list, under 'Seamen, Able' and the sub-heading 'Volunteers—Thames', are his nephew Thomas Boulden Thompson, and Home Popham[1] who was then fifteen and a half.

He and the other 'first-class volunteers', those lads bound for the quarterdeck, now had two years of hard living and tough training in front of them before they became midshipmen, for they had to learn both the art of the seaman and the skills of the officer. For the first, they were expected to go aloft with the sailors, reef and furl sails, man the braces, master the setting-up of masts and rigging, man the boats in harbour, and become proficient at every detail of the sailor's trade. For the second, they were taught navigation, astronomy and trigonometry, the taking of sun-sights with their quadrants at noon, and had to work out the ship's position; and they stood their watch at night.

Their education in small ships such as frigates fell to the chaplain, or the captain himself. Some months after *Hyaena* was first commissioned, Thompson wrote to the Admiralty: 'Having a number of young gentlemen committed to my care, whose education I pay great attention to—and being allowed no schoolmaster to attend to their improvements, I request a chaplain's warrant for the Rev Mr Isham Baggs...'. And Mr Baggs was duly appointed, for his name recurs in correspondence later; but whether through his instruction or that of Ned Thompson, Home certainly profited, to become 'well-versed in the more scientific branches of his profession'.

We have no account of his reactions when he first climbed aboard *Hyaena* that spring, lugging his sea-chest with him; but another 'young gentleman', Captain Crawford described his very clearly, and it is fair to imagine Home's were not very different.

> When I stood for the first time, on a frigate's quarter-deck, I thought I never should be satisfied in gazing—all was new and strange—shrouds, cordage, guns, the whole furniture of the deck and masts—every object was a matter of fresh wonder and astonishment... If I was pleased and indeed agreeably suprised with what I had hitherto seen... I confess that I was not only a good deal *désenchanté*, but my consternation was great, when, after

descending two ladders, I beheld the dungeon (for such it appeared to me) into which my conductor led me, and said that that, the larboard berth, was to be my quarter.

The frigate was low 'between decks'... and, in the half-dozen paces, between the hatchway and the berth, though a little fellow, I knocked my head as many times against the beams. The crib in which I was introduced was small even for a frigate, notwithstanding which the chests belonging to its inmates, were ranged around (none being allowed in the steerage), just leaving in the centre sufficient room to admit a small deal table, which was then covered with a not-over-clean cloth preparatory to dinner. In one corner of the berth was lashed a 'harness' or pickle cask, containing beef that was meant to serve for half the approaching cruise, and which, either from the heat of the weather, or that the preserving process had been imperfectly performed, already began to emit certain unsavoury smells.

The ship was weak, and open in her 'topsides', and at sea, her yawning seams, at every roll, admitted the water, traces of which, in lines of rust, were rendered visible through the dim obscure by means of one lean and meagre tallow candle...

Dinner was soon served by a dirty boy, black and reeking from the galley. It consisted of a piece of beef, baked in a deep tin dish, with potatoes under it. I tried to eat... but my stomach rebelled against food, and it was with difficulty I forced myself to swallow a morsel. Grog for the 'oldsters' and 'black strap' (a very detestable mixture, resembling in taste a combination of sloe juice and logwood) for the youngsters followed.

Home's introduction to the sea-life was probably just like that, set by the twin poles of wonder and nausea, even to the 'yawning seams': *Hyaena*, though a new ship, leaked abominably.

In a later passage Crawford describes the relief, when he is promoted lieutenant, of escaping 'from the depths of the candle-lit cockpit to the more elevated and purer atmosphere of the wardroom; no more to be browbeat, bullied and mast-headed...' Fights, arguments, and the rougher sort of practical joke occupied much of the midshipmen's off-duty time, discipline was rigorous, and night and day they were at the beck and call of the first lieutenant. It was like being at a public school, in fact, with, as Dr Johnson remarked in a different context, 'the danger of being drowned'.

2

When *Hyaena* was commissioned, the American War of Independence was in its third wretched year, and the French had just entered it on the American side. As a result, British shipping, whether in the Channel, the Atlantic, the Caribbean, or off the American seaboard, was under constant threat of attack from French fleets, frigates and privateers. Within a year, the Spanish too, would be drawn into the war, and after them, the Dutch. The high seas were a dangerous place in 1778, and ships sailed in convoy whether they were bound on the long haul to America or to the Antilles, or coastwise in British waters.

The Navy had been allowed to deteriorate dangerously after the Seven Years War, and so urgent was the demand for convoy escorts that *Hyaena* sailed 'in an unfinished state' on June 24, though only to Dublin, with £50,000 for the Irish Treasury, and back with 'the linnen ships from Belfast, Newry and Dublin'—nine ships carrying a cargo valued at the impressive sum of £900,000.

After completing her fitting-out, the ship was in home waters for the rest of the year, but in the spring of 1779 she joined a convoy of 41 ships bound for the West Indies. A French fleet of 24 sail of the line and 13 frigates, under D'Estaing, had come south from New York and was roaming among the islands. In June they took St. Vincent, and were in the very act of attacking Grenada when Admiral, 'Foul Weather Jack' Byron caught up with them. *Hyaena* was told off to shadow them, but took no part in the inconclusive action that followed.[2]

Frigates, then as later, were both the Navy's sheepdogs, endlessly rounding up stragglers, and its watchdogs, investigating every strange sail that appeared over the horizon. The number of ships in Caribbean and American waters on their lawful—or unlawful—occasions was remarkable, and in one period of twenty-four hours *Hyaena* spoke a brig from New Providence, gave chase to and fired at an American privateer, and captured a Spanish privateer from Havana: 'Received on board 37 prisoners, and sent on board her an officer and 5 men.' That was off the coast of Florida, but among the Windward and Leeward Islands the same sequence of sighting and pursuit, identification and occasionally action, applied. Sometimes they lost their quarry, sometimes not; often the quarry turned out to be a British ship; or she might be a 'Bermudian sloop from Turks Island bound for Charlestown, South Carolina, with salt', or a Boston privateer in the process of capturing an English brig. And who was to know whether the next sail, or the next, might not be a French frigate patrolling in the van of D'Estaing's squadron. In those sapphire-blue waters, always with the the islands' mountains on the beam and the brisk northeast trade wind filling their sails, there was rarely a dull moment.

By August *Hyaena* was on her way home with a convoy from Barbados. The West Indian merchants and planters were anxious, with good reason, and importunate; and it seems that they persuaded Thompson to leave his station in order to provide an escort for their precious cargoes: back in England in October, he notes that he had received 'the order for my tryal by Court Martial'.[3]

3

Those eighteen months had been fairly routine, with the savour of some prize money to come at the end of them. But the convoy to which *Hyaena* was attached in January 1780 was a graver matter altogether. Not only was half of it bound for Gibraltar, which had been under close siege since the previous year, and half for the Antilles, but it was in company with a squadron of 22 sail of the line and a number of frigates commanded by Admiral Sir George Rodney, who was on his way to take up an appointment as C-in-C in the West Indies. On their way south, *Hyaena's* log records:

> Took a fleet of Spaniards from San Sebastian's bound for Cadiz... The Convoy consists of seventeen Sail of Brigs, five ships richly freighted of the Carraca Company, and one of 64 which did not discharge her guns. The value of the convoy is computed at £700,000. Also took a French vessel under Danish colours richly laden.

A week later, off Cape St. Vincent, they came upon a Spanish fleet of eleven battleships: *Hyaena's* company had a ringside seat at the action which followed.

> ...at ½ past 12... saw the Spanish Fleet... at 1 the Adml made the signal for Line of Battle abreast... at 10 minutes past 2 the Admiral made the signal to prepare to engage—at 25 minutes past 2 the Admiral made the signal to attack the Rear to Leeward in succession; at ½ past 3 the Spanish fleet bore away... at 22 minutes past 4 the *Edgar* began the Action... at ½ past 5 the Admiral made the signal for a closer engagement. The Spanish Admiral's ship being closely engaged with the *Ajax*, blew up—Bore up for the Wreck, at ½ past 10 passed by two English Men of War taking care of a large ship much disabled, which we judged to be Spanish. The Admiral still continued to chace... At break of day saw 7 Sail, 2 of which were Spanish Ships of War...

The fragmentary notes, jotted down in the ship's log as the action developed and darkness fell, give the feel of that dirty winter's night, with glimpses of the moon between the scudding clouds; but leave to the imagination the piping of the wind, the muzzle flash of the broadsides, the crash and roar and smoke as masts and spars went by the board, the blinding glare as the Spanish Admiral's ship exploded. The tally of the Second Battle of St. Vincent, later known as the 'Moonlight Battle', was one Spanish ship sunk and six captured.

For seventeen year old Home, it must have been an exciting night: did he see himself, one day, sending those most stirring of signals, 'Prepare to Engage', and 'Engage the Enemy more closely', from a flagship's quarterdeck? If so, it was an ambition he was never to achieve, for it was the last sea-battle at which he would ever be present. By a pleasant irony, however, through his work on the flag-signalling code, he would be directly responsible for the most famous signal ever sent, before the most famous sea-battle in British naval history.

But on that blustery night off the Spanish coast such matters lay twenty years ahead, and *Hyaena* returned to her humdrum duties. In February she returned to England from Gibraltar with despatches from Admiral Rodney; in April she was in the Tagus with a prize; and in June she was in Plymouth and Thompson wrote to the Admiralty, 'I am now preparing for sea, though in a shattered condition...'—but whether he was referring to the ship or himself is not clear. A convoy from Jersey to Torbay, then back to Plymouth: 'the People on shore with liberty', the occasion, perhaps, on which they all turned up at the theatre where one of Poet Thompson's plays was being performed.[4] *Hyaena* then went in for a refit, not to sail again until the end of August when she took a convoy across the Atlantic to Sandy Hook, the entrance to New York harbour. She was back in home waters in November, to pick up a convoy and '16 Sail of Transports' with reinforcements for the war, to be landed at Charlestown, South Carolina.

In those busy waters she continued to collect prizes: two ships and the American privateer which had taken them, and in the West Indies in the New Year, five more ships, including a French and a Spanish privateer; and, in March, three Dutch ships from Surinam 'with very valuable cargoes, and one with Slaves and Ivory from Guinea.'

In the same month, writing from Barbados, Thompson notes: 'I am now by command of the Admiral going to take Berbice and establish the colonies of Demerara and Essequibo according to capitulation.' What had happened was this: the previous month the Dutch colonies in South America, named after the three rivers, had surrendered when a British squadron had descended on them and captured all the ships in the Demerara River. Now *Hyaena* was being sent there to complete the conquest and supervise the change of sovereignty. It did not prove particularly strenuous, though the Spaniards from their settlements on the Orinoco to the north proved troublesome; mostly the ship lay in the Demerara River, until, in October, the Proclamation announcing the Sovereignty of the British Crown was read and the inhabitants took the Oath of Allegiance. Soon afterwards Thompson sailed north once more to the Antilles where three French Squadrons, 136 sail of the line, were rampaging up and down the islands.

4

Home Popham had now been at sea for three years. He was no longer a 'youngster' but a midshipman and, it seems, doing the job of a lieutenant. Quite suddenly, after those years of obscurity in the gunroom—and very junior members of a ship's company, even when selected for a commission, do not figure in their Captain's letters nor in the log—he appears by name, and in rather odd circumstances.

On 23 April 1781 *Hyaena's* log recorded that she had sent a supply of Gunner's Stores on board a sloop with the curious name of *Shelanagig.*[5] This was in the Demerara River, and she sailed two days later with two sail 'under her convoy'. The following month she joined forces with Rodney and the main West Indian fleet in Carlisle Bay, Barbados. On board her was Home Popham, a fact which only emerges later because of what happened to her.

The *Sheilanagig*, to give her her more usual spelling, was a small ship of 14 guns, with a complement of 40, one of the quick-sailing vessels employed for shadowing, gathering intelligence, carrying despatches and other similar duties; and it was for the second of these that Rodney had need of her. About 24 May he received news that a small French squadron with 900 troops on board had invested the island of Tobago. He immediately despatched Admiral Drake there with 6 sail of the line and three frigates to try and foil them, while he himself remained in Carlisle Bay with the bulk of his fleet, ready to sail at once if the main French squadron should come south from Martinique. At the same time he sent three of his sloops, the *Fly*, the *Munster Lass* and the *Sheilanagig*, to the island to find out what was happening, look for likely landing places, tell the local people that a British squadron was on the way, and to try to find out where the main French fleet was.

Each of the three vessels was to go to a different bay, in case of accidents: a wise precaution, for on the 30 May *Sheilanagig* was overhauled by one of the French squadron, boarded and captured. She and her company were then taken to Martinique as prize and prisoners.

On 1 September Ned Thompson, still in Demerara, wrote to Philip Stephens, the Secretary of the Admiralty, to say that he was under orders from Rodney to leave the river and convoy a fleet of merchant ships to England, though the orders had not been confirmed. The letter then continues:

> Since writing the above Lieutenant Popham late of the *Shilahnagig* is returned on board the *Hyaena* on his parole of honour[6] from Martinico—Captain Shepherd being taken by the French fleet off Tobago—Mr. Popham left Sir George Rodney at St Eustatius on the 1st of August, who ordered him to join the *Hyaena* and take his passage with me to Europe, informing him that my despatches were sent by a schooner—but thirty days have elapsed, I have every reason to believe she is taken, and the Admirals and every other Senior Officer is gone to America, which makes my situation unpleasing— however I shall wait until the latter end of September to know further of this subject before I determine my departure... as the Trade is ready for sea, and I have no ship to send with them.

Home had brought verbal instructions from Rodney that the ship was to escort the convoy home and take with him the Admiral's despatches, and to report to the Admiralty on the state of affairs in South America: it was for these orders in writing that he was anxiously waiting. They did not arrive; Rodney himself, in ill health, had already sailed for England; and in the end Thompson decided to take the convoy without. He was back in England by the end of the year—to face another court-martial 'on the letter of Sir Samuel Hood'. As on the previous occasion, he was acquitted.

5

In the meantime, Lieutenant Keith Shepherd, Captain of *Sheilanagig*, her master Mr Edward Park and the other officers were back in England on parole, and facing a court martial for loss of their ship. It took place on 23 January 1782 in Portsmouth, and was little more than a formality. Shepherd's letters—to Rodney, Admiral Pye as C-in-C Portsmouth, and to the Admiralty—have not been traced and are not included in the proceedings,[7] but the capture of *Fly* a month or two later was probably very similar. She was taken by a French 74 which, according to Ponsonby, her Captain, 'sailed three feet to our one'. The interrogation in the case of *Sheilanagig* went thus:

Q Did the Captain and other Officers and Ship's Company do all in their power to effect their escape?

A They did.

Q Had you all the sail you could set when you were taken?

A We had all we could set with propriety.

Q What time did you first see the French fleet?

A About six o'clock in the morning.

Q Did the enemy's ships outsail you?

A Very much.

Q Did not the swell that was on your weather beam cause you to near the enemy exceedingly?

A Very much.

Q Could you have fired the lee guns to have done execution?

A No—it was not possible.

The situation is clear enough. After a night at sea, they found themselves to weather of the French squadron at dawn, and being remorselessly pressed down upon the enemy by wind and sea, unable to sail clear and too heeled even to fire their guns. They had no alternative but to strike their colours if they were not prepared to be blown out of the water. Home was not called; the Court accepted the account of the Captain and Master, and they were discharged.

Some time later that year the exchange of prisoners which allowed Home to resume his seagoing career must have taken place, for he was next appointed to the *Alarm*, 32 guns, on the Jamaica station; and in June 1783 he was promoted Lieutenant on Admiral Rowley's recommendation. This was confirmed by the Admiralty fifteen months later on 1 September 1784, when he was described as 'Mr Home Riggs Popham. First Lieutenant. *Alarm.*'

His ship remained on the Jamaica station until the middle of 1783 when she returned home, to be paid off at Plymouth. And there, by coincidence was Ned Thompson, who had just been appointed to the command of *Grampus*, with business on the Guinea Coast. Home was unemployed and therefore on half-pay:[8] what more natural than that he should apply to his old 'instructor and protector' for a posting?

NOTES ON CHAPTER II

1. Thompson also visited Scarborough and Whitby in the tender *Minerva* in his search for a crew, and having found the men he needed shipped them and their baggage 'By the canal boats to Liverpool'. By early June he reported that his complement was almost complete.

2. From ten ships Byron had over 1,200 men ashore sick, 360 of them with fever, 212 with scurvy. Throughout the wars of the second half of the century, the drain on Britain's manpower in the West Indies was appalling: Arthur Bryant gives a figure of 40,000 troops having died there between 1794 and 1796 alone.

3. The connection is clear though unsubstantiated, as the proceedings of the subsequent, 'tryal' are missing from the records. In any case, he was acquitted then, as he was for a similar 'offence' two years later. To resolve the conflicting pressures of the West Indies merchants' clamour for convoy protection, and the threat of French attacks on the islands was often virtually impossible.

4. On her arrival on this occasion or another, Thompson gave his entire ship's company a week's leave, to the horror of the Dockyard Superintendent who was sure half of them would desert. He was wrong. Not only did they all return on time, but when they found that their Captain had one of his plays being performed at the Plymouth Theatre, 'fifty of the crew, with their ladies, presented themselves at the door... and demanded admittance.' When Thompson, who was inside, was told they were there, he paid for them all to attend.

5. Sheela-na-gigs: carved female figures in poses drawing attention to their private parts. Found on churches etc in Ireland particularly, also in England, France and N. Spain, they are one of the many Romanesque depictions of aspects of lust.

6. Parole of honour meant that the captured officer was 'not to serve the King of Great Britain on board any sort of vessel, upon any pretext whatsoever... until being regularly exchanged as Prisoner of War, according to the Agreement made between the Kings of England and France.' A batch of exchanged prisoners was referred to as a 'cartel'. The fact that Home Popham was taken prisioner and spent some months in French hands in the West Indies has not emerged before in the various accounts of his life.

7. Shepherd had been taken in the sloop *Fortune* less than two years before. He was obviously very unlucky or very rash.

8. According to his agent's accounts he was on half-pay from June 1783 to August '84; but there was always a time-lag between an appointment and its acknowledgement by the Navy Board.

CHAPTER III

The Evil Coast 1783-6

1

NED THOMPSON'S appointment had come through Admiral Lord Augustus Keppel, with whom he was on friendly terms, and was for 'the command of the coast of Africa with the appointment of my officers...' Among those he picked were, as in *Hyaena,* Thomas Boulden Thompson and, as 'Extra' or 'Additional' Lieutenant, Home Popham.

Before he joined his ship, Thompson was in London and seeing Keppel regularly: their conversation at the end of July 1783 reveals the intended object of the voyage—although it did not take place until later, and Thompson did not live to complete it. 'I now proposed to Lord Keppel', Thompson recorded in his journal, 'to explore the coast of Africa between the Latitudes of 20° and 30° South'. Between those parallels, i.e. between the present Port Nolloth and the borders of Angola, there were, he suggested, several fine harbours in which the East Indiamen chasing home before the southeast trades could ideally refit. In wartime, especially, this would enable them 'to avoid the enemy without returning the beaten road from the Cape, and the necessity of putting into Rio de Janeiro.' The French were in fact already using the route he suggested, calling at the Portuguese forts of St Philip de Benguela and St Paul de Loanda.

Thompson's idea was approved in principle by both Keppel and the Prime Minister, the Duke of Portland, but postponed for fear 'of alarming our new friends'—by which were meant 'our late enemies,' for although the American War had ended in January the peace terms had not yet been settled, and the various Colonies which had changed hands during it had still to be apportioned between the belligerents—Britain on the one hand and America, France, Spain and Holland on the other. These uncertainties were reflected in the conflicting orders which the Admiralty issued for *Grampus* during the remainder of the year. When she finally left Plymouth in January 1784 she was bound not for the African coast but the West Indies. Lord Howe in his sailing orders, Thompson noted, 'confined my voyage to Barbados, by which he deprived me of every opportunity of promoting my officers, or enriching myself by a freight.'[1]

Then the orders were changed again, and the end of February saw the ship, in company with *Battler*, in Funchal Road, Madeira and bound not for the Sugar Islands but, once again, for Africa, and on a different mission entirely. Madeira was a regular staging-post for ships bound either to or from the East Indies and the Cape, or the Caribbean, and everyone who visited the island, not least 'Poet' Thompson, went into raptures over it. He, his nephew and Wilson, his painter were greatly taken with the splendours of the scenery, and the latter two made 'many beautiful sketches'; while Thompson himself was inspired by a Madeiran legend to write his 'Nautic Poem', *Bello Monte or the Misfortunes of Anna d'Arfet*.[2]

There is something uncommonly attractive about Ned Thompson, and his ship's company, from officers to powder-monkeys, obviously adored him. He combined a high degree of professionalism with exceptional human qualities. Although it is not possible to document it, it can hardly be a coincidence that under his tuition and encouragement during two commissions, Home not only became extremely proficient at navigation and its step-child, hydrography, but took pains to teach them to his own midshipmen when he came to command his own ship. In addition, Thompson may well have been responsible for Home's later interest in flag-signalling, for before they left Plymouth on this same commission, Thompson noted in a list of improvements which he considered necessary in the Navy, 'that ships be furnished with charts', and that he must 'invent a new code of signals'. Moreover, he did actually submit 'a new code and mode of signals' to Lord Howe when they got home, to which he 'received a polite answer in his way.'[3]

2

The final purpose of *Grampus*'s voyage during the first half of 1784 was to make a survey of all the trading forts on the 'coast of Guinea' and report on them. There were nearly a dozen of them along that malevolent stretch of the West African littoral from Abidjan to Lagos; they had been established by the Portuguese, Dutch and British as outlets for the trade in slaves, gold and ivory; and in the aftermath of the American War a number of them were in the process of changing hands, with the inevitable boundary disputes.

In April, therefore, *Grampus* was anchored off the felicitously named Annamaboo Road, and during the ensuing month visited them all. At each the station chief produced his detailed statement for Thompson to check and sign; and these reports give a vivid, and pretty grisly, picture of what was happening along that coast in the years before the abolition of the slave trade. Annamaboo itself was the centre of it, the main market for a great swathe of population which stretched as far as the Volta River, from which the slaves were marched or brought in 'slaving longboats', to be shipped out in the 'blackbirders' for the dreaded Middle Passage to the Indies and North and South America. According to one sailor who visited it, there were a great many ships there 'trading for gold dust, ivory and slaves. It is situated on a sandy beach, close to the sea, which breaks against the fort to protect the English settlers; the land is low and cultivated, but such a surf on the beach that ships cannot land.' There was a small garrison, with thirty-four male and female slaves working in and around the fort, several of the men, according to the station chief's report, 'almost blind'. Trade at that time, he said, was very dull and the natives 'very insolent'. His report continues: 'The trading

Fantine Negroes are the most troublesome and warlike People of this coast, great thieves, restless in temper, braver than other Negroes and always in a state of Riot and Rebellion.'

At Cape Coast Castle, farther east, there was a large garrison; the fort was in good order and well armed with 18, 24 and 42 pounders and over a hundred male slaves—with names like Quashie, Coffee Dick, Mars and Bacchus—classified as tradesmen, canoe men and boys, 'necessary boys', and gardeners, and over a hundred 'serviceable women' slaves. As to the state of the trade, the station chief reported that in twelve months 'Thirteen English ships have sailed from Annamaboe with 5,852 slaves; another at Winnebah with 250 for Charlestown'; and an American with 250 for Boston. They were fetching £4 a head because of the competition. The gold trade was good, the gold being purchased with 'Brazil Tobacco and Indian and British piece goods'; but the ivory trade was indifferent.

And so it went on, at Santa Apollonia, Dix Cove, Elmina, Cape Corse, Fantumquerry—where there were only 7 male slaves, 2 women (Abeneluh and Quendy Coomah) and 2 children, 1 canoe of 13 paddles in good order, but the roof of the fort was in danger of falling in—Ackra, Seccundee and Commende where there was 'No Trade of any kind worth mentioning' and the fort was falling down.

According to the chief at Ackra (Accra), who was ill, the Danes on the Volta were building a powerful fort and were likely 'to secure all the Negro Trade of that extensive river and Eastern country', thereby totally destroying every means of slave commerce to Great Britain. *Grampus* herself visited Volta; but bad weather, sickness, and shortage of provisions—'bread exhausted and water bad and expended'—drove them to Anna de Chavas Bay on the Island of St. Thomas, which is on the Equator 180 miles due west of Libreville, in what is now Gabon and was then known as Cameroun. Here Lieutenant Popham made his first 'Marine Survey' or at least the first of which there is any record, a sketchy and not particularly accurate chart which was published five years later in Alexander Dalrymple's compendious *Nautical Charts*, where it is subscribed: 'Lt Home Riggs Popham. HMS *Grampus*. 1784.'

They were there less than a week, for Thompson—who was himself suffering from fever—felt it urgent that he should hurry home and report, not only the activities of the Danes and the problems of interpreting their treaty but the presence of 'piratical vessels' which were busy along the coast plundering the shipping. By the end of July they were back at Spithead. Among the less probable items of cargo she carried were three 'Angora Cows' which Thompson presented to the Queen, who graciously accepted them, and from Annamaboe, 'a beautiful ballad singing monkey—which died of a flux'.

By September Thompson was back in London with his 'Remarks and Observations': of his young lieutenant's movements we have no certain knowledge, except for one brief, rather cryptic entry in Ned Thompson's Journal in November: 'To Slough in Bucks to search for a rural lodge'... Maria, Tom and Popham with me...' and he adds, 'The joys of life are confined to a few we love.'[4]

3

Not until March of the following year, when his journal ends, is there any mention of Thompson going back to sea. Britain was briefly at peace, and that, for many naval officers, meant no posting and half-pay. In March 1785, however, he records the possibility that he may be sent back to Africa. His friends implored him not to go, for the voyage in *Grampus* to that fever-ridden coast had undermined his health; but when he was finally given his sailing orders, later that year, in the same ship, he went—'for a love of those who sail with me, and to serve them'.

Ostensibly those orders were for a survey of the coast of Southwest Africa, where, as Howe wrote to Byam Martin, 'the Admiralty were even then considering the advisability of establishing a port of call.' Two ships were involved, the 16-gun *Nautilus* commanded by George Tripp, and Thompson's *Grampus* with, once again, his nephew Thomas, and Home Popham with specific duties as marine surveyor. What was not included in those orders was another, very different object of the voyage. With the loss of the American colonies somewhere else had to be found to which those unfortunates sentenced to transportation could be sent, and Thompson had been busy proposing the African coast somewhere between Cape Colony and Namibia as a suitable site for such a colony—of which he would become Governor. He had never been there, of course; his recommendation was based on highly-coloured and wildly inaccurate travellers' tales, notably those of a certain Colonel de Prem, who had commanded the Dutch garrison at the Cape five years before.[5]

On their way, however, the two ships were to return to the Guinea coast to complete their work of eighteen months before. George Tripp later reported the outcome. Captain Thompson, he wrote, 'had settled all the Disputes to the Leeward of Santa Apollonia itself; but as Captain Thompson was very early in the Business taken ill, he could not go through the active part of it, and therefore deputed Lieut. Home Riggs Popham to perform it; and a very arduous task he must have had to effect; the Black People are not easily brought to relinquish that which they think they have a right to.'

For Home it seems that this was his introduction to diplomacy—of the rougher sort—and an experience which would stand him in good stead in later years. *Nautilus*, meanwhile, had been detached to protect Santa Apollonia. That was just before Christmas; in January 1786 the two ships were in company once more at the Island of St Thomas. What happened there is described in the *Naval Chronicle*:

When Commodore Thompson was last on the African station, he caught a fever. The *Grampus* at the time was crowded with a vast number of monkies, parrots and other birds, with a diversity of animals peculiar to Africa, and which the Commodore intended as presents on his return to Britain. The Surgeon appeared on the deck, and informing the crew that the stench arising from these animals had increased the virulence of their

Commander's disorder, and was likely to be of very bad consequence, in an instant the sea around the ship was covered with bird-cages, birds, monkeys and other animals, and every part of the ship thoroughly cleansed.

His distemper, notwithstanding every precaution, continued to gain ground … On the 17th January 1786, he departed this life. His ship was filled with lamentation: the crew conceiving they had lost not only a brave and skilful Commander, but a friend and a father.

The scene, in that steamy climate, with the two small ships anchored in Anna de Chavas Bay, 2,000 miles from that rural lodge near Slough, and surrounded by drowning animals and birds, is balanced precisely on the borderline between tragedy and farce. More practically, it left *Grampus* without a captain.

George Tripp transferred to her, and that left the question, who was to command *Nautilus*? Kirkwood, *Grampus*'s First Lieutenant, was offered the job, but stood down in favour of Thomas Boulden Thompson out of respect for his late captain, and Thomas took over *Nautilus* with the acting rank of Master and Commander, upon, as he put it, 'the unfortunate and unhappy death of my only friend and parent'. And Home went with him. The two ships stayed for two weeks, and then parted company. *Nautilus*, watered and provisioned from *Grampus*, headed south to begin her survey alone.

She remained in African waters until mid-May, and during those four and a half months both Boulden Thompson and Home Popham kept detailed journals. The account that follows is taken from both: Thompson's is the more detailed; together, they present a lively picture, both of that barren land and of the thankless task of surveying its coastline.[6]

4

The passage from St Thomas to Dassen Island, forty miles north of Cape Town, took them fifty-two days, during which they saw no other ship. Having made their landfall and examined Saldanha Bay, they anchored in St Helen's Bay, just round from Cape St Martin. Here Thompson notes, 'I despatched Lieut. Popham, the Surveyor, to investigate the bay and ascertain the situation of the Berg River.'

Apart from the difficulties of surveying a surfbound and virtually featureless coast, their main concern, then and for the whole time they were there, was fresh water, for beyond the shore and the sandhills lay the Namib Desert, arid, waterless and treeless. In contrast, the sea abounded with life, 'a diversity of Sea Fowl about the ship,' Popham noted in his journal, 'and the surface of the water almost covered with Whales and Seals.' The whales 'were not alarmed at the ship, but seemed to approach and investigate a Body, assuming a prorogative (sic) of their element, and of superior size to themselves…' And he goes on with some prescience. 'Had the land promised so much for this voyage as the sea did for the establishment of a Spermacite Factory in this Country, our hopes of success in the undertaking would have been much heightened, little had we to expect from the barren like Aspect of this Iron Bound Shore, on which a heavy surf must ever set.'

He was to make a close and perilous acquaintance with the shore and its everlasting surf next day.

> In this place I was swamped in the Boat while I was attempting to land to take some Angles, and had it not been for the alacrity of the Boat's crew in obeying my orders, we must have been inevitably lost; we were then 9 leagues from the Ship, the sun near setting, every person in the Boat wet through, all our provisions and water lost, drove out by the violence of Wind in the Night to Sea, and did not regain the Ship for near 24 hours.

As a source of fresh water the Berg River was a disappointment, for at that dry time of the year it proved to be salt for fifty miles inland. Popham himself took the boat thirty miles upstream: and there, luckily, he found a Dutch farmer who not only had a well but was prepared to supply them with water and deliver it in carts drawn by ten oxen. The only other people he saw were a Dutch fisherman 'with three or four Hottentot servants drying and salting fish for the Dutch markets at the Cape of Good Hope'. They were the only ship to anchor in the bay, Popham was told, in thirty years. Only fish was plentiful, mullet, bream, rays, and one 'called in these seas the Elephant Fish... a kind of Cat Fish... having a long proboscis'. The ship's seine net was hauled regularly and kept them well supplied.

Thompson reckoned that St. Helen's Bay marked the northernmost limit of Dutch settlement, for there was a landmark with the Arms of the States on the edge of the Berg River; but none of the settlers lived closer to the coast than thirty miles. Certainly these were the last Europeans they were to see; they scratched a living off the land (he was able to buy four oxen, a few sheep and goats, and some cabbages and onions from them) and supplemented their meagre livelihood by preserving fish and selling ostrich feathers. There was, however, a suprising amount of game, deer, hares, partridges and pheasants; there were also jackals and packs of wolves, though they didn't see any. Compared with what lay ahead it was almost a paradise, though a paradise without trees. The weather was as dismal as the land, 'in general hazy, raw, foggy... with the sea breezes which come on at dark and lasted till noon next day... they always brought into the bay a heavy swell.' As a result their examination of the coast was constantly delayed; and because of the swell they were rarely able to anchor at night, but had to back and fill offshore.

Their next disappointment was their total failure to find either Cape de Voltas or the bay and river of that name which appeared on such charts as they possessed. Thompson sent Popham 'on every appearance of a point in shore in the cutter' in the hopes that he would return 'the Harbinger of good News', but without success. 'So inhospitable and so barren a country is not to be equalled except in the Desarts of Arabia...' The only feasible explanation of their failure to find what, on the map, seemed by far the most important outlet on the coast, was that these maps had all been made by 'Inland Travellers'. What they referred to as the De Voltas was in fact, the Orange River, sometimes called the Garieb; but from seaward its mouth was completely masked by sandbanks.[7] The position which Thompson gives in his journal, 28°40S tallies precisely; had Popham been able to land, he might well have found it.

Their next call as they roamed northwards was at the Bay of Angra Pequena, site of the modern Lüderitz in Namaqualand. They arrived there on 11 April, with the whole ship's company suffering from 'colds, sore throats, Rheumatizms and agues', owing to the constant damp. Although they found no drinkable water here either, they did meet their first natives, and investigated a tall granite cross standing on the northern horn of the bay. Popham described it as a 'pedestal', Thompson, more accurately, as 'a cross wrought of the natural marble of the country.. on the east and west sides is an inscription neatly carved in Roman characters... but wholly defaced; on the end of the arm which points to the south, I plainly made out the Arms of Portugal... the carving of this pedestal is far from being crude, and it must have cost some time in erecting...' If they had been able to decipher the inscription, they would have learnt that the cross had been placed there by the Portuguese navigator Bartholomeo Diaz, on his pioneering voyage to the 'Cape of Storms', as he called it, and beyond, exactly 300 years before.[8]

There was another monument at Pequena, 'a square board nail'd on a spar about 24 feet long'; and this, Popham says, 'I immediately landed for, to get the piece of board for information, and the spar for fuel, which was now become a very valuable article.' This inscription, also much worn by wind and weather, commemorated the visit there by Lt de Frégate, Monsieur Bart, in *La Vénus* on May 16, 17--: a date which Thompson was able to complete as 1733, when Bart charted the bay, 'a survey lately published by Mr Dalrymple from the original manuscript'.[9]

5

Nautilus included in her complement a botanist, Mr Howe, who was having a most unrewarding time. Ever since St Helen's Bay, where he did discover some unfamiliar 'bulbous plants', his forays ashore yielded little: at Pequena a plant resembling 'a small geranium', and that was all. Popham, however, found something very different in the sand: 'several prints of human Feet (which did not exceed the size of those of a Boy of ten years old), and some of wild beasts ... but no sign of Hut, Habitation, Smoke, Wood or Water could be seen from the adjacent hills.' Later, he saw 'a man with several dogs attending him', who avoided him; and, in great excitement, what he thought was a spring. But it turned out to be nothing more than a kind of tank or reservoir, possibly dug by the natives to store water during the rainy season but now barely damp.

He was pushing off from shore when:

we discovered several Natives with Dogs approaching us, this was a temptation to return; in a little time there were seventeen assembled with twenty-three Dogs—I endeavoured by every gesture and act of friendship to communicate with them, laying on the ground Knives, Trinkets, Brandy Biscuits &c which they picked up and seemed much pleased with—two of them advanced from the rest with an apparent wish for me to lay down my Arms. This I did, and tho' the only one out of the Boat, they would not suffer me to touch them, but made signs for me to follow them—which I did so far as I thought it prudent—for if 17 Men should not trust me to approach near enough to communicate, I had a plausible right not to trust myself to the power of those 17, without the reach of my party's Assistance.

I lost nearly two Hours in fruitless Arguments with these savage Hunters (Excepting one who was the Headmost in advancing, with every cannibal low cunning). They were of low stature, of different casts as to their Complexion, but none quite so black as the Negroes, thick lips, flat Noses, and are the ugliest fellows I ever saw, making themselves still more so by the addition of Grease, and Dirt, which they rub on their skins, and plaister their platts of Hair with...

And that was really that. A further attempt, by Thompson, to communicate with the natives was equally frustrating, and on 19 April they departed after Popham had completed his survey. 'This place,' he wrote in his journal, 'afforded as little refreshment, scarce any Fish and no Flesh; the Ship's Company eat the Penguins and reported them excellent; I wish my palate could have agreed as theirs did, but I thought them much too fishy to eat as fowl.' 'It is much to be lamented,' Thompson summed up, 'that so fine a harbour as Pequena should be formed by such a barren, unfruitful soil, apparently doomed to everlasting sterility.' Two centuries later, the seaward fringe of the Namib Desert is still barely inhabited.

The problem of navigating and surveying along a barren, unapproachable and largely unknown coast, with few recognisable features and no water, come very clearly out of the two journals. Fog held them up; water was rationed to one quart per man per day; and when, at Pequena, Popham came upon a tree 'thrown up some five feet above high water mark', it was a real find and was chopped up for the galley fire.

Slowly they pressed on northward. 'Running along the shore at a distance of about 4 miles,' Popham noted, when the fog cleared sufficiently, 'and seldom out of the sound of the surf,' they found themselves off a 'line of perpendicular rugged cliffs which were named Easter Cliffs, and from-our Latitude I imagined it is what has been laid down in the Charts for the Gulf of St. Thomas, equally erroneous with the other Geographical Description of this Country.'

On the 27th they came to another inlet, Walwich (now Walvis) Bay, 'well sheltered from all winds and you lay there as in a mill pond'. The beach was littered with driftwood—where from, they wondered, there was not a tree in sight—and in the evening 'a party of natives came to the waterside and suffered us to join them.

Saluting us accordingly to the custon of the Country by rubbing our faces with some rancid fat, which they had in the horn of a cow', and chanting the words 'Borasso! Borasso!' This lot were considerably more friendly than those at Pequena—too friendly for comfort!—and showed an unexpected fondness for brandy and tobacco; tastes which, Thompson reckoned, they could only have acquired by previous contact with Europeans, probably from the Portuguese to the north.

Popham surveyed the bay, and he and Thompson accompanied the native party back to their village, which Thompson sketched: no more than a huddle of rough shelters made from the branches of shrubs, one of the few forms of vegetation. Howe, the botanist, discovered a 'small thorny plant' possibly the prickly pear, which he identified as a kind of cucumber, and which, with milk from their cattle, supplied the people with their main nourishment. Popham noticed that the women—of whom there were very few and very hideous—had the top joint of their little finger cut off, and he wrote off the whole tribe as 'being part of the laziest and most filthy Nation in the Universe.' The sight of one of the women picking the lice out of her husband's 'clotted wool' and eating them 'with vast pleasure and satisfaction' did nothing to mitigate this impression. As a result of the flies, the smoke of the fires in their huts and the blowing sand, every one of them had sore eyes, with the eyelashes, Thompson noted, 'eaten away by a small fly... which the country is full of, and the eye is the first place they attack'. No wonder they all carried what Thompson calls 'a flapper' made of a fox's or jackal's brush attached to a stick.

Walvis Bay, for all its excellent shelter, was surrounded by swamps, out of which 'arose thick fogs and putrid exhalations', giving them all more agues. This sounds very like malaria, and their remedy for it, the 'Peruvian Bark' * was effective. But there was still no fresh water to be found: wherever they dug they found it brackish and 'nearly as salt as the Ocean'.

6

They left Walvis Bay on 2 May and almost immediately ran into trouble. 'In the evening it fell calm and the ship driving fast in shore by the impulse of a very heavy swell that broke in a tremendous surf upon a steep Beach, we were compelled to anchor'—'an irksome situation', Popham noted, which lasted for two days. The peril of their situation was potentially acute. If they had been driven ashore, *Nautilus* would not have lasted more than a few minutes in the breakers; and supposing that any of her company had succeeded in fighting their way through the surf, what hope of survival would they have had, without food or water in that desolate place? Some future voyagers might one day have come across their bleached skeletons among the dunes and a few scraps of precious driftwood—as they did themselves at their next anchorage, Fish Bay. There, on the low sandy isthmus

---

* Bark of the Cinchona Tree, which yields quinine.

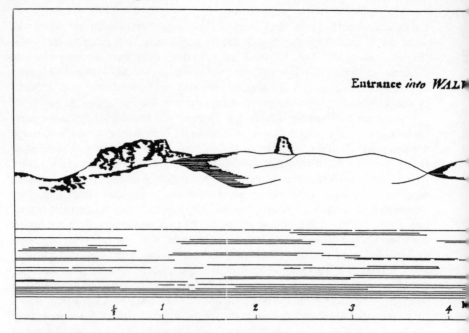

Entrance *into* WAL

Sketch of Walwich Bay, SW Africa, with HMS *Nautilus* (1786); 'well-sheltered from all winds and you lay there as in a mill pond'.
The drawing is probably by Popham who surveyed the bay.

known as Tyger Island which formed it, they came across 'a large piece of lump leather, and the runner tackle of a large boat, the blocks of which were painted green and did not appear to have been exposed there above a year', but no clues as to what vessel these relics might have come from.

Home Popham's chart of Fish Bay, 'certainly the most barren spot, I had seen on the coast', amply confirms his impression of its utter desolation.[10] There was, however, a great amount of driftwood, and 'an abundance of fish, of a great variety and all excellent' including 'Soals, Breams, Snappers, King Fish, Albacores, Jew Fish, Skait, Thorn-backs and Rays...' The seine was hauled once or twice a day, and brought in so much that a lot had to be thrown back. But there was still no trace of water. Thompson wrote, 'While the survey of the bay was completing, I used every endeavour to find fresh water, but in vain; I also penetrated with a party as far as possible into the country, but to my mortification beyond every hill we persevered to ascend, we still found one which rose higher, nor did I perceive the least sign of vegetation', only 'the tracks and dung of beasts' and a

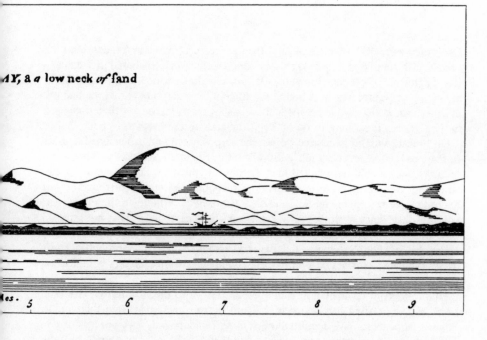

AY, a a low neck *of* fand

les. 5 6 7 8 9

bird like a crow, the second land bird seen since St Helen's Bay almost two months earlier.

Although Fish Bay was sheltered, except from the north, and had a depth of between 7 and 15 feet, without fresh water it could hardly be recommended except as a temporary refuge for small vessels; and on 16 May they weighed and sailed north again towards Cape Negroe. With Popham sailing in the cutter as close to the surf as he dared, they searched for the cape, and the river that was said to lie beyond it, and saw no sign of either. 'Among the many various errors we found in all the charts respecting this coast,' he noted, 'none can be more egregious than their description of Cape Negro, which they lay down as a long cape stretching to the westward ... from 16°04′ to 16°27′ south lattitude.' Instead, all they found was 'a continued straight shore, barren sand hills and dark hummocks, with a flat beach and a high surf.' In fact, on modern charts there is a cape of sorts, Ponta Albina, south of Porto Alexandre, after which the coast of Angola inclines east of north towards Benguela. But in any case their work was done.

'In compliance with my orders and instructions', Thompson recorded with almost audible relief, 'my researches terminated, and I hauled to the northward, nor did any man feel a regret at leaving so dreary a coast, along which we had sailed nearly 1,200 miles... without seeing a tree or procuring a drop of fresh water'.

7

Once they were 150 miles from land they picked up 'the clear Trades', and the 'few Aguish complaints began to recover'. Six days later they anchored in St James's Bay, St Helena. There they found the *Dutton*, East Indiaman, 'and a French Bark, belonging to Nantz, who was bound for Angola for a cargo of slaves; he had put in here in some distress having made the island by mere chance, when he supposed himself by his reckoning to be 60 or 70 leagues to the eastward of it.'

On June 1, with all hands recovered, the ship watered and provisioned and the rigging refitted, they weighed and sailed for England. Normally, Thompson remarks, they would have called in at Ascension Island for turtles, which would have been 'very grateful to us, to whom provisions had not been frequent'; but his orders were to press on home as fast as possible. Which, in the event, was not very fast. They were beset by calms and light airs, and it was not until 23 July, after a tedious passage of 53 days, that they finally dropped anchor at Spithead. About the only consolation was that they had not lost a single man through sickness or accident: the satisfaction with which Thompson records the fact is indication enough of its rarity.

Home Popham immediately submitted his charts to the Admiralty. The First Lord, Howe, writing to Commander Byam Martin in August, said that 'Lieut. Popham appears to have acquitted himself, as I understand, very successfully in the discharge of his late commission...', but that did not mean that the Admiralty had a job for him. Once more he was back on half-pay. Nevertheless the voyage, and the work of the surveyor, arduous and unpleasant though they were, soon proved useful to him, and laid the foundation for his reputation among his contemporaries as 'one of the first marine surveyors of his time'.

As to where he was, and how he spent his time, during the next empty six months there is no direct evidence; but it is reasonable to suppose that he was in London, in the company of his eldest brother William,[11] then a Colonel in the East India Company's Bengal Army and back in England after outstanding service under Warren Hastings. William had married the previous year and was living in Dover Street: Home's only surviving letters from this period are also from Dover Street. Conjecture is supported by the fact that during this period his thoughts turned to India. Which other member's of Joseph's large family, Home's full and step-brothers and sisters, he saw or visited, we do not know. There are brief references in two of William's letters, written some years later, to 'our sister', but that is all.

One thing Home did do at about this time was to have his portrait painted.[12] It is not a very good portrait, and it has been described as probably having been painted 'by a provincial artist on tour at a naval establishment' and positively dated as before 1787 (by an Admiralty order of 17 November that year, full dress uniform was restored for lieutenants, 'the most significant detail being the innovation of the celebrated foul anchor to the buttons... in Popham's pre-1787 uniform the buttons have a rose or star'), the combination of circumstances neatly fit Home's at that time. But why he should have had his portrait painted at all is anybody's guess.

The fact is that in 1786 Mr Home Riggs Popham, Lieutenant in His Majesty's Navy but for the time being unemployed and therefore without official rank, had few ties and probably not much money. His father had been dead for twelve years; and now Ned Thompson, his protector and benefactor, was dead too. If he was going to make something of his life, he had better take drastic action—which is exactly what he did. And for the first time he revealed the qualities of enterprise, impulsiveness and grasp of detail which were to persist throughout his life.

NOTES ON CHAPTER III

1. Captains of naval vessels which carried cargo were paid for it (cf. *Narcissus* bringing the specie back from Buenos Ayres: Chapter XIV).

2. 'How long is it since the Royal Navy had seen a Captain who kept a painter, and was his own poet?' asked the editor of the extracts from Thompson's Journal in the *Cornhill Magazine*. Or, as Thompson himself said of his Muse:

   > If Prose and Rhyme, alas, should jar
   > She's half a poet, half a tar.

3. Lord Howe was First Lord 1783-8 and was working on his own improvements to flag-signalling, to be issued six years later as *The Signal Book for the Ships of War* (see Chapter XII). Thompson said of him in 1785, 'he is now so very unpopular throughout the Navy that all try to pluck the Trident from his hand.'

4. He had grounds for his melancholy: the entry for 20 Nov runs: 'The dullest and severest birthday I had ever encountered—my boy ill—my wife mad—my friends unsatisfied and pressing me for money.' Despite which, he offered Dr Johnson £200 because the Sage in his last illness, was desperately poor.. Johnson in his reply said 'he had never heard of such generosity'.

5. The background for the search for a new convict colony, and the part played by Edward Thompson, are fully covered in a paper by Randolph Vigne, MA, FSA, which he presented to the Australian Historical Association Conference at Sydney University in 1988: 'The Botany Bay that Failed: Commodore Thompson and the Namibian Coast Scheme', and which he kindly sent me. Thompson's death, and his nephew's report on that desolate region, ensured that Botany Bay was chosen instead.

6. Confusion, in the published references to this voyage, is caused by the fact that while Popham says that he was surveying 'on the Coast of Caffraria', that region on contemporary maps is shown on the *southeast* coast of South Africa, between the present ports of Durban and East London and now called Transkei. There it was bordered by 'The Country of the Wild Hottentots', and 'Wild Boskeman's Country'. The land to the north of Cape Province was at this time largely unexplored, and 'Caffraria' was used loosely to describe the whole area of what is now South and Southwest Africa, Namibia and Angola.

7. 'Mouth of the Orange River, or Garieb ... forms inside a big bay with some sandbanks like little islands. This mouth cannot be seen from the sea because of the sandbanks that lie in front of it, which cause breakers for quite half-a-mile from the shore... Thus even a small boat cannot enter here from the sea'. (From Notes to a map by C.D. Wentzel of Ensign Butler's Expedition, 1752: included in 'Pioneer Travellers of South Africa,

1750-1800', Vernon S Forbes.) Between 1685 and 1783 there were only seven such travellers: they included a Scottish gardener, and a Frenchman, Le Vaillant, who exaggerated wildly.

8. The remains of the cross, the Padrao, set up by Diaz were discovered by Dr Eric Axelson of Witwatersrand University in 1953. Two years later Quentin Keynes, the owner of T.B. Thompson's Journal was able to give Axelson a copy of Thompson's sketch of it; and in 1985 the two men met at the spot to discuss the 50th Anniversary of Diaz's visit, with the idea of erecting a replica of the original. (See the 'The Pillar in the Mist' J. Kinahan. Staats Museum, Windhoek, Namibia, 1988)

9. Alexander Dalrymple, then Hydrographer to the East India Company, published his collection of charts from various sources in 1785. Twelve years later he was appointed first Admiralty Hydrographer, in which capacity he and Home Popham were to cross swords. (See Chapter XVI: 2.)

10. Four of Popham's African charts, as well as his later ones from the Red Sea, are in the Hydrographic Department, MOD (N), at Taunton.

11. Lt-General William Popham (1740-1821) made his name in the first place by storming the 'impregnable' fort of Gwalior in 1780; and in the following year captured Patita and Bijaigarh. In 1785 he married Mary, daughter of Sir Willaim Thomas, Bt. He was MP for Milbourne Port, 1787-90, and returned to India in 1799 and fought in the Fourth Mysore War.

12. The portrait is in the National Portrait Gallery. Originally attributed to Sir William Archer Shee or the American artist Mather Brown, it is now catalogued as 'Artist Unknown', and tentatively dated c1783. It could have been painted then, after his return from Jamaica, between the two African voyages, or after the second. Professor Dorinda Evans, in her book *Mather Brown, Early American Artist in England,* dismissing the suggestion that it was by him, draws attention to the fact that 'the surface of the face is strangely uneven, the paint throughout was too dry when it was applied, and the drawing of the right arm is too awkward for Brown.' The comparison with Mather Brown's portrait of Home Popham twenty years later clinches the point. The portraits of Home and his elder brother William were given to the National Portrait Gallery by Bishop George Popham Blyth, Archdeacon of Rangoon, who became first Anglican Bishop in Jerusalem in 1887. How the portraits came into his possession in the first place is not known.

CHAPTER IV

Hazards of the China Trade 1787-93

1

ON 12 FEBRUARY 1787 Home Popham wrote to the Secretary of the Admiralty:[1] 'Having had the permission of Lord Howe to apply for leave of absence, to go to the East Indies to follow my private affairs: I beg you will do me the favour to move their Lordships to grant me two years leave of absence for that purpose...' Their Lordships did not see fit to grant his request. First of all, they stipulated that he must get permission from the East India Company to visit their settlements; and then, when he said he only wanted to go to the Danish settlement of Fredericknagore,* that 'they do not think fit to give leave of absence to any Officers on half-pay to go to the East Indies, unless they are employed in the service of the East India Company'. After a further letter from him, however, they somewhat grudgingly gave in, but only on condition that he gave up his half-pay.

Popham, so far as known, had no private affairs in Fredericknagore, nor does he seem to have had the slightest intention of going there. Indeed, writing some years later, he put the matter rather differently. The American War being over and 'there being then no further employment' for him, 'it was proposed to him to enter on a Mercantile Enterprise from Ostend to the East Indies; which he acceded to without any further consideration on the subject, than of the opportunity it would afford for activity and improvement in the various branches of his profession, more particularly Practical Astronomy and Marine Surveying.'

This, in its way, is no less disingenuous than his original request, for, like several other of his activities throughout his life, it is tinged with the ambiguity which made him suspect to many of his contemporaries. It was, in short, true—but it was not the whole truth. No doubt, since the Navy was his profession and he was an ambitious young man, he wished to improve his qualifications; but it is as certain as anything can be that he saw in it an opportunity for activity and improvement in his finances. The 'mercantile enterprise' was more important than the 'practical astronomy': he went East hoping to make his fortune, and he very nearly succeeded; and the story of the next six years was to surface over and over again in the future and supply a handy weapon for his enemies. 'The less said about that the better,' remarked Fletcher Wilkie in 1805 when drawing a word-sketch of him, and immediately implied a certain disreputability.

That the adventure began in Ostend virtually ensured that, for it was a free port, and a haven for smugglers as well as merchants and sea captains busy contravening

---

* Now Serampore, 15 miles up the Hooghly River from Calcutta.

the monopoly of the East India Companies, the British 'John Company' included. Because it lay within the Austrian Netherlands, and was therefore part of the Austro-Hungarian Empire which stretched from the Channel to the Danube and as far south as Tuscany, the Imperial writ ran there as well as in Genoa. Robert Charnock with whom Popham was to have considerable dealings, was, it was said, notorious for smuggling goods, particularly tea, to England.

There are several versions of how Popham travelled to India that first time: that he was employed as navigator on an Indiaman, or as master of one, or that he was taken on by the East India Company as a hydrographer. None of these appears to be true; while his own statement that he 'proceeded to Ostend, and from thence to India', although certainly true, is hardly illuminating. Illumination is provided from another source altogether. Under the date 13 April 1787, in 'a list of ships fitting or fitted out at Ostend on private account chiefly destined for China manned chiefly with Englishmen left unemployed when the Commutation Act put an end to smuggling tea...' is the following entry: '6. The *Madona* (sic) Captain Popham. A L'ancre dans la Tamise d'où ce vaisseau doit revenir pour Ostende.'[2]

Can this be the Home Riggs Popham, late of HMS *Nautilus* and currently unemployed, on leave of absence from the Royal Navy having given up his half-pay in order to 'follow his private affairs in the Danish settlement of Fredericknagore'? Everything suggests that it is. We do not know what he was doing between July 1786 and March 1787, but it seems extremely likely that he spent part of the time in Ostend, exploring the possibilities for going into commerce and buying the *Madonna*, *before* he applied for leave. Because the voyage out East was all arranged, he was even prepared to give up his half-pay.

By his own testimony, he went to India in 1787,

> where he followed his commercial pursuits without interruption or restraint, and without being aware that he was violating any law of his country by so doing: That he was well-known to Lord Cornwallis, then Governor-General of Bengal, and graciously and kindly received by him; and at his Lordship's request, whilst *lying with his Foreign Flag at Calcutta*, he undertook to make a survey of Laccam's Channel and Harbour, of which he made a report that obtained his Lordship's approbation.[3]

That is all, but note the key phrase 'whilst lying with his Foreign Flag'. That can only mean that he had his own ship, and that she was evading the Company's monopoly by sailing under foreign colours, no other than those of the Austrian Empire, Tuscany or Leghorn, much used by the Ostenders when challenging the pretensions of John Company.

The next slight but positive piece of evidence as to what he was up to in 1788 comes exactly a year after he was reported as being in the Thames in the *Madonna*. It occurs in a letter by one John Adolphus Pope, a sailor, and is dated April of that year, in Rangoon.[4]

The arrival of the *Vienna*, Capt. Williams, and the *Indian Trader*, Capt.

Kipling, has added much to our society. They are both come from the Nicobars, laden with cocoanuts. This is one of the chief articles of trade and the profits are immense. The *Vienna* is a ship under Imperial colours, wholly manned by Europeans and belonging to Captain Popham, a brother of our old messmates.

Ignoring for the moment the enigma of the last six words,[5] it would seem that some time after his arrival in Calcutta, Home sold the *Madonna* and bought the *Vienna*. Corroboration for this comes from another source. During that year he went into partnership with a certain John McArthur[6] to purchase a ship, the 500 ton *Stadt van Weenen*—the Flemish rendering of *City of Vienna*. The purchase date is not known; what is known is that at the end of the year, both the ship and her then cargo, consisting partly of Indian piece goods, were mortgaged to the firm of Archibald Paxton & Co. and she sailed for Ostend.[7] There, later on, as *La Ville de Vienne*, her name was changed to *L'Etrusco*. In the meantime, i.e. during 1788, Home was employing her, under the command of Captain Williams, in local—and extremely profitable—trading.

If this is correct, he was 'following his commercial pursuits' with considerable energy and success. But he was also indulging in other pursuits as well; for he had met a young lady, Elizabeth Prince, the daughter of a captain in the Company's military service (in which Home's brother had distinguished himself). William Hickey, who was in Calcutta at the time, knew all about the affair. Among the English community was a Mr Carter who, as a boy, had had a remarkably fine voice which had entranced Lady Hamilton, but which had gone on adolescence. He had therefore come out to Bengal to teach music and singing.

Amongst those who had benefited from Carter's instructions [Hickey noted], none did so in so great a degree as Miss Prince, now Lady Popham, the wife of Sir Home. The lady possessed uncommon powers of voice without knowing what to do with it or how to avail herself of the advantage Nature had blessed her with. Under Carter's management she became a proficient, and had candour enough to admit how greatly she had benefited by his advice and directions.

But Carter not only taught Elizabeth to sing: he fell desperately in love with her, proposed, and was 'positively refused'—whereupon he quitted India. And Home and Elizabeth were married.[8]

Hickey gives only one other titbit of Calcutta gossip connected with the pair, and that concerned a Mr Hesilrige who, at the age of forty, 'was so inconsiderate as once more to engage in the holy state of matrimony, marrying a wild and giddy girl of fifteen, daughter of Mrs Grey, the sister of Sir Home's lady.' All of which suggests that Home had found his feet as rapidly in the limited but lively society of the Honorable East India Company in Bengal as he had in the profitable complexities of East Indies trade .

And so, at the end of 1788, with a new ship and a newly-wedded wife, he sailed for Ostend, determined to return to his commercial pursuits in those opulent waters as soon as opportunity offered.

2

In the Memorial which he addressed to 'The King's Most Excellent Majesty in Council' in October 1803, and for reasons which will become clear later, Home Popham wrote: 'The Peace continuing, and the service of your Majesty's petitioner not being otherwise called for, he engaged in a second voyage to India, for which he obtained a large outfit from the house of Robert Charnock & Co. of Ostend, and sailed from thence to Calcutta in the year 1790.'

This bland outline of events reveals scarcely anything of his actual activities that spring of 1790; any more than it reveals that, although the Peace was continuing, a mere 170 miles away France was in uproar. More of that later: what he was actually engaged in during February and March was the re-mortgaging of his ship *La Ville de Vienne*, henceforth to be known as *L'Etrusco*, to the Leghorn firm Messrs Valle & Borghini, for £5,000 at a rate of 1¼ per cent, on condition that at the end of her round voyage she should be delivered to Leghorn, or, failing that, he should pay a fine of '$1,000 of 8 reals Leghorn money'. Valle & Borghini produced a Genoese captain, Francisco Coppi, of whom Popham was to 'make use' in order to acquire a passport for a voyage to the East Indies and permission to sail under the Tuscan flag from Prince Leopold, the Austrian Emperor and among his other titles, Grand Duke of Tuscany. To such labyrinthine legal dodges were merchants and shipowners driven in their determination to evade the monopoly of the East India Company. From Charnocks he loaded a cargo of masts, spars, iron, lead, copper, marble and bale goods; and his second mercantile enterprise was ready to sail.

Before the ship left Ostend in July, however, Home received a cautionary letter from his brother William, who wrote:

> Be assured, our friends in Bengal shall know of your intended visit there by every means in my power. I hope you will attend to the necessary ceremonies respecting the flag you sail under, even to the number of Englishmen you carry with you as part of the ship's company; orders are positively sent to India to be very strict with respect to foreign ships, and yours, I have reason to believe, will be particularly marked. Do not give way to ideas contrary to this opinion of mine, lest you and your friends should materially suffer...

What was all this—'necessary ceremonies', 'particularly marked', 'materially suffer'? Was he setting out to break the law? In order to answer this question, it is necessary to look at the powers of that remarkable organisation the 'United

Company of Merchants of England trading to the East Indies', i.e. the Honorable East India Co. William Pitt's India Act of 1784 had brought it under government control, but it continued to enjoy its monopoly of British Far Eastern trade for some years yet. Though the Act curtailed the political powers of the Company by making it subject to the government of the day through a Board of Control, not until 1793 was it actually compelled to allow some British merchants to trade on its sacred preserves, and thereby lost the power granted to it by an Act of 1718 by which it was authorised to seize any British subject trading independently, or under the auspices of the Ostend Company. But 'there were not wanting enterprising spirits who sought to make a profit by taking services with its foreign rivals'[9], or employing the fiction of sailing under a foreign flag.

The years between 1784 and 1793 were therefore a period of transition from total to partial monopoly, as far as trade in British bottoms was concerned. The Company could not curb the legitimate commerce of genuine foreign companies—Dutch, Swedish, Danish—with their own settlements in India, nor with the 'Country Ships' trading locally. But what it could do, under the 1784 Act, was fine 'British subjects ... trading to India under the authority of a foreign Prince of State' £500 for each offence.[10]

The answer to the question, therefore, is that Popham was not quite breaking the law, but he was taking a considerable risk. If his legal fiction were exposed and *L'Etrusco* judged to be a British ship sailing under false colours, he would be liable to arrest and deportation; while if she were regarded as honestly trading under the Imperial flag, he would be liable to a £500 fine. That he considered—obviously with William's measured advice—the risk worth taking was, in the first place, because he had friends in government in Bengal, and in the second, because of the widespread evasion of the law, the endemic corruption by the Company's servants. They were using foreign ships to send home their ill-gotten gains, and, as one writer put it, 'Hence originated a clandestine connection with the Foreign Companies, which has been kept up ever since.' Popham, in short, reckoned he could get away with it.

4

Their first port of call after leaving Ostend was Funchal. Here they took on a cargo of wine, including the 'best pipe of Madeira on the island (which they say is the London particular), and of the very best quarter cask of malmsey', as requested by William, who added, '... I could wish both were the oldest of the kind to be had'. And from Madeira Popham wrote to Robert Charnock, settling various outstanding bills and reporting the purchase of another ship, the brig *Donna Anna*, of which no more is heard. In their reply Charnocks remarked, inter alia, that 'The prospect here for your return cargo is very flattering, as every obstacle to your returning direct to this port is removed. These countries are again under the dominions of the House of Austria'[11]

The ship called in at Cape Town and picked up a number of extra hands who were to sail with Popham for the next three years. For the next leg of the voyage the only source of information is *L'Etrusco's* brash young owner himself, in a speech in the House of Commons eighteen years later, when he was no longer young but no less brash. Defending himself against charges of illegal trading in the ship, levelled against him by a Mr Lushington, he described the voyage and provided his own justification for it.

> ... with respect to his trade in India; he had had it in his intention to go to Salapore [sic], but his ship striking a rock in Mozambique Channel, he had been induced, to save his crew, to make for Bombay, where he witnessed vessels taking in goods and trading contrary to the law, *which was evidently relaxed in their favour. How then was he wrong in availing himself of this relaxation?* * From Bombay he went to Madras, where similar proceedings were freely carried on, under the same colours as his, and attended with the same circumstances.

The same dispensation, he maintained, held good in Calcutta where

> Lord Cornwallis knew at that time that he was a British subject, and that he was in command of a foreign ship. It was in his Lordship's power, as Governor-General, to have put him under arrest and to have sent him back to England; but on the contrary, that Noble Lord... had *abstained from noticing* the trade in which he had been engaged.

Better still, though Popham did not mention it on this occasion, *L'Etrusco* was promptly pressed into Company service. On the Malabar coast, where the Company's forces were involved in one of their wars with Tipoo Sahib, they were short of food and the ship was commissioned to supply them with rice and grain. En route for Bombay, however, she came up against the full force of the Northwesterly Monsoon—'very violent'—which drove them eastwards across the Bay of Bengal, and they fetched up at 'the Company's New Settlement on the Prince of Wales Island in the Streights of Malacca' now known by its native name of Penang.

Here while the gale damage to the ship was being made good, Popham displayed another facet of that energy and initiative which, throughout his life, either commended him to his superiors or landed him in hot water. He not only 'undertook an examination of the navigation of the whole island, and discovered a South Channel between the Island and the Malayan Coast, which would allow ships drawing up to 24 feet to use it', but wrote, and later published, a detailed account of the island's climate, produce, and suitability as a naval and mercantile base.[12]

---

* Author's italics. *L'Etrusco's* arrival, and the auction of her cargo of 'Europe Goods' was reported in the *Calcutta Gazette,* 7 April 1791.

The southern channel was a boon to ships leaving the island for China, for until then they had to beat up against the monsoon and round the northern tip before they could set course, and in 1792 Popham himself piloted five of the Company's Indiamen 'besides many country ships' through it to clinch the matter. Characteristically, in his book about Penang and its virtues he included a number of testimonials from ships' masters who had made use of it. For this useful piece of hydrography, and his earlier work on the Hooghly River, the Governor-General in Council 'directed that a piece of plate may be prepared, bearing an inscription expressive of the occasion on which it was given'.

There are two paragraphs in the Public Letter from Bengal to the Court of Directors in London, dated 25 November 1791, which go a long way to explaining his immunity from prosecution while he was operating outside the law in Indian waters, and were to serve him well when he returned to England eighteen months later. 'Unemployed as Mr Popham is under the Company, his zeal and the gratuitous direction of his professional talents to the advancement of the public good… claimed more than common notice…' is the first. In the second, they request that these services 'may be represented in the terms they merit… to the Lords Commissioners of the Admiralty of England'.

How could they invoke the letter of the law against a man who had, quite voluntarily, proved himself so useful?

5

The supplies bound for the Company's hungry troops on the Malabar Coast were transhipped on to one of the Company's own ships, and *L'Etrusco* took on a miscellaneous cargo of 'beetle nuts and rattan canes' according to one of the crew, 'and sailed thence to the Malay coast, where she took on other goods of the same kind, and likewise some pepper, which she carried to Calcutta'.

So towards the end of 1791, Home Popham was back in Bengal, having had, it seems, a good year's trading; for the next thing to happen is that he is buying another ship.

If the story at this point becomes somewhat complicated, it is partly because some of the documents involved are missing, but mainly because that is precisely what the transactions were. In essence, Popham sold his (mortgaged) ship *L'Etrusco* (no more is heard of her having to be returned to Leghorn) and with the proceeds 'and other sums acquired by outward investments' bought in her stead the American-built *President Washington*, changed *her* name to *L'Etrusco*, took her to Canton and, in partnership with two European merchants there, loaded her with a valuable cargo consigned to Robert Charnock & Co. in Ostend.

So much for the bare outline: what in fact happened was this. After the original *L'Etrusco*'s return to Calcutta, Francisco Coppi, the 'Captain of the Flag' in whose name the Tuscan passport had been issued, abruptly left the ship, apparently because of some grievance over his share of the rice cargo bound for Bombay.

His departure put Popham in a spot, from which he extricated himself by simply sailing for Bombay on a further voyage without him, and therefore without legal colours. By doing so, as his Calcutta merchant John Burgh pointed out, he not only gave Coppi a weapon, but put the ship and her cargo in jeopardy as his insurance became invalid.

Coppi himself apparently intended to lay an information against Popham, accusing him of breaking the Company's monopoly. 'Be on your guard,' Burgh wrote in mid-July 1791, 'all this might have been prevented; but alas! my friend, you have been indeed too precipitate...' John Burgh, a friend indeed, took every possible step to frustrate Coppi's plans, though this was not easy since 'he works like a mole in the dark'. However, before Popham returned to Calcutta at the beginning of November, the matter had been resolved by a Higher Power. 'That bare-faced Italian who', as Burgh wrote, 'we have not seen or ever desire to see unless he was about to take his last swing on a ladder,' had died the previous month—from, one must presume, natural causes.

One danger had been removed, but there were others, and Popham himself was now doubly vulnerable. 'If I am more apprehensive,' Burgh wrote, 'that something of the kind may happen from many circumstances which I have heard, and know also that your enemy, Robertson, is now at Bombay, and who would most likely exert himself to oppress you if such an opening for doing it should be found.'

In the meantime Popham was being invited to take part in an even more dubious enterprise. A commercial agent by the name of Pendergast was organising freight and passengers for Popham's return voyage to Europe, and wrote to him from Dacca: 'Let me know... your terms for freight, and whether you are bound direct for Ostend... and inform me whether you can effect the landing of a few bales of very fine goods in England at the usual terms... Do not be offended by my proposing illicit commerce to you... there are many houses in London whose principal attention is given to this line of business.' It was, Pendergast assured him, simply a way of circumventing 'the exhorbitant charges at the India House and infringing their monoply rights.'

Popham's reply has not survived; but in any case he was already involved in a more ambitious, less dangerous, and he hoped more lucrative plan. On Christmas Day 1791 he wrote to Robert Charnock about it in a letter that gives some idea of the tightrope he was walking in his determination to make his fortune: 'some friends advised me to buy a new ship that had just arrived from America, for the purpose of lowering the freight and carrying home a number of passengers.' With the prospect of peace between Tipoo and the government, he reckoned 300 people would be looking for passage home. However, he had no sooner agreed to buy the *President Washington* (980 tons, armed with ten French 6-pounders and small arms) than the peace negotiations broke down, and even worse. '... the Bengal Banks, from whence the sources of all my promised funds were to have arisen, failed... it was a settled plan of the Black Moneyholders to break the Banks... This was such a stroke, that it almost got the better of the little philosophy I possess, on reflecting with astonishment that such an event could take place in so short a time.' The purchase price was $78,000 Spanish, say £21,450, but without specifying how he proposed raising the money, he assured Charnock that he was going ahead.

Which he duly did. According to one of the sailors, the American owners of the *President Washington* took over the old *L'Estrusco*; from somewhere or other Popham produced not only the balance, but another Tuscan subject, one Giacomo Pons; and on 2 January 1792 the Tuscan Vice-Consul transferred the captaincy to Pons. Significantly, it was to Pons that the Americans had sold the vessel: Popham was not mentioned. So, with Coppi out of the way, with his new ship and many of the original crew, and sailing once more under the Tuscan flag, Popham left Calcutta for Penang.

6

He had probably sailed just in time, for in a letter of 18 February 1792 he was warned that 'Captain Fenwick, in his friendly letter to the Council, had mentioned the *President Washington*, as your property, engaged in illicit trade...' and orders had been issued to investigate. 'In so arbitrary a government,' his correspondent went on, ''tis impossible to say how far things may be carried, especially when such malicious reports are listened to and taken up in so serious a way.' Things were getting rather too hot for his comfort in Bengal.

Popham had slipped up at home, too. His leave of absence from the Navy had been only for two years, and that had long ago expired. William had reminded him of the fact back in March 1790, adding that when he applied for an extension 'it must not be for India as... they will require a certificate from India House; you may make it for Africa, or the West Indies and America, which may be for two years.' Last time it had been for Fredericknagore: this time he neglected to apply at all; and in April 1791 he had accordingly been struck off the list of lieutenants. Ironically, this coincided almost exactly with the Governor in Council writing to India House, commending his survey of Lacams Channel, and asking them to pass the commendation to the Admiralty. Then, and indeed throughout his career, Home Popham showed a talent for making life difficult for himself.

According to the later testimony of one Isaac Sioblin 'of Obo in Finland, mariner and late butcher', the new *L'Etrusco*

> loaded a cargo of rice and saltpetre (at Penang) for account of the East India Company, which she delivered at Madras, and likewise some bales of cotton: and having there taken in more cotton, she returned again to Pulipenang, where she was hove down and underwent a repair, during which period the cotton was stored, but afterwards reshipped, together with some lead, rattans, pepper, and beetle-nuts, which she carried to Whampon, where it was delivered into boats for the purpose of being carried to Canton...

That was the voyage on which Popham piloted the Company's ships through the

South Channel, thereby adding to the contradictions of his status in Bengal.

The ship arrived in Pearl River in September 1792; and on 23 October an agreement was signed between Home Popham, Charles Samuel Constant de Rebeque of Geneva, and Jean-Baptiste Piron, a Frenchman, for the provision and freighting of a cargo from Canton to Ostend. De Rebeque put up the greater proportion of the cash, Popham and Piron contributing a share each.

Canton, at this time, was the only port in China open to European traders, and they were only there on sufferance. They were not allowed into the city, but were restricted to their own small mercantile community along the waterfront, while their ships had to anchor down river at Whampon. There were two key people in any transaction in this extraordinary closed, yet thriving, oriental trading-post: for the companies, the supercargoes, European agents who knew the labyrinthine regulations of the Chinese bureaucracy, and were expected to combine their roles, as one writer puts it, of 'merchant, banker, linguist and diplomat'; for the Chinese, the guild or *Hong* merchant, whom the visiting trader contacted on arrival and through whom alone he was permitted to deal. Despite everything, 'the rules and regulations, the exactions and indignities', despite the problems of language and custom, the trade especially in tea, silk, porcelain—was booming. At the time when the *L'Etrusco* was there, exports from Canton to England were running at £1.5 million a year—and all without a single written contract—and the profits were enormous.

De Rebeque had worked for both the British and French East India Companies, and had a cargo ready for shipment; but 'finding (the ship's) tonnage too large and his funds not sufficient to employ the whole of it', he went into partnership with Popham and Piron.

In the meantime another complication had arisen. Giacomo Pons fell ill and was advised by his doctors that the voyage would probably kill him; so command of the ship was handed over to the ship's doctor, a Venetian named Balthazar Georgi, who had joined at Calcutta, and, fortunately, possessed Tuscan citizenship. The Gilbertian appointment of the surgeon as captain was, of course, a legal fiction; it was done, as Popham himself said, 'for greater caution'. Popham himself was regarded as master, and only when they reached home waters was nominal authority handed over to Georgi.

By the end of the year the three partners had mustered a mixed cargo worth about £50,000 comprising some 80 chests of china (table sets, 'flat blue plates', 'soup ditto', and nearly 20,000 'blue bowls'[13]); a quantity of 'powdered sugar candy', camphon and Souchong Tea, yellow nankeens, and baskets and chests of china plant, benjamin, rhubarb and sago.[14] The chests of china would have been stowed at the bottom of the hold, where they would serve as useful ballast—600 pieces were reckoned to weigh 500lbs—with the lighter items stacked on top.

This was the bulk cargo, belonging to the three partners. In addition, several of the consortium had private cargoes of their own. Popham certainly did, though there are no details of it, for he was later to be accused of smuggling it ashore at Ostend; and so did Georgi. His is listed in full, and it suggests a lively commercial imagination. There was silk, lamb skins, 100 fans 'of rosewood and yellow, finely-cut', 36 clocks, '40 pounds pearls of madreperle'; a 'large and very rare collection of Chinese paintings on paper, water colours, beautifully executed'; he also had sea otter skins, '2 pieces of Mallay silk cloth, gold worked', '10 bundles of dragon-blood canes', 1400 Malacca canes, 300 tooth-pick cases, 5 boxes of preserved ginger, and among much else, '2 large figures, viz a Chinese Mandarin and Lady, dressed in the custom of the country, moving head and arms'... Suddenly one is transported from the go-downs of Canton, and the thronging traffic on the Pearl River and the anchored ships, straight into those elegant 18th century drawing-rooms: the ladies in their embroidered silks and satins sipping their Souchong tea from Nanking porcelain bowls; the gently stirring fans, the glass-fronted cabinets with their arrays of carved figures; the men with their malacca canes; and, after those gargantuan 18th century meals, taking a small glass of tincture of rhubarb.

China was the very fount of the luxury trade.

7

L'Etrusco sailed from Whampon on 2 January 1793, thereby 'saving the monsoon' and ensuring a fair wind for Africa. On board, besides Home Popham himself and de Rebeque, travelling as supercargo, and a cosmopolitan crew of a hundred or so (twenty-six of them English), were two or three passengers, one of them being Captain Grey, Popham's brother-in-law and the father of that 'wild and giddy girl' who had married Hesilrige in Calcutta. They called at Penang, and made a fast passage to St Helena where they arrived on 30 March and stayed for ten days.

Two weeks out on the last leg back to Europe they were spoken by a Portuguese man-of-war, and learnt that war had broken out between the Maritime Powers and Revolutionary France, and that the Austrian Netherlands, including Ostend, had been overrun by the rabble armies of the Revolution. What happened next, as described by Vincent Rivaz, de Rebeque's London agent, somehow epitomises this whole voyage, from the closed, mysterious world of silks and oriental dyestuffs, Hong merchants and unsmiling mandarins, with its dreams of wealth and its fraudulent ship's papers, towards a once-familiar one, now torn apart by revolution and the death of kings.

> ...on receiving such information, he the said Charles Samuel Constand de Rebeque, with the privity and approbation of the said Home Riggs Popham, made... an exact copy of the said Bill of Lading, and also of the said Invoice, leaving out the name of the said Jean-Baptiste Piron, and stating the whole of it to be for his account...

The last thing these adventurers needed was to be picked up by a British frigate.

Later on, one of the sailors was to report that he had overheard the Mates talking in the hold. They had discovered that there was French property on board, and were afraid that 'if they were overhauled by an English man-of-war, that the ship would be made a prize of war, and they would lose their wages'. There was also a rumour on board that they were 'to proceed to America to get colours, to carry the ship more safely to Ostend'. According to another member of the crew, the *L'Etrusco* sailed sometimes under Tuscan and at other times under British colours; and although she had an American jack on board, and other national colours, these were purely for use as signal flags.

Their fears were real enough. As one of the sailors remarked, they were 'troubled' three times before they reached their home port, once by a Liverpool privateer, once by HMS *Diadem*, and finally by an armed cutter off Dunkirk. Fortunately, on each occasion, they were allowed to proceed unmolested. Short of food and water, they put into Crookhaven, in the extreme southwest corner of Ireland. There—and at this point the ironies of the story start to multiply—*L'Etrusco* joined company with two East Indiamen, the *Swift* and the *Pitt*, was escorted with them by a Revenue Cutter to Cork, and because of the danger from French privateers convoyed on to Spithead by HMS *Diadem*. Neither the cutter nor the man-of-war seems to have taken any particular interest in her; though, for fear of impressment, the English members of the crew were kept below while she was in British waters.

Off the Isle of Wight *L'Etrusco* parted company with her escort and headed for Ostend, picking up a pilot off Hastings. That night according to the testimony of John Marck, mariner of Copenhagen, 'several boats came alongside near Dungeness; and… several chests of tea and one chest of Rhubarb were taken out of the ship and put into boats; and… Captain Popham went on shore near Dungeness, before the said boats came alongside, to a partner of one of the owners… but whose name he knoweth not.' It may have been mere coincidence that a Mr Wenham, the son of one of Robert Charnock's partners, happened to be living near Hastings.

Popham was to deny categorically that such an incident had taken place: and, if bond had been broken and some chests of tea were missing, then they must have been given to the pilot as a *pour-boire*. Or perhaps to ensure his silence.

That was the night of 14 July. Next day, between Dunkirk and Ostend, an armed British cutter came alongside and the ship was boarded by a lieutenant. He and Popham had a long conversation, 'walking the quarterdeck', and then he left. There is no record of what was said, but as the *L'Etrusco* continued on her course undetained, it is reasonable to assume that the officer, having examined the ship's papers and questioned Popham, decided she was on her lawful occasions. *L'Estrusco* dropped anchor in Ostend Road the following day. They had run the gauntlet of privateers and British men-of-war, armed cutters and the Revenue; they had reached their destination.

8

Ashore, Home Popham had a wife, and a two-year old son whom he had never seen. Almost before the anchor touched bottom a boat was hoisted out, the homecoming presents of tea, lengths of silk, one can guess what else, were loaded into it, and he was rowed ashore and one of the sailors, a Dutch lad, helped him cart it all home. And what a homecoming it must have been. He had been away almost exactly three years, he had had adventures galore, and he had come back with a decent fortune. In the end the gods had smiled.

At about midnight that same night, Lieutenant Mark Robinson of His Majesty's Frigate *Brilliant*, which was anchored not far away, rowed across with a small armed party, sprang aboard, and formally seized the *L'Etrusco* as a Prize of War.

9

Whatever the rights and wrongs of the case—and the wrangling went on for fifteen years—it is difficult to find justification for Robinson's action. Although Britain, to the fury of neutral nations, maintained the right to search, and take in for examination, ships sailing under neutral flags, in July 1793 Austria was in alliance with her and so a ship sailing under the Tuscan flag was in fact not neutral at all but friendly. The tatterdemalion *sansculottes* of Revolutionary France had indeed occupied the Austrian Netherlands briefly the previous year, but had been sent packing by a joint Austrian, British, Hanoverian and Hessian army under the Prince of Coburg in March 1793; Ostend was, and for the rest of the year remained, in Allied hands. However doubtful *L'Estrusco*'s papers might turn out to be on close scrutiny—and admittedly the 'Ostenders', as they were known, were notorious freebooters—on the surface they were in order. Mark Robinson had seized a vessel ostensibly belonging to an allied nation.

That his action posed problems for the authorities in England may be deduced from the fact that three weeks elapsed before orders were issued for her to be brought back, first to the Downs and then up the Thames to Deptford. During this dismal period Popham, according to one of the more vicious current slanders, offered Robinson £40,000 to clear off. Since Popham's entire investment amounted to little more than this sum, his strenuous denial rings true. If anyone suggested such a bribe, it is more likely to have been de Rebeque; but if it ever were offered, Robinson declined it.

What is certain is that Popham set off almost immediately to London, first of all to try and sort matters out, and secondly to apply for reinstatement on the list of lieutenants and so make himself available for naval service—and get back on the payroll.

Meanwhile, the crew of the ship were taken ashore to Deal and subjected to 'Examination taken in Preparatory' before a magistrate, and with the assistance of an interpreter. During these hearings the story as recounted in this chapter was repeated, with minor differences and in a variety of tongues. This evidence, with submissions by Home Popham, de Rebeque and Georgi, and statements by Robinson and others, was then submitted to the High Court of the Admiralty for judgement. There, despite a claim 'on the ground of Jurisdiction and Territory' on behalf of his Imperial Majesty, *L'Etrusco* was adjudged a Prize of War, and she and her cargo were forfeit to the Crown.

During the course of the next few years, this verdict was upheld by the Lords Commisioners for Hearing Appeals in Prize Causes; but the contestants persevered and the case, described by the King's Proctor as 'peculiar' and 'without precedent', started its long, long journey through the courts, to end up in all its complexity as a set of Parliamentary Papers which were finally laid before the House of Commons in 1808.

NOTES ON CHAPTER IV

1. The letters are in 'Papers presented to the House of Commons respecting the Ship *L'Etrusco*, etc...', Feb. and March 1808. These, running to over 100 pages, provided much of the information in this chapter. See Parliamentary Papers (Misc), Vol X.

2. In 'The John Company at Work' by Holden Furber the following occurs: 'The managers of private India ventures from Ostend never sought publicity... Unquestionably, many of the Ostend voyages were wholly British... The *Eagle*... and the *Madona*, Captain Popham...' and he mentions ships 'flying Tuscan, Savoyard, Genoese or even Russian colours'. 'They were the mystery ships of the illicit trade and may often have changed their colours to suit the occasion.'

   British ships involved in this trade ran a double risk: besides the vengeance of the East India Company, the Royal Navy waited to pounce on them and impress any British seamen on board. On 4 August 1790, Popham's second voyage, the Admiralty ordered Rear Admiral Sir Richard King, C-in-C the Downs, to intercept *L'Etrusco*, 'commanded by Lieutenant Home Riggs Popham, of His Majesty's Navy... now at Flushing, bound to the East Indies, whose Crew is wholly or principally composed of His Majesty's subjects...' and 'to take out of her every person of the above description...' In the event, Popham slipped through unmolested. He ran the same risk on his return, of course.

3. This is the only known chart of his which has not been traced.

4. This reference and that in Note 2 were kindly given me by Mrs Anne Maier, editor of Pope's letters.

5. None of Home's brothers or step-brothers fits here. But his elder brother Thomas (b.1741) had a son Joseph (b.1772) who became second mate of an East Indiaman. At fifteen or sixteen he could have been a messmate of Pope's and been mistaken for Home's brother, since there would have only been ten years between them.

6. This seems likely to have been the John McArthur, a purser in the Navy, who like Popham worked on improving the flag-signalling code, and in 1791 became secretary to Admiral Howe.

7. Almost exactly 20 years later Paxton's brought an action for debt against Popham and McArthur, claiming that they were still owed £3,575 on the money lent to buy the cargo. The case was heard in the Court of King's Bench before Lord Ellenborough, CJ, and

three judges. Popham and McArthur argued, first, that the debt had in fact been met by the sale of the goods; and second—and impudently—that Paxton's had sold diverse goods to the partners for them to export from Calcutta to Ostend 'illegally and against the Statute, and without the licence or authority of the East India Company' on 1 December 1788. Judgment was given for the defendants. (*See* Fast: *Reports of Cases in the King's Bench*, Vols 9, 7 & 10.)

8. In the Register of Bengal Marriages, Vol 4, 1788. No. 51 the entry reads: POPHAM, HOME/MOFFAT, ELIZABETH which would appear to confuse matters, especially since F. W. Popham states, in *A West Country Family*, that Home married Elizabeth *Prince* in Bath in 1790. In fact, Elizabeth was Elizabeth Moffat Prince: a combination of the Bengal register and Hickey's gossip settles both the lady and the place.

9. Cambridge History of India Vol V, p 313.

10. 'All his Majesty's subjects residing in Great Britain, Island of Guernsey, etc. America and the West Indies, are strictly prohibited from trading to, or being in, India, unless licenced by the Company; and the ships and cargoes of such illicit traders, and also their persons, shall be seized by any of the Company's Governors or Agents, and the illicit traders shall be sent to England to answer for their offences... British subjects trading to India under the authority of any foreign Prince or State, shall forfeit £500 for every such offence.' India Act, 1784. 24 Geo III.

11. Revolution in France spread to Belgium in 1790, soon after Popham left, but was suppressed by the Emperor Leopold. As Charnock wrote to him in January 1791: 'As soon as the Austrians were in force, say 20,000 men... the mighty Patriots' army dispersed, and "like the baseless fabrick of a vision", left not a trace behind: so much for politics; now again to business.'

12. *A Description of Prince of Wales Island in the Straights of Malacca with its Real and Probable Advantages...etc.* Originally pub. 1791; and, complete with charts, in 1799. C. Northcote Parkinson remarks that although Penang did not turn out to be either as salubrious or as productive as Popham claimed, 'this settlement was genuinely useful in more ways than one', notably as a base against the Dutch in Batavia. Fifteen years after Popham wrote his *Description*, but only six after the full edition was published, it was made a Presidency by the Board of Control, Stamford Raffles was appointed Assistant to the Chief Secretary, and most of Popham's recommendations were carried out.

13. Essentially, two completely different kinds of 'Nankin Porcelain' were imported into England. One was the 'blue and white' ware, decorated with the familiar willow pattern and other, similar, *Chinese* designs; the other was specially made and decorated to order for the European trade, with designs—ships, landscapes, mythological subjects and coats of arms—faithfully copied by the craftsmen in Canton. Popham's cargo almost certainly consisted of the former.

14. Nankeen was a yellow cotton cloth: China plant was the root of *Smilax China*, of the same family as Sarsaparilla; benjamin is gum benzoin, a balsam extract used in varnishes for paintings and furniture, in ointment, and as a stimulant and perfume, rhubarb root was a medicinal, astringent root-stock used as a purgative.

CHAPTER V

The Duke of York's Admiral 1793-6

1

WITH THE seizure of *L'Etrusco* and her cargo Home Popham's free-booting days abruptly ended; in July 1793 he was unemployed, no longer a naval officer, and with a wife and a son to support. How much, if any, of the money he had made in the Far East he had managed to put aside is unknown; the agreement with de Rebeque and Piron strongly suggests that he put every penny he could lay his hands on into the venture; yet, within a few years, he was maintaining establishments in London and the Isle of Wight, while constantly complaining of being short of cash. Among his contemporaries he had a distinct reputation for cupidity.[1] He certainly needed his pay, and fortunately for him the country was at war and already had an army on the Continent.

As soon as he got home he started to badger the Admiralty to reinstate him on the Lieutenant's List and find him some employment; and in a manner that was to become characteristic of him, mustered every argument he could think of to support his request. He cited his West African charts and Lord Howe's commendation, his discovery of the South Channel at Penang, quoting letters of praise for it from masters of ships who had used it;[2] and he did not fail to mention the eulogy from the Government of Bengal to the Admiralty, and the presentation of plate that accompanied it. He also said that he had given up his half-pay voluntarily—which was a lie—and he pulled every string he could.

His first four letters had no effect; but in August a slightly more emollient one to the Secretary of the Admiralty was to have the desired result: 'As it is possible you may be too busy tomorrow to admit me, I hope you will nevertheless bear me in mind with Lord Chatham should you see him, as my friend Sir Harry Martin intends to make a particular intercession on my behalf with his Lordship on Friday for the appointment of Capitaine du Port at Dunkirk.[3] If appointed, he hopes, he says, to recommend himself to the Duke of York by his exertions in arranging the Port and 'superintending the disembarkation of the heavy artillery stores that may go over'.

This time his request was attended to, and in September, a lieutenant once more, he was despatched to Ostend as Agent for Transport to the British Army in Flanders, commanded by George III's younger son, Frederick Augustus, Duke of York. Since Ostend had been his home port, as well as his home town, for the previous five years, the appointment made sense; but it did not pass without comment. 'This appointment of Popham', Brook Watson wrote to the Admiralty, 'I find makes much noise at Ostend—the employ he has been in has raised it—

he's very clever, knows almost everything... the Navy Agents who are great men in their way and very much wish to give themselves airs...' And others were to share these opinions.

2

To Home Popham's biographer the war in the Lowlands from 1793 to the end of 1795, and his part in it, present certain problems, for the disastrous outcome of the former is only matched by the triumphant reputation bestowed on him by the latter, and the totally disproportionate effect which it had on his entire future career. It was, indeed, the fulcrum on which that career turned, but which also imbued it with an abiding ambiguity.

While he was on his way home from China, France had declared war on Britain, unwelcome news which they had heard north of St Helena; and during the spring and early summer Pitt and Dundas had cobbled together an alliance with Austria and Prussia, and an army of sorts, which sent the raggle-taggle soldiers of the Republic scampering back where they came from. The road to Paris lay open; but instead of advancing, the Prince of Coburg settled down to besiege Quemoy, and the Duke of York broke off to beseige Dunkirk. There appeared to be no urgency, since the French were obviously bent on self-destruction. In Paris during this dreadful summer of The Terror, Robespierre and the Jacobins were wielding the guillotine like a scythe and half the country was in revolt against them.

However, in August 1793 Lazare Carnot, a Captain of Engineers from Burgundy, was given the task of reorganising the French Army, a task which he carried out with such skill and demonic energy that when they attacked the Allies in September they defeated both the Germans and Austrians, at Hondeshcoote and Wattignies, and the Duke of York had no choice but to call off the siege of Dunkirk and retreat along the coast to cover his base at Ostend. By 25 October 12,000 French were besieging Nieuport, which was held only by a tiny garrison of a mere 1,300 men.

Here the newly appointed Agent for Transport first showed his resourcefulness, for he formed the local fishermen into a corps of Sea Fencibles which 'were of so much use during the siege' that the Commander-in-Chief personally acknowledged his debt to them.[4] After three days the French gave up: Ostend was safe, for the time being, and the Agent for Transport had had his first opportunity to recommend his exertions to the Duke of York. There were to be plenty more.

The French forces now swung south to recapture Toulon, surrendered to Hood in August, and the winter lull settled over the Flanders front. Popham was back in Ostend doing his proper job: doing it with rather more zeal than suited the Port Captain.

Lieutenant Popham had a letter from the Navy Board enclosing a list of thirty-nine transports, [Captain Bisset wrote plaintively to Evan Napean at the Admiralty on 13 December.] What I think singular and a little extraordinary is, although Sir Henry Martin knew the character I was sent over in, my name is not mentioned at all; and Lieutenant Popham is instructed to take his orders and concert and arrange everything regarding the embarkation with the Commanding Officer, so it would appear that the Board consider me as a dead letter... Lieutenant Popham should be instructed to concert necessary arrangements with me...

However, a fortnight later his tone has changed, and he was writing of

Mr Popham's exertions and activity in the whole of the business— and I must do him this justice to say, I think him uncommonly clever and clear-headed— and I don't think they could find a man in all the Naval department so well calculated for the Department as he is...

In the fairly thankless administrative job of organising the embarkation and disembarkation of troops and stores for the Army, of ordering and despatching transports, he was thoroughly proving his worth. A mastery of detail was one of his outstanding qualities.

It is not known who coined the sobriquet 'The Duke of York's Admiral', or when, but in March 1974 His Royal Highness wrote to the Admiralty requesting that Lieutenant Popham be appointed to superintend the Inland Navigation in Flanders, and that he be promoted to the rank of Master Commander. The first request was granted: the second was not—or not yet; but he had certainly made his mark at GHQ.

3

The Spring campaign of 1794 began well for the Allies, for on 24 April a French offensive under Pichegru was routed by the Duke of York at Beaumont. 'Had Coburg followed up this brilliant exploit, 'Arthur Bryant wrote 'Beaumont might have proved one of the decisive battles of history': for, once again, they might have swept through to Paris and thereby brought the Revolution to an end. But Coburg did not follow up; and, worse still, when a joint Allied advance was launched three weeks later, the Austrians failed to turn up and the British found themselves surrounded at Turcoing and were hard put to it to escape to Tournai. 'The Emperor's white-coated columns', Bryant notes drily' 'did not march to the sound of the guns. Instead they stayed and listened to them.'

It was the turning point of the campaign. The French, reinforced, attacked again in June, divided the Allies at Charleroi, and when the Austrians retreated east towards the Rhine forced the British to retreat also, northwards. Tournai was lost, then Ghent, then Antwerp. Ostend had to be abandoned; and thereafter the whole Channel coast to the mouth of the Scheldt was in French hands.

There is no indication as to when or how Home Popham organised the escape of his Elizabeth and young William Craddock from Ostend to England. He was certainly kept busy; and at the end of July the Duke of York wrote to the Lords

Commissioners of his 'entire approbation of the conduct of Lieutenant Home Popham, whose unremitting zeal and active talents have been successfully exerted in saving much public property on the leaving of Tournai, Ghent and Antwerp; these and many other meritorious services' prompted HRH to ask the Admiralty to promote him, but to let him stay 'in his present employment, where his service is essentially necessary.'

Benjamin Tucker, who missed no opportunity of imputing to Popham dubious motives and behaviour, noted that, as to his becoming the Duke of York's Admiral, 'those who were in the Duke of York's suite on the Continent, can, no doubt, furnish many curious anecdotes touching the circumstances which occasioned Sir Home to outstrip the ordinary course of professional advancement... he became so useful and necessary to HRH...' But, in the manner of such insinuations, 'the anecdotes' are left to the reader's imagination .⁵

However, the facts are plain enough. In territory seamed with rivers and waterways, a resourceful naval officer adept at boat operations and in this case one who always had suggestions and solutions on the tip of his tongue, could not fail to be an asset to a young Commander—the Duke and he were of an age—trying to hold an army together during a long, disastrous retreat. For the French renewed their offensive in September, and by early November the British were on the south bank of the Waal at Nijmegen, with the enemy in hot pursuit. On the 4th HRH wrote to Dundas from his headquarters in Arnhem:

> Upon further consultation with Lieutenant Popham of the Navy, who has 100 British seaman with him, and to whom I have committed the entire charge of the Bridge, it appears that even if the enemy succeeds in destroying it, he will be in possession of the Means of keeping up a communication, and of withdrawing the Garrison when it shall become necessary.

Whether Popham actually constructed the pontoon bridge, which consisted of sixty vessels, or was merely overseeing one that already existed, is not clear from the various descriptions. But three days later the French were able to range their artillery on to it, and in the course of a three hour bombardment succeeded in sinking one of the boats 'and did much other damage'. On the 9th, he wrote :

> This, however, we repaired by 7 o'clock in the evening when 9000 men of the Garrison, and all the British and Hanoverian Artillery were retreated; leaving about 4,500 men behind. The next morning the French had so completely got the reach of the north end of the Bridge that they prevented our working, and by night we had seven boats sunk together, over which we made a slight platform to retreat the remainder of the Garrison with the assistance of the Pont Volant and I recommended in the strongest manner to His Royal Highness to do so that night, if he meant to save them by the passage of the Waal.

At 9 the Orders arrived, and the whole Garrison was saved except for about 300 Dutch who were crossing in the Pont Volant* when the Mast head was either carried away by too Broad a Sheer or shot away, which made the boat swing stern to the stream as the inner end of the Hawser was made fast, and the Dutch soldiers would not suffer the Boatmen to cut the Hawser after they had let go an anchor and endeavour to shear them to the Northern shore.[6]

'Even under these circumstances,' HRH wrote to Dundas, 'Lieutenant Popham would have saved them...' Throughout the campaign the Dutch, who loathed the British, behaved equivocally at best, with overt hostility for most of the time.

Once across the Waal, what was left of the British Army (21,000 were down with typhus) was given a brief respite, and early in December 1794 the Duke of York handed over the command to General William Harcourt and returned to England. Before he left, his solicitations on behalf of his Superintendent of Inland Navigation were heeded; and on 30 November his ADC, Hewgill, wrote to Home Popham:

I have the pleasure to acquaint you, that the last mail brought a Letter from Lord Chatham, expressing, in very handsome terms, his readiness to obey His Royal Highness's commands, and adding, that you should immediately be appointed Master and Commander: I trust it will hardly be necessary for me to express my happiness on this occasion; but I cannot offer you my congratulations without lamenting... that the former application had not been attended with success... for otherwise, in consequence of your late exertions and signal services at Nimuegen, you might now have been promoted to the rank of Post Captain. All I can say is, that no favourable opportunity shall be lost in your attainment of this object...

Unwittingly, the Duke of York left behind him the makings of one of the most appalling chapters in the history of the British Army.

4

According to the conventions of 18th century warfare, fighting ceased on the onset of winter, to be resumed in the spring; but the armies of the Revolution, their commanders under the threat of the guillotine if they failed, could not afford to respect them. Pichegru and Moreau, far from retiring into winter quarters, continued to advance; and very soon acquired an additional ally. After the heavy rains of late autumn, with swollen rivers and widespreading flooding, came frost, hard and unrelenting. By Christmas Eve, when the British were faced with crossing

* *Pont Volant*, a floating bridge, in this case operated by a hawser running from one bank through blocks on the two masts of the vessel, to the far bank, by which the occupants hauled themselves across. When the foremast carried away, the boat, still held by the hawser running through the after sheave, swung her bow away downstream. Whereupon the Dutch Commandant, who was up forward, panicked, crying '*Tout est perdu!*' and causing confusion among the troops. The boat ended up on the French side, and the Dutch were all captured.

the Neder Rhine in their unending retreat into Germany, Popham wrote to Lt-Col George Don, the Deputy Adjutant-General, of the possibility of crossing on the ice, but it was not yet thick enough to bear. 'The River has risen two feet in the night', he wrote on Christmas Day 1794, 'Pichegru may amuse himself by looking at the snow... I wish you a Merry day.' But two days later the French were across the Meuse and the Waal; and on the 30th December there was a thaw and Popham was back bridge-building, using local boats known as 'bylanders'. 'Every possible exertion ought to be used to compleat the Bridge,' he wrote to Don, 'which I think will be the first finished in the Rhine.'

On New Year's Day 1795, with irony: 'I suppose it was not *supposed* in my Department to think, but as a servant of a distressed Army, I hold it good to make propositions for their relief... I not only give my assistance to the Commissariat, but I trust to any individual in the Army when they apply to me'. That army was scrambled across the Rhine, partly by boats hauled over by horses, and the retreat continued to the Yser, with the French hard on their heels. There were continuous demands on the Superintendent for Inland Navigation for ships to evacuate the sick and wounded, and for gunboats to guard the waterways when they were not frozen. Which they very soon were, for in the middle of January a cold spell of arctic quality whipped across Europe and lashed the dispirited troops as they struggled northwards from Arnhem across the flat and desolate wastes of Gelderland. Sir John Fortescue described the rout, for such it was, in a memorable passage:-

> Those of the Army that awoke on the morning of the 17th January saw about them such a sight as they never forgot. Far as the eye could reach over the whitened plain were scattered gun-limbers waggons full of baggage stores or sick men, sutlers' carts and private carriages. Beside them lay the horses, dead; around them scores and hundreds of soldiers, dropped to sleep in the arms of the frost; there a group of British and Germans round an empty rum cask; here forty English Guardsmen huddled together about a plundered waggon; there a packhorse with a woman lying alongside it, and a baby swaddled in rags, peering out of the pack, with its mother's milk turned to ice upon its lips—one and all stark, frozen, dead. Had the retreat lasted but three or four days longer, not a man would have escaped.

As it was, more than 6,000 soldiers died in four days.

On 20 January the French entered Amsterdam, and a few days later captured the Dutch fleet, frozen in in the Zuyder Zee, by galloping across the ice. Holland was lost and, although the Government was not ready to admit it, so too was the campaign.

5

The best place now for evacuating the sick and wounded was Emden, but the French were already advancing through northwestern Holland and would soon be at the west bank of the Ems. To keep the river open Popham needed gunboats, and in February he was on the island of Nordeney looking for suitable vessels. The owners were asking £1,500 each: 'will buy one or two but no more', he wrote to Don. By the time he got back to Emden, having been frozen in on Nordeney, the French were at Delfziel and, as he wrote, 'having armed vessels becomes a matter of most absolute necessity'. And in the same letter, 'I shall do everything in my power to get the Buoys placed to facilitate the navigation of the River.'

His energy was inexhaustible, his speed of movement dizzying, his labours unending. Apart from the search for gunboats, and the problem of arming them, there were embarkation points to be found and prepared, troop transports and hospital ships to be met and piloted in, embarkation of men, sick, broken, lost, in their thousands, to be organised. On 20 March he wrote to Don from Emden: 'I passed the Fort of Delfziel last night in a cutter and brought her [HMS *Daedalus*] into the harbour, as I thought it would give confidence to the Masters of the Hospital ships in going down. The sick will be all embarked by or before noon tomorrow.' And he remarks in parentheses that he had been delayed outside for *seven days* 'by the cruel perverseness of the weather'.

At last the Government decided that the campaign was a lost cause, and the evacuation of all but the cavalry and a force of artillery—left to look after George III's beloved Hanover—should go ahead. In mid-March 12,000 British and foreign troops, and many of the sick, were being shipped out; but there were always more trickling in. On 6 April Popham wrote to Don that he was embarking the Newcastle Division, six to ten battalions a day, but he must, he tells Don, know the number of sick 'so that I may appropriate hospital ships accordingly'. And the letter continues: 'There are many sick and convalescents arrived, I do not know to whom they belong; and where they are to apply to for relief as they have no surgeon with them, nor is there a person on the medical staff.'

In truth, the ramshackle administration of the Army, which had failed throughout the campaign, had collapsed completely. Fortescue's damnation of Henry Dundas, Secretary of War, was no exaggeration: 'his idea of putting an army in the field was to land raw men on a foreign shore, and expect discipline, arms, ammunition, clothing, victuals, medical stores and medical treatment to descend on them from heaven.' It was then left to men of the calibre of George Don and Home Popham to rescue what and whom they could.

On 23 April Home Popham, already being referred to as Captain by Dundas in correspondence, was in Bremen 'purchasing hammocks and other necessaries for the thirty-three sail of *unfitted* Transports which have arrived in the Weser... to receive all such Corps or people as General Dundas* may think proper to send to England.'

It was a grim and desperate business, and it continued well into the autumn, as dribs and drabs drifted in to Stade on the Elbe looking for a ship to take them

---

* Lt-General Sir David Dundas.

out of reach of the French: 450 Choiseuil and 432 British Hussars, 315 from
3 Corps, 55 Artillery officers, 74 exchanged prisoners, 300 horses, '380 persons
of all descriptions' and a further 200 horses, a miscellaneous collection of
'Brunswickers'. Popham's letters have the factual, harassed tone of a man distracted
by the number of calls on his time and energy, but only in a private letter to Don
on 23 October does he reveal the strain he has been under.

> My dear Don I pray you to persuade the General to keep back one regiment
> for we really have not ships enough to accommodate the whole: make up
> the complement 786 and I am your man. I never was so fag'd with Dogs
> and Devils, I wish the Business was at an end, and if ever I have anything
> more to do with Transports, you may transport me to Botany Bay.
>
> Yours truly, Home Popham.

A week before he had been in Hamburg, chartering ships 'on the part of his
Britannick Majesty's Commissioners for conducting His Transport Service', at a
price which those Commissioners would regard as excessive when the accounts
came in the following year. The repercussions from this continued all through
1796 and rightly belong later, but the letter Popham wrote to Lord Spencer, the
First Sea Lord, on the subject throws a vivid light on his responsibilities in Germany
in 1795.

> In addition to the duties attached to my situation with the Army [he wrote
> from Sackville Street early in December 1796] Admiral Christian applied
> to me in July 1795 to take up ships for the removal of certain Corps from
> the Continent; and the number of these Corps increased, till the whole Army
> was comprehended; when I was informed by the Transport Office that Mr
> Secretary Dundas relied so fully on my being able to obtain the perfect
> accommodation required, that no Transports would be sent from England...
> I was urged to every exertion by General Dundas, who not only stated the
> critical situation of the Army, particularly the British Cavalry, but directed
> me to report to him the best place for that valuable body of men to cross
> the Elbe, in order to effect their retreat to Denmark in case of necessity.
>
> At the same time I was pressed to the immediate execution of this Duty
> by Mr Dundas, and most particularly entreated by Admiral Christian, who
> then presided at the Board, to hasten the equipment of the ships, and not
> to consider Money in this instance.
>
> In vain were repeated applications for Officers to assist me; none were
> sent; I had to organise a service, in a Country where every person was
> naturally inimical to military operations... you are enabled to judge of my
> exertions in the equipment of near Eighty foreign Ships, and the embarkation
> of as many foreign Troops, as they were competent to hold, most of whom
> were averse to their removal from the Continent, and some of whom were
> in a state of Mutiny at the time; independently of this, I had to embark all

the British Cavalry that came to the Elbe...

... I trust you will think I was equally fortunate in my dispositions, when your Lordship is informed, that in 1795 I embarked nearly forty thousand Infantry, and six thousand Cavalry without the most trifling accidents occurring to either Man or Horses; and precisely the same good fortune attended my similar operation in 1793, and 1794.[7]

6

The evacuation continued to the end of 1795. One of Popham's letters to Don was headed 'On board the *Mary Francis* off Thillingfleet', 6 December 1795, with '300 horses and 380 persons of all descriptions'; and in another letter of the same time he writes, 'for while there is a soldier in the Country our work will never finish.' But, as he said in his letter to Lord Spencer 'I am confident, my Lord, all that Man could do, to carry the spirit of my Instructions into execution, was done; I performed every Iota of the Service committed to my charge, and quitted the Continent in January 1796.'

And he quitted it with the rank of Post Captain. The previous March the Duke of York had written personally to Spencer, referring to Popham's 'uncommon exertion in many difficult and important employments' and his 'very essential use to the Army under my command'. 'Under these circumstances,' he concluded, 'I am induced to recommend him to your Lordship's protection, and request that he may be promoted to the rank of Post Captain.' Spencer replied two days later testifying 'my respect and obedience to your Royal Highness's pleasure, to promote an Officer who has deserved so well of his Country,' and the appointment was duly gazetted on 4 April 1795.

Popham's rise from Lieutenant—and one under something of a cloud—to Post Captain had been accomplished in under twelve years, from Commander to Captain in less than eighteen months. In the light of what he accomplished on the Continent, under the most adverse and dispiriting circumstances, the promotion was no less than he deserved, and it was not its rapidity which the Navy resented—Nelson, after all, rose from lieutenant to captain in under two years—but the fact that it had been the doing of the Army. For this the Navy never entirely forgave him; and the fact that he had become a Post Captain without ever commanding a naval ship, least of all a ship of the line in battle, in their eyes compounded the offence. He was not, in Tucker's dismissive phrase, 'a Naval quack'; but nor was he, in the style of Tucker's hero Earl St Vincent or the captains and admirals serving in the battle squadrons, a 'tarpaulin'. By chance he was on his way to becoming something rarer, a specialist in a number of fields only indirectly connected with the navy's main tasks of defending Britain, her colonies and her trade: combined land-sea operations, hydrography, signalling and scientific invention. That he also happened to be a first-class seaman merely adds to the ironies that surround his life and career.

One of those ironies was there to greet him on his return to England. Because of the irregularities alleged against him by the Board of Transport, and despite his promotion and the royal favour which had led to it, the Admiralty did not see fit to employ him, and he found himself back on half-pay. In January 1796, the month he got home, Elizabeth presented him with a daughter, to be christened Caroline, so it seems he must have been in England some time in the spring of 1795, though there is no mention of it in his letters.

NOTES ON CHAPTER V

1. Benjamin Tucker, admittedly biased, insinuates that he was always on the make; and Lady Holland, in her Journal, refers to his 'money getting spirit'. From his own letters it is clear that, in common with other naval officers, money was a constant anxiety; all the more so for him since he spent it freely, on publishing his signal books, on charts and navigational equipment and on his *Description of Prince of Wales Island*, not to mention lawyers' fees.

2. Printed in his *Description of Prince of Wales Island*.

3. In fact Dunkirk, though under siege, was still in French hands, and remained so.

4. HRH to Gen. Sir Charles Grey, 2 Nov. 1793: Home Popham 'has conceived the idea of arming the fishermen of Flanders in defence of their own towns; and he received orders for that purpose from HRH the Duke of York, through Sir James Pulteney, the Adjutant-General, and formed a body of them into a regular corps for the defence of Nieuport. He was entrusted with the command of them himself; and to their utility Sir Charles Grey, and other officers, bore the most ample testimony.' *Naval Chronicle*, Vol XVI, 1806.

5. From the notes by 'B. T. Esq. Late Secretary to the Admiralty' written in a minute hand on the account of Popham's court-martial in the British Library.

6. The letter ends: 'I cannot sit longer at my desk from a violent pain in my chest and shortness of breath.'

7. According to Tucker, 'the extreme dexterity and economy he displayed in measuring and hiring the Transports at Hamburg [in 1792] – upon which the ungrateful Transport Board remonstrated against his accounts and refused to pay them – in this case too, he was compelled to fly to his grand Panacea of a Pamphlet to vindicate his injured character...' And so on. The 'Pamphlet', if it existed outside Tuckers imagination, has not been traced; but in a curious letter to Nepean written on 21 November 1796, Popham complains that he has 'been kept in a state of expensive idleness during the most active part of the war, for the profession to which I belong...' At the heart of the Transport Board's charges was the accusation that the agents Parrish & Co. overstated the tonnage of the ships chartered, and hence the charter fee, by £10,000 and also overcharged on everything else from printing to brokerage and warehousing. Because Parrish were acting under his authority, he 'could not be entirely separated from any blame'. The matter appears to have been resolved, for no more is heard of it. Across the corner of one of these letters is scribbled, presumably by Nepean: 'Send a note to Mr P. (I mean *Capt.* P.) desiring him to call here tomorrow at 3'.

CHAPTER VI

The Threat
of Invasion
1798

1

IN THE spring of 1798 England was edgy with rumours. Ireland was in uproar, the very presence of the Protestant English in the balance as open rebellion replaced mere civil disobedience, its leaders convinced of help from France; while across the Channel, Bonaparte's troops seemed poised for the invasion of England herself. To counter it, the Channel Fleet kept up its constant, vigilant blockade off Brest, and at the mouth of the Thames and in the Downs a considerable force of sail of the line, frigates, gun-brigs and other vessels was kept on permanent alert. They had detailed orders from the C-in-C, Lord Keith, to remove all buoys and lights; and if the invasion flotillas were encountered, any vessels carrying soldiers or horses were to be run down and sunk, and no prisoners were to be taken. This ruthless procedure was not to apply to vessels of war, and in the case of the transports was 'only dictated by imperious necessity'.

Bonaparte was reported to have more than a quarter of a million men—an exaggeration—ready for the attempt; and despite all the measures being taken, it was accepted that a proportion of them might land on the English coast. To oppose them, Britain had a regular Army of 32,000 men at home, 25,000 Fencibles (a Home Guard enrolled for the war) and a force of Militia which had been increased to 100,000—on paper, at least—the previous year. On top of these were the largely amateur, and largely unarmed, volunteers, a motley collection of 40,000 estate servants, bank clerks, shopkeepers, lawyers and what-not, with little but their bare hands, a few blunderbusses and patriotic enthusiasm with which to drive back the Revolutionary hordes. Their determination was kept at boiling-point by horror stories of French atrocities, and by wild rumours of a tunnel being constructed under the Channel, or a bridge over it; of fleets of balloons to carry men and guns across; and of barges 2000 feet long and 1500 feet wide propelled by windmills. With so much to go on, the cartoonists had a field-day.

During all this frenzy of preparation Home Popham was in a curious and invidious position. Thirty-six years old and a Post Captain, he had never commanded a man-of-war larger than a sloop or any other ship apart from the two L'Etrusco's—and that was hardly a recommendation for employment on sea duty in the Royal Navy. He was unpopular in his own Service and dependent on the good offices of patrons: Henry Dundas, the Minister for War; Lord Spencer, then First Lord of the Admiralty; the Prime Minister William Pitt and the Duke of York. His only notable service had been ashore in Flanders, on what the *Naval Chronicle* describes as 'a new kind of service for a seaman', in which he had given 'the first proof of what may be expected from Naval Officers of science, even on shore'. Now he was unemployed and on half-pay and, as he was fond of pointing out, with a growing family to house and feed. Indeed, it had been augmented by two daughters, Caroline and Mary, in the preceding two years. The *L'Etrusco* affair was still bogged down in the Admiralty Court, and his appeal against forfeiture was pending. Such a succession of disappointments and anxieties might well have reduced him to despair, but throughout his life he showed remarkable resilience in the face of adversity, and even now, amid all the distractions that bedevilled his private and professional life, his vigorous imagination was busy.

In Flanders he had organised the local fishermen into a kind of maritime militia which he termed the Sea Fencibles.[1] They were recruited initially to man the flotillas of gunboats, but also distinguished themselves during the defence of Niewport. Might not a similar corps be useful in the present emergency at home? In 1798 he submitted to the Admiralty his 'Outline of a Plan as an Auxiliary Defence of the Coast of England against invasion, by the Establishment of Sea Fencibles'. The gist of the idea comes in the third paragraph: 'It is accordingly proposed to enrol the seamen and seafaring men resident in the towns and villages on the coast, and train [them] to artillery, with a positive assurance that they are never to be called out, unless for actual service, or for the purpose of exercising.'

Every sea-coast from Cornwall east-about to the Forth would be divided into districts, each with a number of beaches to guard. There would be a Captain and Commander for each county, and they would be responsible for training the men and for calling them out in an emergency, or 'when the weather is favourable for the enemy to attempt a landing'. They would be paid a shilling a day when they were on duty, whether for training or the real thing, and would be protected from impressment.[2] These local seamen—'so able and a hardy race of men', as General Sir Charles Grey, commanding the southeast district, described them—were uniquely qualified to act as a coastal defence force. Many had their own boats; they knew the creeks and inlets of the Thames Estuary and the East Coast as nobody else did. Their number included smugglers, though they presented a special problem since many of them had been outlawed and were on the run: Popham had to arrange a special dispensation for them.

Once established, the Sea Fencibles were to man 'doggers, galliots and other flat vessels fitted to carry two or more long heavy guns, manned with an officer and twelve people', and to undertake general coastal protection and 'attack or annoy small Privateers, or retake any vessels that may have fallen into the enemy's hands.' They would be supplied with provisions, and be entitled to prize money. They could also be used to man the coastal forts.

The Sea Fencibles [Popham wrote] are not to be forced to serve out of the district they undertake to defend, unless the enemy make good a landing, when they will in course follow their Commanders, who will be furnished with half pikes to arm the men of his district, and these pikes will be made longer than a musket with its bayonet fixed, that the Sea Fencibles may have an opportunity of charging the enemy with advantage in any general action, of storming such redoubts as the French may throw up, or any other work they may presume to make in England.

The scheme for the Sea Fencibles was swiftly accepted by the Government, and in April Popham was appointed Commander of the district from Beachy Head to Deal, as likely a stretch of coast as any for the threatened invasion.

2

The Sea Fencibles were never to be called upon to perform any of these heroic, indeed suicidal, feats, and their main interest lies in the light the scheme casts upon its author: his thoroughness, his quick imagination, his enthusiasm which was always liable to surge into over-enthusiasm. On 6 April, immediately after his appointment, he wrote to General Grey submitting '... such ideas as have suggested themselves to me on the practicability of the enemy's landing in the above district':

> From Sluys, Ostend, Nieuport and Dunkirk the same wind (i.e. E to ENE) will carry them through the Queen's Channel and South Channel up the Swale, and the distance from Sluys... to Feversham, will not exceed thirty leagues; and I believe it will scarce be necessary for me to say that they have more schoots and billanders in Holland than they can have occasion for on such an expedition, and that the turbot men are as well acquainted with the coasts of Kent and Essex and the channels leading to the Thames as our own pilots.

He goes on to analyse, beach by beach, bay by bay, port by port, the advantages and disadvantages each presents to the invader. This paper[3] fell into the hands of the French and was obviously studied with close attention. To the paragraph 'The fleet in the Downs and the Goodwin Sands are such securities to the coast between the two Forelands that little is to be apprehended in that space', Bonaparte himself added the note 'The Commander has not observed that with a southerly wind the fleet in the Downs and Goodwin Sands cannot prevent the French from coming to land on the coast between Margate and Ramsgate',—to which the editor of the Spencer Papers had added drily, 'Bonaparte here seems to have had his chart upside down'.

Popham is especially interesting on the subject of Rye.

> From Rye Old Harbour to Hooksledge ... there is an uncommon fine beach of sand and shingle, on which with an easterly wind a debarkation... may be made. ['This is the opinion of all the authorities I have consulted', noted Bonaparte.] In this space there is a harbour of more consequence than people are in general aware of; it is formed by a natural beach thrown up parellel

to the shore and at right angles with the entrance of Rye New Harbour...*

He has not yet completed a survey of it, he goes on, but has seen fifteen square-rigged vessels lying there, and 'large cutters drawing 11 feet of water' use it, though they take the ground at low water. A French note to this passage concludes that '700 or 800 vessels of the flotilla could enter. If the channels are found to be defended it would be easy to take them in reverse.'

Popham closes his paper—and this reflects his impulsive energy:

I am now building at Dover a row-galley to carry one heavy gun, and I think the Admiralty will give orders for others of the same description to be built. Indeed they have applied to the Treasury at my instance to order three smuggling vessels lately taken by the custom-house cutters, to be delivered over to me for the purpose of being lengthened and fitted as galleys; and when I get these vessels under my orders I think I shall be able to prevent the French row-boats from coming near this coast, either to reconnoitre or annoy our trade.

Elsewhere Popham argues that the invasion force will rely not only on specially built flat-boats but on the fishing fleets in the Channel ports—at least 800 vessels. 'I think the fishing-boats ought to be seized,' he continues, 'and if it can be managed to make the coup general, it will not only deprive the enemy of a number of Transports, but the best pilots (i.e. the fishermen themselves) for the Sussex coast.'

'I think the fishing-boats ought to be seized...': in that sentence, perhaps, there is a glimpse of the next project to fire that flammable imagination. But in the meantime, and since the goddess of irony rarely failed to overlook whatever Popham did, it is necessary to note that Bonaparte, after his lightning tour of the invasion harbours in February, had reported to the Directory (for he was still not sole master of France) that the French lacked the essential command of the sea, and that without it an invasion of England was too risky. Although the building of the invasion fleet would continue, he was already laying his plans for a very different, and even more ambitious expedition: to Egypt, and after Egypt, India. While Home Popham was planning his next stroke to forestall the Corsican adventurer, the latter was mustering in Toulon and Marseilles the warships and transports and troops for his great enterprise in the east: one which, in due course, would also involve Captain Home Popham.

3

Defensive measures against impending invasion were all very well, but they alone were not enough to appease the aggressive temper of Henry Dundas. 'We cannot

* The coastline here has, of course, changed considerably since.

so effectually annoy the enemy,' he wrote to Spencer, 'or keep alive the spirits of our country as by constant unremitting offensive operations during the whole summer.' With this robust approach Home Popham was in entire accord; and in the spring of 1798 he produced a scheme of his own, one well calculated to 'annoy' the enemy, and to find favour with the Minister for War.

His original Secret Memorandum 'submitted for Lord Spencer's consideration, on the possibility of destroying the Sluice Gates of the Bruges Canal and the lock gates leading into that Canal from the Harbor of Ostend' is undated, but he must have written it in March, or even earlier, for by the middle of April and soon after he had been appointed to command the Kent and Sussex Sea Fencibles,[4] he and General Sir Charles Grey produced a joint appreciation of the forces that would be needed to carry it out.

The object of the operation was this. The Saas Lock at Ostend was the seaward entrance to and exit from, the canal which linked the Channel to Bruges and Ghent, and so to the West Scheldt and the port of Flushing. The canal provided a safe inshore route for the invasion barges being built and collected in Belgium and Holland: cut that link and they would be forced to go outside, where they would come under the attentions of the patrolling frigates of the Royal Navy.

His plan, Popham goes on, is 'the result of long deliberation and... founded on a perfect knowledge of the places...' The canal from Bruges to Saas, 13 miles, is he says, as much as 100 yards wide in many places, and has a minimum depth of thirteen feet: it also provides an ideal place for fitting-out any number of vessels, and is out of sight and beyond the reach of the Navy. If the destruction of Ostend Harbour itself were included, this would deprive the enemy of an excellent haven, 'as I have seen 70 sail of transports and nearly as many more vessels of different descriptions go out in one tide'; moreover, like Dunkirk, the place is a nest of privateers. Even without the immediate threat of invasion, he argues, demolition of the lock would be worth doing since the canal was a major artery for bringing naval stores to the Channel ports from Holland: a good point, when the only alternative would have been horse-drawn waggons lumbering over unmetalled roads.

For the actual operation Popham suggests that they would need a total of seven frigates for carrying a total of 2,000 'effective men', plus a company of Artillery 'furnished with Petards for blowing the Bason gates to pieces, four howitzers and 6 heavy field pieces.' In addition they would need eight gun and bomb brigs, two carronade brigs, and a number of cutters and sloops of war, as well as flat-boats for landing the troops. Some of the men would immobilise the ferry that crossed the harbour from the town, while 500 would make straight for the lock-gates. The rest would act as a covering force. Some of the brigs would bombard the docks and town, while others diverted attention from what was happening at the lock. The sloops and cutters, meanwhile, would be busy cutting out or setting fire to whatever ships happened to be in the harbour. All in all, it was to be exactly the kind of daring enterprise to appeal to the eager young midshipmen, lieutenants and captains of the 18th century navy.

The most effective time to blow the gates, he suggests, would be half-ebb, 'as the water will have an amazing fall, after which it will be impossible for any Boats to cross the Harbour, indeed I imagine everything will be torn away and carried to sea by so great a body of water coming down at once, nor is it possible to say what mischief may be done to the upper canals when the lower water is drawn off.' Mud and silt will clog the harbour; perhaps, he suggests, a vessel might be sunk in the fairway so that it forms a shoal—and the canal banks might well collapse.

As his imagination soars, Popham muses whether, while they are about it, they might have a go at the connecting canal which linked Bruges to Nieuport and Dunkirk. There are occasions when he seems to deserve Arthur Bryant's description of him as 'that clever but incurably plausible naval officer, Captain Home Popham'.

4

Dundas, Under-Secretary William Huskisson and Grey were all enthusiastic; Spencer, the First Lord, less so, particularly when Grey pressed for Popham to command the expedition. As he wrote to Dundas on 25 April, he deplored 'this peremptory sort of nomination of *naval* commanders by land officers'—particularly when the naval officer concerned has so forcefully recommended himself to the 'land officer' responsible for the nomination.

> Captain Popham, [Spencer continued] should remember that he is a very young captain,* that he never commanded a ship-of-war of any description (as far as I know) in his life; and I am not without apprehensions that his being placed in command of a squadron on this occasion may give great disgust and offence to the profession who are sufficiently irritable on these matters. Had any common transports been employed, I should for these reasons have preferred employing him as an agent for transports, the sort of line in which alone he has hitherto been known in the service, and in which he has very much distinguished himself...

The only way out was to give him a ship *armé-en-flute*, i.e. fitted out as a transport, and ensure that the captains of all the other ships were junior to him. And this is exactly what happened: Popham was given the 26-gun *Expedition*, with an apologetic note from the junior Sea Lord, Admiral Sir William Young[5], which really touched him on the raw—as one suspects it was meant to. In a memo to Grey, Popham wrote, quoting Young's letter:

> 'I am sorry you are put into so ill-conditioned a ship—we will lend you one lieutenant and twenty men from the *Irresistible* which will enable you to do tolerably well.' This is a neat mode of carrying on service and a cool

---

* He was 36, but with only three years seniority as a captain.

mode of expressing his opinion that the twenty men will enable me to do *tolerably* well—I shall keep this letter to show that the sanguine Marine Execution Man only expected *tolerable well-doing*[6] [And he continues:] The Captain whose men are to be borrowed will in course suppose it done by my application and as it is without any previous notice to him will naturally think I have behaved unlike a gentleman and call me to account on my return—It may probably be what Mr Young wishes—that I may go out with a halter round my neck.

Planning by Grey and Popham continued in a flurry of details: powder in boxes for blowing up the dock works; enough petards to breach six pairs of gates; pioneers' tools for undermining; a small, fast-sailing hospital ship to be added to the fleet, and so on. The troops were to be embarked from the Isle of Thanet, without camp equipage since it was hoped that the job would be completed in ten hours.

While the preparations were in train, however, Spencer appointed a senior officer over Popham. At the news of this, the latter says he 'behaved complacently and cool'; but suggests to Grey that a word from him, emphasising the value of his local knowledge and the fact that he knows the land commander designate, General Eyre Coote, might, 'have more weight than all the jealousies of the *Under* Lords.' He ends this odd letter, with its personal under and overtones, with a request for 13-inch bombs in place of 10-inch for the diversionary operation against Flushing (which, in the event, was cancelled). Every detail is dealt with in these operational notes, every contingency foreseen; and when, early in May, Popham came to issue his 'Operational Orders', it was as the officer in command of the naval side: Grey's intervention had had the required effect. 'The ships under my command,' they begin, 'being intended for a Secret Service, the Captains and Commanders are requested not to say or do what may induce speculative opinions related to any expedition whatever. The ships will sail at very short notice...'

The orders themselves were a model of clarity and precision. Armed cutters were to be stationed as path-finders in the approaches to the harbour to lead the expedition in; six vessels were to bombard the town from the NNW, and 'be ready to set fire to any vessels on the east side, cut them out or sink them. Fourteen vessels—bomb and gun brigs—would take the eastward side for the same purpose, while *Expedition*, with *Ariadne* and *Minerva*, would lead in to the beaches where the first 600 were to land. They would be put ashore in flat-boats; the artificers with their tools would be disembarked at the same time in the *Expedition*'s own boats. Other ships were to land the guns, one 6-pounder and two howitzers; and two more waves would follow the first, one of 450 men with some artillery, the last of 364 men, with two more guns. 'Also,' the order continues, 'it will be necessary to land a certain number of seamen for the purpose of co-operating with the Army in a variety of instances where their professional knowledge may be of much assistance.' And he adds: 'Captain Popham trusts that the Officers and Seamen will so co-operate with the General and the Army that they will seem but one Corps which in every situation must ensure success to His Majesty's Arms'.

Each boat would be under the immediate command of a midshipman, and captains were to make sure that boats' crews were composed of 'sober steady men' 'as the safety and facility of the enterprize will much depend on the Management of the Boats'. Contingency plans were outlined in case of 'a precipitate retreat' being forced on them by enemy numbers; and a special section of the orders was devoted to the central purpose of the expedition, the destruction of the lock-gates, and the 'Miners'* who were to do the job.

5

Just as everything was falling neatly into place, Home Popham was summoned to the Admiralty: he was to rejoin his ship as quickly as possible, take her to Portsmouth, pick up the 10th Regiment, and sail for Ireland, which was known to be on the very verge of rebellion, with lively hopes of French aid. However, as he wrote to Grey from Dartford on his way back, 'as I past the Horse Guards I overtook Mr King the Under Secretary who had just received excellent News from Ireland...'

As a result, and under pressure from Huskisson, Nepean the Admiralty Secretary, and Grey, those orders were cancelled. At Dartford, where he changed horses, he says, 'I left London at half-past twelve, and I am now hustling with four horses to get to sea tonight.' The panic was over; and on 11 May he wrote to Coote from *Expedition*: 'At last arrived here with my untutored, undisciplined crew. I was obliged to work the Cat today and the other Lieutenant felt so incompetent to my quicksilver Motions that he has written to resign.'

The original plans had included an associated series of operations against Flushing to destroy the 200 invasion schoots there, and also an assault on the Frisian island of Ameland, but both were abandoned. In his letter to Grey from Dartford, Popham also mentions an intention to bombard Calais, Dieppe, Fécamp and St Valéry 'by way of feint, and to draw the attention of the Enemy away from our great Object...', but in the end the Ostend expedition was launched without these diversions—and it was not the Enemy that caused the trouble.

6

On 13 May Home Popham wrote to Spencer from Margate to say that all the troops were embarked, but unsettled weather was holding them up. It continued to do so; and although the expedition sailed on the 14th, it was not anchored off the Belgian coast until four days later. The following day, in the courteous manner

* i.e. Sappers. At this period the NCOs and privates of the Royal Engineers were known as 'The Royal Sappers and Miners'.

of the age but rather oddly in view of the earlier emphasis on secrecy and surprise, Eyre Coote and Popham sent a joint ultimatum to the Military Commandant calling upon him to surrender Ostend or to suffer bombardment.

This preposterous demand Muscar, the Commandant, and his *Conseil de Guerre* utterly rejected: they would be put in their shrouds (*ensevelis*) beneath its ruins first. The operation was put in train immediately.

> At 1 am we anchored [Popham wrote in his Despatch to the Admiralty,] soon afterwards the wind shifted to West and threatened so much to Blow, that the General and myself were deliberating whether it would be better to go to sea and wait a more favourable opportunity; when a Boat from the *Vigilante* brought the Pilot Vessel alongside which she had cut out from under the light house Battery and the information obtained from the Pilots under separate examinations so convinced us of the small force at Ostend, Nieuport and Bruges that Major-General Coote beg'd he might be landed... even if the Surf should prevent his retreat being so successful as he could wish.

In short, the force was to be landed against Home Popham's better judgement. An added incentive for going ahead was the news that a large number of schoots from Flushing were even then in the canal en route for Ostend—exactly the traffic the operation was designed to stop.

The troops were therefore bundled ashore, most of them before the shore batteries were aware of it.

> *Biter, Hecla* and *Tartarus* [Popham's dispatch continues], Bombs, very soon opened their mortars and threw their shells with great quickness and precision. The Town was on fire several times and much damage was done to ships in the Bason—by 5 o'clock all the Troops ordered to land... were in shore with their Artillery, Mines, Wooden Petards, Tools and Gun Powder, and before 6 o'clock I heard from General Coote that he had no doubt of blowing up the Works. I now became very anxious... from the state of the weather...

Some of the gun-vessels were taking a pasting from the shore batteries, so Popham called them off, but sent one of the transports and two of the frigates in to draw the fire of the batteries away from the troops ashore, and some of the other gunboats in to cover the embarkation. 'At 20 minutes past 10 I had the pleasure of seeing the explosion take place, and soon after the Troops assembled on the Sand Hills near the shore; but the sea ran so high that it was impossible to embark a single man'.

Indeed, the wind had been strengthening all the time; so much so that *Minerva*'s contingent, who were to be the last ashore, had wisely been turned back. There was nothing to be done but lie off and wait till the next day and hope that the wind would have moderated.

Which, indeed, it did—but it was too late.

This morning (the 21st) at daylight, I went on shore in the *Kite* for the purpose
of giving every assistance, but I had the mortification to see our Army
surrounded by the enemy Troops, and as I had no doubt the General had
capitulated, I ordered all the ships to anchor further out and I sent in a Flag
of Truce...

Coote had been wounded trying to rally the Light and Grenadier Companies of
the 11th, who were giving ground to superior numbers of French troops. The whole
force was in fact surrounded; they had lost more than fifty officers and men, and
the only alternative to surrender was annihilation. Information from shore, however,
was quite unequivocal: 'that the sluice gates and works are completely destroyed
and several vessels intended for Transport burnt, I have this morning heard that
the bason was quite dry, and that the works destroyed yesterday had taken the
States of Bruges five years to finish.' Home Popham's triumphs were invariably
to exact an unjustly swift retribution of disaster.

7

'I hope you are convinced,' Popham wrote to Grey next day, 'the Plan was well
laid, the enemy taken by surprise, and the Object accomplished within the time
specified, but I cannot contend against the elements'. He was hoping to arrange
'an exchange of Honor' of French prisoners (not from this operation but from
others) 'for everybody, at all events Mr Coote...' In the same letter, he adds: 'if
before I return any person dare hint at an atom of Neglect or want of Judgement
on my Part, I beg, as the Father and Patron of the Expedition that you will desire
the most publick Enquiry into my Conduct...'

Feelings of deep-seated personal insecurity take one of two forms: either a refusal
to justify one's actions, or an almost ingratiating eagerness to do so. Home Popham,
for reasons which one can only guess—the loss of his mother at birth, his curious
position as the youngest child of one family yet the eldest of a second; his rootless
youth; a sense, in a class-concious age, of being an outsider—took the second
alternative. Over and over again during his often controversial career he felt
compelled to justify himself, either in print or, when he became an MP, in speeches
in Parliament.

On this occasion, however, no defense was required. 'I have been received',
he wrote to Grey, 'by everybody exactly as you assured me I should and as I know
you wished...'; and indeed he had nothing to be ashamed of. Sir Julian Corbett
summed it up as 'a thoroughly well-designed and brilliantly-executed enterprise';
its commander, in this his first important combined operation, had handled his
squadron of 27 miscellaneous vessels with great skill and assurance; the 'great
Object' had been spectacularly achieved; and if the aftermath had proved a disaster,
well, as he said ruefully to Grey, 'you cannot fight the elements'.

In any event, although immediately after it he admitted to being much dejected, his irrepressible spirit quickly recovered, and within a week he was promising to send Grey 'the Heads of my next Proposition'. 'I again offer you my gratitude; I owe all to you and I hesitate not to declare this most publickly. God bless you My dear Sir.' The Ostend expedition had been an important step in his career, and General Sir Charles Grey's support had largely ensured that it took place.

NOTES ON CHAPTER VI

1. 'Fencible' = Defensable 'fit and liable for defensive military service'. Shorter OED.

2. But only, the Admiralty added, 'under such restrictions as the Admiralty may judge proper to those men who enrol themselves as Sea Fencibles.'

3. A translation, or rather a précis, exists in the *Archives de la Guerre*, annotated partly by Bonaparte and partly by other hands.

4. In early May, after he had been ordered to Ireland, Popham wrote to Grey: 'I must settle all the Sea Fencible business, and let a Captain meet me at Hastings to supercede me in the employ which is not done yet...'

5. Nine years later Admiral Young would be presiding at Popham's court-martial! Described by contemporaries as 'a Pavement Admiral' and satirised by Marryat as Sir Hurricane Humbug.

6. 'Good God!' Grey wrote to Huskisson when he heard this, 'what does Admiral Young mean by doing things by halves? Mr Dundas must interfere or all will go wrong—and get what was required yesterday, two lieutenants and an order for 70 men from the guardship in the Downs, for without that addition the *Expedition* frigate cannot sail.'

CHAPTER VII

A Gift from the Tsar 1799

1

BETWEEN MAY 1798 and May 1799 Captain Home Popham was ashore, but as he was to say of himself in another context, 'by no means idle'. Professionally, he was in command of the Sea Fencibles between Deal and Beachy Head; and since he was living at Standen in the Isle of Wight, was compelled to do quite of lot of travelling. He was regularly in London, for he had much business there. In November the Appeal against the fortfeiture of L'Etrusco came up before the Law Lords, and was dismissed. It would recur at regular intervals over the next ten years.

At about the same time, 'being a Gentleman well versed in several branches of knowledge, particularly marine surveying, and that part of practical astronomy which is subservient to the purposes of navigation, who has upon several occasions distinguished himself by his zeal for promoting science...'[1] he put himself forward for election as a Fellow of the Royal Society. He was recommended by seven Fellows, and was ballotted and elected on 18 April 1799. It is disappointing to have to report that, although they thought he was likely to prove 'an usefull, and valuable member', there is no record of his having taken part in any of the Society's transactions. This did not deter him, however, from putting the letters FRS after his name; indeed, in the book which is published in 1799 he spelt it out in full.

The work concerned, 'A Description of Prince of Wales Island,' was published in a very handsome edition printed in London by George Cawthorne,[2] and included not only the chart of the South Channel but another, of the Indian Ocean and the Bay of Bengal, with the different routes to be taken by ships during the Southwest and Northeast Monsoons.[3] It also included numerous details of the island's produce, sailing directions, and testimonials to the author; and it may well have influenced the Board of Control of the East India Company to raise the island's status to that of a Presidency six years later and build it up into a port of call for their ships, with dockyards and an arsenal.[4]

In the broader context of the war, there had been a series of events in the Mediterranean which, in a curiously oblique way, were to have their impact on Home Popham. In May 1798 Bonaparte set out with a formidable fleet of warships and transports for the conquest of Egypt. On the way the expedition stopped at Malta and demanded the surrender of the island from the Knights of St John whose headquarters it was. They handed it over without a fight and Bonaparte sailed on, leaving a strong garrison to hold it.

The Knights Hospitallers, or the Knights of St John of Jerusalem[5] to give them their full title, were a composite body, and in their disarray elected Paul I, Tsar of Russia, to be their Grand Commander. Paul, who had succeeded his mother Catherine the Great two years before at the age of forty-four, is summarily dismissed by historians as 'mad', 'half-mad', or 'a petulant maniac'. He was certainly pretty odd; but this is hardly surprising in view of his life up to the time of his accession. Catherine had kept him a virtual prisoner in the castle of Gatsina, had deliberately excluded him from affairs of state, and regularly threatened to cut him out of the succession. His main occupation had been endlessly drilling a tame squad of soldiers; he suffered from a bad digestion and convulsions; and his behaviour veered wildly, from magnanimity to rage. 'In Russia,' he remarked to the Swedish envoy on one occasion, 'only he is great to whom I am speaking, and for so long as I am speaking.' He was not the most suitable person to be entrusted with absolute power.

To Paul, Bonaparte's capture of Malta was a personal affront. In his more quixotic moments—and the word is used deliberately—he dreamed that with the help of the Knights he would save Europe from the twin horrors of Revolution and Free-Thinking. 'He is more particular ,' Popham was to write later, 'and more jealous in his function as Grand Master than he is as Emperor of Russia.' To recover possession of the island for this spent Order of Chivalry was an obsession.

When, therefore, in the winter of 1798 Pitt began to try and build yet another coalition with Austria, Prussia and Russia, with the primary objective of driving the French out of the Low Countries, Paul proved agreeable. In addition to a hefty advance payment and a monthly subsidy, he was promised the return of Malta. A Russian army under Marshal Suvorof was already on the march for Italy: another, it was hoped, would join the British and Austrians in an assault on the Netherlands.

2

Captain Home Popham FRS received his orders from Henry Dundas, the Secretary for War, in mid-May 1799. 'The disposition manifested by the Emperor of Russia', they began, 'to act in concert with His Majesty against the common Enemy affording a reasonable ground of hope that the Court of Petersbourg may be prevailed upon... to assist with a body of Russian Troops in any operation.. against Holland'... 'I have received His Majesty's Commands to direct you to proceed to that Capital with all possible Expedition.' What Popham was expected to do was to secure the allocation of 20,000 soldiers from the Tsar and organise the transports in which to ship them, if possible via 'the Canal running from Kiel to the Eider, by means of this River establishing a Communication between the Baltic and German seas.' If that proved impossible— and he was to ascertain the precise limitations of the canal—he was to arrange for them to disembark at Lübeck and march to the Elbe. He was to find out whether enough shipping was available, how much it would cost to charter and convert it, and whether the work could be carried out locally. All this was to be done with the utmost caution, secrecy and speed, and in collaboration with the Ambassador, Sir Charles Whitworth.[6]

Why Home Popham should have been chosen for this particular mission is clear enough. As Agent for Transport in Flanders he had achieved both reputation and the patronage of the Duke of York, and his stock stood high with the Government ministers concerned: Pitt, Dundas, Lord Spencer at the Admiralty and Lord Grenville, the Foreign Secretary. He was expert in the movement of troops by water, he was an excellent navigator, and he had just the plausibility and charm that might work with a difficult customer like Paul. Whitworth had described Paul as irritable, and 'one in whom, I am sorry to say, vigour of mind and patience under adversity are so much wanting as they are necessary.'

On 18 May, Popham left Yarmouth, in the lugger *Nile* spent a week in Hamburg looking into the question of hiring transport, found out the exact dimensions of the locks on the Holstein canal (90 by 26 by 9 feet) and the sailing directions for entering, and reached St Petersburg on 3 June.[7]

The Tsar kept him waiting ten days for an audience; but when they did finally meet they quickly became on the best of terms. Paul happened to be in a genial frame of mind; and once Popham had explained the plans for the forthcoming expedition, the Tsar's resistance to providing the troops gradually melted. After some persuasion, he agreed to provide the transports as well. Never was Popham's charm used more effectively: within a week he was writing from the naval base at Kronstadt that the Emperor had told him 'to divest myself of every ceremony and only look on him as an individual'. Formality was dropped, he was introduced to the Empress and the princes and princesses, and was dining with them en famille. With justified complacency he could write later that the Tsar would do anything for him. The same could not be said of Admiral Kouchelev, however, for, Popham wrote, 'he effectually foiled me by pretending only to understand his Native language.' Popham and the Tsar, one presumes, conversed in French, though it is not mentioned. Nor, unfortunately, is there any record of Popham's personal impressions of the Tsar, 'his minute nose perched like a comma on his face, rendering his expression both proud and petulant'.[8] In his portraits he looks like a spoilt small boy dressed up in a uniform too big for him.

With the Tsar behind him, Popham found all the objections of the senior officers swept aside. The troops for the expedition were swiftly selected, and the work of converting the necessary shipping put in hand; and Popham, armed with the Imperial authority, can be visualised bustling between the Palace and the dockyard. Before very long he is telling Paul exactly what was wrong with the organisation and what improvements were needed—'which struck him so forcibly that he ordered their adoption and I cannot muster up bronze enough to tell you the civil things he said on this occasion'.[9]

There was praise for his progress from everyone involved: from George III, who 'signified his approbation of your exertions and conduct since your departure from this country', from Whitworth, from Grenville, and notably from General Stamford, the Prince of Orange's envoy. He, whom Popham 'dismissed as a well-informed old man, rather of insinuating manners', and more of a politician than a soldier, produced perhaps the shrewdest assessment of Popham's character of anyone. 'I find in Mr Popham,' he wrote to Grenville at the end of June,[10]

> a man full of zeal, talent and knowledge. He seems to me to have been born
> with the kind of courage which has no doubts, a man to whom the most
> difficult things seem easy. At the same time I observe mingled with all these
> qualities, a degree of ambition which he brings to every enterprise and which
> causes him to want all the credit for himself.*

If the subject of this cool analysis had seen it, he might not have been quite so
condescending when, in a later passage in his letter to Huskisson, he wrote about
'this old man, a General before I was thought of...' who arrives in Russia to find
that 'a Naval Officer has annihilated his proposal' before he ever got there; and
worse, 'this Naval Speculator' had so far found favour with the Tsar that he has
the ships and troops already organised. 'I declare I felt for the old gentleman, and
as I always like to soothe instead of irritate', he sets out to mollify him. Popham
was thirty-seven and had good reason, no one could deny, for feeling pleased with
himself.

Equally, he was aware of it and the dangers that attended it. 'Jealousy is a damned
thing', he wrote in the same letter to Huskisson 'and I have been so bit by it I avoid
it as I would a Rattlesnake.' But he could not avoid it, as he well knew. Explaining
that the Tsar wants him to command the expedition, he admits to being afraid, if
captains senior to him are involved, 'of some old Fleet character being started by
Admiral ----- as a bugbear to prevent my commanding.' The answer, he thinks, might
be to ask the Tsar to appoint him as Admiral in the Russian Service for the time
being, and to serve in a Russian ship. 'In fact,' he concludes, 'I'll do anything to
secure the object and I think I know the country [Holland] so well I cannot fail.'

The tone of self-congratulation in his correspondence did not escape the notice
of those at home. In a letter to Lord Grenville, his brother Thomas wrote, 'I think
he [Popham] has infinite merit and deserves infinite praise; I will not quarrel with
him for desiring to make that praise exclusive.' His self-esteem was not to be at
all diminished by the events of the last days of July.

3

RUSSIA
Extract of a letter from Cronstadt, August 2.
Our countrymen who have been employed at Revel, in conducting the
Embarkation of the Russian troops, have been honoured with great marks
of attention from the Emperor and his Family.

His Imperial Majesty requested the *Nile* Lugger, in which Captain Popham
went to Petersburgh, to be brought up close to his Palace of Peterhoff, where
he went on board, accompanied by one Nobleman. The Lugger was

---

* Cf. Admiral Joseph York's opinion, quoted in Popham's letter to McMahon.

immediately got under weigh, and there being a fine breeze of Wind, His Majesty was highly surprised and gratified at the swiftness of her sailing. After a two hour Cruise, he was landed again at the Palace, when the Lugger gave him a Royal Salute.[11]

Popham, in a long letter to Huskisson describing the event, says that the Tsar was quite unattended, and this gave him the chance to discuss the forthcoming operations, and to 'cultivate his good opinion and confidence.' The sequence of subsequent events is not clear, but the success of the expedition was obviously unqualified. Thus, the Letter from Cronstadt:

It appears that the account he gave of the English Vessel had greatly excited the curiosity of the rest of the Imperial Family, as next day Captain Popham was honoured with the company of the Emperor, the Empress, four Princesses, and three Princes, with their retinue, when they were of course treated with a sail, at which they were highly delighted, and with great condescension partook of some Ship beef and biscuit. The Emperor was particularly attentive to every thing on board the Lugger, visiting every part of her; and when the Sailors were hoisting the sails, he insisted on helping for once to set the sails of a Vessel belonging to his gracious Ally, and actually hauled the rope with the men. The Empress begged that the Crew would sing 'God Save the King', which was instantly complied with to Her Majesty's entire satisfaction.

Popham does not mention this charming occasion in his letters to Huskisson—though he must have made much of it in his letter to Elizabeth and the children—probably because his next piece of news was even more portentous.

Immediately on my return to the Palace I was desired by Count Rastopsin to attend the Emperor in his cabinet when he said, Sir, I know I have no right to confer any Order of Merit on you except provisionally, but as I feel it my duty to recommend you to His Majesty's protection, I shall at the same time request his permission to make you a Commandant and Chevalier de l'Ordre Illustre de St Jean de Jerusalem; and I shall now take the liberty of knighting you in my own Dominions and investing you with the Order as a mark of my approbation of your zeal and conduct since your first arrival in this country.

In a parenthesis at this point in his letter, Popham says: 'Sir Charles Whitworth's conversation on the subject of this Order placed me in a very delicate situation...', and his inclination is to decline it,

but his Imperial Majesty drew his sword and Count Rastopsin desired me to kneel which I in course did; the Imperial sword was put I believe more than once on each shoulder, when the Count Rastopsin brought the Order which the Emperor placed round my neck, and on rising gave me his benediction...

Popham therefore accepted the honour with due respect and gratitude, but took the precaution of sending it to England in case Dundas objected, or the King refused permission for him to wear it. In the event neither happened; and at the end of September George III duly granted his Royal Licence and Permission to receive and bear (in his own country) the insignia, etc. The Tsar also presented him with a snuff box set with diamonds, and the Tsarina gave him 'a valuable ring'.

The remark about Sir Charles Whitworth's 'conversation' needs clarification. In the Tsar's almost mystical enthusiasm for the Knights of Malta and his position as their Grand Commander, he was sprinkling KMs around like confetti. Every member of the Corps of Horse Guards, his personal pride, wore one; and he was so free with them to British officers that in December George III put his foot down. Popham and Admiral Lord Duncan were allowed to 'receive and bear' theirs, but no one else. Perhaps, Count Woronzow, the Russian Ambassador in London, wrote to Lord Grenville, the latter might gently suggest to the Tsar that some other '*marque de sa Bienveillance*' might be substituted. In an affair replete with irony this was perfectly in accord. The final twist was still some months ahead.

4

There was not much other frivolity during Popham's two and a half months at the Court of St Petersburg, if his letters are anything to go by. The Russians were not geared to this brisk British captain who knew exactly what he wanted, was determined to get it, and had the Tsar's authority to see that he did. 'Our quick motions' he wrote to Huskisson as early as 21 June, 'have made so compleat a revolution [in the Russia Navy's methods] that I wish I may get safe home; you cannot send for me too soon.'

'If only Admiral Cuchelev's zeal had kept pace with his stupidity,' he was writing a month later, 'we should have had Imperial ships for the embarkation, and all filled by next week, but he is an incorrigible old sloth and hates an Englishman as much as he despises activity; I have had much difficulty to keep my temper with him; however the business is now over.'

As for getting home, there was no chance of that. 'Upon the whole,' Huskisson wrote to him in mid-July, '...it will be best that you should remain in Russia... endeavouring in the meantime to render the favour you enjoy with the Emperor conducive to every arrangement that may tend to promote harmony and good understanding between His troops and ours when they come to act together.' And in the same letter, which contained the details of the forthcoming expedition, '...it is intended that the Duke of York should take the command of the whole combined army... and of course He will be glad of your assistance in a country where interior navigation is so much recoursed to.' (All these letters are superscribed either 'By

Named Messenger' or 'Under Flying Seal'.)

For at home plans had been finally worked out. Beyond the ultimate goal of defeating Revolutionary France, still under the control of The Directory, there was an immediate aim of securing the Dutch coast—always a British obsession—and with it, restoring to independence, under the exiled Prince of Orange, Holland herself. To achieve this Pitt and Dundas were relying heavily (too heavily, it turned out) on the readiness of the Dutch people to rise against the French occupying forces. In picturing the campaign as part of an insurrection, they overlooked the blend of apathy and hostility which the Dutch had evinced six years previously.

Nor was this the only lesson of the Flanders campaign which they forgot, or chose to ignore. In 1793 the government had raised an army of outstandingly poor quality by the iniquitous 'bounty' system: now Pitt and Dundas, having undertaken to provide 30,000 men, threw open the ranks of the regular regiments to Militiamen and, worse still, members of the Supplementary Militia. 'The ministers,' Fortescue wrote, 'after all the bitter experience of the past six years, had not yet learned the difference between an army and an assembly of men in red coats.' Even by these doubtful means Pitt was only able to raise 10,000, the Militiamen arriving at the camp between Canterbury and Deal 'in growing numbers and in every degree of intoxication', as Arthur Bryant caustically describes them.

The plan of the campaign to be prosecuted by this ill-organised force had something of the same optimistic vagueness. Half a dozen possible points for the initial landing were considered, from Walcheren in the south to Den Helder in the north, with various sideshows— staunchly favoured by Home Popham, who argued his ideas in long letters from St Petersburg—such as landings on Goeree or the Frisian Islands; but when the expedition finally sailed on 15 August, Sir Ralph Abercromby decided to make his initial landing at Helder, at the mouth of the Zuider Zee, having been forced, as Fortescue puts it, 'to leave England in a hurry, with inadequate forces, no Prussian allies, no proper intelligence, no Russian support, and merely with the hazy purpose that he *should go to Holland and do something.*'

The Russian support was, at least, on the way—just. After weeks of ceaseless cajolery, bullying and hard work, Popham had at last seen the 10,000 Russian soldiers on board the transports provided by the Tsar; with a further 6000 awaiting ships from England. With infinite relief, he handed over the responsibility for actually delivering them to Captain Daniel, and left in the *Nile* for Copenhagen and Harwich.

'God bless you, my dear Popham,' Whitworth concluded a long letter just before he left, 'no one wishes you health and success more ardently than your sincere friend...' Without Popham's extraordinary way with the Tsar, he knew, it was unlikely that the Russian contingent would have got away when it did, if at all.

As a postscript to the whole bizarre episode, and a tiny illustration of the kind of problems that arose, a week before they left the Russian Commander, General Herman, demanded that his troops should be provided with 'the black rusk of this country which he endeavoured to persuade me had more nourishment than the English biscuit.' The Tsar, who of course was already familiar with it, was called upon to arbritrate. He agreed that 1lb of the latter was worth 1½lbs of the former. What the soldiers thought of it is not recorded; but as they are described as living on boiled grain and quas(?) 'and even ate with relish the tallow which they scraped out of the ship's lanterns washed down with train (whale) oil, they probably did not mind either way.

5

The last decade of the 18th century seems to have specialised in vile weather. The winter of 1793-4 had been arctic; that of 1799-1800 was even colder; and in the autumn of 1799 it rained incessantly. It also blew. For a week the British expedition was hove-to off the Dutch coast in a gale; headed inshore when it eased—which gave those ashore a useful warning—and then had to lie off for a further week. When the troops were at last able to disembark, tired, hungry, wet and seasick, there was still a sea running and a number of the ships' boats capsized as they ran into the beach (no 'flat-boats', i.e. landing craft, had been provided). Nevertheless, and despite some hard fighting, the army landed successfully and secured a foothold. Against all the odds, the first and most dangerous part of the operation had succeeded.

A further success followed. Admiral Andrew Mitchell took his Squadron through the channel between Den Helder and Texel Island into the Zuyder Zee where the Dutch fleet was anchored and summoned them to surrender. Since the sailors had already hauled down the Republican flag and hoisted that of the House of Orange, their Admiral had no alternative but to obey. Thus bloodlessly the British came by twenty-five men-of-war, seven of them ships of the line, though none were in very good shape.[12]

Popham stopped briefly at Copenhagen where—and it is an example of his thoroughness—he had 70,000 gallons of water ready in casks for the coming fleet, and sailed on to Harwich. On 27 August, the day Abercromby was putting his troops ashore, Admiral Checkayov's Squadron was at Elsinore; they reached the scene of battle a fortnight later, but not overland.

By that time the Duke of York had arrived and taken overall command; and Popham, after a very brief stay in England, joined him,[13] and went to work in his usual energetic fashion. 'I have made every arrangement for the Inland Navigation in the Commissary Department, and I am sending by water some boats and guns to a situation nearest the Harlemeer... [for] when we are ready to proceed to Amsterdam.' At the same time he was urging Admiral Dickson, 'no very enterprising officer', to put gunboats on the canal that runs the length of the Helder peninsula, and down the Zuider Zee side, to threaten Amsterdam. Even before he left England, he was sending Lord Spencer at the Admiralty his ideas as to how the campaign should be conducted, as well as asking to be given a pendant, that is, the rank of commodore, and a ship to command, 'to give me more efficiency when it is right to bring into the interior the gunboats and other armed vessels to co-operate in any plan of attack; besides which the ship, if she is well manned, will furnish me with assistance to build bridges and to facilitate our movements in a variety of instances.' He succeeded in getting three gunboats on to the canal, where they did useful work when the Allied advance began on 19 September.

He hardly needed a pendant to establish his authority, however, for shortly before the attack began the Duke of York appointed him his Naval Aide de Camp, subject to the approval of the King. 'You are, I hope, Sir, convinced', Popham wrote to Dundas, 'I want power and authority but to use it for public good.' He was, in fact if not in title, now the 'Duke of York's Admiral'; and he did not hesitate to advise him on military matters, sometimes in opposition to the soldiers.[14]

Of the details of the wretched campaign of the following four weeks, the less said the better. The Helder peninsula was a wicked place down which to advance, the countryside intersected with dykes and with a single causeway pacing the canal; but an excellent place to defend. The only hope of success lay in advancing as fast as possible to Haarlem and Amsterdam before the French could muster reinforcements, but this Abercromby had refused to do. He was a canny old man, and without adequate transport, horses or artillery, short of food and water, and with an army consisting largely of raw recruits, he would not take the risk. Even after he had defeated a French/Dutch assault on 9 September he stayed put, though there was little to stop him breaking straight through.

The Allied advance, when it did begin on the 18th, was in the measured assessment of Admiral Mitchell, 'unfortunate'; which is to say that it was a shambles. To start with all went well. The Russians rushed forward—two hours before zero hour—in a disorganised, heroic mass and captured the town of Bergen. Then the French counter-attacked, General D'Herman was taken, and his troops retreated as precipitately as they had advanced, plundering the Dutch villages as they went. Abercromby, having captured Hoorn on the shores of the Zuyder Zee, stayed there, while the battle raged twelve miles away without him. At the end of the day the Allies were approximately a mile and a half from their starting-point.

The next attempt, delayed by more gales, also promised well at the start with the capture of Alkmaar, and a new line all of fifteen miles from where they had started five weeks before. By this time Popham had four gunboats on the canal, armed with 18 and 24-pounders, and they fired between 80 and 100 rounds each before three of them were sunk—a bagatelle he mentioned in a postscript in a letter to Spencer. But poor intelligence (the French, despite a spirited counter-attack during the day, regarded themselves as beaten; the British thought they had been reinforced), appalling weather, the indiscipline of the Russians, the country, lack of transport and the weakness of the High Command, decided the day—and indeed the campaign. By 4 October the entire army had straggled back almost to its original line. Though no one, the politicians least of all, was yet quite ready to admit it, it was all over.

From time to time, through the torrential rain and the smoke of battle and inter-Service recrimination, one has glimpses of Captain Sir Home Popham, KM (though he was not yet using his title): on 4 October, writing to Spencer from the Alkmaar Canal of 'the wonderful gallantry of the British troops' and the prospect of driving the French over the Meuse; and in the same letter, 'I am just going into Alkmaar specially despatched by HM (HRH?) and the Prince of Orange to arrange some points with the Regency.' In a letter from Spencer to Admiral Mitchell, 'I hope Captain Popham will be able to collect and arm a good number of schuyts in the canals about Alkmaar and form a tolerable flotilla'. He had already asked more than once for more small gunboats, 'Under the positive conviction of the service they will render the army.'

They were duly despatched from England; meanwhile, Naval ships off the North Sea coast, and the schuyts and gunboats on the canal, were able to give the army support on both flanks; but to no avail, for the heart had gone out of the campaign. Popham's letter to Spencer of 12 October gives at least some of the reasons:

> There is no doubt but we might have got to Beverwick, and probably to Haarlem, but previous to our possessing these places we must have had two pitched battles, and we should have been further removed from our only port, and probably the worst port in Holland for a military depot; the roads also nearly impassable, and the country driven before the enemy left us but few resources... the people in this Province are more attached to their present Government than in any other, and Alkmaar was always notorious for being the most disaffected city in Holland.
>
> We are just now embarking our wounded... I declare to you on my honour that in the whole course of my service I never had half so much to do as I have at present. The variety of services I have attended to cannot be described...

6

On 19 October the French offered an armistice, and the Duke of York accepted. Although Popham, in his letters to Spencer just before it was signed, was arguing that to occupy the West Frisian Islands and part of the coast of Friesland itself would be better—and easier—than complete evacuation, the suggestion was ignored. The British had 10,000 men sick, the Russians 5,000; on the 28th Popham was writing to Spencer, 'I congratulate you on our at last having a fine day, and we are profiting of the opportunity it gives us of embarking troops at all points, and I trust that before night we shall be able to get on board at least 10,000 men.'

The evacuation—from a lee shore and at the end of a wild autumn—went better than he had ever hoped when, only four days earlier, he had clamoured for 'all the small vessels in England, and every Tub, Boat and large Hoveler' drawing less than 16 feet to help carry the troops off the beaches. 'The large ships off the Sandheads are dreadfully exposed, and embarking troops in them is very precarious.' As it was, three ships of war and one transport were wrecked, and several hundred men were lost; yet, since there were on 12 October 126 transports off Helder—'the worst port I ever was in'—and 45,000 men not to mention the horses to be evacuated, it could have been much worse.

As for the Russians, the first idea had been to ship them straight home; but when that proved impracticable because of the lateness of the season, Popham argued that they should be sent to the Mediterranean to reinforce Suvorov: but he and his army were already in retreat from Massena in Switzerland. Instead, they were taken first to Yarmouth and then to Jersey where they seem to have behaved with rather more propriety than might have been expected, until they were finally repatriated the following year. By then, however, a number of things had changed, as Popham was to discover.

One of the reasons for those changes can be be traced in Popham's correspondence from Holland during October. After the capture during the first offensive of General D'Herman (he of the black rusk), the Russian command fell to General D'Essens, 'a most ignorant dog' acording to Popham. Under him, Russian morale collapsed; and on the 24th Popham noted that their army was in a state of disintegration. And as for D'Essens himself, 'I kept my temper with him till yesterday, when I was obliged to turn him out of my quarters'.

From England, the General sent back to his master in St Petersburg the most damaging reports of the campaign, 'the whole tendancy of it', as Dundas, who had read the correspondence, wrote to Grenville a month later, 'is to create ill blood between the two courts. Is this to go on? Or if we do not publicly state to the Emperor our dissatisfaction with the conduct of this general, are we not responsible for all the mischievous consequences likely to result from it?'

There was an obvious choice for the task of remonstrating with the Tsar, and so Popham was to be sent back to St Petersburg in order to put the record straight and restore confidence between Britain and Russia—a mission which forms the substance of the next chapter.

On 9 October 1799, the day the army in Holland retreated to its original line, General Bonaparte landed at Fréjus on the Côte d'Azur to wild popular acclaim. Exactly one calendar month later, by the *coup d'état* on the 18th Brumaire, he took the first step on the road to absolute power.

NOTES ON CHAPTER VII

1. From the citation on his Certificate of Election: Vol V: 332.

2. Kindly lent to me by its owner, Mr Quentin Keynes. Although Popham's Preface is dated March 1799, the book must have been published late in the year, as he subscribes himself Sir Home Popham, Knight of the Sovereign Order of St John of Jerusalem (as well as Captain in the Royal Navy, and Fellow of the Royal Society), and he did not receive his knighthood from Tsar Paul until the end of July.

3. The monsoon blows from SW from April to September, then in October changes to NE: this was the 'engine' for the great two-way sailing ship trade routes.

4. Thomas Stamford Raffles, the founder of Singapore, was appointed Chief Secretary to the Council under the Governor, the Hon. Philip Dundas. There were only a hundred or so Europeans.

5. The Knights of St John was founded as a charitable order c1048, but later took on a military role. By the end of the 18th century it had reverted to its original function of tending the sick and poor; but had also become rich, comfortable and corrupt.

6. Henry Dundas to Popham: Most Secret. 10 May 1799. W. L. Clements Library.

7. Lug-sailed vessels with three masts, armed with 8 to 10 guns and carrying a crew of 40-50 men, luggers were used by the Royal Navy as despatch boats. The French equivalent was the *chasse-marée*.

8. Peter Ustinov in his autobiography *Dear Me*, describing the statue of Paul in the Peterhof Palace.

9. Popham to William Huskisson (1770-1830), at this time one of the Secretaries in the War Office. He later became an MP, and in 1823 President of the Board of Trade. At the opening of the Manchester-Liverpool railway he fell on to the track, was run over by an engine, and died of shock. His letters are notable for their longwindedness.

10. The original is in French. In the same letter, he says: 'Grâces à l'activité de M. Popham, la chose se presse avec toute l'ardeur possible.'

11. Naval Chronicle, 1799. Vol II. There is a curious, and unexplained, footnote to this story. In a letter to an unidentified, but noble, correspondent in 1814, acknowledging congratulations on his promotion to Rear Admiral of the White, Popham continues: 'Your Lordship must be aware of the intimacy with which I was honord by the *present* Emperor of Russia when I was employed on a mission in that country, and that His Imperial majesty used to sail with me on the Neva. The Honourable mark of distinction which I wear emanates from him and I have a small Pension attached to it *for saving his Father's life...*' There are several riddles here. The *present* Tsar, in 1814, was Alexander I ; but it was his father Paul (who was murdered in 1801) with whom Popham was on such close terms, and who knighted him. As for saving Paul's life, no other reference to it has been found. The letter is in the collection in the W. L. Clements Library.

12. Whatever the British do, 'an Austrian observer said, 'they always succeed in adding to the number of their ships.' And Sheridan remarked that, in addition, the nation had gained some useful knowledge: viz. no reliance could be placed on the PM's knowledge of human nature; Holland was a country intersected with dykes; and that the weather in October was not as good as it is in June. *(Years of Endurance, p263)*

13. Dundas to Grenville, 11 Sept 1799. 'Captain Popham came here yesterday morning, and it is my intention to send him to Holland. He knows every inch of the country remarkably well, and, besides that, I think he may be of great use to keep all things smooth and well with the Russians.'

14. 'I must, in justice to HRH,' Popham wrote to Spencer on 17 October, 'say that I think, after all the attention he gave my arguments and entreaties, he was not far from being convinced my positions were right. However, it was decided against me'.

CHAPTER VIII A Winter Journey
1799-1800

1

BACK IN London, Popham wrote to William Huskisson, then Undersecretary
of State, on 21 November:

Previous to my departure for Russia, and during the course of various
services in which I was engaged under Mr Dundas, you frequently expressed
to me his approbation of my conduct, and gave me assurances it should
not go unnoticed, particularly about the end of last year, when I candidly
stated to you my situation, both as to the extent of my Family[1] and my
circumscribed Fortune, and so far convinced you of the impossibility of
keeping two establishments, that you desired me to sell my place in
Hampshire and fix myself in London, and that 'I should have an appointment
in England or abroad,' these were I believe your precise words; and I did
not hesitate to comply with your wishes.

I can fairly state that in the last two years which is the period I have been
directly or indirectly under your auspices that I have spent near three
thousand pounds but I do not assert that this sum was totally devoted to
the Service or incurred solely on that account, though I assure you that the
expence of changing Houses, moving and other extraordinary and incidental
charges has amounted to more than half of what I assert to have spent; and
if considering my own personal exertions, and the circumstances I now state,
you think I am entitled to any retribution or remuneration, I have no doubt
you will put it in train of being given and that also before I again set off
for Russia.

Why he should have chosen to live on the Isle of Wight in the first place is
unknown. Certainly there were Pophams there; indeed, a John Popham
commanded the Isle of Wight Militia during these years and became deputy
Lieutenant of Hampshire; but the family connection was tenuous. Home Popham's
branch had moved from Somerset to Ireland during the 17th century, while John
was descended from Sir John Popham, Elizabeth I's Lord Chief Justice and master
of Littlecote, and his grandson Alexander, one of Cromwell's Colonels of
Horse.[2] Nothing, therefore, can be deduced from that, any more than can the
fact that five years later Home Popham became MP for Yarmouth, IoW.

That still lay ahead. No doubt the 'other extraordinary and incidental charges'
were at least partly due to the L'Etrusco litigation. That venture, which should

have made him a rich man, reduced him instead to a permanent state of financial anxiety; and the £500 a year which was granted to him for his services in Holland and Russia—perhaps as a result of this letter to Huskisson—though useful, hardly solved his problems, for without a posting, that is command of a ship, he was on half-pay.

2

In accordance with what he had written to Huskisson, Home Popham and his family had settled, for the time being, in York Place on the recently-developed Portman Estate, west of Baker Street. But he was already standing by for his return visit to St Petersburg; and by early December he had received a letter from Sir Charles Whitworth assessing the problem he would be facing: '...the impression which You, who so well know the extreme susceptibility of our friends here, may expect—I much fear the Game is completely up— and that we shall find it in future a very difficult task to persuade the Emperor to entrust to us his troops'.

That the full significance of Whitworth's letter had not got through is clear from the memo of Popham's, undated but clearly from this time: 'In case the Emperor again proposed to give me Rank in Service, what am I to do? Am I to go to the Crimea, Tartary or Italy if the Emperor desires me?—in short, am I implicitly to obey the Emperor's directions?' Then, ever the practical Agent for Transport, there follows a reference to a Mr Cumming of Riga, who is to be told to look into supplies of 'beef, spars and timber for the Navy Board'. Then, 'as soon as the Baltic opens, four fast sailing-cutters or Luggers should be sent to Lubeck and Cronstadt for the communications; but they ought to be coppered as it is attended with difficulty careening them.' And looking further ahead, 'gunboats and Mortar boats should perhaps, be put in hand, for the canals in case we should again go into Holland and Flanders.'

The note, intended for no eyes but his own, throws an unusually candid light on his particular amalgam of ambition, imagination, and hard seaman's sense, and makes it easier to understand both his appeal to the politicians—he was always ready with some intriguing scheme or other—and his regular indiscretions. What further complicated judgement was that he was also extremely good at his job. It is also quite clear that whatever Sir Charles Whitworth said, Home Popham had no doubt whatever that when he returned to St Petersburg he would be resuming his former amicable relationship with Paul.

This is confirmed by the line, scribbled at the end of the memo 'Letter to Sir H. Popham. Pension.' Cryptic but for the letter he wrote to Huskisson on 7 December:

...you promised a letter to show the Emperor on the subject of my Pension; I think it would be still better and have a greater effect if His Majesty would write a few lines to the Emperor, saying that in consequence of his

accommodation he had ordered it to be granted. You must make it appear
to have risen entirely by the Emperor's patronage [the Tsar had, indeed,
suggested it when he dubbed him KM] and your object ought to be to throw
me on his future protection; I know his Imperial Majesty so well, that he
would consider such a letter as the strongest mark of friendship on the part
of the King, and it would do away with a number of our supposed sins...

But all these agreeable prospects were to be dissolved in the acid of the Tsar's
instability.

3

Captain Sir Home Popham, KM, FRS, special envoy to His Imperial Majesty Tsar
Paul, finally left Harwich in HMS *Ariadne* just after Christmas 1799, heading for
the Elbe. The weather, which had had such a disastrous effect on the Texel
operation, had achieved new extremes of severity as the winter advanced, with
the Baltic frozen and ice reported even off the German coast. So bad were
conditions that he had, at one point, considered travelling to Russia by way of
the Mediterranean, but had been dissuaded. It might have been a good idea.
   A full month after his departure he wrote a long letter to Lord Grenville:

We experienced a great deal of unsettled weather after our departure...
frequent thick fogs, and Easterly winds, and had passed thro' many Miles
of drift Ice off Ameland... I intended to land on Norderney Island, for
this purpose we were beating up the coast with the wind from ESE to SE
but it increased to a heavy gale and flew suddenly round to the SW threatening
to come to NW which it very soon did; and under this appearance, our having
been four days in the direct track of vessels coming from the Elbe and
Weser, without seeing a sail; and the quantity of ice we had been surrounded
with, I agreed it was too dangerous an Experiment to try the Elbe, and
concurred in the propriety of running to the Eastward for Norway, Sweden
or Jutland...

They were heading for the mouth of the Skagerrak, intending to make Marstrand,
north of Goteborg; but the wind flew back to the east and they were forced to
put into Blint Sound, just round the southern tip of Norway between Kristiansand
and Arendal,

where the pilots assured us it was the severest winter they ever remembered,
that the Cattegat was frozen over, and it was a mass of ice from the Skaw
to Gottenburg, with much drift ice on every part of the Coast of Sweden.
On this information [he continues] I tried the roads between Blint Sound
and Arendal, and found them almost impracticable; the whole Country was

covered with snow and the narrow Sledge path in many places filled up by every squall of wind with the drift from the adjacent mountains, in fact the travelling appeared not only very tedious, but in some respects dangerous. We were the whole day going twelve miles and often obliged to walk, especially over the Rivers in three feet of snow.

The party struggled to Arendal, where the local pilots said it was possible to go coastwise, but only in the brief daylight in order to find a way through the icefields; so Popham chartered a cutter, the *Swift*, and succeeded in working his way north to the entrance to Oslo Fjord, where the vessel was immediately frozen in. 'However by the assistance of a number of men from the different Islands, and their ice boats, we cut the vessel out on the second day, and got as high up the Fjord as Moss, from where I am setting off for Stockholm...'. He apologises to Grenville for going into such detail; it is only to show that he is making every effort to press on, 'not that I can promise myself any remarkable Expedition, as I hear it is with difficulty the high Roads can be kept clear of the drift of snow from the extraordinary quantity that has fallen since Christmas.'

He was right not be too sanguine. Although he had found allies in the Ankers, 'the most powerful and opulent in Norway', who arranged for the roads to be cleared as far as the Swedish frontier, he still had to retrace his steps to Moss (he wrote again to Grenville from Christiana, now Oslo, on 31 January) to pick up the main road from Goteborg to Stockholm at Uddevalla instead of taking the more direct route north of Lake Vanern, which he was told would almost certainly be impassable.

And so they set off north and then northeast through the frozen countryside, with temperatures varying wildly from very little below freezing to 9 to 12 degrees during the day, and dropping to 25° below zero at night.

4

While Home Popham and his men were struggling to cross Norway and Sweden, Whitworth in St Petersburg was growing desperate: desperate for news—'We have at the moment ten mails due from England', he wrote to Grenville on 4 February; desperate at the Emperor's increasing animosity towards Britain; desperate for the arrival of Popham who alone, he feels, may be able to swing the Tsar back into a more compliant frame of mind.

On 21 February he wrote to Grenville again: 'I have no account whatever either of or from Sir Home Popham. I confess I begin to be alarmed, having received post from England with letters from his family, posterior to the date of his departure.'

A week later Whitworth at last had news of the errant Captain. Thanks to the snow-clearing arranged by the Ankers, they had reached Stockholm from Goteburg on 9 February and, the Gulf of Bothnia being impassable, had set off five days later by way of Torneo at the extreme northern end of the Gulf, just south of the Arctic Circle and on the borders of Sweden and Lapland.

Sadly, though hardly surprising, there are no letters describing that 600-mile journey through the epically-named Vasternorrland with its snowy forests and sparse habitations, and at that time of the year its abbreviated daylight. All that can be gathered, apart from what imagination supplies, occurs in a letter he wrote to Grenville after his arrival at St Petersburg, in which he refers to 'the difficulties and obstacles, which I experienced in my journey by Torneo, where he had 36° of frost by Reaumurs Thermometer'.

But on 6 March Whitworth received a letter from him, dated the first, from Uleaburg (now Oulu) on the northeast shore of the Gulf of Bothnia where he was 'detained by indisposition'. More than indisposition was to hold him up from now on. The Tsar's hardening attitude towards Britain was already clear: Captain Harcourt, whom Popham had sent on ahead to explain matters, was held up at the Russian frontier awaiting the Tsar's permission to enter the country; and the same thing happened to Home Popham when he reached it a fortnight later. But at last, on 25 March, Whitworth was able to write with unmistakable relief: 'I have pleasure to inform your Lordship that Captain Sir Home Popham is this moment arrived.' The journey from Harwich had taken 88 days.

5

To have averaged something like 25 miles a day over the 1,100 miles from Stockholm was an astonishing achievement; and the irony of it was double-edged. In that Whitworth was receiving letters from England by 21 February—a week after Popham had set off from Stockholm—it is apparent that conditions in the south had moderated sufficiently for normal winter traffic, either by sea or overland, to be resumed; but by then Popham was already committed to battling his way northwards, and probably had no information on what was happening in Germany and the southern Baltic. That was the first cut of the whip. The second was that however quickly he had managed to reach St Petersburg, it would have had no effect on the outcome.

He realised this almost at once. Apart from the delay in obtaining permission to enter the country at all, he was writing to Grenville within a week of his arrival: 'hitherto I have not been able to obtain an interview with Count Rastopsin, or even the commonplace civility of an answer to two notes I addressed him on this subject, after having done myself the honor of calling, on my arrival at his house.' The atmosphere, like the weather, was sub-zero.

For the whole of April he and Whitworth tried desperatley to fulfil their mission, and their letters are replete with a kind of baffled exasperation at the complete reversal of the Tsar's attitude from that of a bare nine months before. On 2 April Whitworth reported that he was not allowed to despatch a messenger, and that the Tsar had applied to His Majesty to recall him 'because he was dissatisfied with my conduct.' And on the 10th: 'We continue, Sir Home Popham and myself, in the same anxiety, or more properly speaking Despair ...Sir Home Popham urged, with his accustomed warmth and energy, all those arguments with which his intimate knowledge of His Majesty's Intentions and the present situation of Affairs could furnish him...' But to no avail. His request for an audience was refused; and on 18 April Whitworth, noting the Emperor's 'unfriendly and irritable disposition towards the English', wrote to Grenville that if Popham failed to get an audience, 'he proposes returning with the utmost expedition to England, where his services may be usefully employed.'

The audience was never granted; and the only word received from Paul during that maddening month was a verbal message, delivered by Count Panin, 'that if he, Sir Home Popham, wishes to leave, His Imperial Majesty could not think of detaining him... and therefore wished him a good journey.'[3]

So much for that punishing slog through the winter wilderness; so much for the fantasies of being granted a pension, or being offered a post in the Imperial service; so much, too, for those moments of glory last summer, the sailing picnics aboard *Nile* with the Tsar and his family, those friendly têtes-à-têtes in the Peterhof Palace, the knighthood, the pension. Home Popham returned, in no pleasant humour, to England where, in due course, his talents would be called upon. Paul, on the other hand, now an ardent admirer of Bonaparte—they even planned a joint expedition against India which, since Paul forgot to ascertain how far it was, and neglected to supply the Army with food, never crossed the Russian frontier—was a marked man. On 24 March 1801 he was cut down in a Court conspiracy by Count Pahlen, to be succeeded by his rather more prepossessing son Alexander.

NOTES ON CHAPTER VIII

1. According to F. W. Popham's *West Country Family*, Home Popham had at this time one son, William Craddock (b. 1791), and two daughters, Caroline Emily (b. 1796) and Mary (b.1797). Another son was born in 1801, a daughter in 1804, and two more sons, Brunswick Lowther and Strachan Irving, in 1805 and 1809. Two more sons born between 1791 and 1796, died young, and there were two other daughters.

2. His armour, and that of his brother Edward, 'General-at-Sea' in the Commonwealth, hangs in the great hall at Littlecote.

3. Seven years later, Rear Admiral Sir Charles Stirling was to suggest that the reason the Tsar would not see Popham on this occasion was because he was afraid of having his mind, and his policy, changed by his erstwhile friend. (See Stirling's letter to William Marsden: Ch. XIV.) This seems a reasonable explanation of his behaviour—in so far as it was susceptible to rational explanation.

CHAPTER IX

A Rotten Job in a Rotten Ship 1800-3

1

'UNDER SAIL,' Captain Sir Home Popham wrote to William Marsden, Secretary of the Admiralty, on 3 September 1800, 'I find the *Romney* the crankiest ship I ever was in, and she cannot bear a Port open at the time the *Isis* has all hers up.' Francis Chard, the ship's carpenter, agreed: 'The Ships Lower Deck ports in a wery bad state when ther is any sea and meakes a deal of water they have bin Reported for 2 years and grows worse... the Ship works a baft partickerlery a bout the Round House and Poope.' Popham suggested a number of modifications, including the removal of the 'poope', an addition, which would relieve her of some top weight and make her 'a better-man-of-war, a faster sailer... and last many years longer'.

These strictures are worth remembering in the light of later events, but the justice of them was to be vividly demonstrated a couple of months later. Popham had been appointed to the ship in August, and had already had enough experience of her to form a keen, and unfavourable, judgement.

On his return from Russia in May he had had a rare three months ashore (in July he was writing to Marsden from Chertsey) and when he joined *Romney* it was for a brief and bloodless operation against the Danes. This stemmed, as had Popham's miserable month in St Petersburg, from Tsar Paul's growing admiration for Bonaparte, who encouraged him to reintroduce the Armed Neutrality of the North,[1] in protest against Britain's claim to the right to search neutral vessels. If the Scandinavian action were allowed to succeed it would close the Baltic to the vital British trade in grain, timber and naval stores, and put more than 100 sail-of-the-line at Bonaparte's disposal, so when, in the summer of 1800, Denmark claimed immunity from the British right to search and seize, and boldly sent a convoy through the English Channel, the Navy first fired on and then seized the escorting frigate *Freya*, and took her into the Downs. To the diplomatic crisis that followed, the British Government acted with speed and resolution.

While Sir Charles Whitworth, now accredited to the Danish Court, was instructed to discuss the affair with Count Bernstorff, his arguments were reinforced by the arrival off Copenhagen of a British squadron consisting of seven sail-of-the-line under Vice-Admiral Dickson, a squadron of which *Romney* was a part. The Danes capitulated, and the British agreed to repair the *Freya*. The respite was to be brief—six months later Nelson would destroy the Danish fleet at the battle of Copenhagen—and the incident would hardly be worth a mention but for the fact it was while the squadron was off Elsinore that Home Popham conceived his ideas for the extension of the naval flag-signalling code, his most secure claim to a place of honour in the history of the Royal Navy (see Chapter XII.)

By 31 August the incident was closed, and Popham sailed for England with despatches from Dickson and Whitworth. With *Isis* in company, he was impressed with the differences in sea qualities between the two ships. On her return, *Romney* went into Sheerness where she remained for the next two months.

2

Affairs in the Baltic, the state of the *Romney* and his new signal code were not the only matters to occupy Popham's energetic mind and free-ranging imagination that month. On the 19th he submitted 'for Mr Dundas's attention, a paper concerning the proposed expedition against the French occupation of Egypt, a paper which as vividly as anything he ever wrote displays those qualities. After a summary of the problems of climate and provisions (in which, he suggests, among other things, that they should call at Cyprus for horses), he recommends that the troops should be supplied with 'shoes made to come up about two inches above the ankle bone and to go with a lace to prevent the sand coming in'—the first 'desert boot' in fact. In particular, the men should be forbidden to march barefooted, 'as I have witnessed so many fatal consequences both in the East and West Indies, & the Coast of Africa ... from a *jigger* or worm which insinuates itself into the skin...', and he goes on to suggest that troops should be sent from India to Suez to take the French in the rear. In addition, 'three or four ships should sail in the ensuing week from England for the Red Sea and push their way up to Suez ... it will operate as a great demonstration in favour of Sir Ralph Abercromby's Army, it will cut off the retreat of the French, and this naval force will be ready to co-operate with the first or second Battalion of Seapoys that arrive..'

'I am aware,' he goes on, 'that a variety of difficulties and objections will be stated to everything I have suggested if it is known the ideas came from me, but I am ready to meet them and enter into fair discussions with any Person who may conceive he knows more of the relative situation and interests of the different countries, or has more practical or geographical knowledge of them than myself...'

Whether the idea of such a 'pincer movement' had already been mooted, and a letter from Dundas to Lord Spencer suggests that it had, in the same letter Dundas wrote:

> ... when I revolve the question again and again in my own mind, I am the more eager for obtaining the services of Popham for that purpose, for there is mixed with it so many considerations of a political nature, and where the naval officer will have to act with and conciliate the Sherif of Mecca, and others on both sides of the Gulf [i.e. the Red Sea], that I am persuaded no person can execute the business to satisfaction who does not go there fully in the knowledge (beyond what any official instructions can give) of the full extent of my ideas upon it.

Significantly, in the light of the feelings which Popham's unprecedented promotion had aroused, he continues:

> I don't see how any question of interference of rank can occur. It is a special and appropriate service in which he can act under the instructions of the Secretary of State, and in the execution of which there is no prospect of prize or any other temptation to excite the jealousy of any naval person.

A point on which Popham himself was bitterly to agree.

He received his orders on 1 November; that night *Romney* shifted her anchorage to a position off Margate, and it came on to blow. At 10 the next morning they let go a second anchor and brought down the topgallant masts to reduce windage. The log tells the story of the next twelve hours:

> PM. ...clear'd the Sheet Cable tier. At 1.30 parted the small bower cable and let go the Sheet Anchor. The gale increasing to a violent Hurricane with rain, the ship on her beam ends, the wind veering to the Northward, the sea breaking over her upper works, washing in her Bucklers* from the sea within. People employed fothering** the ship. At the Pumps. At 2.30 cut away the Mizen Mast [it 'was so excessively bent', Popham wrote in his report, 'that it went over the side by one blow from a small hatchet: eased her a little, but she did not right']. Lost the two cutters on the quarters and one quartermaster being entangled with the rigging. At 3 cut away the Main Mast and 3 '26' carronades, 32-Pounders with the shot and Barkes on the main and quarter decks. The ship brought up but driving at intervals. People employed clearing the ship of the wrecks, at the Pumps and serving the cables with Hammicks, raising Mouses thereon to prevent the ship being filled with water. 'The gale increasing to a perfect Hurricane, more resembling a Tuffoon (sic) in the China Seas... the wind was now so violent that it was impossible for any man to stand without holding...'

That was the climax. The wind eased, and they started to set up a jury rig, hove up the sheet anchor, and fired a gun for assistance. None was forthcoming; and by that night they had a jury mizzen rigged and some sail on what was left of the foremast. The fore topmast had been brought down when they cut away the mainmast. Under this rig they limped back into the Thames, in company with eight other large ships, all under jury rig. The last log entry for the day runs: 'Serv'd each person of the Ist and 2nd Watches with half allowance of Wine'. They needed it.

They finally succeeded in warping the ship into Sheerness by their own efforts, and at once began stripping her out, for everything, including the provisions, was soaked. Later the Master Attendant came on board and warped her along-

* Bucklers: wooden shutters placed against the inside of a hawse hole to prevent the water from coming in.
** Fothering: staunching a leak by lashing canvas over it.

side the hulk *Assurance* to have new masts fitted. The Admiralty, advised of the disaster, were forced to admit that 'under the circumstances he [HRP] has stated, their Lordships are satisfied with what he has done'. At the very least, he had saved his ship.

3

The dockyard worked fast. Within a fortnight new masts and rigging were being set up; and at that time 100 tons of 'hospital stores' arrived with, to dispense them through the ships of the squadron, 1 inspector, 2 surgeons, 1 apothecary, 1 purveyor, 5 hospital mates, 1 clerk and 2 hospital servants. Before the end of the month the ship was ready for sea, and during the first week of December the Squadron mustered at Portland. Apart from *Romney* it consisted of the *Sensible* (36), *Wilhelmina* and *Sheerness* transports, and the sloop *Victor*, carrying 1,500 men of the 65th Regiment of Foot. The regiment was to relieve the 61st at Cape Town, and the latter were to be landed at Suez, join up with contingents from India, and march across the desert to Cairo to link up with Abercromby's 16,000 who were already on their way through the Mediterranean. For a country at that moment without a single ally, and Bonaparte, master of half Europe, threatening invasion, the strategy was almost impudent in its daring.

As for Home Popham, the conveyance of the troops to Egypt was only part of his orders, a routine matter. Far from routine were the instructions, hinted at in Dundas's letter to Spencer, issued to him by the Secret Committee of the Honourable East India Company. The gist of them was contained in a letter from the Committee to the Governor General of Bengal, Lord Wellesley, dated 2 December 1800.

> Sir Home Popham, who has proceeded with a squadron to the Red Sea… has been authorised by us to negotiate and conclude engagements with the Sherriff of Mecca, and other Chiefs in that sea, for the revival and establishment on a proper and permanent footing, of the general commerce between these countries and India, which formerly was so advantageous to our Indian possessions, and particularly to Bengal, but which, from the oppression of the Arab government has now fallen into decay and almost total ruin; and Sir Home Popham is directed to follow such instructions as he may receive from you for his guidance in the accomplishment of our wishes…

First Commissioner for India, and thus the controller of the Company's patronage and military operations, was Home Popham's friend and patron, Henry Dundas.

The Squadron sailed on 6 December, and set course for their first port of call, Funchal, which Popham had last touched at in *L'Etrusco* ten years before. As the ships lumbered southward, with *Wilhelmina* and *Sheerness* always

lagging—'they sail so infamously ill', Popham reported—shipboard routine continued
with its regular round of damaged gear, and floggings 'for theft and prevarication',
'for stealing the water', 'for disobedience and contempt'. Regular star sights were
taken. One of Popham's passions was for marine surveying and its mother art,
navigation. 'As I knew I was to go over a great tract of unexplored sea,' he wrote,
'I took with me at my own expense, a Draftsman, whom I taught Hydrography
on my passage out. My chronometers and other instruments cost me upwards of
£1,200.'[2] He had on board no less than eight chronometers, four of them made
by Arnold; and he was meticulous in teaching his midshipmen the elements of
navigation. The Articles of War were read regularly, in accordance with Admiralty
orders; the rigging was as regularly set up; and whenever opportunity offered seams
were caulked, for *Romney* leaked abominably. The passage to Madeira took them
two weeks.

Just before they left England, Popham wrote to Dundas asking him to look into
the *L'Etrusco* affair, which was still unresolved after some seven years despite
the dismissal of his appeal by the Court of Admiralty. 'I can bear the idea of having
lost my all', he wrote, 'without repining, but hate Charnock [the Ostend merchants]
to suffer.' Money was, as usual, a preoccupation; and from Funchal he submitted
to the Admiralty a claim for travelling expenses in connection with the squadron;
and also for his half-pay from 17 December 1798 to his appointment to the *Romney*
'as I was employed part of that time by the Secretaries of State in Russia.'

At Madeira they took on twelve Lascars, one of whom soon departed this life,
and four British seamen, as well as beef, wine, water, and ten live bullocks, and
sailed again on Boxing Day. They crossed the Line during the first week in January
1801, and dropped anchor in Table Bay on 10 February. During the passage they
lost one seaman through a fall from the main t'gallant mast; and in between holding
Divine Service and setting the old ship to rights (blacking her sides, caulking outside
and in, cleaning the 'tween decks, ventilating and painting—all vital to the health
of the ship's company) her captain had time to think of other matters.

As always, his thoughts, which he eagerly communicated to various members
of the Cabinet in letters and papers, were wide-ranging and constructive—and
absolutely nothing to do with the job in hand. To Spencer and Grenville he
suggested an expedition to take the Danish fleet, 'an act of humanity as well as
policy', in order to prevent the Baltic becoming 'a Russian Sea'; to Huskisson in
February, and to Wellesley three weeks later, he agitates for Dundas to 'continue
his intention of devoting this force to South America'[3]—supporting evidence, if
such were needed, that Popham's Buenos Ayres adventure five years later was
not the impulsive act which it is usually made out to be. Gratuitous advice of
this kind shows also how high this very junior captain stood in the estimation
of certain members of the Government of the day, as well as helping to account
for his unpopularity with many of his colleagues.

At Cape Town the 65th Regiment was duly put ashore and the 61st embarked
in their stead, and on 1 March the little squadron headed east and then north for
the Mozambique Channel and the Red Sea. Of the troops from India, 300 were

already on their way under the care of Rear Admiral Blankett; the rest, having been held up at Trincomalee through fever, had been shipped to Bombay by Arthur Wellesley (the future Duke of Wellington and the Governor General's brother) without authority. But for his illness, Arthur Wellesley would have commanded them in Egypt, with Sir David Baird as his Second-in-Command.

Blankett, in command in the Indian Ocean, was a sick man and Popham was to relieve him; but neither he nor Admiral Rainer, the C-in-C East Indies, had been clearly briefed by Dundas as to Popham's responsibilities. To make matters worse, relations between Rainer and Wellesley were strained: the arrival of a captain of junior status with wide, but ill-defined, duties, and the ear of both the Secretary of State and the Governor-General, could not have been better calculated to create a climate of misunderstanding and tension.

Trouble began as soon as Popham reached the Red Sea, in the third week in May. Blankett had left orders that the troops were to rendezvous at Suez; at Jidda,[4] Popham found General Baird with the Indian contingent, and conflicting orders from India that they were to be disembarked at Coseir on the NW coast of the Red Sea, below the Gulf of Suez. This was accomplished a fortnight later; and Blankett, who had landed his troops at Suez and was still there, was not pleased, for it appeared to be an act of direct disobedience on Popham's part. Ten days later he himself came down to Coseir in *Leopard* and specifically authorised Popham 'to direct the ships and transports at this anchorage, the same as before the Admiral's arrival, as it cannot be better done...' – a barbed compliment which made quite clear who was in command, and put Popham firmly in his place as little more than agent for transports, his old role under the Duke of York.

Blankett was to use his authority once more. 'I have omitted stating', Popham wrote to Wellesley in his report of 20 July, 'that it was my intention, at the particular instance of General Baird, to have accompanied the Army with a body of seamen across the Desert, and to Cairo; but Admiral Blankett was so averse to the measure, that on quitting Cosier, he put every discretion out of the question, by ordering me to Mocha before he would make his dispositions to leave me in command of the Red Sea...' He died on 14 July, and was buried at sea 'with all the honours due to his rank'.

Baird set off, without Popham and his seamen but with the Sepoys from India and the 61st, at the end of June; but although he moved fast, largely by water once he reached the Nile, he was too late for the battles. Abercromby had forced his way ashore at Aboukir Bay near Alexandria on 8 March while Popham was still south of Madagascar, and after a brisk action had established himself, somewhat precariously, on the road to Alexandria. He and John Moore defeated the French in an advance on the port on the 21st, but were unable to take it: and Abercromby himself, wounded during the battle, died of gangrene a week later. General Hely-Hutchinson, who succeeded to the command, left Alexandria invested and set off with a mere 9,000 British and Turkish troops for Cairo. The city, although occupied by 13,000 French soldiers, surrendered on the 27th June – three days before Baird left Coseir. Thus the only troops of the 'pincer movement' to be present belonged to the detachment landed at Suez a month earlier by Blankett; and they had a fearsome march across the desert, losing a score of officers and men from thirst.

The first part of Home Popham's commission had now been fulfilled; and with the formal transfer of power and Blankett's death, he was free to exercise his responsibilities with reference only to the Governor-General. 'I trust that your Excellency will see the propriety,' he wrote to Wellesley on 20 July, 'of making Commanding Officers absolute, if they were even not inclined to be so; for the moment the executive power is divided, different interests are pursued, and responsibility, which is the very soul of energy and zeal, is so lessened that apathy supersedes ambition, and every plan is rendered abortive...' There is no direct reference to Admiral Blankett, but the implication is clear; what the letter did not take into account was the presence in the same theatre of operations of Admiral Rainier.

The troops collected in the Red Sea with such labour may have missed the action, but that labour was by no means wasted. French influence, which had permeated through Upper Egypt and along the shores of the Red Sea itself (the rulers of which owed their first allegiance to the Ottoman Porte in Constantinople) had now been eliminated. That, as Popham wrote to Lord Elgin, the British Ambassador at the Porte, should make his mission to the Arab chieftains a little easier.

4

This, the other part of his work in the Red Sea, he began at once; indeed, on his way northward in May he had visited the Sheriffe of Mecca, and had quickly summed up where that gentleman's sympathies lay: equivocal towards the Porte, friendly towards the French, and 'with a decided antipathy towards the English'. This judgement was shared by the Bombay Government's 'Political Native Resident', Mirza Mehendy Ally Khan (Popham's spelling) who was in fear for his life from, as he put it, 'that Diabolical and Black principal of Poison'.

If it had not been clear that Popham was going to find himself in very murky political waters on a first meeting, it became so on the second, at the end of June. The Sheriffe, who had taken the throne by deposing and imprisoning the rightful ruler Abdallah, and was prevaricating until it was certain whether the English would succeed in expelling the French, began by querying Popham's credentials. In a letter to Elgin, Popham asks him to send the Sheriffe verification – or better, have him deposed, since 'he is universally detested from his tyrannical and rapacious conduct'.[5] The scheme was warmly approved by Baird – not a man to be restrained by protocol.

Meanwhile, they were in deeper water on board the *Romney*. In a gale in July she was making twelve to fourteen feet of water an hour, and every pump in the ship had to be employed to keep her afloat. In this condition they sailed for Calcutta with despatches from Baird for Wellesley, leaving Captain Sause of the *Sensible* in charge at Coseir. They arrived in the Hooghli on 9 August and went straight into dock.[6] On the 11th Popham was summoned to meet Wellesley, and as the latter was about to set off for Oude, went with him.

The burden of their discussions on the journey may be deduced from the Memorandum which Popham submitted to the Governor-General ten days later. Two of the Arabian Emirates were involved at this early stage: Sennah, roughly the modern Yemen, with its port of Mocha and its rich coffee trade which, Popham suggested, might be turned into a Company monopoly 'though without the appearance'; and Mecca, with its port of Jidda and its crafty and unscrupulous Sheriffe. Its importance lay in its suitability as an entrepot with the markets of Mecca and Medina to take goods imported through Jidda; but the problem was its ruler. 'I cannot altogether bring myself to decide the question about the Sheriffe of Mecca,' he wrote, but one way or another—blockade or bombardment —he must be taught a lesson. 'Residents' should be installed to keep an eye on things; and two shoal-draft vessels with 'battering guns' should be built specially, 'which, as commanding the destruction of the towns, would keep the whole country in a state of subjection'. Popham was not a man to recommend half-measures either.

In the meantime *Romney* was undergoing a major refit. Rotten planks in her hull, of which there were a great many, were being replaced, new spars made, casks of beef that had putrefied were sent ashore, and the whole ship was fumigated and 'smoaked' to destroy the vermin. While all this was in progress the crew lived on the hulk *Norge* alongside, but life was no easier for them than in their own ship: one man was given 36 lashes for 'drunkenness, abuse, and attempting to drown himself', while two others were punished for 'Abusing a Centinel'.

By the end of October the main work was done and the ship dropped downriver to Kedgeree, near the mouth, to recover her guns and take on shot. The Prize Agent came on board and paid each man 20 rupees; and on 22 November Home Popham had a visitor, his eldest brother Major-General William Popham, who was duly saluted with fifteen guns. That is all that was said about their meeting; but it is clear from a letter that Home wrote to Henry Dundas on the 1st that they had met before, and that one of the subjects they discussed was the possibility of his getting into Parliament. 'I owe him [Lord Moira][7] a great deal for his attention, and his exertion to get me into Parliament; my brother offered me a seat, and his Lordship tried every channel to accomplish it... My brother continues the same disposition, and a negotiation is again on foot...' This would explain why he had written to Evan Nepean, the Secretary of the Admiralty, at the end of October, asking him 'to press their Lordships [to] allow me to quit that station [the Red Sea] and return to Europe.'

No doubt William, who had been in India off and on since 1768, was able to brief him on the latest developments in a country where the French were a continuing menace—as indeed they were in the Indian Ocean, the Bay of Bengal and the East Indies. Had not a brand-new frigate, *La Chiffonne*, arrived at Mahé in the Seychelles some months earlier, having captured the *Bellona*, and if allowed to roam at will, would pose a constant threat to the returning East Indiamen.[8]

From England news arrived of the invasion of Portugal by Bonaparte's unwilling ally Spain; and this at once suggested that France might attempt to take over the Portuguese colonies in the East, notably Macao. If this happened it would virtually close down the Company's trade with China, for Canton, the only outlet, would be cut off. Whether the danger was real or not, it was none of Home Popham's business: nevertheless, and in the full knowledge that Admiral Rainier was sending two line-of-battle ships there, Popham suggested that he himself should convoy a small military force to 'secure the settlement against attacks', as he put it.

Wellesley and the Bengal Council agreed, and Popham was directed to go ahead. As always, he knew exactly what he was doing and how far he was stepping beyond the bounds of his responsibilities: as always, his headstrong and impulsive enthusiasm overruled his judgement; nevertheless, it was with considerable circumspection that he wrote to Rainier on 5 December:

> The extreme delicacy which, on the one hand, it was my duty to observe, of undertaking any service in these seas without your sanction or command; and the extensive mischief which, on the other, I might be able to prevent, by giving convoy, at least as far as the Streights of Malacca, to the armament intended for Macao from this country, reduced me to a situation of much embarassment; and... I cannot but feel great anxiety that it should be honoured by your approbation.

That approbation was not forthcoming.

December 1801 was not a good month for him in other ways. Just before he left for Penang to face Rainier, he wrote to David Scott, the East India Company's Secretary in London:

> Lord Wellesley has imbibed some little prejudice and jealousy because I have acted so decidedly [In this case, in withdrawing ships which he regarded as surplus from the Red Sea]... he is very flattering in his panegyrics, but I know confidentially he *hates* me, and any man who has the sense to generate suggestions for the public good...

The day before he wrote that, there had been a nasty accident on board *Romney* as she was being made ready for sea. From the log: 'Scaling the lower deck guns, the flash from the touch-hole of one of the guns in the Gun Room communicated to a Powder Horn overhead and its explosion fired 18 more, by which three officers and 11 men were severely scorched.'

They sailed a week later, and arrived at Penang on Boxing Day. There is no transcript of the interview between Rainier and Popham, but there is no doubt of its tone.

> I could not exactly learn [Popham wrote to Wellesley after it] from the particular mode in which the Admiral expressed himself, whether he

conceived I had acted properly... I was very conscious I had; I therefore took
no notice of a variety of innuendoes, tending to reprobate those Officers who paid
attention to the remonstrances of the Governments in India, under any case, even
of the most extraordinary emergency...'[9]

Rainier was obviously furious. He commandeered *Romney*'s provisions and stores
to furnish two of his frigates, despatched them to Macao, and packed Popham
off back to the Red Sea with a flea in his ear. Within seventy-two hours of his
arriving at Penang he was off across the Bay of Bengal, in Madras in the first
week of January 1802 and anchored in Mocha Roads five weeks later. Hard is
the life of a man who, nominally independent, finds himself serving two masters.

The odd and rather endearing thing about Home Popham is that he was perfectly
well aware that he largely had only himself to blame. As he wrote to Wellesley
back in September, when he had been touting ideas of expeditions against Mauritius
(known then as the Isle of France), Manilla and Batavia (Java): 'I am aware, in
many instances, my ideas want pruning, I am equally convinced some are
inadmissible; and I know from the latter habits of my life, I aspire probably too
much at the possession of power...' But he does not want power for its own sake,
only so that he can apply it 'to the performance of whatever service may be entrusted
to my direction.' And as for those ideas, 'they I confess are owing to the *speculative
formation of my brain*'. (Author's italics.)

One of them, recurring even among all his present preoccupations, was that
of an expedition against the Spanish colonies. 'I have previously told Lord
Wellesley,' he wrote in a private memo to an unnamed correspondent at the end
of August, 'that Mr Dundas proposed sending me to South America when the
Red Sea service was finished, and I have reason to believe this opportunity was
taken of employing me by the Secret Committee that I might have a greater field
to recommend myself.' And he goes on to suggest that perhaps he might qualify
for an annuity from the East India Company, 'owing to the enormous expense
I have... as a Commanding Officer on a combined service wishing to keep up
an intimate connection with the Army.'

5

From February until the end of August 1802 *Romney* was back in the Red Sea,
ranging from Mocha in the south to Suez in the north. In March Popham had
planned to visit Cairo at the invitation of the Turkish Pasha Mehmet (or
Muhammed) representing the newly restored authority of the Ottoman Porte, and
to discuss with Baird the return of his troops to India. But plague had broken
out in Cairo, and Popham was afraid that it might be carried to Suez by pilgrims
visiting Mecca. He therefore postponed the journey and turned his energies towards
making sure that it did not reach the squadron. The steps he took—virtually putting
every ship under his command in quarantine—and his orders for putting them into

effect were models of sense and clarity; and a Committee of Health was formed with instructions to inspect every ship to see that they were being obeyed.

In the event the plague did not reach Suez, but the precautions he introduced are a good instance of his thoroughness and sheer professionalism. For all the 'speculative formation of his brain', he was a damned good captain, as well as being a very fine seaman.

As far as visiting Cairo was concerned, however, the 'speculative' part was in command, and with the health of the squadron assured he was able to accept the Pasha's invitation and in May set off, escorted by an officer of Mehmet's household 'with a troop of dromedaries and many led horses'. On arrival he was cordially entertained; and in the discussions which followed on conditions for future trade between Egypt and India, stepped well beyond his brief. For in truth he had no business to be there at all. His embassy was to the Arab fiefdoms bordering the Red Sea, not to the Turkish satrap in Cairo, and he was to have his knuckles rapped by Wellesley as a result. If he had been less enterprising, though, we should have been deprived of the splendid image of him in full dress uniform trotting across 80 miles of desert, surrounded by the Pasha's camel corps; an image far removed from, but no less vivid than, his trudge round the Gulf of Bothnia a mere two years before. There is a sheer exuberance about Captain Sir Home Popham, KM that disarms criticism.

Back in Suez in June, and having seen Baird and his troops safely—he thought—on their way to India, he sailed for Jidda. Three days later, at the entrance to the Gulf of Suez in a strong gale with haze:

> At daylight saw a ship to the westward with ensign hoisted at the mizen peak, Union down, supposed to be the *Calcutta* on shore. Made the *Duchess of York* signal to speak her, at 6 wore ship... at 1030 came to with both bowers in 12½ fathoms.. hoisted out the launch and sent her on board the *Calcutta* to take the men out...

She had 331 officers and men of the 80th Regiment and 79 native Indian followers aboard, and she had driven ashore at 3 o'clock that morning. They were only half a mile off, but there was a heavy surf and the one boat they launched was swamped with the loss of seven lives. In a letter to Baird the CO of the regiment Lt. Col. Harness, described what happened next:

> We had now no boat remaining;—the gale increased... At 7 o'clock three ships appeared in sight; but so much to the leeward, with the sea and wind... little hope was entertained of their affording any assistance. However, we soon discovered one of the vessels to be HMS *Romney*; which about 10 o'clock, anchored at about two miles and a half from the *Calcutta*, when Sir Home Popham directed the *Duchess of York* to anchor at middle distance from us; and at 12, the *Romney*'s launch came on board. By nine in the evening, every man of the 80th, except the seven drowned in the longboat,

COMMERCIAL AND MILITARY

SIGNALS

FOR

THE SHIPS IN THE SERVICE

OF

THE HONOURABLE EAST INDIA COMPANY.

LONDON:

Printed at the Minerva-Press,

FOR THE HONOURABLE EAST INDIA COMPANY,

BY W. LANE, LEADENHALL-STREET.

1804.

was taken on board the *Romney*.

It is the skilful position Sir Home Popham took up, so as to enable his boats to sail to and from the wreck... and to the dexterity and perserverance of his well-trained boats' crews, we are eminently indebted for the salvation of so many lives.

The humane personal attention of Sir Home Popham to the comforts of the troops, many of whom reached the *Romney* in a very weakly state, will long be remembered with the warmest gratitude.[10]

Next morning *Romney* started to drag her anchors, and they had to cut and run; the troops were put ashore, to be picked up by the *Wilhelmina* and taken on to Madras.

There is no mention in the *Concise Statement** nor in the log, of hydrography, nor was it any part of Popham's instructions; and yet, during the eighteen months he was in the Red Sea and entirely on his own initiative, he surveyed it from end to end, and compiled and had drawn in great detail a complete chart in two sections, north and south. There are sketches and plans of Suez, Jidda, Tor Harbour, Mocha Roads, the Straits of Jubal and Aden; and notes as to where water and cattle may be obtained, with occasional warnings such as 'Extreme caution should be observed in intercourse with the natives'.

The reason for undertaking what must have been a long and arduous labour is inscribed on the charts: 'I very soon perceived that there was no accurate chart

* See next Chapter.

MARITIME

SIGNALS

OF

THE HONOURABLE EAST-INDIA COMPANY.

compiled at their request

by

Sir Home Popham.

Opposite and right: The title-pages of Popham's two signal books for the East India Company.

of that dangerous intricate Navigation, which induced me to avail myself of the situation I held to form the present one.' And he acknowledges the help he received from the officers both of the ships in the squadron and the chartered vessels, 'most of whom were in possession of Time-pieces and many fully competent to superintend the task.' His eight chronometers, he says, 'were constantly used in small vessels under the direction of such Officers who had qualified themselves by unremitting attention to the Science since we left England...'

The two Red Sea charts are far the largest and most detailed he ever made, and may be said to justify, if only in retrospect, his election to the Royal Society. That they were a valuable addition to the knowledge of the area there can be no doubt, and a French chart of 1834 makes acknowledgements of them. The charting of the seas and oceans was still, and despite the formation of the Admiralty Hydrographic Office seven years before, a haphazard business in which navigators had to rely on charts produced by individual captains as need arose, occasionally by specific surveying voyages such as that of the *Nautilus*, or those captured from foreign ships.[11]

6

All this of course, was, subordinate to his main task, that of restoring the Company's commerce with the Arab states. The guidelines were laid down by the Secret Committee in a letter of 10 November, before *Romney* left England, and in a despatch from Wellesley, dated 16 October 1801. The former was mainly concerned with detailed points about duties payable, Residents' rights and duties, bribes to Viziers, and other day-to-day matters. The latter, which included certain specific conditions which Popham was to include in his negotiations, also contained a number of general instructions. He was, for example, to impress on the rulers 'the dignity of your situation as the Representative of the British Nation'; but he was not to visit Courts in the interior, as these rulers were not sovereign princes but officers of the Porte. Any 'presents' he made to the various Chiefs should be modest: presents alone would not secure concessions. But, Wellesley continued: 'It is our intention that you should exercise the sole and exclusive power of conducting the political negotiations... under my authority'; and to confirm that power, he was to have a company of Sepoys and twelve troopers, letters of credence, money drafts, an expense account, and an allowance of 2000 rupees a month.

Armed with this authority, Popham headed for Jidda—to find matters even worse than he had anticipated. The Sheriffe had not merely rid himself of the Porte's representative by that diabolical and black principle of poison, but was himself incommunicado. 'If I had anything to communicate to him,' Popham reported to Wellesley at the end of June, 'I might write to him at Taif [a place famous for its gardens, some distance from Mecca] as he was there eating fruit, and it was too much trouble to come to Judda', a reply of sublime insolence, but hardly surprising from one who was in the habit of referring to the English as hogs, and anyone who had anything to do with them as 'the slaves of hogs'.

Assuming that there was little to be gained by remaining there, Popham discharged the English harbourmaster and sailed south to Mocha. From there, at the end of July, he sent Wellesley a long report summarising his recommendations for the future conduct of Britain in general, and the Company in particular, in its relations with the Red Sea states. It is a remarkable document, in the first place for its insouciant suggestion that the East India Company should aim for a total monopoly of trade between India and these states, excluding the local Arab dhows, keeping the French out, and virtually turning it into a British lake. As the Peace of Amiens had been signed four months before, overt acts against France could hardly be countenanced—but her influence could still be undermined.

'The possessions of the Company', he wrote, 'have been so extensive... that it has long ceased to be considered simply as a Commercial Body; and the success which has attended a more enlightened Government, manifested the propriety of viewing it as a vast empire...'

Popham goes on to describe in great detail—and this is the second remarkable feature of his report—the patterns and value of the trade in the area: Egyptian wheat supplying the ports of the eastern shore of the Red Sea as far south as Al Qunfudhah, while farther south they rely on supplies of wheat and couscous 'which is the staple food of the lower class' from the interior of Arabia; Mocha coffee, '36,000 Mocha bahars... about 8,000 tons' of which 'two-thirds... is sent up the Gulph for the Egyptian and European markets; the remainder goes to India, Muscat, and occasionally by American or other foreign vessels'; and 'gums, drugs, and other commodities which may be included in the general productions of Arabia and Abyssinia, and will form a very valuable part of the export commerce of the Gulph.'

This trade, he estimates, should be worth over one million rupees a year; and in an appendix to his report he gives a breakdown of the kinds of goods appropriate for the Mocha, Jidda and Cairo markets, with the estimated value in either Mocha Dollars or, oddly, in German Crowns. From an almost totally incomprehensible list ('Baftaes Nowsarry', 'Cusseedy', 'Muccarmas of all sorts', 'Kinkhobs', 'Soosey Tooltthein') the eye picks out others intelligible if not familiar: Soft Benares Sugar, Moongey Rice, Chintz Menea; or under 'Gruff Goods', Vermillion in Cakes, Tin in Bars, Jenjoo 'or Ginger', Cloves, Cinnamon, Benjamin (shades of *L'Etrusco*!) or, under Bengal Goods, 'Cassmere Shawls', Persian Tobacco, Ambergrease. And so on. Even the quinquiremes of Nineveh did not carry a cargo as spicy as that; the list has all the redolence of the *sukh*. It is also a notable example of Home Popham's ability to master the most intricate details of matters which were largely unfamiliar.

To understand the commerce of the Red Sea was one thing: to come to terms with the rulers of that commerce was another. From Mocha he set off to visit the Immaum of Sunna, head of the Kingdom of Yemen. His mind, it seemed, had been poisoned against the British by the Nawab of Surat—so successfully that on the journey across the desert, even protected by his company of Sepoys, Popham suffered considerable indignities. In a furious letter to the Vizier, written on his return to Mocha on 25 August, he wrote that '... the Ambassador [i.e. himself] is really unhappy that his duty obliges him to represent to the Vizier, that from the moment he left the gates of Mocha he was daily insulted and plundered...'

At Mansurah, one Sheik Aklan of Dorebat surrounded the party with armed men and demanded 500 dollars and one of their tents; at Kerrah they were held up for four days by the Dola of Tais; and at Orash 'one of the Sheiks levelled his piece twice at the Ambassador, within ten yards; and declared he would shoot him because he had no money about him to give the Sheik'; and later,

> 'a party seized on the dromedary of one of his suite, struck him, took away his sword, and tore his coat (the uniform of His Majesty) from his back... The Ambassador takes the liberty of observing to the Vizier, that he would have repelled some of these insults with his body-guards of Seapoys, and probably put most of the Imaum's subjects to death, who were concerned in such atrocious acts; — but as his character is supported by that all-powerful nation to which he belongs, he considers it beneath his dignity to command so contemptible an atonement; nor does he even look upon the destruction of Mocha, Loheia and Hodeida, which he could accomplish in a few hours, by His Majesty's squadron in the Red Sea sufficient reparation...'

Nor was even this all: 'another act of aggression' consisted of 'enticing his Majesty's subjects to desert from their ships, and embrace the Mahometan religion'—apparently with some success.

Coming to terms with people like these was obviously not going to be easy, and Popham turned his attention to the Sultan of Aden, who seemed likely to prove more amenable, and whose harbour in Popham's opinion, though not in Admiral Blankett's, was considerably safer than the open roadstead at Mocha. The Sultan had in fact already approached the Bengal government offering a commercial treaty; and Popham now submitted to him, via his son, 'the outlines of a treaty for his father's consideration'. Apart from its immediate advantage—the port of Aden was to be open to all British subjects, and the duties to be levied on goods going in and out were to be kept to between one and three percent—the fact of such a treaty existing might well bring the Immaum of Sunna to a more amenable frame of mind. For the first time during his long and exhausting embassy Popham sounds quite optimistic.[12]

7

Throughout it, his task had been complicated by the changing situation in Europe. First there had been the Spanish invasion of Portugal; then, in October 1801, the Preliminary Treaty which was to be the basis for the Peace of Amiens the following year, was signed in London. The news of it reached Suez at the end of April 1802.

Under its terms Egypt was restored to the Porte; and although no one trusted Bonaparte, the French, for the time being, were no longer enemies. The nuances of the situation had been ignored by Home Popham as he tried to negotiate with the Arab rulers, persuading the Immaum of Senna 'to take measures for preventing the French from having a footing in Arabia', interfering in a quarrel between the Porte and the Sheriffe of Mecca, and initiating separate negotiations with the Pacha of Egypt. All these, Wellesley wrote in a stern letter on 20 June 1802, were completely contrary to his instructions from the Secret Committee: in future he was to restrict himself to the Red Sea states, and avoid becoming involved in politics.

Popham's reply to these strictures on his conduct does not appear among the Wellesley papers; but in August he repeated his request to Admiral Rainier of a year before to be relieved, and two months later Rainier agreed. By then *Romney* was in Bombay for another docking, having left Aden, her last Arabian port of call, early in September.

The Red Sea with its enervating climate and its devious rulers with their petty squabbles was behind him, and he was able to turn to more congenial matters. From Bombay towards the end of October he wrote to Lord Spencer, 'I have employed every means to execute Lady Spencer's commissions...' and says that he is bringing back 'some very fine black wood-logs... which carries a higher polish for tables than any wood I ever saw. I also expect before I quit Bombay to get some very opulent wood for chairs.' And a month later he wrote to Wellesley to say that his promised Red Sea charts were not ready, and he will send them later. The following day, 27 November 1802, just before setting sail for England, he wrote his last letter to His Excellency the Most Noble the Marquis Wellesley, KP, Governor and Captain General over All the British Possessions in the East, &c. &c. He has not had, he says, so much as a farewell word from his Lordship; and he goes on to recite his services over the last two years.

> These very exertions and the effect they had on several occasions, have raised a Host of Enemies in every Presidency, particularly in Calcutta, and the length to which that rancorous spirit of revenge has been carried, even within my knowledge, would astonish you... I am aware I was a very unpopular character at Calcutta, because I ordered all the provisions shipped for the Army in Egypt to be surveyed; and some were reloaded and condemned on the quays: - nor was it my good fortune to be on the best terms with Mr Louis [the Agent]... I mention these circumstances, because I know many people, from jealousy and envy, have in the most insidious manner, presumed to arraign my general conduct...

The letter ends:

> I now however quit India after a laborious service—in a country where no opportunity has presented itself by which I could gain either military Fame or Fortune; in my own profession I have rather incurred the torrent of

jealousy, and I doubt if I have made a friend except the Commander-in-Chief, and the Army in Egypt.

Was he exaggerating? Like many clever, sensitive people, Home Popham veered between extremes of elation and depression, and beneath that often jaunty self-confidence there lurked an equal vulnerability. That he had enemies there is no question; and they were at work in England as well as in India. Back in March the Commissioners of the Navy Board had started an investigation into the cost of the repairs to the *Romney* and *Sensible*, with the result that, although the bills were honoured, the amounts were 'impressed', i.e. charged, against Popham and Louis, and the former's pay had been stopped pending an inquiry. (See Chapter X.)

At the same time, his 'laborious service' in the Red Sea was clearly recognised. While *Romney* was on her way home, Wellesley wrote to the Court of Directors in London praising Sir Home Popham's 'zeal and alacrity... in promoting the interests of the Honourable Company', his 'active and able exertions' in the public service both as regards the Egyptian expedition and the force intended for Macao. And the Governor General in Council continued:

> The conduct of Sir Home Popham, during his political mission to the Arab States, furnishes equal proofs of ability, industry, and attachment to the public service; and although the Governor General in Council deemed it to be his duty to express his dissent from the policy of Sir Home Popham's proceedings in Egypt and other places... His Excellency highly approves the general tenor of Sir Home Popham's conduct on the coast of Arabia and the Red Sea.

Undiluted praise was not something that usually came his way, for he was a man who provoked reservations.

Romney arrived at St Helena at the end of January, to find a request from the Company to await the arrival of seven Company ships and convoy them to England.[13] They duly appeared, and under *Romney*'s protection sailed again in mid-February. The voyage was uneventful and they only saw a couple of other ships. On 12 March the log reported: 'Saw two strange sail bearing NNE. Made sail in chace. Fired a gun (shotted) to bring the chace to. Sent a boat on board. A Portuguese ship from the coast of Africa to the Brazils.' A month later: 'At sunset the extremes of the Scilly Isles... At 9 saw the Lizard Light', and on 12 April, 'saw the Eddystone'.

After a brief stay in Plymouth, where they picked up forty-two Greenwich pensioners as supernumeraries, they anchored in the Downs on the 18th, and hauled alongside the *Rochester* hulk on 20 April 1803. They had been away for two years and five months.

NOTES ON CHAPTER IX

1. First established in 1780, during the American War of Independence. Popham mentions a convoy of 'near 80 sail of vessels engaged in the Baltic trade', which gives an idea of its importance.

2. Details of some of the chronometers on board, and their accuracy, are described by one of the officers in the *Naval Chronicle* in 1803. The first really accurate chronometer, by John Harrison, passed its test on a voyage to Jamaica the year before Popham was born. Lt.Cdr. A. C. F. David points out that to have eight of them, except in a ship engaged in exploration, was most unusual, and stemmed 'presumably from the fact that Popham prided himself on his surveying ability'. (Private letter to the author.)

3 Plans to attack the Spanish colonies in S. America went back to 1780, were revived by Francisco Miranda in 1797, were a frequent preoccupation of Popham's—who submitted a long paper to Dundas on the subject—and reached a sort of fruition in his Buenos Ayres adventure of 1806.

4 And see C.Northcote Parkinson, *War in the Eastern Seas*. In a footnote in the *Concise Statement*, Popham notes: 'Alluding to the Telegraphic Signals, or Marine Vocabulary, which was used for all communications between the Army and Navy by General Baird; and since my return to England I have printed a Second Edition.' See Chapter XII.

5 In Feb 1802, Elgin wrote to the Court of Directors of the Company, suggesting that he should meet Popham in Cairo to discuss the problem of the Sheriffe of Mecca, but sent the embassy secretary, Straton, instead.

6 The city of Calcutta is 75 miles from the sea up a winding channel in the Hooghly River, littered with shoals. There had been doubts about its ever becoming a major port; yet, in spite of all its disadvantages, Fort William became the headquarters of East India Company government in India. Anchorage in the river was poor, and loss of anchors and cables was put at £3,000 per annum. It is worth noting that the founder of Calcutta was one Job Charnock.

7. Moira, Francis Rawdon-Hastings, 2nd Earl of. Soldier, Later Master General of the Ordnance in Grenville's Ministry of All the Talents, after Pitt's death. In 1813 Home Popham took him to India on his appointment as Governor General, but that is another story.

8. Popham had learnt before he left the Red Sea that a French warship was in those waters, and despatched the *Victor* on a reconnaissance; but Admiral Rainier had already sent the frigate *Sybille* and on 19 August she sailed boldly into Mahé, flying French colours, and in sixteen minutes of 'pretty warm work' took the *Chiffone* from under the shore guns. It was just as well: *La Chiffone* was brand new, and reputed to be the fastest sailer out of France.

9. A month later Wellesley replied, 'I am extremely concerned to learn... the unfavourable and erroneous view His Excellency Vice-Admiral Rainier appears to have taken of the liberal and zealous aid which you have offered...'

10. Col. Harness's letter was forwarded to the Duke of York, who sent it on to the Admiralty, 'where', Popham remarks, 'with many other testimonies of my service, it remains a Dead Letter'. Of this incident, he wrote elsewhere that 'nothing but such boats as the *Romney*'s for which you know she was famous though at least two of them were stove..' could have saved the *Calcutta*'s people.

11. The Admiralty Hydrographic Office was created in August 1795 with Alexander

Dalrymple as the first Admiralty Hydrographer. In 1807 Popham was a member of the Admiralty Chart Committee which laid the foundations of the Admiralty Hydrographic Service. (See Chapter XV.)

12. The treaty was duly signed by HP and dated 6 Sept 1802. Article 1 read, in part, 'That there shall be a commercial union between the Honourable East India Company... and the subjects of Sultan Ahmed Abdool Kureem.' It backed up the political relations established three years before, and survived until 1839, when the British occupied Aden.

13. The Court Minutes of the Company for 13 July 1803 read: 'Resolved that the thanks of this Court be given to Sir Home Popham.... for his ready compliance with the request of the Governor of St Helena to remain there... until some of the Company's homeward bound ships should arrive at that Island, and for his care and attention in convoying seven... to England, and that Sir Home Popham be presented with the sum of 500 guineas for the purchase of a piece of plate as an acknowledgement of those services...'

That 'piece of plate', an elegant silver tea kettle on a stand complete with spirit lamp, and engraved with Popham's crest and inscription, is now in the possession of Mr Boris Reford of Montreal, to whom I am indebted for both the photographs and the information.

CHAPTER X

'Enormous and Extraordinary Expenditure'? 1803-5

1

WHEN HMS *Romney* arrived home Britain was on the brink of renewed hostilities with France. Into this tense siuation sailed men who, in their captain's words, 'many of them, had been seven or eight years in the ship; and some had nine years pay due.' These men had been promised fourteen days' ticket of leave after they had helped fit out some newly-commissioned ships in Sheerness Dockyard, but this was revoked. '...From the peculiar circumstances of the times', said the Admiralty order, 'it was impossible to grant leave of absence; and therefore trusting that the men would display their wonted zeal, and enter for some ship in the harbour; or otherwise they would be drafted.' The Fleet had mutinied six years before for reasons such as this.[1]

Home Popham had just finished the unspeakable task of reading this letter to his assembled ship's company and, not surprisingly, 'every seaman seemed almost to wish my instant destruction', when he was abruptly summoned to meet Sir William Rule, the Surveyor of the Navy. He had brought from London a warrant from the Navy Board empowering him to go aboard *Romney* and examine the report on the ship's condition, the repairs she had undergone and the ship's stores which had been purchased while abroad. Although Popham knew that his accounts were under investigation, the high-handed way in which the matter was handled angered him: but he was helpless. Rule, accompanied by the Commissioner of the Navy Board, the Builder, the Storekeeper, the Master Attendant and other dockyard officials, proceeded on board. When they had concluded their examination of the ship, they took ashore with them various members of the ship's company to attend what Popham calls a 'Committee or Court'. Popham himself was not invited, but insisted on attending.

The burden of the inquiry resolved itself into a number of questions. What had been the condition of the ship on her departure from England, and on her arrival at Calcutta? Were repairs necessary, and were those that were carried out essential? Had there been wanton and wasteful expenditure on stores? And why had the work been done at Calcutta and not at Bombay, where there was a naval dockyard and an ample supply of ship's stores? To all these Popham had unequivocal answers, and the first is worth quoting. 'I then requested to put one question, namely, "Whether, if the *Romney* had not received the repairs in question, considering the weather we experienced, she would not, in all probability, have gone to the bottom?"' The question was disallowed. But perhaps the oddest aspect of the business was that the ship's own officers—the lieutenants and the master—were not called, nor was Popham allowed to bring them forward as witnesses, and only the warrant officers were examined.

This was not the only curious facet of an inquiry that bore the signs of a vendetta against Home Popham, but which was in fact even more complicated, for it was linked with a campaign against the First Lord of the Admiralty, Earl St Vincent, whose sturdy attempt to reduce the corruption in the naval dockyards had stirred up a tumult of resentment.[2] The two are indissolubly connected through one man, St Vincent's secretary, Benjamin Tucker; and to understand the 'case' against Popham, it is necessary to look briefly at what had been happening at the Admiralty and the Navy Board while he was in the Red Sea.

With the fall of the Pitt Government early in 1801, Henry Addington, the incoming Prime Minister, had appointed Admiral Sir John Jervis, ennobled after his great victory of Cape St Vincent four years before, as First Lord. A noted martinet, he saw his chance, with the signing of the Peace of Amiens, to tackle the notorious abuses in the Navy which were said to be costing the country £1M a year and jeopardising both ships and sailors' lives.

The malpractices ranged from the building slips to the stores, from the clerks to the prize agents. Everyone was on the fiddle. Shipwrights had an unpleasant habit of cutting the centre section out of copper bolts, replacing it with a wooden trenail, and selling the metal. The theft was disguised, and a number of ships were lost through structural failure caused by these 'devil-bolts'. Condemned stores were taken ashore and then sold to another ship as fresh; pensions—'smart money'—were conned out of wounded and sick sailors by land-sharks who got them drunk and sold them clothes at exorbitant prices on credit; prize agents held back, often for years, money due to their clients. Clerks were suborned by 'hampering', i.e. bribes of hampers of wine and ale, dockyard stores were stolen and sold outside, so that many breweries were found to be using 'king's casks'. And so on and so forth. Agents purchasing naval stores abroad were not above selling them to the enemy. There was plenty of scope for reform, and bitter resistance to it; but St Vincent was not a man for half-measures: his commissioners descended on the dockyards, uncovering fraud and corruption wherever they went and detailing them in a series of reports, the first in 1802. Necessary as this cleansing process undoubtedly was, St. Vincent's economies left the Navy considerably weakened when war was resumed in May the following year.

St Vincent's henchman in the work was Benjamin Tucker. As a purser in the Mediterranean Fleet, he had served under St Vincent, had eventually been appointed his secretary, and had gone with him to the Admiralty. His loyalty to his master was fanatical; and his offical positions, first as Second Secretary of the Admiralty, later as one of the Commissioners of the Navy Board[3] with the ear of the First Lord, gave him a great deal of power. He was an industrious and able civil servant who would stop at nothing to further his master's interests, malign his master's enemies, or defend his master's reputation. However, in Captain Sir Home Popham he had picked an adversary who was more than a match for him, and he never forgave him.

As far as Home Popham was concerned, the Commissioners of the Navy Board who were called upon to investigate the charges against him concerning the work done in Calcutta on *Romney* and *Sensible* issued their report in October 1802. Everything, they said, was in order and there was no case to answer. The Admiralty, however, were not prepared to let the matter rest: they referred the report back to the Board, where it was picked up by the recently appointed Junior Commissioner to the Commitee of Stores, Benjamin Tucker, and his version was very different.

Not only did it accuse Popham of taking *Romney* and *Sensible* to Calcutta for repair—and unauthorised modifications to the latter—when the proper dockyard for the work was Bombay; but the amount of money spent there was out of all proportion to the work done, something like £70,000. And that was not all. There were discrepancies, Tucker said, between the number of sails damaged and their subsequent replacement, between anchors and cables supplied and those lost, and a dozen other such matters. Behind it was an implication that, by appointing Louis as Acting Naval Officer, he had formed a conspiracy to cheat the Admiralty. This damning document, compiled virtually singlehanded by Tucker, was read by the other Commissioners and they passed it, merely excising 'objectionable' expressions and those 'containing asperity', and it was delivered to the Admiralty in February 1804.

From the moment Sir William Rule held his hearing in Chatham after *Romney*'s return, Popham tried to obtain details of the charges levelled against him, without success. And at the same time the Navy Board was demanding full details of the bills he had drawn in Calcutta and the Red Sea, but refused to see him to discuss them. Over and over again during the summer of 1803 he requested an interview with St Vincent, but received merely a chilling reply, referring him 'to the Board, through their Lordships' Secretary, respecting any steps which he may be desirous of having pursued with regard to the subject therein mentioned'. It was all both sinister and frustrating.

However, Sir Home Popham, as one naval historian puts it 'was very capable of taking care of himself', and in August 1803 he had privately printed A CONCISE STATEMENT OF FACTS RELATIVE TO THE TREATMENT EXPERIENCED BY SIR HOME POPHAM SINCE HIS RETURN FROM THE RED SEA and submitted to 'such of his Majesty's Ministers, and other distinguished personages, whose friendship and protection, I am proud to boast, have not, in the slightest degree, been diminished, by the cruel and vindictive attacks on my character, honour and reputation...' One copy went to Prime Minister Addington, who asked Popham to restrict its circulation, and assured him 'on his honour' that he had never heard St Vincent either directly or indirectly say anything against him.

There are, nevertheless, good grounds for believing otherwise.[4] St Vincent disapproved of the Sea Fencibles because they kept naval officers ashore when they should be at sea; and he treated him with an indifference close to hostility when asked for an interview. Popham himself mentions in the *Concise Statement* that 'liberties had been taken with my name, which were supposed to have originated from the tenor of Lord St Vincent's conversation'. Add to the resentment in the Service towards his rapid promotion and his lack of battle experience the fact that he was a favourite of the Tories, especially Lord Melville, the former—and prospective—First Lord, while this was a Whig administration, and the case becomes clear. The ruthlessness of the politics of patronage spared no one.

The *Concise Statement*, 212 pages long and assembled as it must have been at top speed, is a curious piece of work which illuminates Popham's character in ways which he certainly did not intend. Its form is that of a selective anthology of letters to Popham and by him, covering his two and a half years in the Red Sea, and including whenever possible eulogies on his conduct such as that following the *Calcutta* rescue. Its tone is self-justificatory, and often self-congratulatory as well, but it disposes of a number of the calumnies which were circulating about him in naval circles. To take two examples, it was Admiral Rainier, not Popham, who appointed Mr Louis; and it was on Rainier's orders that he went to Calcutta instead of Bombay. It quotes extensively from his correspondence with Wellesley, although this bears not at all on the subject of the inquiry being carried out by the Commissioners of the Navy Board: its function is to demonstrate his abilities as commander of a squadron, as a seaman, and as an envoy.

No wonder that it infuriated Benjamin Tucker, beavering away at his report in the offices of the Navy Board in Somerset House; but it did not justify his response. For what Tucker did was to publish a pamphlet, entitled 'Observations on a Pamphlet... said to be "A Concise Statement ... etc..." To which is added a Copy of the Report made by the Navy-Board to the Admiralty'—the report, no less, than that on which Tucker had been working, which was confidential and which Popham himself had been given no chance to see.

The tone of the 'Observations' may be gauged from one or two extracts:

> There is, it is true, some apology for Sir Home, who has served but little, where the characters of any of our Admirals could have been learnt; yet, if the brilliancy of his own exploits, in teaching the midshipmen of the *Romney* to observe the transit of a star over the meridian, had not blinded him...

And a little later:

> Sir Home talks of envy and jealousy having operated against him; surely he cannot mean to apply that insinuation to either of the late Sea Lords of the Admiralty! Of what trait in his character, of what feat, during his career in the public service, can he fondly have imagined them to be jealous? Are not the public yet to be informed of these wondrous exploits... and will it not be confessed... that if any such exploits had been achieved by him, they would have *lost nothing in the telling*?

And so on. But Tucker went further. This unpleasant document, complete with its leaked report, was then circulated through the fleet, and even on board the ships of the squadron of which, by then, Popham was in command.

Stung, as well he might be, Popham produced a second, revised version of the *Concise Statement*, which included both Tucker's 'Observations' (of course anonymous) and a pamphlet written in his defence—though not, one is led to believe, at his instigation—by 'Aeschines',[5] This was published early in 1805, but by then a number of changes had occurred to operate in Popham's favour. The Addington Ministry had fallen in May 1804, and St Vincent had been replaced at the Admiralty by Lord Melville.

2

Romney's problems were by no means Home Popham's only preoccupation during the eighteen months after his return. In addition to publishing the *Concise Statement*, he produced the second printed version of his *Marine Vocabulary* signals* during 1803; and in August the *L'Etrusco* affair, already ten years *sub judice*, surfaced once more. Three Law Lords, sitting in the Council Chamber in Whitehall, rejected Popham's petition to have the ship and her cargo, or their value, restored to him. This might have appeared to seal the matter once and for all, but he was not beaten yet. On 24 October 1803 he deposited in the Council Office a 'Humble Memorial and Petition' to 'The King's Most Excellent Majesty in Council' in which he outlined both his own naval career and the lethargic progress of the case through the High Court of Admiralty, the Lords Commissioners on appeal (in 1796 and again in 1798) and finally its rejection by the Law Lords. What this meant was that, as he stated in his petition, the 'Property, which, having been proceeded against as a Prize of War, has been adjudged to your Majesty, and is subject to your Majesty's most gracious disposal'. As such, the money became part of the Droits of Admiralty,** the fund out of which prize money was paid: Popham was humbly requesting '...that your Majesty will be pleased to direct the aforesaid remaining proceeds of the said Ship and Goods to be paid to him, or to grant him such other relief as in your Majesty's wisdom shall seem meet.' In the following month, de Rebeque, one of the three partners in the ill-fated enterprise, also petitioned the King on the grounds that Popham was still in debt to him and the money owing should be paid to him out of whatever was granted to Home Popham. According to the latter's petition, de Rebeque had already had £12,197 18s 8d, and the felicitously named Skeýkinqua—who appears here for the first and last time—£16,242 11s 3d, by direction of the Appeal Commissioners; and there was nearly £40,000 still lying in the Registry; and this in spite of the fact that the ship herself, which had cost £20,000, had been sold off for a mere

---

* See Chapter XII. But Popham managed to include in the *Concise Statement* a letter from Admiral Rainier in which he asked for 'a copy of your ingenious telegraph signals'—though the letter in question was mainly concerned with the appointment of Mr. Louis.

** See Chapter XIII, Note 6.

£7,050. These were large sums of money, and Popham could ill afford to let the matter go by default.

In addition to all this, during 1803 he was working on the drafts of his Red Sea charts, and pulling as many levers as possible to get into Parliament.

That was the summer in which the war, halted briefly by the Peace of Amiens, broke out once more. Across the Channel that July Bonaparte was inspecting the barges built and building for the invasion of Britain, and the 150,000 troops mustered in the Channel Ports waiting to cross in them. Rumours about the invasion achieved astonishing imaginative heights: balloons, a bridge, even a tunnel, were being prepared for the transit of Boney's armies; and, bred by the rumours, a patriotic fervour of almost hysterical proportions. Every able-bodied man was in uniform; and, according to Lord Auckland, '...I am convinced that, should an invasion be tried, you would see all the ladies letting their nails grow that they might scratch at the invader.'[6]

The rumours might be extravagant, but the threat was real enough as Boulogne harbour was hurriedly enlarged to accommodate the convoys of barges creeping close inshore to their embarkation points. To protect them from the attentions of British raids and cutting-out expeditions, the entire French channel coast was turned into a fortress 'of iron and bronze', one field gun to every league—almost as if the expected invasion was to be in the opposite direction. And night and day, summer, autumn and winter, the British squadrons cruised up and down from Rochefort in the south to the Texel, on guard against the emergence of the French fleets without which the invasion barges would never be able to leave their moorings. This was the situation, and this the mood of Britain, bold, resolute, defiant, in May 1804 when the Addington Government fell, Pitt returned as Prime Minister, and Lord Melville replaced Earl St Vincent at the Admiralty.

With the change of government, Popham got his wish and entered Parliament as Member for the rotten borough of Yarmouth, Isle of Wight, a seat in the gift of the Holmes family at a reputed price of £4,000. In May also a mysterious American made his appearance in London, a clever, equivocal figure with whom Popham was soon to be involved. Elizabeth had just presented Sir Home with a daughter, their third, at their residence at York Place, Portman Square; and early that summer they bought a small estate, Titness Park, near Sunninghill in Berkshire. From there, in July, Popham wrote to Melville: 'I have not been altogether idle; my chart of the Red Sea has received its last correction from the Engraver and will be presented to you tomorrow or the next day...' He had, he said, seen 'Mr Francis'; and he went on: 'Lady Popham is at present in the country, but I expect her in town on Friday... I am certain she will do herself the honour of waiting on Lady Melville...' It is one of the very few references in his letters to his wife and family; and it makes clear that the relationship between Sir Home and Lord Melville extended beyond the formalities of office.

3

Although it means running ahead of events, it is convenient to round off the *Romney* affair here. In September that year, 1804, Popham finally obtained from the Admiralty, Tucker's report, though not the papers on which it had been based. He had already refuted the charges, in so far as he had been able to learn of them, in the *Concise Statement*; had even taken Counsel's opinion as to whether he had a remedy at law, and was advised that he had not; but now injury had been added to insult. On 16 December he wrote to the Commissioners of the Navy Board: 'It is impossible for me to express what I feel on hearing that your report to the Admiralty dated February 20th of the present year, is printed and sold in the booksellers' shops in London... with their signatures on it', and he requests them most forcibly 'to trace the channel which has taken from the archives of your office a paper under consideration of the Admiralty, and forced it on the public'.

This was the pamphlet 'Observations...' which Tucker had circulated through the Fleet. The very day after Popham's letter, the Commissioners wrote, denying all responsibility; and, after further pressing from Popham, issued, early in 1805, their Fourth Report. This was nothing less than a complete retraction of Tucker's accusations, and it laid the blame unequivocally on him. Tucker, it was now admitted, had made a number of 'errors'. 'We have too much reason to apprehend that the Report is in many instances inaccurate...', they conceded; and, to clinch the matter, 'In short, we can scarcely think that there ever were such extraordinary means resorted to, to produce a particular effect, as have been in the framing of this most overstrained account.' Benjamin Tucker, it may be noted, had already been transferred, and had been appointed a Secretary to the Admiralty.

The business was still not quite over, however. On 5 February 1805 the Hon. Charles Kinnaird, MP for Leominster, raised the matter in the House of Commons 'as much to defend the honour and character of the gallant officer,... as to prevent an improper and useless squandering of public money.' His desire to defend Popham's reputation did not, however, stop him reciting the charges brought against him in detail; and Popham, who was present, defended himself stoutly.

That there was more to it than simply the question whether he had or had not squandered public money emerged from one particular passage in Kinnaird's speech. He had heard on good authority, he said, that the previous Board of Admiralty—i.e. that in which St Vincent was First Lord—had 'designed to institute a criminal prosecution' against Popham. 'The change of administration, however, by which the late weak and inefficient Board of Admiralty had been changed for a capable and efficient one and had prevented them from carrying their views into effect.' It had become, in short, a party question, ammunition to be used against St Vincent by the enemies which his investigations and economies had roused.

As a result of Kinnaird's initiative, the '*Romney* Question' was referred to a Select Committee, and this duly reported on 8 July. The members of the committee were given a vast amount of material to consider, including the shamefaced and apologetic Fourth Report of the Commissioners of the Navy Board. This did not merely show that Tucker had succeeded in multiplying the actual expenditure by a factor of ten, but pinpointed precisely the Admiralty's responsibility in the matter.

As to the first, one example among many will suffice: a 'smoke-sail', rigged to keep the smoke from the galley chimney from smothering the quarter-deck, was stated to have cost £73, and Tucker had made much of this. The actual cost, however, had been £7 6s 3d! As to the second, a number of absolutely damning facts emerged. For one, Tucker had been transferred from the Admiralty to the Navy Board directly after the Board's first report which had cleared the accounts; and it was he who, with the help of one clerk, compiled the report which concluded that the repairs to *Romney* and *Sensible* had cost £70,000—whereas the true figure was slightly more than one-tenth of that.

The Select Committee confirmed that Admiral Rainier, not Popham, had appointed Mr Louis: and they discovered also that the Bosun, Mr Ewen Bartholomew, had been impressed as soon the *Romney* docked at Sheerness and held on board the *Zealand* 'with the sole view of extorting some evidence against Sir Home's conduct; though he declares that he never could allege anything against him; and that he never sailed with any Captain who paid more attention to the health, comfort and discipline of his ship's company, or who was more economical with respect to stores.' The Committee also established that the Board's refusal to allow Popham to state his case or answer the charges in person was in response to a direct order to that effect from the Admiralty, even though this was contrary to normal practice.

In the light of these revelations, and a great deal of study of the documents in the case, the Committee had no difficulty in stating, when it reported to the House in July, that 'the charges brought against the integrity of Sir Home were wholly unfounded and that it appeared on the contrary to the House that he had discharged the trust reposed in him with ability and fidelity, and so as to have powerfully conduced to the benefit of the public service.'

His vindication was thus total, although, as is the way in such affairs, some of the mud slung at him proved all too durable. There was one illuminating disclosure in the Committee's findings. They found that the Report published with Benjamin Tucker's 'Observations' and 'circulated very generally, and with considerable industry, through London, through the sea-port towns, and through His Majesty's fleet at Portsmouth; and in the Channel, and off Brest, in that squadron in which Sir Home Popham was then himself employed' had been published 'by the advice of Lord St Vincent's friends, and with the concurrence of Lord St Vincent himself, to whom he (Tucker) had shown a manuscript draft of it before it was published.'

That made clear beyond any possibility of doubt where the inspiration for the whole shabby business originated.

Long before this fortunate outcome, however, the officer concerned had become involved in what was, even for him a very odd kettle of fish indeed.

NOTES ON CHAPTER X

1. *Concise Statement*, p3-4. In addition to the material concerning operations in the Red Sea, the proposed expedition to Macao, etc, the Concise Statement of 1805 contains a useful chronological list of the letters and papers in the *Romney* inquiry with notes and quotations, and also the Fourth Report by the Commissioners of the Navy Board.

2. Admiral Sir John Jervis, Earl of St Vincent. Despite his fully warranted reputation as a disciplinarian, he was open-minded enough to embrace Nelson after the Battle of Cape St Vincent (1797) for his brilliant, but unorthodox, tactics in HMS *Captain*. St Vincent's economy drive when he was First Lord caused bitter controversy: in a letter to Melville on 6 July 1803, Popham wrote: 'We are in very low spirits, and there is no chance of anything active to arouse us. The Marine Lord has compleatly paralysed the British Navy and opposes every proposition from Downing Street.'

3. The Admiralty was the operational arm of the Navy, the Navy Board the administrative arm responsible for maintenance and supply: relations between them were by no means always as close or as cordial as they should have been.

4. In a letter to Melville 6 January 1803, Popham wrote of 'the exertions which have been made to keep me out of Parliament... in one instance a Memorandum was drawn out and when the Agent of the principal presented it to the Banker to put in the name he said, there is but one person in the kingdom who is objectionable and that is H.P. I afterwards learnt Lord St Vincent had found out by his spies the negotiation was nearly concluded, and interested himself with the principal to object to me.'

5. 'Aeschines' (Athenian orator, 4th century BC) was the *nom de plume* of the pamphleteer Blagden, who served a term in gaol for an attack on the Board of Admiralty in general, and St Vincent in particular. The tone of his 'Few Brief Remarks', which run to a mere 60 pages, suggests that his views had not been modified by his experience: phrases such as 'the supercilious and arbitrary proceedings' of the late board of Admiralty; 'the Noble Earl... aided by the vindictive insinuations of his upstart coadjutors' and so on, abound. Popham could hardly have had a more trenchant apologist.

6. Quoted in *The Years of Victory*, Arthur Bryant. For a splendid panorama of that year of invasion scares, see his Chapter III. Popham, in his letter to Melville of 6 July, argues for 'a demonstration of offensive operations as the best mode of Defence for this Country' as it will keep the enemy coast 'in a continued state of alarm, and change the attention of the First Consul to defensive instead of offensive operations.' Melville agreed wholeheartedly, and Popham was given his chance: see the next chapter.

CHAPTER XI

Secret and Unethical Weapons 1804

1

'ABOUT THREE years ago,' an anonymous correspondent wrote to the *Naval Chronicle* in 1808, 'a man of grave and mysterious carriage of body, made his appearance in a certain class of fashionable society in London, under the name of *Francis*. It was shortly *whispered* about that he was a *Yankey* American, of some consequence, whose real name was *Fulton*.'

The 'Yankey American' who appeared in London in May 1804 under the assumed name of 'Mr Francis' was, indeed, Robert Fulton; and he had been brought secretly to England from France via Amsterdam according to an agreement with the Addington Ministry. Fulton is remembered primarily for his steamboats and for his submarine, the *Nautilus*, which he demonstrated successfully to the French naval authorities in the Seine in 1800, and with which he proposed attacking the British squadron off Brest. The news leaked through, and the ships were alerted, but nothing came of it—although Fulton took the *Nautilus* there in 1801, carried out successful underwater trials in the Rade, and apparently spent the summer prowling around offshore looking for victims.

Despite the modest but undeniable success of the submarine (Fulton and three others remained submerged for three hours at a depth of 25 feet), he had already turned his attention to the other half of the destructive equation, the 'submarine bomb'. In a trial in which this primitive torpedo was towed by pinnace to within twenty yards of a moored 40 foot sloop and then launched, it hit the target and destroyed it.

On the strength of these experiments, Fulton was summoned by Bonaparte to demonstrate *Nautilus*. Far from responding to this command with the alacrity that might have been expected, Fulton first disclosed that the vessel no longer existed, he had dismantled her and sold her for scrap; and second, refused even to show the First Consul the drawings without a prior agreement as to terms. A combination of Fulton's unco-operativeness, a change of incumbent at the French Ministry of Marine, and the start of the process that was to lead to the Peace of Amiens, concluded his attempt to interest the French in submarines, torpedoes and mines. 'Go, Sir,' the new Minister of Marine, Denis Decrès, is reputed to have said to him, 'your invention is good for the Algerians or Corsairs, but understand that France has not yet abandoned the ocean.'

Fulton, though, was not yet quite finished with France. During the following two years he teamed up with another American, Robert Livingston, to develop a steamboat; and having built and tested a 70-foot model, offered Bonaparte the idea of a fleet of them to be used for the invasion of England. Advised against the idea by the Academy of Sciences, he rejected the idea until it was too late: when, in July 1804, he changed his mind, Fulton was already in England.

2

Robert Fulton, born in Pennsylvania in 1765, had started his working life as an artist, and had practised as such in England when he arrived in London, for the first time, in 1787. But he also dabbled in engineering, and was employed on various canal-building schemes before moving to France in 1797 and turning his attention to underwater warfare. That he had a fertile and ingenious imagination there is no doubt, even if few of his inventions were original: both *Nautilus* and his mines and torpedoes derived, directly or indirectly, from the work of another American, David Bushnell. Bushnell had built his 'portable engine to sink ships', the *Turtle*, in the 1770s. It was a true submersible, driven by hand-cranked propellers and fitted with an auger, like a narwhal's horn, in the bow. This was to be screwed by hand into the ship's bottom, and a mine attached to it. Bushnell's one attempt to use it in anger, against HMS *Eagle* in New York harbour in 1776, failed for a number of reasons but ultimately because the single crewman could not persuade the auger to penetrate the timber and it snapped. Bushnell then turned to the idea of the unmoored mine, and actually tried them out in the Delaware River, but with no more success.

Fulton developed and extended Bushnell's ideas, and, in trying to attract sponsors and their money, endowed them with a grandiose philosophical theory. They would, he argued, put an end to war, since a weak country armed with them would have strong nations at its mercy. The argument, although a shaky one at best, was not lost on St Vincent. 'Pitt', he is reputed to have said, 'was the greatest fool that ever existed, to encourage a mode of war which they who command the seas did not want, and which, if successful, would deprive them of it.' A remark which, from the perspective of two world wars and the unrestricted use of submarines, has the ring of prophecy. This, at any rate, was the mysterious American who, eager to sell his ideas to the highest bidder, slipped into England in May 1804, under the pseudonym of 'Mr Francis'.

His ideas for a submarine were submitted to a committee consisting of Sir Joseph Banks, President of the Royal Society; the chemist, Henry Cavendish; William Congreve, inventor of the rocket[1]; the engineer, John Rennie; and Sir Home Popham, representing the Navy. They were not impressed.

But 'the tenacity of the inventor', as someone remarked-of Fulton, 'is usually second only to his poverty.' And Fulton was very tenacious indeed. The submarine might not have found favour with the British authorities: perhaps his 'submarine bombs' would have a more enthusiastic reception. By working on George Hammond, the Under-Secretary of State at the Foreign Office, who had been instructed to deal with him; and on Home Popham who, predictably, found in him a fellow spirit, Fulton finally succeeded in negotiating an agreement with the Government. It was sealed informally in July at a breakfast at Pitt's house, at which Popham was present, and formally on the 20th of the same month with a document signed by Pitt, Melville and Fulton, and witnessed by Popham.

In it Fulton, 'the inventor of a plan of attacking fleets by submarine Bombs... agrees to disclose the principles of his scheme to Sir Home Popham and to superintend the execution of it...' subject to the following conditions. He was to receive £200 per month while on this service for his trouble and expenses, with a further sum not exceeding £7,000 to be set aside to cover his 'mechanical preparations'. HM Dockyards and Arsenals were to supply all the necessary materials; and if it turned out that the government were unable to use the finished weapons, two commissioners would be appointed to assess them. If they passed them as potentially effective, Fulton would get £40,000. He would receive the same sum if the weapons destroyed 'an enemy decked vessel', as well as half the value of all ships so destroyed for as long as he was supervising the job. Once his services were over, he would continue to receive a quarter of the value for fourteen years; and he undertook not to divulge the plans and drawings to anyone else for the same period. All monies were to be paid to him within six months; and his claim would stand, even if improvements to his original scheme were made by other people.

3

'Mr Francis' had his contract with the British Government—but what, precisely, was he offering? The submarine had been dismissed by the committee, so what was meant by 'submarine bombs'? If confusion has arisen, the reasons are twofold. First, because the weapons were novel the terminology is inexact and the same word was applied to several different ones; and second, because, on Popham's own evidence, he and Fulton began working on two different but related ideas simultaneously. One was a primitive variation on the *Nautilus*[2] which Popham refers to as a 'plunger' or 'plunging boat'; the other was the submarine bomb, known variously as a 'carcass', 'coffer' or 'catamaran'. The former was intended to tow the latter into position. For reasons which are discussed later the term 'catamaran' caught the popular imagination, and the Press, and those who found the whole subject risible, latched on to it. One other point is worth mentioning: as the whole project was supposed to be secret, the information which leaked out tended to be garbled.

That Popham and Fulton worked closely together on it is clear from their letters. Fulton regarded Popham as a friend, was flattered to be asked to breakfast with Sir Joseph Banks, and enjoyed having his brains picked by Popham on the subject of South America, on which he purported to be an expert although he had never been there, and which had been brought to the attention of the Government, once again, by the return to Britain of the Venezuelan patriot Francisco Miranda with his schemes for an expedition against Caracas.

Home Popham wasted no time in setting to work, and on 12 August he wrote to Admiral Lord Keith, C-in-C of the Channel Fleet and the man responsible for frustrating Napoleon's invasion plans, from Lymington in Hampshire:

...you are so well aware of the difficulties which generally arise in proposing any new mechanical operation, particularly in our dockyards, that you will not be surprised that I could not get a plunger made till Saturday morning... We tried experiments yesterday, last night and this morning, and although the thing did not row so fast as I expected, yet it had more buoyancy and the men in it went with much confidence... I am pretty confident it will row three knots as soon as it is completed. The experiment about the distance which it can be seen is very satisfactory. It was veered astern about ten o'clock last night, and although there was considerable glare from the moon it was scarce perceptible at 25 fathoms, and quite out of sight at 35, nor could any trace be discerned half way up the main rigging...

Five days later, he wrote again:

In my letter from Lymington I stated that I found it much better to row the plungers with two pairs of sculls, and they have been made accordingly and instead of steel, which was the original intention, we have wooden ones... fitted in a socket the same way, which the steel ones were, which your Lordship saw at Putney.

This does not sound like a description of a submarine; so what was it? According to the description by the Port Commandant at Boulogne, where one was captured in October[3], 'it is seventeen feet long, and eight and a half broad, and carried at its two extremities a barrel of combustibles; two men placed in the middle, rowed with two oars each.' This suggests some kind of oar-propelled 'explosion boat', and quite unlike anything proposed by Fulton. A more detailed, if less reliable, description is given in a letter to Lord Grenville from the Marquis of Buckingham, written at the end of September:

...I have now obtained a detail of the wonderful expedition fitting in the most secret recesses of Portsmouth-yard, under the advice and direction of Sir H. Popham, who, I know, is higher in your good books, than in mine; for I think ill of him. The project is to tow a fire-vessel without masts, and level with the water, thirty-two feet long, into Boulogne harbour. The eight boats that perform this miracle are rowed *under* water, each by two men whose head and shoulders only are above water. The experiment has been tried in the basin at Portsmouth *by night*, and the boats moved very rapidly.

The whole will be ready by about the 14th October, and will be tried, as I suppose, at the spring tides... under Sir Home's orders! In all this charlatannerie I have no faith.

This does not tally with the rowed explosion vessel which the French authorities found ashore at Boulogne, nor indeed with any other descriptions of what was going on at Portsmouth and Lymington that summer: it was mere rumour. Setting aside for the moment the specific purpose of the plunging boats, there were other 'new curiosities' being developed simultaneously under Popham's supervision, the carcasses or coffers, and casks.

We have tried an experiment with a tin lantern made in a particular way [he wrote to Keith on 17 August] having a tube in the lower part, and that tube fitted with a slow fire composition and put in a cask charged with gunpowder and combustible balls; the cask has ballast boxes below to keep it steady, and each boat may carry two to throw overboard when it may be judged expedient to do so. They are about the size of a forty-gallon cask and will I think do a great deal of mischief.

This was one type. Others, the carcasses proper were made of copper lined with lead to ensure that they were watertight; and were fitted with a clockwork timer which was started by pulling out a pin, like a hand grenade. Whoever had this job was specifically ordered to bring the pin back as proof.

Work on the various devices continued into September, involving as it did not merely the shipwrights at the dockyard but clockmakers to build the timing mechanism, and Woolwich Arsenal to provide and despatch the explosives. Although Home Popham was responsible for the weapons, when, early in October, the first operation was launched against the flotillas in Boulogne harbour, the command went not to him but to Keith, and he was relegated to 'a civil situation', the technical expert, with responsibility but no authority.

The attack on Boulogne was part of a continuous campaign designed to disrupt Napoleon's invasion plans and, if possible, lure the French flotillas out beyond the protection of their shore batteries and into action—a lure they normally resisted. Abraham Crawford, who wrote of his experiences as a lieutenant during the night of 3 October 1804, described it in genially sardonic terms.

For several days prior to the attack there was a great display of our force before Boulogne... for no object that I can conceive, except to put the enemy on his guard, and give him timely notice of our intentions. Besides the *Monarch*, Lord Keith's flag-ship, this force consisted of two or three ships of 50 and 64 guns, four or five frigates, a few gun-brigs. Besides these there were a few sloop-rigged vessels, prepared as fire, or rather explosion vessels... filled with combustibles and powder, and supplied with explosive machinery similar to that which was fitted to the carcasses or coffers.

Home Popham issued his General Orders for the attack on the 1st October. Three distinct weapons are mentioned: plungers, carcasses and casks; and they were to be towed to position upwind of the French ships, their timing mechanisms to be set to fire them progressively, and then released.

> As the wind was light [Crawford wrote] the explosion vessels were taken in tow by the larger boats, the whole being covered by the gun-brigs... the lighter boats, such as the galleys, were provided with coffers, and were intended to approach so near, and in such positions, that in setting these machines adrift, there would be every likelihood of their taking effect... Burning and blowing up seemed alone the order of the night...
>
> The French (how could they be otherwise) were perfectly awake to all that was going forward... The enemy's sentinels hailed and discharged their muskets nearly at the same moment; and long before the carcasses could be set adrift, the whole bay was lit up by vivid flashes of musketry that was soon increased to almost noonday brightness by a blaze of artillery from the flotilla and batteries...
>
> Meanwhile the explosion vessels were advancing under sail to the different points against which they were expected to act; and just before penetrating the line of the flotilla, their officers and crews jumped into the boat, which each vessel towed astern for the purpose, abandoned them to their fate. One by one, in a few minutes... they exploded, and shot in columns of flame into the air, adding by the splendour of their meteor-flight to the brilliancy of a scene, which, with one melancholy exception, proved nothing but a grand and expensive, though harmless *feu de joie*... Thus ended this costly *feu d'artifice*, which had been concocted with much thought and ingenuity...

The one 'melancholy exception' was the crew of a French pinnace, 'the captain of which', as Admiral Bruix reported to Napoleon, 'seeing a fireship, which appeared to be towed by a canoe with a sail, ordered it to be boarded... hardly, however, had they come near the fireship, when it blew up; the pinnace was destroyed...'

Bruix confirmed that three kinds of weapon were employed in the attack: 'the first were sloops, cutters and other vessels; the second were a kind of coffers twenty feet long and three feet broad, without any mast; the third were a kind of barrels, filled with combustibles and which were so contrived as to explode by a piece of mechanism. The vessels were filled with several pieces of hollow wood, which were filled with inflammable matter, and which was lighted with matches... but it seems the effect was not well-calculated, for they did no harm.'

Bruix reported eleven explosions, so it is clear that detonation presented no problems; what remained to be solved was some way of guiding the weapon to its target. Among the audience at the Boulogne fireworks display was the Minister for War and the First Lord of the Admiralty, Lord Melville (formerly Henry Dundas) in the frigate *L'Aimable*. His presence provided rich scope for the balladeers.

5

The new weapons, known as *Infernals* in the Fleet, were dubbed 'Catamarans' by the Press. The word as applied to the twin-log rafts of the Coromandel coast and Ceylon had been familiar in England for more than a century.[4] Its use in this context suggests that the carcasses were linked in pairs for this operation, but the evidence suggests not: Fulton was working on the idea, and Lord Keith, writing to Admiral Louis in January 1805, says: 'I think that the best way of endeavouring to make use of them is by setting them on in the strength of the tide, two and two, or attached to a buoy by a line with cork floats and with hooks like fish jiggers fastened to it, or something that might catch a cable, and leave the current to press the carcasses under the bottom...'

Whatever the truth of it, the novel weapons were so blanketed in rumour and speculation, so fogged in mystery, that any name for them might have been equally applicable. Among the populace at large they were a subject for ribaldry and derision: among professional seamen and others of a more thoughful mind, their implications were more sinister. The French, reasonably, referred to them as cowardly, 'a horrible attempt against the laws of war, by seeking to destroy an enemy without exposing themselves to any dangers'. British reservations tended to be either moral or technical. There were those who agreed with the French that such weapons, 'employed in the darkness and silence of night, against a helpless and unsuspecting enemy... ought never to be resorted to'; there were those who did not believe that they would ever work; and those who, like Lord St Vincent, were afraid that they might work all too well. Five years later the debate was still running, and a correspondent wrote to the *Naval Chronicle* in 1809:

> But coffers and rockets, bad as they are, are nothing to what may be expected... Battles in future may be fought under water: our invincible ships of the line may give place to horrible and unknown structures, our frigates to catamarans, our pilots to divers, our hardy, dauntless tars to submarine assassins, coffers, rockets, catamarans, infernals... How honourable! How fascinating is such an enumeration! How glorious, how fortunate for Britain are discoveries like these!

That these various doubts–with the usual doubts about Home Popham himself–had spread through the Channel Fleet is apparent from a letter from Melville to Keith, written a few days after the Boulogne operation.

> I have no right to control the private judgement of any officer, but I have a right under certain circumstances to insist that they shall keep their opinions to themselves, at least till they are asked, and it is impossible not to animadvert on the conduct of a Rear-Admiral with a flag flying in your fleet assembling himself and others in the house of the Port Admiral, there to hold an unreserved conversation criticising a plan which His Majesty's

Government had adopted and were acting upon under the Commander-in-Chief of the fleet... I am well aware that Sir Home Popham is an object of envy with some, of jealousy with others, but as he is attempted to be run down, it is the duty of the Government to run him up. To the conviction of all of us he has served Government for many years in various capacities zealously and well... I am perfectly aware that Sir Home Popham, acting in your fleet *without a commission* was in a very awkward predicament, and naturally the ardour of a zealous mind might produce some of the observations you have heard, but as he was the person who was placed in that awkward predicament a liberal-minded man ought to have been the more disposed to overlook any little inaccuracies which might occur in the execution of so novel and complicated a service.

There is no doubt that to more conventional naval officers—'Nelson's sailors'—riding out the winter gales off the long lee shore of the French coast, maintaining month after month the blockade of the French squadrons in Brest and Rochefort, Popham must often have seemed no more than a flamboyant dilettante who used his influence with Pitt and Melville and the other Tory politicians to secure preferment, promotion and pensions. They might approve of his signalling system and respect his charts, but he was not one of them.

Popham himself, meanwhile, undeterred by the dislike of others, undisturbed by doubts of himself, unworried by the failure of the operation, continued to advocate the potential efficacy of the 'infernals'. Back in Dover on the 4th, the day after the Boulogne fiasco and after a busy night, he still found the energy to write Melville a ten-page letter about the attack and its future implications. It was, he insists, 'a sort of practical experiment on the Enemy', no more, designed 'to establish a certain point'; he rejoices that '... Your Lordship was present at all the explosions, and had an opportunity of conversing with the principal Officers concerned', and will therefore be in a better position to assess the value of these new weapons.

As for himself, Popham continues, 'I am perfectly satisfied that the enemy will not in future consider himself so secure in Boulogne Roads as he has hitherto done, and I am equally confident that this mode of warfare offers to the superior Fleet only, the greatest advantage on many occasions.' It will have reduced the danger of invasion, certainly from Boulogne; and if the French do try and concentrate a number of ships there, 'the application of a few carcasses will make their situation anxious and alarming'. It should even be possible to reduce the British blockading fleet, and rely on close surveillance by small vessels, reporting via a chain of similar ships by—naturally—Popham's telegraphic signals.

If it all sounds just a trifle over-confident, it is true that a month later Melville was writing to Keith, '... the alarm created everywhere by the operations at Boulogne exceeded everything we have ever supposed. The Pannick [sic] has been conveyed to other ports, particularly Brest, and the pannick has laid hold of the army intended for the invasion at every place from whence it was intended to come.

It may require further consideration how far something should now be done to keep up and increase the pannick.'

As a tailpiece to Boulogne, a little light relief from the extravagant hopes of the operation's protagonists, and a whiff of healthy scepticism, the following verses from *Cobbett's Political Register* are worth quoting, at least in part.

THE CATAMARAN

AN EXCELLENT NEW BALLAD

(In imitation and to the tune of '*Malbrouk s'en va-t'en guerre*')

DUNDAS is gone to Boulogne He has a *pawky* plan
To burn the French flotilla, 'Tis called *Catamaran*.

DUNDAS is come off Boulogne; He is a prudent man,
He wisely takes *L'Aimable* For his Catamaran.

DUNDAS our tars haranguing Now shews his new-made wares;
As at some prating pedlar *Jack* turns his quid, and swears.

See fireships, my frog-toasters, To entertain John Bull;
Of brimstone and of bottles They, like some heads, are full.

See here my casks and coffers With triggers pulled by clocks!
But to the Frenchmen's rigging Who first will lash these blocks?

Catamarans are ready (Jack turns his quid and grins)
Where snugly you may paddle In water to your chins.

Then who my blocks will fasten, My casks and coffers lay?
My pendulums set ticking And bring the pins away?

Your project-new?' Jack mutters, Avast! 'tis very stale:
Tis catching birds, land-lubbers! By salt upon the tail.

So fireships, casks and coffers Are left to wind and tide;
Some this, some that way wander, Now stern before, now side.

Ships, casks and coffers blazing Now bring Vauxhall to mind:
As if ten thousand galas Were in one gala joined.

There in that blaze go fifty! And there go fifty more!
A hundred in disorder There run upon the shore!

From them the joyful tidings Soon flew to London town:
By hundred and by thousands They burn, sink, kill and drown.

Now longs DUNDAS for morning His triumphs to survey;
But lo! the French are lying Just where before they lay.

Lord Keith sent home a letter, He scarce repress'd a laugh:
DUNDAS steals to his office To work his telegraph.

But now to them, who never Did England's hopes deceive,
Our Soldiers and our Sailors, Their business let us leave:

May Pitt from colonelling Retire upon half-pay;
And Admiral Lord MELVILLE The yellow flag display!*

6

'From the violence that party newspapers write and endeavour to frighten us from the further use of our new instruments of attack on the enemy fleets, large and small,' Melville wrote to Keith on 11 October, 'Mr Pitt and I are of course become more eager to omit no fair opportunity that may offer of striking such strokes as may throw themselves in our way.'

There was no shortage of targets. That autumn Napoleon, Emperor since 7 May, was at Boulogne and harrying the Channel coast shipyards to build even faster the barges destined for the invasion of Britain. Already, at Étaples, Boulogne, Wimereux and Calais there were over 1,000 of them, with 200 more at Le Havre, Cherbourg and Brest. 'Eight hours of a night favourable to us will decide the fate of the universe,' he had boasted a year before. Landsman that he was, he imagined that boats could be built in a day, and 2,000 launched across the Channel on a single tide. Whenever the flotillas sneaked out for exercises they did so under the eyes and guns of Keith's watching fleet, and rarely with impunity.

Even if Melville had not been the fire-eater that he was, Popham and Fulton between them were not prepared to abandon their 'new curiosities' after one unsatisfactory experiment: While Fulton was asking Keith for a mere '...2 or 3 decked ships, 1 frigate, 2 gunbrigs, 2 bombs, 2 or 3 cutters and from 30 to 40 boats', manned by 'picked men of sober character and cool deliberate courage' as a special force for future operations, Popham was arguing the need for 'being thoroughly prepared to act offensively' and offering to go again as a 'volontier' if Melville could not provide him with a command.

'I confess I don't like that kind of anomalous service,' Melville wrote to Keith, 'and I rather think you seem to agree with me... I think there is a great awkwardness in any person serving in a situation where he is neither the object of military command, nor entitled to give orders which others are bound to obey...' Popham, with the habit of command combined with his special knowledge of the new weapons, had obviously put up the backs of the regular ships' officers at Boulogne—hence the meeting at the Port Admiral's house—and he asked Melville to try and arrange for him to be given 'the authority of a Flag instead of a private Pendant'. A week later he was appointed to the *Antelope* 'so that he may be ready

* The 'Yellow Flag': an Admiralty fiction designed to move senescent admirals off the active list and into retirement.

to take any part in the service under you [Keith] that may be advisable or that the season may permit'.

That service would not finally be decided on for another month: meanwhile both Camaret, at the entrance to the Rade de Brest, and Rochefort, south of La Rochelle, were considered as possible targets. By late November, however, Keith had decided on Fulton's suggestion to try to destroy a couple of shore installations, the Pile Battery off Boulogne and Fort Rouge near Calais. 'I should think one explosion vessel and one large carcass best suited for the purpose of each,' he wrote to Popham on the 26 November; and Popham, Fulton, Captain Plampin of *Antelope*, and Captain Owen, who had been at the Boulogne operation, made their preparations.

The second Boulogne attack, on the Pile Battery, was postponed, but on 8 December *Antelope*, the *Susannah* explosion vessel and a number of small vessels left Dover for Calais. The operation took place the same night. It was not a success. The hero of it was undoubtedly Lieutenant Hew Stewart of HMS *Monarch*, who took charge of the *Susannah* and succeeded in jamming her bowsprit among the piles on which the battery stood—and in getting away in a boat afterwards. Mr Bartholomew of *Antelope* and a Captain Brownrigg towed the two carcasses in, but failed to place them. In due course the *Susannah* exploded with spectacular, if rather disappointing, results. The cutter *Fox*, sent in next morning to assess the damage, reported:

> As I proceeded towards the shore I saw a great quantity of planks and timber floating... I did not discover any alteration on the east side of the Fort, but when I got to the westward I could plainly discover the most part of it damaged and the breastwork knocked down, and I have every reason to believe it was very much injured by such a number of people being assembled there and seemingly at work upon it.

Although the result failed to come up to expectations, the arrival of the flotilla off Calais 'on the close of the evening', the covering fire from the gun-brigs, the return gun and musket fire from shore, and the culminating blast from the *Susannah* as she blew up, must at least have alarmed the 80,000 troops stationed there in readiness for the invasion, and the crews of the luggers, caiques, peniches and *bateaux plats* assembled to convoy them on it.

In his report to Lord Keith, Popham wrote:

> I very much regret that Mr Bartholomew could not fetch the fort, for I am positive he would have lashed the carcass to the piles. He, however, very prudently returned with it to the *Dart* and although something prevented the second carcass from going off, which evidently had been striking against the piles, yet he recovered it and brought it on board...I have great satisfaction in stating that not an officer or man was hurt.

7

To call these operations, and later ones in which Home Popham was not involved, a fiasco, would be to overstate matters, even if their effect was moral rather than physical. They form one odd little chapter in the history of submarine warfare; a chapter which would be unimaginably expanded a century later, in the North Sea, in the Dardanelles, in the Channel and the Western Approaches, and in the long, icy swells of the Denmark Strait. At that particular period, however, the experiments led nowhere.

The author of *The Catamaran* summed up the problem in two lines: 'So fireships, casks and coffers/Are left to wind and tide...' Fulton's carcasses and plunging boats contained in embryo two weapons, and a delivery system for one of them, which later in the century would be developed separately and with devastating success. One was the mine, the other was the torpedo, while the true submarine would combine with the second to produce a weapon system entirely worthy of the odium directed against it both when it was in its infancy and its maturity. But in 1804 the weapons were as confused as the terminology used to describe them, and no sure method of bringing them into contact with their proposed victims was devised. Oddly enough, Fulton did have one solution in mind, but failed to pursue it; and that was the moored mine fitted with a contact fuse. He had suggested this while he was still in France, but it was ignored, and he seems to have forgotten about it.

There was to be one more operation involving carcasses, again at Boulogne, and almost exactly a year after the first. By this time Fulton had devised the system of linking two of them on a long line so that, as it fouled the anchor cable, they would be swept one each side against the bottom. According to the French, they succeeded in cutting the connecting line and they floated away, exploding harmlessly out of range: according to Fulton, the carcasses were set too deep and failed to make contact. Either way, it was another failure and Fulton was growing desperate. Not only was faith in the weapons—such as it was— fading, but his supporters were disappearing as well. In December 1804, immediately after Fort Rouge, Popham had been appointed to HMS *Diadem*, and fully expected to be in command of an expedition against Venezuela with General Miranda; as a result, connection with Fulton—though not with his weapons—came to an end. In April 1805 Melville, subjected to a vote of censure for financial irregularities in the Navy Treasurer's office, resigned[5], to be replaced by Lord Barham, a far less enthusiastic ally.

In a last, dramatic effort 'to convince Mr Pitt and Lord Melville that a vessel could be destroyed by the explosion of a Torpedo under her bottom', as he wrote later, Fulton managed to procure the *Dorothea*, and on 15 October 1805 succeeded in blowing her apart so convincingly that 'she separated in the middle, and the two ends went down; in twenty seconds, nothing was to be seen of her except floating fragments'.

The demonstration was sufficiently impressive for a 'torpedo' attack to be planned against the French fleet in Cadiz; but before it could be launched Trafalgar was won, and 'this species of warfare, unmanly, and I may say assassin-like', as Crawford put it, became unnecessary. In any case, six weeks before, Napoleon had left Boulogne and its clustered, useless flotillas of invasion barges and was marching eastward.

For Robert Fulton, 'Mr Francis', all hopes of revolutionising naval warfare—and making a fortune—were over. Demanding £10,000 for coming to England in the first place, £100,000, for demonstrating the effectiveness of his weapons, £2,400 a year for life and £60,000 to keep his secrets to himself, he finally had to settle for £15,640—which was not too bad—and left England in disgust in October 1806, to return to America where, six years later, he busied himself trying to sink British ships during the War of 1812.

Eighteen months after the Calais affair Lord Keith wrote to the Admiralty:

> Lieutenant Robinson has charge of the following vessels and effects left at Dover by Sir Sidney Smith, Sir Home Popham and Mr Francis: 1 cutter, *Atlanta*, ex-pleasure-boat; 2 boats; 1 long, 10-oared galley; 4 hovelling lug boats—possibly useful as explosion or fire boats; 4 fast rowing boats; 4 gigs fitted with cork as lifeboats, one plunger and model… one plunger and one catamaran. The watch locks are out of order…'

NOTES ON CHAPTER XI

1. 'Ammunition without ordnance, the soul of artillery without the Body', as he lyrically described the rockets.

2. Fulton also used the expression 'plunging boat' to describe *Nautilus*.

3. Cobbett's *Political Register*, Oct 1804, in which various French accounts of the Boulogne operation are printed in full.

4. In the *Shorter OED* a catamaran is defined as 'a raft or float consisting of two or more logs tied together', with a date: 1597. Or 'a kind of fire-ship or torpedo', 1832.

5. Popham defended Melville against the vote of censure, which was passed by only one vote.

CHAPTER XII

Problems of Communication 1800-12

1

'THIS VOCABULARY', Home Popham wrote in his Introduction to the original edition of his *Telegraphic Signals or Marine Vocabulary*, dated 1 November 1800, 'was originally made to facilitate the conveyance of messages from the *Romney* off Copenhagen, to Admiral Dickson off Elsineur.' The occasion was that brief, bloodless browbeating of the Danes in August of that year, and *Romney* was having to pass on to the Admiral signals from Lord Whitworth, the Ambassador, ashore, a task for which Lord Howe's *Signal Book for the Ships of War* had not been designed.

'Its utility', he goes on, referring to his own *Vocabulary*, 'was in that instance so obvious, and so generally allowed by the Captains of the North Sea Squadron, that Sir Home Popham conceived it might be brought into more extensive practice, and has already given copies to different officers... and sent it to Lord Spencer', the First Lord of the Admiralty. And in the following two short paragraphs he sums up, with rare economy and precision, why it was needed, and what it could do.

It is by no means intended to interfere with the established signals, as a single signal is certainly the most efficient for military evolutions.

It frequently however happens that officers wish to make communications of very essential moment far beyond the capacity of the established signals, and it is presumed that this Vocabulary will afford such convenience.

In order to understand the justification for that claim, which has ensured for Home Popham a place, modest but secure, in the history of the Royal Navy, it is necessary to look briefly at the state of flag-signalling before he had his brainwave.[1]

2

At the root of the matter was the connection between signalling and *The Permanent Fighting Instructions*, that bible according to which commanders were bound to fight sea-battles. First promulgated in 1673, these 'instructions for the Directing and Governing of His Majesty's Fleet in Sailing and Fighting' became during the next century both permanent and mandatory, and they were transmitted from the

TELEGRAPHIC SIGNALS;

OR

MARINE VOCABULARY;

WITH

OBSERVATIONS ON SIGNAL FLAGS,

AND THE

BEST MODE OF APPLYING THEM.

—————

By SIR HOME POPHAM,

COMMANDER OF THE ILLUSTRIOUS ORDER OF ST. JOHN OF JERUSALEM,
F. R. S. CAPTAIN IN THE ROYAL NAVY.

—————

London:

PRINTED FOR T. EGERTON, MILITARY LIBRARY,
WHITEHALL.

———

1812.

flagship by specific flags. The signal flag was a way of issuing a limited number of commands: it was not a way of carrying on a conversation, nor could it be used for asking questions or sending any messages not included in the *Instructions*. The flag signals were, as one recent writer puts it, 'generally speaking, a one-way communication system'.

As the 18th century with its naval battles wore on, and tactics changed, individual admirals produced *Additional Instructions*, each with its own flag, with results that were increasingly chaotic. Admiral Rodney's to take one example, needed 40 flags and 7 pendants, but the essential limitation remained. If the commander wished to send any other message to his captains, the only way he could do it was by sailing within earshot and bawling through a speaking trumpet or by sending a boat, neither of which was entirely practicable in heavy weather or amidst the thunder of battle.

Nor was it only during a battle that the need to be able to pass information—of all sorts, far beyond the range of the existing code—from ship to ship became important. There is a vivid illustration of this in a letter to Popham himself from an unknown correspondent, written in February 1805.[2]

Captain Patrick Campbell late of the *Doris* meant to call upon you to say how much the late Captain Jervis lamented he had not your Telegraph Signals to communicate to Sir Charles Cotton the sailing of the French Fleet from Rochfort. He was three days in Company with the British Fleet, and the weather was so bad, he could not communicate the information he wished, that at last judging it important to do so at all risques, he got into his Boat tho' the weather still continued so bad and was drowned. Thus had these Telegraph Signals been in use, a knowledge of the Sailing of the Rochfort Fleet would have been communicated three days sooner, and the Life of this Officer and some of his Boat's Crew saved. Captain Campbell says to the Southward, they are in use amongst all Ships, but off Brest etc, not known.

To clinch the point, only eight months later in the same year the Hon. Henry Blackwood, Captain of the frigate *Euryalus*, wrote to his wife two days before Trafalgar, while engaged in keeping the French and Spanish fleets in Cadiz under surveillance:

Within two hours, though our Fleet was at sixteen leagues off, I have let Lord N. know of their coming out... At this moment we are within four miles of the Enemy, and *talking to* Lord Nelson by means of Sir H. Popham's signals, though so distant, but repeated along by the rest of the frigates of this Squadron.

Opposite: The title-page of the 1812 edition of the *Marine Vocabulary* which finally decided the Admiralty to include it with the official *Signal Book for the Ships of War*.

These two words in italics sum up precisely the change which Popham's *Marine Vocabulary* was in the process of bringing about; but the two letters illustrate also the lack of consistency that was still bedevilling ship-to-ship communication. Nelson's fleet had the book; Sir Charles Cotton's squadron, doing the same work a thousand miles to the north, had not.

Home Popham was not the first naval officer to try to impose some order and method into flag-signalling. Of those forerunners, the most important was Admiral Lord Howe, whose *Second Numerary Code* separated the *Instructions* from their flags, tabulated the latter into a logical sequence, and related them to numbered messages in the Signal Book. At the same time he reduced the number of flags to twenty-four, and redesigned some of them to make them more easily distinguishable. With additional improvements by Rear-Admiral Kempenfelt, Howe's work was adapted throughout the Navy as *The Signal Book for the Ships of War* in 1790.

This was a considerable advance; but, although with a three-flag hoist the sender could transmit nearly 1,000 messages, and with a four-flag hoist nearly 10,000, he could still only refer to what was in the *Signal Book*: if the words he wanted were not there, the possible number was purely academic. Nor would it ever have been possible to provide a fixed form of words to cover every eventuality.

3

This was the point at which Home Popham, struggling with the *Signal Book*'s inadequacies off Copenhagen in August 1800, made the imaginative leap that was needed. This consisted of the simple but fundamental realisation that language is composed of sentences, sentences of words, and words of individual letters. Therefore, if the sender of a message, any message, is provided with an alphabet he can transmit any words; and if he has a vocabulary of ready-made words he can build out of them any sentence. What was required was a system that was both simple and comprehensive, an appropriate wardrobe of flags, and—perhaps the most difficult part of all—an acceptance of the principle so general that every ship in the Navy would be able to *talk to* every other ship.

If what he says in his Introduction to the first edition was literally true he worked extremely fast, for *Romney* was in the Baltic for little over a month: yet by November, when it was printed, he was able to suggest not merely that it had been put to use there, but had already been seen and approved of by the 'Captains of the North Sea Squadron'.

That is by the way. The fact of the matter is that when the first edition appeared it consisted of a flag system of his own devising, and a thesaurus—an 'entick' or 'dictionary', he calls it—of 1,000 words which he calculated were those most commonly needed in the day-to-day business of the Navy at sea. Words not in the vocabulary could still be spelt out laboriously letter by letter. It was the first step on a journey that was to occupy a great deal of his time for the next fourteen

Home Riggs Popham as a lieutenant (c. 1793).

Left: Edward Thompson, Popham's first captain. The subscription reads: Formerly Commander of His Majesty's Forces in the Kingdom of Guiana and afterwards Commander-in-Chief of His Majesty's Ships on the Coast of Africa.

Opposite: Sketches of the natives of Namibia initialled T.B.T., ie, Thomas Boulden Thompson, Captain of the *Nautilus.*

Right: Sketch, also by Thompson, of the *Padrao* erected by Bartolomeo Diaz in 1486 during his voyage to the Cape of Good Hope. It later disappeared, and a replica has since replaced it to mark the 500th anniversary of his landing.

THE CROSS ON PEDESTAL POINT

THE ARMS

MAN IN PENGUIN BAY

MAN IN WALWICH BAY

WOMAN IN WALWICH BAY CAFFRARIA

MAN AND WOMAN IN WALWICH BAY

CHART
of the
SOUTH CHANNEL
from
Prince of Wales Island to
Sea.

TO THE
Governor General in Council
of
FORT WILLIAM

This CHART of the South Channel from Prince of
Wales Island to sea, is Inscribed as a Testimony
of Gratitude,

by His faithful, and
obedient Servant,
Home Popham

Calcutta Decer 26th 1791.

Mud

Mud
Flat

FORT CORNWALLIS

QUEDA

COAST

Prays River

PRINCE of WALES ISLAND

Mud Bank

this Bank extends far to the
Southward all Mud soundings

Edge of the Mud Bank, Soundings irregular

Scale of Yards

Scale

Yards

British Statute Miles

Geographical or Nautic Miles

No of feet

Prays Beacon
North Beacon on the Long Sand
Middle Beacon on Do
Beacon on the middle ground
Jingo or South Beacon on the Long Sand
South Beacon on Prays Sand
Mud Flat Beacon

Blue Flag
St Williams Red
Do
White
White
Red
Blue
St Williams White

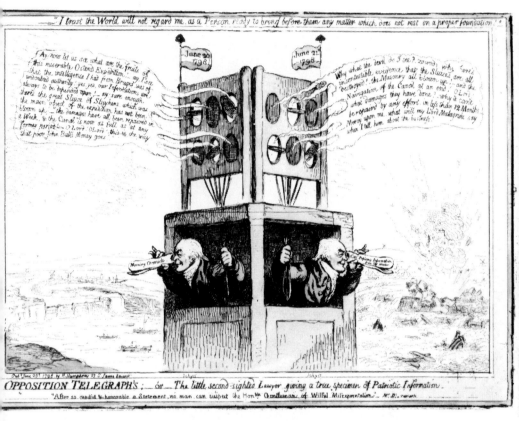

Above: 'Capt. Pop'em's information from Captain Winter' on the righthand telescope at Henry Dundas's eye, the *Morning Chronicle* on the left. The subject is the demolition of the Saas Lock at Ostend in June 1798. In the left-hand balloon, 'Ay, now let us see what are the fruits of this miserable Ostend Expedition! . . . ' ie, nil; the lock is undamaged and the harbour calm. In the right-hand balloon, ' . . . the Sluices are all destroyed! . . . the Masonry all blown up! . . . and the Navigation of the Canal at an end . . . ' Below, a scene of devastation. The cartoon by Jekyll was published 23 June.

Opposite: Popham's chart of the South Channel between Prince of Wales Island (Penang) and the mainland of Malaya, 1791.

Opposite: Paul I, Tsar of Russia and, incidentally, Grand Commander of the Knights of St John.

Right: Engraved portrait of Popham by Hastings, undated, but probably soon after his promotion to captain in 1795, when he would have been in his middle thirties.

Left: The silver tea-kettle presented to Popham by the Court of Directors of the East India Company in thanks for his convoying some of their ships home from St Helena in February 1803. Beneath the inscription is the stag's head which appears in his coat of arms.

The landing at Lospard's Bay, Cape Colony, January 1806. Some of the troops are already drawn up ashore on the left, and there are other figures, possibly the Dutch sharpshooters, lurking by the shore on the right.

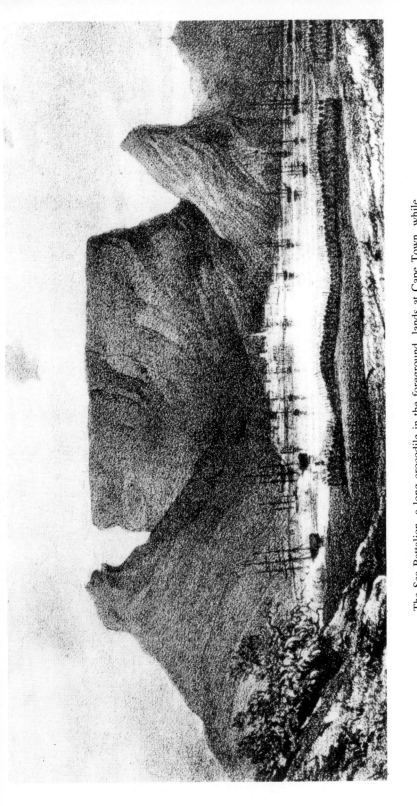

The Sea Battalion, a long crocodile in the foreground, lands at Cape Town, while the ships of the squadron 'coast the enemy's shore, throwing shot among his troops and people'.

At Quilmes on the River Plate, twelve miles below Buenos Ayres, the boats carrying Beresford's 71st Regiment head for shore through water which was extremely shallow and to all appearances ...

Buenos Ayres from *Narcissus*: a deceptively peaceful scene.

Above: Sir Home Popham, KM, FRS. An engraving obviously taken from Mather Brown's portrait, though suffering subtle changes in the process.

Above: Seals discovered in respectively the Africana and Cultural History Museums in South Africa. *Left:* Arms of POPHAM: Argent, on a chief Gules, a bezant between two bucks' heads caboshed Or. *Crest:* A stag's head and neck erased proper. *Motto: Me Juvat Ire Per Altum. Right:* Arms of Popham and his wife, PRINCE: Gules, a saltire Or, surmounted by a cross engrailed Ermine. (From Encyclopaedia of Heraldry, London 1844).

On 14 August 1809 the battleships added their bombardment of Flushing to that of the rockets and artillery of the army ashore, the town surrendered, and the passage into the West Scheldt was secured.

Left: King Christophe of Haiti (1767-1820), 'dressed in a plain green coat, decorated with the grand cross of the Order of St Henry, white satin breeches, and crimson Morocco boots . . . His hair . . . perfectly grey, his countenance very intelligent . . . '

Right: Portsmouth Signal Station (Detail), by an unknown artist, with one of the semaphore arms raised. It was built on the Square Tower at the end of the Platform or Battery two years after Popham's death.

Below: A similar, but more lively version of the same subject by E. W. Cooke. Here the semaphore arms are at rest and there is a hoist of three flags flying from the mast.

The memorial to Home
Popham in the churchyard of
St Michael and All Angels,
Sunninghill, Berkshire; and two
details from the plinth
depicting his skills in
navigation and hydrography,
and in flag-signalling.

years. In 1803 with the second edition he took the second step, including an assortment of rather less useful words, and nearly a thousand sentences 'most applicable to military or general conversation'.

This was the vital principle on which his *Marine Vocabulary,* and his reputation as a pioneer in naval communications, rests. As Professor Michael Lewis says, 'It is the basis of all subsequent systems in which the flag is the principal medium: and it enabled the Admiral, *for the first time,** to say exactly what he liked by signal.'

How did it work in practice? As Popham made clear in his original introduction, he does not 'interfere' with the existing flags of the official *Signal Book for the Ships of War,* which retained their single-flag connotations, e.g. 'Enemy in sight', 'Engage the enemy', and so forth. But to each of the twenty-four he gave a letter of the alphabet: I and J shared a flag and, oddly, V and U changed places; and a special pendant told the receiver that the signal referred to his *Vocabulary,* not to the *Signal Book.* If a word was to be spelt out, a pendant referred the receiver to the numbered letters, while other pendants, guidons or long vanes[3] indicated words and sentences. These were all subdivided into 'classes' and numbered. In the example he gives, he takes fifteen flags, the minimum number he considers practicable. 'The number of flags to be used is the number of "Classes"', in his own words, so that each flag of the fifteen, when flown uppermost, denotes a 'class'; that is, it directs the receiver to the relevant section of the *Vocabulary.* The rest of the signal pinpoints the exact entry in that class, these entries being arranged alphabetically. Exactly the same system applies to the sentences.

Taking his fifteen flags, Popham demonstrated that according to the arithmetic of 'combination', as he called it, with two at a time 210 signals can be made (15×14); with three at a time 2,730 (15×14×13); and with four at a time 32,760. Given 24 different flags, with four hoisted at a time the possible total rises to 267,720. In order to achieve this, Popham calculated, a flag lieutenant would need to have in his signal locker '24 flags, 1 guidon, 7 pendants, and 3 long vanes—a total of 33 pieces of buntin' (sic).

Apart from its remarkable range and flexibility—and in this, as in other respects, it was unique—Popham's elucidation of his system has an agreeable commonsense about it. 'Prepositions and articles will be used as seldom as possible, and the sentences will be made short. In verbs, the number, person, tense and mood, must be applied to the sense of the sentence . . . But when it happens that the exact word is not in the vocabulary, one nearest synonymous will be adopted . . . '

The most famous instance of a flag lieutenant having to find the 'one nearest synonymous' was, of course, during the few minutes before the Battle of Trafalgar. 'Mr Pasco,' Nelson said to his Signal Lieutenant, 'I wish to say to the Fleet, England Confides That Every Man Will Do His Duty. You must be quick, for I have one more signal to make, which is for Close Action.' But 'confides' was not a ready-made word in Popham's *Vocabulary* and would have had to be spelt, so Pasco suggested 'expects' instead, which was. 'That will do,' Nelson said, 'make it directly.' The next signal to flutter out from *Victory* that afternoon came not from

* His italics

Popham's code but from the *Signal Book,* and consisted of one flag only: Number 16–'Engage the Enemy More Closely'.

Home Popham could hardly have anticipated that his *Telegraphic Signals or Marine Vocabulary* would enable England's favourite Admiral to make the Navy's best-known signal just before the most famous naval battle in British history, and there is no record of his having ever referred to it. In more practical matters, he reveals the warmth and concern which, according to a later witness, made him a captain popular with his ship's company. In the Introduction to the 1803 edition of his signal book he wrote:

> The general port signals may also be expeditiously communicated from the Commander-in-Chief's ship, by which the wear and tear of boats will be materially saved, and the necessity of their bearing up for Portsmouth Harbour in bad weather obviated. When this is the case the boats frequently get very much damaged, and the crews desert, or *get ill by lying in their boats with their wet clothes on.**

4

In 1803 he produced at the request of the East India Company a version specially suited to the needs of the Indiamen.[4] He had just returned from the Red Sea where he had been working closely with the Company's ships, and where, he says, he had found his signals invaluable for keeping in touch with General Baird ashore. In the same year he published his second edition–all this at his own expense–and he continued to work on, and expand, both the basic vocabulary and the sentences over the next eight, extremely busy, years. In 1805 it was officially issued to the Navy, but separate from and supplementary to the *Signal Book,* and was by no means in general use that year.

But its reputation was already unchallengeable, if not unchallenged. In the autumn of 1811 their Lordships ordered him to send up his 'new manuscript Telegraph', the fruit, Popham said, of 'many years labour and many months incessant application'–but it was not quite ready. 'I wish', he wrote to John Barrow at the Admiralty, 'the introduction of a Synonimous [sic] Table had not occurred to me, it is far more difficult to accomplish than I expected . . .' And, indeed, it must have beaten him, for no such Table was ever included.

But now, just when his system, proved and approved for a decade, was about to be finally adopted, he found it was being challenged by a Mr Ciara, whose method was being promoted by Admiral Berkeley. Popham at once suggested that a committee be set up to decide on their respective merits; but when he saw Ciara's–and the Admiralty sent him several rival systems to examine that year–he was fairly caustic, referring to 'Admiral Berkeley and the foreign officer, who,

* Authors Italics

whatever may be his merit in the line of his profession, does not appear to have well examined the principle on which combinations are formed . . . ' So much for Mr Ciara who, with his signal system, vanishes.

In April 1812 the Admiralty convened a committee of eight flag officers and captains to scrutinise and report on Popham's latest version; and on the 29th they submitted their findings. The members, who must have been familiar with it in its earlier form already, were unanimous in finding that 'the principle on which the Code is founded is simple and comprehensive; it also combines everything that can be wanted to complete one General Code for every Service, and we consider that its adoption will be of the greatest utility to the public service.' They also thoroughly approved of 'his marine vocabulary which we find to be considerably enlarged and improved retaining at the same time all its former simplicity.' In the light of this wholehearted approval, Popham was directed by their Lordships 'to revise and arrange the Admiralty Signals agreeable to your new Code, and in doing so likewise arrange a Sett of distingishing Pendants as recommended by this Report, laying the whole before their Lordships as soon as the same shall be ready to be printed.'

Enlarged it certainly was. It now contained 6,000 'Primitive Words' exclusive of inflexions, 30,000 'Real Words', 6,000 'Syllables'—mainly for use in sending names e.g. NEL-SON—and a wide selection of Sentences, plus Tables of Geographical Names, Military Phrases and Technical Terms, Provisions and Stores. As before, any word not included could be spelt out. The only thing missing was that dreaded 'Synonimous Table'. It is, in short, a work of almost lexicographical complexity; and considering that he had been for much of the preceding eight years not in his study at Titness Park but at sea on active service, the achievement becomes all the more remarkable.

Delightfully, too, the commonsense of the original remains. Expletives, he says, should be avoided; and:

There are many abbreviations, which, though they are considered barbarisms in writing, are tolerated in familiar conversation, and are well adapted to telegraphic communications; and perhaps the rude and inartificial, but generally very concise, modes of expression employed by children would furnish many useful models of the language best adapted to signals.

It is impossible not to feel affection for a man who could make such a recommendation to the grave Admirals of the Royal Navy.

5

The only drawback was that in the same month as that letter from their Lordships was written he received his orders for Spain, and for the twelve months from April

1813 he was at sea, conveying Lord Moira to India, during which admittedly fairly uneventful voyage the revision, as he wrote to Melville on his return, 'occupied by far the greatest part of my time'. All the same, he was able to submit the final draft within a week of arriving back at Spithead, and it appeared in its definitive, official form in 1816.

The job was done at last, but his restless, inquiring mind was already engaged on another method of communication altogether. As this is really a separate subject, however, it will be considered in its proper place.

NOTES ON CHAPTER XII

1. *'Telegraphic Signals or Marine Vocabulary* by Sir Home Popham, Commander of the Illustrious Order of St. John of Jerusalem, FRS and Captain in the Royal Navy.' The original Introduction of 1 Nov 1800, and the second, with Instructions, of 18 April 1803, are both reprinted in the 1805 edition, the earliest extant. Both that, and the later ones, are in the Admiralty Library, and the 1812 Edition is in the BL.

2. 19 February 1805, signature illegible. WLC Library. The escape of the Rochfort squadron under Admiral Missiessy took place in January in a snowstorm, on orders from Napoleon to attack the West Indian islands. Dominica was taken, but not held.

3. *Pendant or pennant:* a tapering flag. *Guidon:* similar to a pennant, but narrowing to a point or fork. *Vane:* a short, blunt pennant.

4. Maritime Signals of the Hon. East India Company: Compiled at their Request by Sir Home Popham. 1804. Admiralty Library, EC65. No. 103 'You detain the Convoy by your Inattention'; no. 160 'Are the Natives friendly?'; no. 161 'Are they numerous?'

CHAPTER XIII

'A Good Deal of Cleverality' *1804-6*

1

IN THE summer of 1804, with the return to office of his old patron William Pitt, Home Popham achieved his ambition of entering Parliament as Member for Yarmouth, Isle of Wight. His election may not have been of much benefit to the town's inhabitants, but it gave him a taste of the status which he was always striving for – and a platform upon which he could defend himself.

Becoming an MP was only one incident in a period in his life as busy as it was varied. There were his Red Sea charts to see through the printers, and the charges arising out of that cruise to be challenged in a new edition of the *Concise Statement* – a business that was to drag on into 1805. Another matter destined to drag on even longer surfaced again in 1804, that of *L'Etrusco,* which James Heseltine the King's Proctor described as 'very peculiar' and passed on to 'the discretion of His Majesty's Government'. With no solution in prospect, it was costing everyone concerned a fortune in legal fees.

In spite of the accusations – of smuggling, of embezzlement – which were a gift to his enemies, Popham still had the confidence of his Tory political patrons, especially when it came to dealing with some of the odder and more persistent supplicants for government support. One of the most persistent was a certain 'Count' Francisco de Miranda, a Creole from Venezuela with a Canary Island shopkeeper for a father and a coloured mother. As a young man he had joined the Spanish colonial army, but had been dismissed, fined, and sentenced to ten years' imprisonment in Oran for illegal trading while on an official visit to Jamaica. He had escaped, travelled all over Europe, and visited Russia where, in a curious parallel with Home Popham, he became the confidant of the Empress Catherine, the mother of Tsar Paul I. In 1784 he had found his way to America, met Jefferson and Alexander Hamilton, and drew up a plan 'for the independence and the freedom of the Spanish-American continent . . . with the co-operation of England' – a country which, in fact, he had not then visited. In 1790 he appeared and had a long interview with Pitt, to whom he expounded his plans – for which he said he would need 12,000 men and fifteen sail of the line. Pitt, involved in the squabble with Spain over Nootka Sound, pumped him, nourished his dreams, and when the dispute was settled, quietly dropped him. Bitterly disillusioned – 'Pitt is a monster . . . I am sold for a Treaty of Commerce with Spain' – Miranda tried to dun the government for a pension, failed, and went off to France to fight for the Revolutionary armies.

He was back in England in 1798, was again warmly welcomed by Pitt, and again put off with fair words. During 1803 and 1804 he found an ally in Sir Home Popham. In November of the former year Popham sent a secret paper on South America to Mr Secretary Yorke at the Admiralty[1] in which he outlined past projects for attacking one or more of the Spanish colonies, and went on to say, 'This subject has since been frequently agitated; and as I officially knew that I was to have the honour of directing one part of an expedition . . . I, in course, lost no opportunity of informing myself on every point at all connected with an operation of such importance. It is a topic that has occasionally occupied the attention of the ablest statesmen for a series of years.' And a little later: 'General Miranda's intelligence and correspondence with that country are so well known to Government . . . I have been long in the habit of strict and confidential intimacy with the General.'

A year later it looked as if it was all settled. 'I shall receive Miranda on board in forty-eight hours after his arrival at Spithead,' he wrote to Melville on 24 November 1804 while he was waiting to launch the carcass attack on Fort Rouge, 'and sail, looking for the rest of the squadron to follow . . . ' He adds, in an uncharacteristic moment of self-doubt, that he wonders 'if I appear too much alive to the beneficial consequences of this project', meaning Miranda's. But once again the South American adventure was abandoned, and Popham was appointed to *Diadem* and given the command of a less controversial expedition.

2

On the day that Pitt returned to power, Bonaparte was declared Emperor of the French; two months later he moved to Boulogne, the better to chivvy the shipwrights who were building the invasion barges and to contemplate his coming triumph. There, seated upon the throne of King Dagobert and dressed in a toga, he reviewed the 80,000 troops poised for the *Soit Nommé Descente en l'Angleterre,* and had victory medals struck in anticipation of its outcome '*frappé à Londres en 1804.*'[2] Hubris could hardly soar higher.

Across the Channel which he had yet to cross, other Frenchmen observed the charade with mature distaste. Chief and most vocal among them was a naval officer of Royalist sympathies, Baron d'Imbert.[3] With him and his fellow conspirators Home Popham was also briefly involved that hectic summer. The Baron had put forward a scheme for capturing the French fleets blockaded in Toulon, Ferrol, Rochefort and Brest. Four or five picked Royalist officers would land in France, contact their former colleagues on the ships, and persuade them to slip their moorings and allow themselves to be captured by the British squadrons in the offing. As an operation, even when narrowed down to one squadron in one port, Brest, it never sounded very convincing; and despite a voluminous correspondence, much of it concerned not with the plot but with the pensions being paid them by the British government, it came to nothing.

To turn from the melodramatic to the domestic, during his time in *Romney*

Popham devised and produced a thirty-one page manual entitled *Rules and Regulations to be Observed in His Majesty's Ships*. These, he says in its Introduction, datelined Deal, December 1804, he used in *Romney*, and since there was no single standard publication on the subject throughout the Navy, they might fill a real gap.[4] The booklet is too long to reproduce, but even in extract it demonstrates its author's thoughtfulness towards his ship's company—the obverse of his impulsive, multi-faceted imagination.

The 'General Rules' give a detailed picture of the routine of shipboard life, from the issuing of beer and water to precautions to be observed with the galley fire, from the airing of bedding to the scrubbing of the 'tween-decks; and it is full of delightful domestic touches. 'The men are always to take off their shoes and stockings when washing, as they will be found comfortable and dry afterwards'; and, 'As the boys are naturally idle and very dirty . . . ' the Master-at-Arms is to keep a sharp eye on them. 'Neither Captain nor Officers are to be suffered to pick the choice pieces of salt or fresh meat'; and warrant officers' and midshipmen's lights are to be out at 9 o'clock at sea and 10 o'clock in harbour. Health and cleanliness are emphasised all the way through, and this does much to explain Wilkie's comment on the health of Popham's men on the voyage to the Cape.

The booklet ends with 'Exhortations and Injunctions to the Ship's Company of His Majesty's Ship *Diadem*'[5], the ship to which he was appointed that December; and these, he suggests, should be printed on card and 'affixed to each of the seamen's births' (sic). They begin:

As every well-disposed Sailor must be convinced, that neither comfort nor happiness can exist in a dirty, disorderly Ship, Sir Home Popham hopes that the Ship's Company will consider themselves interested in keeping the Ship clean, and stimulating each other to do the duty of their respective Stations with cheerfulness and alacrity. It will always be his most anxious wish to study their comfort, and promote their happiness, by every mode in his power, consistent with the rules of the Service; in granting leave at a proper time, or any other indulgence that can be pointed out. . . .

There follow ten injunctions. They are to carry out their duties with alacrity and in silence, keep themselves 'clean, sober and honest', and they are 'neither to swear, or use any blackguard expressions', nor are they to gamble, fight or quarrel. And on Sundays, dressed in their best clothes, they are to 'behave themselves devoutly, and as becometh brave Seamen and good Christians.'

After all that, it is disappointing to have to report that, according to the logs of both *Romney* and *Diadem*, his sailors were by no means invariably well-disposed, or clean, or sober, and were even on rare occasions known to strike their superior officers—for all of which offences, according to the custom of the Service, they had the skin flayed off their backs. But he was not, generally speaking, a flogging captain; and one gets the impression that, he ran a taut and happy ship.

3

That same December of 1804 HMS *Diadem* joined the Channel Fleet under Admiral Lord Keith, with whom Home Popham had worked on the Fulton project. One of his officers was a young Marine, Lieutenant Robert Fernyhough, whose journal and letters, with those of his three brothers, were collected and published by the eldest of them in 1829. His first entry is dated 20 March 1805 at Spithead; he had then been in the ship for three months, much of the time cruising off Brest, and was just back after three weeks at sea.

> We sailed again in a few days, hearing that the French fleet was at sea, consisting of twenty-four sail-of-the-line. Our orders were communicated by telegraph, to unmoor and proceed to sea with every line-of-battle ship. It was so unexpected, that we left our Captain behind.

One can imagine Home Popham ashore, frantic with frustration!—but nothing happened, and they were back again early in May.

Robert's narrative continues:

> On the 20th May, we weighed anchor and stood out to sea again, with the Channel Fleet; not a little harassed by the enemy, for they would not leave the protection of their batteries. They would sometimes make a feint to come out, but when we attempted to near them, put back again. On Tuesday last we alarmed them in good earnest; the Admiral signalized to form order of battle, and led the fleet consisting of thirty-two sail-of-the-line, twelve of which were three-deckers, so close into Brest, that the French could count every ship singly. The British colours floating in the wind, proudly bidding defiance, ports open, matches lighted, our hearts true to the honour of old England . . . Our spirits were high, our hearts panting for a trial of strength, but nothing could move the enemy. After cruising in vain, for some weeks, we returned to Spithead to prepare for a long and distant expedition.

So ended Home Popham's only experience of serving with the battle fleet: it could hardly have been more disappointing; though, with a pinch of luck, they might have had the reward of patience. For in those early months of 1805 Napoleon was issuing ever more urgent orders to his Admirals in Toulon, Rochefort and Cadiz, to break out through the British blockade, gather in the West Indies, and rendezvous off Boulogne in June to cover the invasion. Another five months and *Diadem* would have been present at Trafalgar. However, the Admiralty had other plans. 'You will readily conceive, with what anxiety we look forward to our future proceedings,' Robert Fernyhough wrote. 'Sir Home Popham advises every officer to stay by the *Diadem,* as our cruise may be profitable . . . ' Rumours about their probable destination, deliberately circulated by the Government, had everyone baffled. Major Alexander Gillespie of the Royal Marines, then a lieutenant, who sailed with the expedition and subsequently wrote an excellent account of it, recorded that at Portsmouth in July, 'A great many packages and letters were daily shipped, addressed for Constantinople'—a ruse intended to suggest that they were bound on some diplomatic mission; but then a number of horses were embarked, one of them draped in a blanket stamped *Sir David Baird*. 'All instantly concluded that our future vocations wanted not the auxiliaries of pen, ink and paper, but those of shot, shell and gunpowder.'

Their conclusion was justified. *Diadem* sailed for Cork, passing on the way the Royal yacht *Royal Sovereign* with His Majesty on board. *Diadem* saluted her with twenty-one guns, and Sir Home was summoned 'to wait on His Majesty by his command'. And in Ireland the expedition was ready and waiting: *Belliqueux, Raisonnable* and *Diomede,* sail-of-the-line—two frigates, two gun-brigs, twelve East Indiamen, sixty transports, complete with horse, baggage and hospital ships—'so that we cut a very respectable appearance when we got on the "blue waters". I should not forget to mention,' Gillespie continues, 'that among other "Varieties of the Season", we had a female convict ship from Cork. These ladies enlivened us now and then with choice specimens of their conversational powers, whenever we came within hail.'

Before they sailed, Sir Home received two cheering items of news: one was that, through Pitt's influence, he had been granted £17,000 from the Droits of Admiralty;[6] the other was a letter from the Admiralty dated 31 July, authorising and directing him to hoist a broad pendant 'so soon as she [*Diadem*] has left the Island of Madeira . . . and to wear the same (in the absence of a Flag Officer) until you shall receive further orders.' That is to say, he was to be appointed Commodore of the expedition, once it was headed for its true destination.[7] More will be heard of both these communications, for the ripples from them were to go on radiating for years.

The destination of the huge convoy swinging at anchor in Cove (Cobh) that August was, in fact, concealed until its commander opened his secret orders once they were well on their way. Gillespie and Popham himself had believed that Miranda was behind it, that the expedition was to rendezvous at Trinidad and, so Gillespie thought, 'our debarkations were to have been effected upon the banks of the Oronoco'. 'Whether this project found opposition in the Cabinet,' Gillespie continues, 'or from whatever other cause, the destination after some time was changed.'

The reality was different, as both Baird's and Popham's orders make clear. All the troops were bound, eventually, for India: on the way, however, five regiments, amounting to 4,000 men, were to divert and capture Cape Colony, which had been taken from the Dutch ten years before but returned to them under the terms of the Peace of Amiens. With the Low Countries occupied by Napoleon, it represented a threat to British lines of communication with India and the Far East. Once recaptured, part of the squadron and sufficient troops to garrison it were to remain at the Cape while the rest continued their voyage to the East, for there was always the possibility that the French might attempt to re-take it. The precise interpretation of these orders was to be the subject of much argument later on.

4

HMS *Diadem* was a 3rd Rate of 64 guns, which is to say that she was one of the smallest ships of the line to merit the title of battleship. Such ships had practically disappeared from the 'line' by then: *Diadem*, twelve years old, had been employed as a troopship for the previous seven years, and that was her role now. On board were 900 men of the 38th Foot with, among the officers, a Captain Fletcher Wilkie who was also to write his memoirs. Between him, Gillespie and Robert Fernyhough, the events of the next eighteen months and the actions of Captain Sir Home Popham received a great deal of sharp, first-hand scrutiny and documentation. Also on board, according to the *Naval Chronicle,* was the Captain's eldest son William Craddock, later to become an admiral, then sixteen.

Their first port of call was Funchal, and Wilkie gives a wry description of the run south.

> After knocking about in the Bay for some days, we made good our passage to Madeira after a tedious voyage of a month . . . we approached its lofty shores under the influence of extreme thirst; aware that we should visit the island, we had not laid in any white wine, our beer and porter had all been wasted, and burst; and latterly, as we got into warmer weather, we had no beverage but strong port-wine, and water that had been seven months in the transports, which we were obliged to punish with whisks, to flog the offending hydrogen out of it, and to hold both nostrils when in the act of deglutition. It may be easily imagined with what avidity we gazed on the clear running streams when we got on shore; we drank Madeira and water by the bucket, and devoured grapes by the bushel.

They left this paradise at the beginning of October, and on the 4th the log records: 'At 11 hoisted the Broad Pendant of Commodore Sir Home Popham, KM, etc, etc, the different Men of War saluted with eleven guns each, which we returned with three salutes of eleven guns each. The East Indiamen and Transports cheered as they passed, which we returned cheering them.'

Then the convoy divided. Of the 120 ships, 65 headed direct for India while the rest, 16 East India Company ships and 34 transports with the warships, set course for Cape Town. The day after hoisting his Broad Pendant, the Commodore made one or two appointments among the ships of the squadron, including bringing Captain Hugh Downman of *Diomede* aboard *Diadem* as his Captain, and promoting his own First Lieutenant, King, and giving him the command of *Diomede*. There was, on the face of it, nothing unusual in the Commodore of a squadron wishing to hand over the day-to-day running of his ship to a Captain, especially as he had all the responsibility for the naval operations which lay ahead; but this apparently simple and fully justified action was to have unpleasant consequences later on. At the same time the Commodore despatched Captain Ross Donnelly in *Narcissus* to St Helena and on to Cape Town—under false colours, if necessary—to gather all the intelligence he could about the garrison, and the shipping in Table Bay.

Because the expedition had been unable to provision fully in Madeira, Popham decided to call in at San Salvador, now Bahia, in Brazil; and as they rolled their way southward—'the ship's company amusing themselves with the usual ceremonies in passing the Line'—Fletcher Wilkie had plenty of opportunity to jot down 'a word or two about our Commodore'; words, which because they form one of the few detached, first-hand impressions of him, deserve to be quoted. Home Popham was now forty-three, and had had a more than normally varied and controversial naval career.

I should certainly say [Wilkie wrote] that he was not what is called one of Nelson's sailors—nor was he what another Navy man of some celebrity named a 'soldier on board ship'. He had led a sort of miscellaneous life—he had been employed on gunboat service, forwarding pontoons and such duty, under the Duke of York in Holland—who ever afterwards remained his friend; he was then concerned in some private trade—the less said of that the better; at length he was appointed to his present command. He possessed what the Scotch call a good deal of 'cleverality'—was very conversant with the details of landing and embarking troops—had made considerable improvements, and given greater scope to the code of telegraphic signals—could run up the repairs of a ship, to make them cut a reasonable appearance in the annual expenditure—and could plunder an enemy's dockyard in the most complete and scientific manner. In his manners and address he was gentlemanlike and insinuating—and his powers with the pen need not be doubted, as they got him from between the horns of a dilemma, perhaps more awkward than was ever previously encountered by any public man.

Amongst his own officers he was very popular—he took them always wherever there was a prospect of prize-money—and everything in the shape of promotion, that fell at all within his power, he gave to the Squadron. To do him justice, also, as regarded ourselves, he spared neither trouble nor expense to ensure the health of the troops. We had fruit served out in abundance both at Madeira and Bahia—and at the latter place he bought the entire cargo of a ship with London porter, which was served without discrimination to all hands. We had roomy ships, great attention to cleanliness—and all these combined brought us to the Cape in the most perfect health . . . We embarked 903 rank and file from Cork, and landed 901 at the Cape—one man having died of consumption, and another detained on board by accident. I question if, in any other of the most favourable situations in the world, the result would have been equally good, out of a body of 900 men thus confined for six months on board ship.

On this last point, one naval historian has said: 'Those who have studied the statistics of disease in other expeditions will realise that Popham was at any rate Nelsonic in one important respect.'

One hundred and fifty miles off the northeast corner of Brazil lies the San Rocas reef. It is lit now, but it was not then, and as it barely breaks surface was a serious hazard for any ship heading for Recife or San Salvador. The Commodore had sent a dozen transports on ahead because they were short of water, with the frigate *Leda* to take care of them. Aware of the danger ahead, Popham lent Honeyman, *Leda's* Captain, one of *Diadem's* chronometers. Despite this, two of the ships, the *King George,* transport, and the *Britannia,* East Indiaman, struck the reef and were lost. *Leda* herself touched, but got off. It turned out that Honeyman did not know how to use the chronometer and had been relying on dead reckoning. Remarkably, from the two ships wrecked there were only three casualties.

After this mishap the squadron and the remaining transports arrived safely at San Salvador, where they replenished their stores which, besides the London porter, included water and 'sixty-six pipes of sound port'. On 26 November they set sail once more for South Africa. As they crossed the South Atlantic, the Commodore and General Sir David Baird worked on the detailed operational orders for the landing; and Popham produced not only a detailed chart of Table Bay and the immediate coast, but two sets of special flag-signals, the first covering the ships and the regiments on board each, the second the various possible landing-places. On 4 January 1806 the log records: 'Saw the land ahead . . . at 8 the Cape of Good Hope bore SE by E, 8 or 9 leagues', and on the following day the whole convoy was brought to anchor off Robin Island.

5

The first problem, as it had been off the coast of 'Caffraria' in *Nautilus,* was the surf, and Popham and Baird went off in a boat to reconnoitre. Meanwhile, as Robert Fernyhough reported, 'we now made preparations for our debarkation, fired guns, and hoisted English colours; a broad hint to the enemy of our errand, which was quickly taken, for the town appeared in great confusion. We saw a party of cavalry, riding in various directions.'

The Highland Brigade, consisting of the 71st, 72nd and 93rd Regiments, were duly got into the boats; but the wind blew up as the morning advanced, and they all had to be brought disconsolately back aboard again. Conditions were equally bad the following morning, but later in the day calmed down and it was decided to attempt a landing at Lospard's Bay, ten miles or so to the west of the town. One boat capsized, nevertheless, and 'thirty-five fine fellows of the 93rd were drowned'; but only one was killed by the Dutch sharpshooters stationed on the dunes, and they were soon driven off.

While the Highlanders advanced against relatively light opposition, Baird called for the Marine Battalion to be landed nearer the town to cut off the enemy's retreat. Fernyhough, who had been promoted to Adjutant by Popham, went with them. 'It is astonishing to me, how we did land through such a tremendous surf,' he wrote to his brother, ' . . . the nearest point we could get to the shore, was forty or fifty yards, so we were obliged to wade that distance, up to the middle, before we could reach it. I was completely ducked, for in getting out of the boat a sea came and dashed me over head. . . . To my great annoyance, I found an excellent pistol spoiled . . . and all my ammunition rendered useless.'

The expedition now had more than 5,000 men ashore, and Baird, having sent the outposts packing, began his advance towards the town. Governor-General Jansens had settled for a battle, and had his men—about equal in numbers, but including 36 Chinese 'artillerists', who later joined the British—arrayed in two lines on rising ground. For a time the Dutch put up a stiff fight, but then Baird's Highlanders went in, and they fled. Jansens himself left Cape Town to its fate and retreated up-country with a nucleus of his army, and the British at their heels. But the pursuit soon faltered in what Baird in his despatch described as 'a deep, heavy and hard land, covered with shrubs and scarcely pervious to light bodies of infantry; and, above all, a total privation of water under the effects of a burning sun, had nearly exhausted our gallant fellows in the moment of victory.'

But victory was not long delayed. While the fleet 'constantly coasted the enemy's shore, throwing shot among his troops and people' with devastating effect, and a party of seamen from *Diadem,* commanded by Popham himself, made a spirited effort 'to occupy a position in the Reit valley and co-operated with the Army', Baird advanced on Cape Town and called upon the garrison commander to surrender. After some delay, a flag of truce appeared and terms were quickly agreed. Fletcher Wilkie, meanwhile, set off with a detachment of Marines after Jansens. The latter's intention had been to try and stir up the natives to harry the British: instead, he gave himself up. The Marine party returned to heartening news: no less than Nelson's victory at Trafalgar, two-and-a-half months earlier.

To the victors of Cape Town the victory at sea seemed to set a seal on their success. The retaking of the colony had been almost bloodless; the inhabitants, by and large, welcomed them; and there was the pleasant prospect of prize money ahead. 'I expect to share between two and three hundred pounds for this capture', Robert Fernyhough wrote; and Popham and Baird, dividing the commanders' share between them—an arrangement that was to draw a sneer from Benjamin Tucker: what had the gallant Commodore contributed beyond cruising up and down off the coast?—stood to gain a great deal more than that.

In addition, Ross Donnelly on detached duty in *Narcissus* had been doing good work, capturing a French privateer and rescuing her prize, an Indiaman; and later driving ashore a French 32-gun frigate which had been on passage to the Ile de France (Mauritius). Robert Fernyhough and his fellow officers would see no prize money from those successes; but Home Popham, as Commodore of the squadron to which *Narcissus* belonged, was entitled to a share. Or so he imagined.[8]

6

Fragmentary information gleaned from various visiting ships during the next two months suggested that two French squadrons had broken out of the British blockade, which had been relaxed after Trafalgar. But where were they bound? Some reports said the West Indies, others the East; and one, more reliable than most, reported Admiral Linois with at least two sail-of-the-line in the Gulf of Guinea, ready to prey upon returning Indiamen. Vague as all this was, it was enough to keep the squadron on the alert; and, indeed, they spent the first half of February at sea on the look out for them, but only picked up the occasional American or Dane.

Popham himself had no intention of remaining at the Cape any longer than he could help. It is by no means easy to read his mind at this time. Within a week of the surrender he is writing to Lord Melville, saying that he has asked the Admiralty to allow him to go home 'at the fall of the year', and hopes that his 'exertions' may induce Pitt to recommend him 'at least to some situation on the Navy Board'. A fortnight later, in a letter to William Marsden, Secretary to the Admiralty, he says that he does not consider himself 'competent to remain any length of time in command at Cape Town', and asks to be allowed to return to England. In fact, he was due to be relieved by Admiral Troubridge.

Since doubts about his own competence did not normally occur to him, there is no need to take this at its face value: what he meant was that he felt himself wasted, now that the job he had been sent to do was successfully completed, and he wanted to be back at the centre of things. This was hardly surprising. He at last had a seat in Parliament; he had friends in high office; he was bubbling with ideas on everything from troopships to Teneriffe, from carcasses to Caracas, from the blockade to Buenos Ayres, and only back in England could he promote them. And he missed, as any man would, his family. He now had two sons (one with him in *Diadem*) and three daughters, the last born in 1804, and he had seen little enough of them. Although he was now clear of the *Romney* business—he had finally been completely exonerated by the Select Committee of the House of Commons the previous summer—*l'Etrusco* was still a drain on his resources. He had half a dozen good reasons for wanting to get home: until, that is, the arrival in Table Bay of the American ship *Elizabeth* and her plausible and persuasive master, Captain Waine. That quite altered the aspect of matters.

NOTES ON CHAPTER XIII

1. Appreciation of the attack on Rio de la Plata. See ADM1/58 for the full document.
2. *Years of Victory*, p100.
3. The presence of Baron d'Imbert and his colleagues in England dated from 1794. During August of that year, at the height of the Reign of Terror, the Royalists in the South of France handed over the Toulon Arsenal and thirty French ships of the line to Admiral Hood and his blockading squadron. The triumph was short-lived. Both town and ships were recovered when Carnot swung south from Flanders with 35,000 men; and among the 15,000 refugees rescued by the British Navy were a number of naval officers, and d'Imbert. They settled in London and Winchester, were paid a small pension by the Government, and ceaselessly agitated for action against the Republic. Their voluminous

correspondence is among the Melville Papers; the Toulon saga is in *The Years of Endurance.*

4. The pamphlet is bound in with letters from Popham and others in ADM1/58. Neither the *Articles of War* nor the *Admiralty Instructions,* which together constituted Naval Law, covers quite the same ground.

5. The 'Exhortations and Injunctions' were printed separately in the *Naval Chronicle,* Vol 13, 1805.

6. *Droits of Admiralty:* prizes, whether ships captured or destroyed, or any other enemy property, legally belonged to the Crown; but it was customary for the greater part of the value to be distributed to those responsible according to the scale currently fixed by the Admiralty. *L'Etrusco* and her cargo were 'Prize', forfeit to the Crown; but the case was immeasurably complicated by the fact that the claimants included not merely her captor, Mark Robinson of the *Brilliant,* and the Captain of *Dido* which was standing by, but the original owners, Home Popham and de Rebeque, and the consignees, Charnock of Ostend. With the matter still unsettled in 1804, Pitt managed to extract the £17,000 as an interim payment, as it were—even though Popham's claims had repeatedly been rejected by the High Court of Admiralty; and the wretched Robinson had not only got nothing but had spent £6,000 on legal fees. The whole affair was raised in the House of Commons in 1808 by Mr Lushington, the Hon. Member for Yarmouth, in a savage attack on Popham, who was present and replied with his usual eloquent evasiveness—and, as usual, got away with it.

Prize money was obviously of intense concern to both officers and men, and it crops up again in a dispute between Popham and Ross Donnelly in 1807. This was complicated—as the reader will have realised, every dispute in which HP became involved was complicated!—by queries as to the former's status as Commodore of the squadron, and is discussed in later chapters. It was raised again as late as 1819.

7. Even the naval historian W. G. Perrin, let alone Benjamin Tucker, have accused Home Popham of promoting himself to Commodore, but the Admiralty letter of 31 July is clear: to hoist a Broad Pendant was to assume the rank of Commodore. However, 'Commodore' was an ad hoc rank, conferred on the commander of an expedition for the duration of a specific operation or cruise only: when that was completed, the holder normally reverted to plain Captain. The confusion arises out of the fact that in 1805, though not for much longer, the Admiralty recognised two *different classes* of Commodore, one 'with a captain under him', the other without. The former was regarded as a 'Flag officer', i.e. a kind of junior Admiral, with the privileges, particularly with regard to share of 'Prize', of flag rank; the latter, known as a 'ten shilling Commodore', he without 'a captain under him', did not hold Flag rank and did not qualify for an Admiral's cut of prize money. Nor did he receive any extra pay, while the other, superior kind, did. Home Popham assumed—or chose to assume—that the Admiralty intended him to be a 'First Class' Commodore, and acted accordingly. The matter had finally to be thrashed out in court and will be referred to again later.

8. See Note 6 above. Altogether, between October 1805 and March 1806 the squadron captured, recaptured or destroyed seventeen ships: Ross Donnelly's claim for Popham's illicit share was over £2,000.

CHAPTER XIV

Beyond 'the limits of due discretion'?
1806-7

1

NEWS OF the Battle of Trafalgar did not reach the victors of Cape Colony until 9 January 1806, nearly two and a half months after it was fought; while the news of the capture of Cape Town was not received in London until 27 February, six weeks later. At least three months, possibly longer, would pass before Home Popham could receive a reply to a letter home. Thus isolated by time as well as distance was the Commodore of a detached squadron in the South Atlantic in the days of sail; and this time-lag gives an almost hallucinatory atmosphere to events, and the response to them, during 1806. It also laid on expedition commanders a daunting responsibility: if they acted on their own initiative and were successful they could hope for commendation; but if they failed to act, or things went ill, they could expect court-martial.

Popham's orders, before he left Cork, allowed for the possibility that the French might attempt to retake the colony, and for the first three months this was a constant preoccupation. The information on which he and Baird had to work was spasmodic, fragmentary and stale; it seemed certain that at least two French squadrons, one under Admiral Linois, the other under Willaumez, were at large in the Atlantic, but their intentions were largely guesswork. The patrol in February had drawn a blank, and at the beginning of March *Diadem, Diomede* and the frigate *Leda* were back in Table Bay. On the 4th there was a SSE'ly gale, and *Diadem* dragged anchors and fell foul of *Leda*. They were sorting themselves out when a signal was made from the Lion's Rump, the range of hills to the west of Cape Town, for three ships in the offing. 'Supposing them to be French,' notes the log, 'cleared ship for action' (but does not add that both ships and the fort hoisted Dutch colours). 'At 1030 observed one of them standing in for the Bay with French colours.' On she came, all unsuspecting. 'When she came alongside of us,' Robert Fernyhough wrote, 'we hauled down the Dutch colours and hoisted the English ensign, opened our ports, showed our broadside, and ordered her to strike. She lowered her colours, and I was directed by Sir Home Popham to take possession of her, with a party of Marines.'

She proved to be *La Volontaire*, a 46-gun frigate detached from Willaumez's squadron with despatches and, incidentally, a number of officers and men of the 2nd and 54th Regiments of Foot who had been on their way back to England after four years in Gibraltar when their ship had been taken. The other two sail sighted proved to be the *Raisonnable* and *Narcissus,* which had chased her in; but everything pointed to the fact that the rest of the French squadron were probably not far away, though it seemed that news of the capture of the colony had not reached them. In addition, *La Volontaire* reported that Linois, with the 84-gun *Marengo* and the frigate *La Belle Poule,* were on their way home from Île de France with the spoils from a number of captured Indiamen. And yet another French squadron, under Admiral Leiseignuis, was also on the high seas. Immediately Popham and Baird put into operation their defensive strategy, with the troops on standby and the ships anchored under the protection of the guns of the fort.

Yet still there was no sign of them; and later in the month a Hamburg brig arrived and reported that although Willaumez was indeed in the South Atlantic, it was thought that he was bound not for Cape Town but the East Indies or Île de France.[1] On board the brig was a Herr Steetz, an old acquaintance of Popham's from his time in the Low Countries.

The Commodore calculated that if the French *were* on their way they would put in an appearance within ten days, and they remained at readiness. As a precaution, he despatched warning messages to Admiral Cochrane in the West Indies and to Admiral Pellew in the Bay of Bengal.

The ten days passed uneventfully, and Popham became more and more certain that Steetz was right. Breaking free of the anxiety over the safety of the colony, his mind could look ahead. Inevitably it turned towards South America. It is impossible to date precisely when the notion of an assault on the Rio de la Plata moved into the planning stage, but it was certainly during the latter part of March and may have been even earlier. From his long explanatory letter to Marsden of 13 April[2] it is clear that he had been collecting what information he could about the Spanish colonies ever since they called at San Salvador in the previous November; but it was the arrival in Table Bay of the American *Elizabeth* and her ebullient captain, Waine, that provided the final justification.

South America in general, Waine told him, and Rio de la Plata (the province that is now Argentina) in particular, were rich in flour—which was short at the Cape—and all provisions including beef cattle; had fewer than a thousand regular troops in service; would welcome liberation from their Spanish masters; and, most cogent of all, were a mine of wealth. Buenos Ayres, indeed, was the port through which in addition all the rich trade of the Phillipines was channelled. Five hundred troops, Waine argued, would be quite enough to take Buenos Ayres; and to show that he wasn't trying to 'mislead the British', he would gladly 'be one of the five hundred'. He and his ship were at the Commodore's service; but, he added, 'I hope you will not make use of my name improperly as it may injure me greatly'.

Waine's enthusiasm, taken in conjunction with the information supplied by 'Mr Wilson, an eminent Merchant in the City of London', an English carpenter who had been eleven years in Monte Video, and another unidentified Englishman who had been resident eight years in B.A., two of them as interpreter in the Customs House, was more than enough to ignite Popham's combustible imagination; and he set about planning the expedition, and polishing up the arguments in its favour for the benefit of the Admiralty. The first thing was to win Baird over.[3]

The two of them had got on well ever since they had first met at Jeddah five years before: after the capture of Cape Town, Popham had written in his despatch that 'I know of no instance where a stronger degree of confidence and unanimity have been exemplified between the two professions'; and Baird was equally cordial in his. Such harmony in 'a united service' was by no means the rule; in fact, very much the opposite. Nevertheless, and in spite of the confidence he had in his opposite number's judgement, Baird did not like the idea.

His responsibility—for on the capitulation he had, as directed, assumed the Governor-Generalship of the colony—was to its defence, and he had no authority to send any of his troops off on an unauthorised jaunt to another continent. If they were to go anywhere it was back to England, for the order to despatch the transport on to India had been rescinded while they were at Madeira. All of Popham's notorious 'plausibility' was required to win him round and let him have 'a few troops for a short time to bring a question of such importance to an immediate issue'. The clinching—and distinctly dubious—lever that Popham used was to declare that if Baird would not lend him 'the few troops' he asked for, he would go without them and venture it with his Marine battalion. At this barefaced blackmail Baird capitulated and let him have the 71st Regiment, which had formerly been his own. Wilkie, who did not like him, remarks, 'I have mentioned one or two rather repulsive traits [in Baird's character] to show what talent Sir H. Popham must have possessed to have got influence over such a rough diamond, and draw him gradually into his jaws.' Baird was not the only man to submit to that spell, and regret it.

2

The evolution of the expedition against Buenos Ayres illustrates with considerable precision how Home Popham was able to convince himself and others of the validity of a course of action which he knew to be irregular, and which would almost certainly land him—and them—in trouble. Once the bee was in his bonnet, no argument, no misgiving, no ultimate caution, operated.

As far as Buenos Ayres was concerned, he had, first of all, disposed of any qualms about leaving his station: the French had no immediate designs on the Cape, he was sure, and news had come through that India was temporarily at peace. When it came to the positive reasons, every argument chimed with his own convictions, and, *pari passu*, with opinions expressed at his conferences with Pitt, Melville and Miranda. Then there was the matter of their anchorage. The southern winter was approaching and they would have to leave Table Bay because it was too exposed; and as he wrote to Marsden on 9 April, 'It is difficult to decide on the best method of applying the exertions of the Squadron in the ensuing two months to the best advantage.' Perhaps it would be a good idea, he mused, to cruise off the coast of South America in the hope of intercepting Linois' squadron. They would also be able to provision there. This was transparently disingenuous; and finally, on 13 April, the day before the convoy sailed, in a further letter to Marsden Popham came clean. Once more he paraded the arguments in favour, and enclosed a letter from Waine in corroboration. He admitted that he had had to work hard on Baird, but now he had the troops, and he had written to Patten, the Governor of St Helena, asking him to provide a few more (this account of his dealings with Patten was to suffer a sea-change later). He rounded the letter off with an argument which was specious even by Home Popham's standards. Surely, he wrote, it was better to employ the ships in this way, rather than 'allowing the Squadron I have the honour to command to moulder away its natural energy, by wintering in False Bay, and eventually become paralysed after remaining so long as it has done in a state of cold defensive inactivity'?

Surely no one, not even my Lords Commissioners, could dispute that?

'Rumours had been early set on foot about some expedition, which at last gained more consistence,' Wilkie wrote, 'and finally the 71st Regiment received orders to be in readiness—envied by all the rest . . . Accordingly, they were embarked under the orders of General Beresford,[4] and sailed—while we were all dead beat at conjecture where they could possibly be going, one regiment, and the whole squadron! They were too weak for the Isle of France, and we sent them to Macao, and Manilla: at length, coupled with the character of the Commodore, the guessers settled it down into a marauding expedition along the coast of Peru—and it would most probably have been carried on in that style if the broad pendant had been allowed to have things all its own way.'

Just before they sailed, some dismounted light dragoons of the 20th Regiment and six field-pieces were added to the 700 men of the 71st. 'To this reinforcement', Gillespie says in his dry way, 'a regular staff was annexed, which changed its title into an expedition, instead of a predatory enterprise.' Fernyhough, writing on 12 April, also had little doubt what was at the back of the Commodore's mind. 'Our destination is the Rio de la Plata. We calculate on making considerable prize money, if we succeed in our attempt.' And he goes on, 'The Commodore is informed by a Frenchman, now on board (who goes with us to point out where the public money is deposited), that the treasure is considerable.'[5]

Two days later, on 14 April 1806, *Diadem, Raisonnable, Diomede, Narcissus,* the gun brig *Encounter* and four transports hove up their anchors, made sail, and headed NNW on the 1,700 mile haul to St Helena. It was perhaps fortunate for the Commodore's somewhat fragile peace of mind, as Table Mountain dropped over the horizon astern, that no mail had arrived from England since the turn of the year.

3

After leaving the Cape the squadron ran into a gale, and one of the troop transports became separated. 'I was induced to bear up for this island, 'Popham wrote to Melville on 30 April, 'though certainly more with a view to obtaining a reinforcement than of meeting her'—reinforcements which he had, in fact, already asked for, though it added another thousand miles to the passage. (Popham had a habit, when it suited him, of talking of South Africa and South America as being 'contiguous', as if the 22 miles of the Dover Straits divided them rather than 3,000 miles of the South Atlantic.)

'Sir Home', Wilkie, who was not with the expedition, wrote, '...wheedled the Governor out of some men. This was of little use—it only served to get that good and kind-hearted gentleman into a scrape [he was recalled]—and the vagabonds were of little value afterwards—most of them deserted.' Patten 'lent' him 180 men from the permanent garrison; in return, Popham carried out some modifications to the island's semaphore signalling system.

The call at St Helena was completely overshadowed, however, by the news of the death of William Pitt, which had occurred three months before, on 23 January. For Popham this was a devastating blow, and in that same letter to Melville he wrote:

> I consider [it] the greatest national calamity that ever befell our Country, and to my personal feelings it has been such a shock that I shall not easily recover. I did hope from many circumstances that the whole of my conduct would have received his most unqualified approbation, and looking forward to that moment was the greatest pleasure I had. I am now toiling under such speculative promise of approbation, either from different policy, or different sentiments, that I proceed with little pleasure, but as Sir David Baird is equally committed with myself in this Enterprise I trust I shall neither be wanting in zeal or firmness to accomplish it properly.

His dismay at the turn of events runs right through the letter; and it reveals very clearly his awareness of the risk in going ahead with it. With Melville out of office, and now Pitt dead, he had lost his two most stalwart supporters—and who knew, in St Helena in April, what men and what policies would rule in their stead? To whom could he turn now for retrospective 'approbation'? (He did not learn the composition of the new government—that of 'All the Talents'—until the end of August.)

A distinct note of desperation can be heard in this letter, as he recapitulates once again the benefits which will flow: 'a channel of supply for near six million of inhabitants'; the acute need for more export markets now that Napoleon has closed the whole of Europe to them. He even argues that success will improve Miranda's chances 'if it should now be thought expedient to carry it into execution.'

'I trust therefore the measure will be a popular one, even if it should not exactly meet the policy of the present Minister; the latter consideration should however have been my guide, as it originally was owing to the last conversation I had with Mr Pitt... I trust I have judged right, I am sure if that is granted, I shall act right, and thereby make myself I hope worthy the confidence of any Government.'

The little convoy left the island in the first week of May. 'The object of our enterprise,' wrote Robert Fernyhough in high feather, having just been reappointed Adjutant of the sea battalion of 800 men, who were to be given red coats to look like soldiers, 'is to cripple the pecuniary resources of Spain. The signal is made to repair on board; the Commodore and General are now embarking.'

For the next five weeks they endured 'a baffling and tedious progress' as they wallowed southwestwards towards the Rio de la Plata and fame and fortune—or notoriety and disgrace.

4

June 3rd 1806. Soundings of 72 fathoms. Blue mud with specks.'
The fog swirled around them, and there was only enough bread left for another four days: the very gods, it seemed, had turned against them. Although they were in soundings, another nine days elapsed before they entered the river. There Popham and Beresford held a council of war. They had a choice: they could either go for Monte Video and establish themselves there, and then assault Buenos Ayres when they were ready—and preferably with the help of reinforcements from home; or they could make straight for the capital. After a great deal of discussion they agreed to do the second, a decision which, with hindsight, was undoubtedly the wrong one.

There were reasons for either course. In a letter to Marsden written a month later, Popham gave those in support of their decision: that the troops at Buenos Ayres were few and of poor quality, while the best were concentrated at Monte Video; that the former was an open town, while the latter was fortified; that Buenos Ayres, not Monte Video, was the entrepot; and—a pressing point at that moment—they were short of food and B.A. was the more likely to have supplies. Benjamin Tucker was not the only person to point out subsequently why they made the choice they did: there would be more booty there.

Now that they were actually in the river, the enormity of the task they had so blithely undertaken came home to them. The misgivings had started even while they were at St Helena, exacerbated by the realisation that Government support was even more doubtful than it had been before. 'I trust,' Popham had written to Marsden before they left, 'that this small armament will only be considered as a *floating force* to keep up the national characteristic enterprise, and ready to apply to any point of the enemy's possessions which have been neglected...' He had already asked for reinforcements to be sent quickly: gone for good, now, was the brave assurance that with a thousand men they could subdue the country.

The decision taken—and it was made easier by the latest information regarding the city, extracted from a dipsomaniac Scotchman whom they had plucked from a captured Spanish schooner—the expedition was faced with the next problem, that of actually getting to their destination. 'Besides the common dangers of the river,' Gillespie wrote, 'we were often involved in thick fogs, which, with the inequality of sailing in some of the transports, tended much to retard our progress...' The distance from the mouth of the river to Buenos Ayres is 130 miles, the navigation is tricky, and *Narcissus* spent twenty-four unhappy hours on the Chico Bank before she could be refloated. 'In justice to Sir Home Popham,' Gillespie continued, 'those trying occasions evinced a great equanimity of temper, and an unruffled genius, which uniformly marked and directed both his words, and actions. This tribute, and its merits, are greatly enhanced when we penetrate into those conflicts of anxiety that must have ruled within him, struggling at the moment against adverse incidents, and with a mind weighed down by a conscious load of responsibility. Having been personally on board the *Encounter* gun brig,' he concludes, 'with 130 men, which vessel was always under weigh, and in advance of the squadron, and whither that naval chief repaired every morning to guide its movements, I was enabled to remark those testimonies.'

This laborious passage upstream took them almost a fortnight. At Quilmes, where Beresford decided to make his landing, they were still twelve miles from the city, and their presence had not gone unremarked. 'Fires lighted upon every summit,' Gillespie noted, 'and an immense concourse of horsemen from all directions... denoted a general alarm. Our effective army, which was destined to conquer a city of more than 40,000 in population, with an immense body to dispute our way into it, consisted only of seventy officers of all ranks, seventy-two sergeants, twenty-seven drummers, and 1,446 rank and file: making a grand total of 1,635.'

5

During the afternoon of 25 June, Beresford started to disembark his miniscule army, which included the Marine Battalion in their borrowed scarlet coats. The water was so shallow that once again the men had to wade ashore, and by midnight they had all landed safely and bivouacked at the foot of the hill, below the twinkling fires of the Spaniards. The outposts were kept on the alert, but the only alarm, the thunder of galloping hooves at first light, turned out to be not cavalry but a stampede of wild horses.

At 8 o'clock the British began their advance in two columns. They could see the enemy quite clearly—3,000 of them, according to Beresford, with a column of infantry and eight cannon—drawn up on the hill beyond a patch of marshy ground: and the British formed line, ready for the attack which they were sure must come. The Spanish artillery opened fire, but the shot passed harmlessly overhead; and then, on the right of the line, their infantry and artillery started to advance. 'Upon observing this movement,' Robert Fernyhough says, 'General Beresford gave orders for the whole to advance, which was promptly and cheerfully obeyed; first taking off our hats and giving three cheers, the bagpipes of the 71st Highlanders striking up at the same time.'

This brave initiative quickly came to a squelching halt in the bog, and they started to lose men to the Spanish musket fire. 'With some exertion,' Fernyhough continues, 'we cleared this impediment, and continued to advance at double-quick time, till we arrived tolerably near; when the enemy thought proper to retreat with the utmost precipitation, after receiving two or three volleys of musketry, as well as brisk cannonading from two brass fieldpieces, which were fortunately so much to the left of our line, that they avoided the morass, and were enabled to gain the heights in time to fire upon the Spaniards as they retreated.' At the top of the hill they found that the Spaniards had abandoned six brass guns, two of them ready loaded, which they promptly turned on their departing owners.

Between the British force and the city ran the Cuello River, which Fernyhough called 'the Baraccas, a small branch of the River Plate'. There was a bridge across, but they were too late to save it as it was already on fire. That night the two little armies glared at each other across the river, but it was only thirty yards wide and a number of sailors swam across and seized some boats on the far side.

Next morning Beresford pulled back his advance pickets—to the delight of the Spaniards, who read it as a sign of retreat—and then, under cover of the artillery, the whole British forced advanced to the river bank, muskets blazing. While this exchange was in progress, the sailors and engineers constructed a bridge with the boats and, says Fernyhough, 'we forced a passage over, by laying planks from one vessel to another; the enemy again retreating.'

And that was really that, for quite soon emissaries arrived bearing a flag of truce, and with terms of capitulation. Beresford gave them half-an-hour to surrender the city—to which, after some deliberation, they agreed—and his force covered the remaining mile and a half. 'The gates were opened to us,' Fernyhough recorded jubilantly, 'and our gallant little army marched triumphantly into the city, with drums beating and colours flying. We were received by the Bishop and the clergy in their robes, and by the civil authorities of the place.' Next day, the Union flag was hoisted on the castle and a 21-gun salute was fired, to be answered from the river by the *Narcissus* and the troopships.

'We expect to remain here until reinforcements come out from England... as it is impossible with our small force to do much at present. The prize money will be considerable, as the *Narcissus*, which takes the despatches, carries to England 1,086,000 dollars, equal to 30 tons of silver. The whole capture amounts to about 3,500,000 dollars, including Peruvian bark, various articles of merchandise, etc.' Fernyhough then adds, quite inconsequentially, 'Assassinations are very frequent.'

While all this was going on, the Viceroy, the Marquis Sobramente, had discreetly fled, taking with him a large quantity of treasure. A company of the 71st set off in pursuit, caught up with him, and relieved him of the useful sum of 631,684 dollars.

6

'Late on Saturday night last a *Gazette Extraordinary* was published, containing the particulars of this brilliant achievement, which the firing of the Park and Tower guns had previously announced to the public joy' *Morning Post*, 15 September 1806.

'...it cannot be supposed that an enterprise of such importance would have been undertaken, if the Commanders of it had not... received some instructions, probably of a private nature...' *Morning Post*, 16 September 1806.

Sir Home Popham's gamble, it seemed, had succeeded brillantly, and he wasted no time in sending off not only his despatch announcing the capture, but also an ebullient open letter to the merchants of England, outlining the advantages that must accrue from this opening up of new markets. This typical bit of flamboyance, which was received with rapture in Birmingham and at Lloyd's Coffee House, reinforced the suspicions of Popham's enemies. Lord Grenville referred scathingly to 'the Admiral's well-known proneness to bombast', and Fletcher Wilkie mentions sardonically that 'well-known commercial letter from the Commodore'. As always with Home Popham, approval was matched with disapproval; and while the Admiralty inevitably found his conduct highly reprehensible, the Committee of the Patriotic Fund,[6] at their meeting at Lloyd's the day after the news was received in London, 'Resolved that Vases of £200 value each, with appropriate inscriptions, be presented to Major-General Beresford and Commodore Sir Home Popham, for their gallant and disinterested conduct in this successful and important enterprise.'[7]

Almost at once, too, advertisements began to appear in the papers. 'The drooping spirit of commerce is wonderfully revived...', purred the *Morning Post*, 'Every speculative mind is engaged in preparing adventures for that market.' Among those speculative minds was not only that of a Mr Potter who, 'has a quantity of LIGHT STAYS made up that will suit the climate of Buenos Ayres', but those of Messrs Parker & Sewell who, on 1 October, announced the unceasing demand they were experiencing for their SILK HATS for the Spanish market , and which were available for Buenos Ayres, not to mention 'PIANO-FORTES... exceeding cheap'.

The near-hysteria which the news created was not at all diminished by the treatment accorded to the 'specie', when it was landed from *Narcissus* at Portsmouth.

Thirty sailors [*The Courier* reported on 18 September], dressed in the same uniforms as when they attacked the Spaniards on shore, have it under their charge, preceded by a brass field-piece, which they intend to fire a salute with, on their entrance into the principal towns on the road. The Royal Marine band played several martial tunes, at the head of the [eight] wagons; which were decorated by the Spanish flags taken at Buenos Ayres, and three British colours, with R.B. on them, meaning the Royal Blues, the corps of Seamen that landed being so called by Sir Home Popham.

Buenos Ayres was not the only subject to keep the scribes busy that month. On the very day that news reached London, Charles James Fox, who had succeeded to the premiership on the death of Pitt and the formation of the coalition of 'All the Talents', died at the age of fifty-seven.[8] With him died the desultory peace negotiations which had been dragging on with Napoleon since the spring. Fox was succeeded by Lord Grenville as leader of an increasingly shaky Government, in which Charles Grey (Lord Howick; Second Earl Grey on the death of his father General Sir Charles Grey, Home Popham's old collaborator) was First Lord.

During that same fortnight news arrived of a sensational victory over the French at Maida in the toe of Italy by Major-General Sir Charles Stuart with 8,000 troops, facing 52,000 of the enemy and routing them. Like Popham's South American adventure, Stuart's was launched without authority, and using men who were supposed to be garrisoning (in Stuart's case) Sicily and not gallivanting about in Southern Italy. There were other similarities, too: the outcome of both, and the fact that Stuart's naval collaborator was Rear-Admiral Sir Sidney Smith,[9] a sailor whose career was as varied as Popham's, and even more unorthodox.

To lend substance to the suggestion that Popham and General Miranda were somehow acting in collusion, even though their respective theatres of operations were over 3,000 miles apart as the condor flies and more than 5,000 by sea, the latter was reported to have landed in the Bay of Triste, west of Caracas, in the middle of June, with 4,000 men and the (unauthorised) support of Rear-Admiral Thomas Cochrane. Such action on Cochrane's part went far beyond the 'connivance' which was all the Government were prepared to allow Miranda, and Cochrane's name became linked with Popham's as yet another insubordinate commander.

As for Home Popham himself, on 16 September, three days after the news of the capture of Buenos Ayres reached London, *The Courier* reported that they had heard that 'orders have been sent out *commanding* Sir Home Popham *to return home instantly*' and that his promotions have been disallowed. These rumours, they hope, are untrue: if true, however, they should be rescinded, and it should be announced that 'His Majesty has conferred some signal mark of Royal favour upon him'. And the *Morning Post*, on the 23rd, had this to add: 'It is reported, but we hope erroneously, that Sir Home Popham is coming home under arrest. It is scarcely possible that such a proceeding on the part of the Ministers could have any justification.'

Whatever Ministers may have thought of his conduct, the mercantile community, which had seen exports drop from £10M to £2M in two years, were delighted, and were quick to take advantage of the opportunities it offered. 'Nine ships of the first class have already been taken up', the papers reported within ten days of the news arriving, '...and ten times that number will be employed.' The bonanza was on, and Buenos Ayres had already become part of popular mythology. 'A trip to Buenos Ayres is now the fashionable speculation. The *Cocknies* [sic] are inquiring how much farther it is than *Margate*.'

And on the 18th, society news in the *Morning Chronicle* had the following item: 'Lady Home and Miss Popham, and Mr Holloway, her ladyship's brother, from Sunning-hill, Berks, arrived at Grosvenor Square yesterday.'

7

These celebrations referred, of course, to events which had occurred two and a half months earlier: in Buenos Ayres itself in mid-September there was little to celebrate—but *that* news would not reach England until after Christmas.

At first, the Commodore's complacency seemed to be justified. 'Everyone assumed the face of happiness,' Gillespie was to write later, 'hospitality reigned, the laws had their course, and the worshippers of the sanctuary attended as usual, without anyone making them afraid.' Generous terms had been agreed, the British force behaved well, and many of the officers found themselves welcomed into local homes.

Not far below the smiling surface, however, less amiable emotions lay waiting. Rio de la Plata, like the other Spanish settlements in South America, and like Venezuela where Miranda was valiantly struggling to establish a foothold, contained three separate populations: the Spanish government officials; the Creoles, people of mixed blood like Miranda; and the rest, imported negro slaves and indigenous Indians. The Spanish conquerors were disinclined to see their power usurped, least of all by their old colonial rivals and, since the Napoleonic occupation of Spain, current enemies. The local people, on the other hand, while only too glad to see the end of Spanish domination, and believing at first that the British had come as liberators, were not prepared to exchange one colonial administration for another, which was increasingly how matters appeared. Home Popham realised this, but was helpless. In a letter to Lord Howick a couple of months later, he wrote: '...the inhabitants generally have sought so long for Independence, that having in a great measure suspended the Royal Authority in the Capital, they are likely to gain that end, indeed I am satisfied if we could have proclaimed it, they never would have been persuaded to take up arms against us...'

The leader of the uprising was a French officer in Spanish service, Don Santiago Liniers,[10] Chief of the Naval Station at Buenos Ayres, who had been sent down-river to Ensenada on news of the approach of the British squadron. The British, of course, passed Ensenada on their way to Quilmes higher up, and so Liniers was not involved in the occupation of the city. He arrived there two days later under a safe conduct in order, he said, to see his family, and had quickly summed up the meagreness of the occupying forces. According to Home Popham, however, Liniers had given his parole, had come to the city, seen what he wanted to see, then broken his parole by going to Monte Video and raising a force with which to contest the British occupation. Since Popham, in his despatch, was involved in an extended exercise in self-justification, and Liniers had never been a British prisoner and therefore had no occasion to give his parole, the balance of truth inclines towards him.

However that may be, Liniers quite clearly was not the parole-breaking renegade he was made out to be, but an official of the colonial government carrying out his duty—which was to evict the invaders. At Monte Video he collected all the troops stationed there. He also met a certain Pueyrredon, brother-in-law of the

Mayor of B.A., and together with him and two other Spaniards planned the *reconquista*. The British account states that Pueyrredon was responsible for infiltrating arms and men into the city and arranging that when the time came, they would man the flat rooftops as snipers. Liniers says that Pueyrredon simply gathered three or four hundred men 'half of them without arms, with faulty cannons and guns without ammunition', at Perdriel, outside the city, where he drove off Beresford and a superior force while waiting for Liniers to come up from Monte Video. The point is unimportant: the fact is that the weapons and the snipers were in position when the time came, and were responsible for many of the British casualties.

Towards the end of July, when the British had been in occupation for less than a month, Beresford received the first intimations of an intended insurrection. Fernyhough gives a good idea of what they might have to contend with if it came. 'For the size and situation of this city, few in Europe are constructed on a more regular plan, or better calculated for defence against a storm, as every house in itself is a fortification; the top of each being flat, with a kind of breastwork, with loopholes, so that persons might fire from them without being observed...'

After a brief general description of the city and its rigid grid plan of regular streets, its many churches, the cathedral, and 'one very large square, where they have the Cabildo, or common council house', his narrative continues: 'We remained in possession of Buenos Ayres, with our small force, in peace and quietness, till towards the end of July, when appearances began to be a little suspicious. Frequent attempts were made to decoy our men into the country; and about this time, a number of Germans belonging to the 71st Regiment had deserted.' Desertion was to be a problem for as long as the British remained in Rio de la Plata. 'A fellow would ride down to the outposts, leading a horse, give in hand twenty dollars, with the promise of a house and a wife in the interior', Gillespie explains; or it would be done in the more traditional way through drink and shanghaiing. Not all deserters, however, got what they were promised.

Beresford had at once passed the word of coming trouble to the Commodore, who summoned *Diomede* and *Diadem* to Ensenada, and the smaller vessels to Colonia, opposite the city, where Liniers was waiting to cross. Popham's despatch describes the frustrations of the next few days:

> On the 1st of August, in the afternoon, the *Leda* anchored off Buenos Ayres, about 12 miles distant; and on my landing on the 2nd, which I did as soon as the weather would admit of a boat getting on shore, I found the General had just made a very successful attack on about 1,500 Spaniards under Pueridon, five leagues from the town, with 500 men, in which he took all the enemies' cannon...

All numbers mentioned in the several accounts have to be treated with scepticism: the odds tend to be reversed in the English and Spanish versions.

On the 3rd I attempted to return to the *Leda*, in the *Encounter*, which Capt. Honeyman brought within a few miles of the shore for this purpose, as it blew very strong; but the wind freshened so considerably from the Eastward, that we could not get to windward. On the 4th, in the morning, it was very thick weather, and the gale increased so much that it was impossible to weigh. About noon Capt. King arrived, in a gallivat, with 150 men from the *Diadem*, for the purpose of arming the few small vessels we had collected in the harbour; but he was not able to get there till the following day. On the 5th, in the morning, it moderated and I reached the *Leda*; when I received a report from Capt. Thompson, that in the gale of the preceding day the enemy had crossed from Colonia, totally unobserved by any of our ships, except the schooner under the command of Lieut. Herrick… On the 6th and 7th it blew a hurricane; the *Leda* was lying in four fathoms, with two anchors down and her yards and topmasts struck. On the 8th I heard from Capt. King that five of our gunboats had foundered at their anchors; that the *Walker* had lost her rudder, and that the launches and large cutters of the *Diadem* and *Leda* were lost.

For a week after Beresford's initial skirmish, everything went quiet in and around the city. That was the period during which Liniers was ferrying his force across the river. He scornfully dismisses Popham's account of the conditions: 'the wind didn't stop me from casting off with the whole of the *esquadrilla* and entering the Las Conchas river…' He and Pueyrredon now joined forces. News of their approach reached Beresford on the 8th. The atmosphere in the city was tense: 'affairs wore an alarming appearance,' wrote Robert Fernyhough, 'the city was almost deserted, and, in short, we hourly expected an attack.'

What is not at all clear is why Beresford, who had defeated them twice, did not sally out—as he had done before—and attack them in open country, for the Spaniards' combined force only amounted to about 2,000 men as against his 1,200. Popham gives as the reason 'the torrents of rain [which] had rendered the roads totally impracticable for any thing but cavalry; and consequently Gen. Beresford was most seriously disappointed in his determination to attack the enemy at a distance from the town.' If this were so, how was it that Liniers was able to advance? His 'inexhaustible supply of horses', says Popham. Nonsense, said Linier: 'I hardly had enough horses and mules to carry the artillery and ammunition, and almost all my officers were on foot.'

Whatever the truth of it, on 10 August the Spanish force was approaching the outskirts with colours flying, and sent an envoy under a flag of truce to demand the immediate surrender of the British. 'He had a great drum beating before him,' says Fernyhough; 'this unusual mode of procession made some of us smile.' Beresford sent him packing with the message that he would meet them 'at the point of the bayonet.'

By that night they were in the Park at the northwest side of the town, and began to occupy some of the houses 'from which he commenced a brisk fire of musketry, which galled our men severely. This kind of warfare was kept up the whole day without intermission. We had many killed and wounded.' *'August 12th*. Soon after daylight a heavy fire commenced on both sides, which was continued for some hours, when the Spaniards attempted to make a charge up one of the streets, but we gave them such a reception with our guns, loaded with grape and cannister shot, as compelled them to make a hasty retreat, with considerable loss.'

'Our last stand', says Gillespie, 'was made at 11 in the market-place', which was close by the main square, with the castle beyond it and the river behind. The Marines were manning the batteries in the castle, with the St Helena Corps in front of it; but as the casualties, many of them from snipers, mounted, the whole force was driven from the square and into the castle itself, and about 2 o'clock Beresford ordered a flag of truce to be hoisted.

'Never shall I forget the scene which followed the hoisting of the flag of truce,' Fernyhough wrote, 'and the advantage gained over us: about 4,000 ragamuffins rushed into the square, brandishing their knives, threatening us with destruction. The savages paid no regard to our flag of truce, and were firing in all directions.'

Despite the provocation—and the British troops were in fighting mood—Beresford and his officers managed to restrain them, and that evening the confrontation was brought to an end and the terms of surrender agreed. If they had been observed, they would have been honourable enough. The British troops, having marched out of the castle 'with all the honours of war', were to be disarmed and put aboard the transports and returned to England. In exchange, all Spanish prisoners were to be freed. The ships were to be provisioned for the voyage and guaranteed safe passage; and those wounded and too ill to go aboard would be looked after in the city's hospitals until they were fit to travel, when they too would be repatriated. Finally, the property of English subjects in the city would be respected. The document was signed by Beresford and Liniers, Capt. Spanish Navy, and dated August 12th 1806.

About 4 o'clock [Fernyhough recorded] the remains of our little army marched out of the castle, with the honours of war. We hung down our heads sorrowfully, and instead of carrying our swords erect, we dropped them by our sides. We arrived at the Cabildo, and delivered up our arms. This was the most distressing scene I ever beheld, there was scarcely a dry eye amongst us: some of the men, when they came to deliver up their muskets, broke them against the ground, cursing the day they ever took them in their hands.

Fernyhough and the other officers, after an uneasy night under guard in the castle, were left free to find lodgings; he was cordially invited back to the house of the Spanish merchant where he had stayed during the occupation. According to the surrender terms, they all expected this to be a brief interlude before being re-embarked, but:

The Cabildo now put us off from day to day, with the idea that we were to be embarked on board the English transports, still lying off the town, as soon as the provisions could be got ready. However, one morning, to our great surprise, we found that the transports had sailed, having been ordered away by Liniers, who threatened to make prizes of them if they remained longer off Buenos Ayres. We now began strongly to suspect that it was not the intention of the Spaniards to allow us to return to England...

And this was the truth of it. For the next two months they were kept in suspense; then, in the second week of October they were ordered to pack their belongings, which were loaded on to bullock carts, horses were provided, and they were taken up-country, following in the wake of the troops. There, sometimes staying for a time in a village or on one of the estancias, then being arbitrarily moved on, they spent the next nine months. When they were finally released, in July 1807, they were in the foothills of the Sierra de Cordoba, 600 miles from Buenos Ayres. The story of this unusual captivity, though, lies outside the scope of this narrative.

8

Blame for the disaster, and the bitterness created both by it and by the equivocal behaviour of the Spanish authorities, was inevitably directed at Home Popham. Gillespie, with the other officers, believed that the squadron had let them down, both during the Spanish attack and afterwards. '...I can only regret,' he wrote in his *Gleanings and Remarks* published eleven years after the event, 'that his mental resources were in no way equal to meet the difficulty, and that his professional exertions in this hour of danger, fell far short of general expectations.'

This was less than just. Popham went ashore on the 11th to see the situation for himself, and his 'remaining vessels' kept up a bombardment during the final day. Only after it was all over, and believing that the best possible terms had been arranged, did he drop down-river with his depleted fleet, leaving the transports, as he had every reason to believe, to embark the troops. In the light of subsequent Spanish behaviour this may well have been a mistake; though whether the presence of the warships would have made any difference seems unlikely. Gillespie was convinced that it would, and describes it as 'mysterious' and 'a fatal step for us at the time.' What he was not to know was that, for the rest of the month, Popham was carrying on an increasingly exasperated and acrimonious correspondence with Liniers and the Governor of Monte Video, now the ultimate authority in the province as the mob had prevented the Viceroy from returning to Buenos Ayres, trying to persuade them to observe the terms of the original surrender, all to no avail. With contributions from General Beresford, it continued almost until the British were packed off into the country. At first the Spaniards used any pretext to explain their prevarication: the skipper of some small craft going about his business on the river claimed that a musket had been fired at him, and this was taken as evidence that the British had broken the terms; and so on. Eventually, however, it emerged that the terms which Liniers had agreed had been granted on impulse, '*en atencion a su bizarra [gallant] defencia*' as he wrote to Beresford and had been rejected by the Cabildo, which maintained that he had had no right to grant them, and were therefore null and void. Nothing that either of them said made any difference: the correspondence had been a charade from the start. The whole affair merely added to the strains on Home Popham, and increasingly those strains begin to show in his letters.

His anxiety was sharpened by his total lack of communication from England. Indeed, it was not until late August, when an American ship anchored in the river with English newspapers on board, that he discovered who his new masters were. He at once wrote to Lord Howick,[11] the First Lord of the Admiralty explaining that it had all been done for the honour of the Navy: an uneasy letter as well it might be. 'If in the application of my exertions ... it would appear to your Lordship that I have not taken the proper line, I must consider the Error of Judgement a most serious misfortune as checking in any degree the rational expectation I entertained that my conduct would receive your Lordship's approbation ...' He concluded: 'My anxiety and difficulties are also materially increased for the want of some advices from England, as I have not received a letter since I left it, which is nearly twelve months.' Even his astonishing resilience is beginning to fade: it would be put to much greater tests when mail did start to come through.

Towards the end of September while he was still attempting to negotiate the release of the prisoners, the first reinforcements arrived (they had sailed at the end of July), and also the Admiralty's letter of 11 April. It referred to the various appointments he had made on hoisting his broad pendant on leaving Funchal nearly twelve months before, and it did not make pleasant reading. Their Lordships directed their Secretary to acquaint Sir Home Popham, 'that on a consideration of the circumstances under which that appointment took place [i.e. of Downman to be Captain of *Diadem*] they cannot but highly disapprove thereof, as well as the other removes and promotions ... and therefore do not think it right to confirm them.' He is ordered to resume command of *Diadem*, and return the other officers to their original ships; he may, however, continue to wear '*a distinguishing pendant*' until further orders, or until the arrival of a senior officer.

Not a consoling word about the successful capture of Cape Colony, though the bells had been rung in London on 1 March to celebrate that; and no reference to the *broad pendant* which they had authorised him to wear in their original letter, a point Popham made in his reply. Were they, then, demoting him? Or had they only meant him to be a 'Ten Shilling Commodore', that is one without a captain under him, all the time? 'I thought,' he wrote, 'a distinction existed between a Broad Pendant and a Distinguishing Pendant'; and he went on to imply that he had no intention of obeying their instructions, either with regard to his status or the appointments.

His justification for such irregularity comes out in a long and revealing letter he wrote to Howick on the same day: it was the intention of Lord Barham, the then First Lord, that he should wear a broad pendant, and although it would be 'indelicate' to give him the proof in a letter, prove it he can.[12] Popham had just heard from Baird that he was sending two regiments of infantry and 300 cavalry from the Cape: with them, he plans to go first for Maldonado with its excellent harbour at the mouth of the River Plate, sixty miles east of Monte Video, and then for Monte Video itself; though he is painfully aware of the responsibility he is being forced to take on in planning such military operations without higher authority.

> Nothing can be more melancholy [he writes in a sudden gust of self-pity] than my situation, and it is impossible for me to express to your Lordship how sincerely I feel the unqualified disapprobation which the Board has conveyed to me, of every part of my conduct; it has compleatly paralysed all my exertions, and harrasses [sic] me with the constant reflection, that whatever I now do must subject me to the risk of increased censure ...

Grasping for anything that will offset this disapproval—and he still does not know what reception will be accorded officially to the capture of Buenos Ayres, never mind its loss, though his friends in England approve of the first—he continues:

> I know, my Lord, I have many Enemies, and many who would shrink at the disgrace attending an honest exposition of the cause by which they were influenced; I also hear that the particular notice which the late Lord Nelson, and many other distinguished officers have taken of my telegraphic signals has considerably increased the misfortune I mention...

Popham was always aware of the jealousy of his fellow officers towards him for his rocketing promotion and the 'protection' he enjoyed from a number of politicians, and it increased the defensiveness that was as much a part of his character as the over-confidence. Both, reverse and obverse, image and reflection, are displayed in letters like this one, with all their lack of dignity; a lack of which, throughout his life, he seems sublimely unaware.

With the arrival of the first instalment of reinforcements under Colonel Backhouse from England, Popham launched a swift and almost bloodless assault on Maldonado, the possession of which, with the island of Goretti captured at the same time, ensured their command of the entrance to the river. Monte Video would have to wait upon the arrival of General Auchmuty with the main force, for Popham had no great opinion of Backhouse— '...not that I expect he will trouble me much on that score [their future plans] unless he is aroused by others from his natural torpitude'.

Even these problems, personal and professional, pressing but insoluble as they were, were not enough to quench completely that active and inquiring mind. Later in November he was writing to Howick again, suggesting that every ship on foreign service should carry two field-pieces so that, in a combined operation, the army would have at least some artillery to be going on with. He had, indeed, already tried to buy several brass guns in high order at Rio Grande, 300 miles up the coast, but failed 'on account of the number of departments which such a proposition must necessarily pass through'. Another of his schemes was to take the Portuguese fortress of Santa Teresa, 'which ... would give us a free intercourse with the northeast part of this province and implicate the Portuguese in the war in this country.' The difficulty—one of the difficulties, though he does not mention the others—was, as usual, the dearth of news. 'It is impossible to say whether European Portugal is at this moment our Friend or our Enemy.'

9

On 3 December 1806 all such speculations were brought to a summary end, for on that day HMS *Sampson*, flying the flag of Rear-Admiral Charles Stirling, dropped anchor in the river. Dutifully, Captain Sir Home Popham took down his broad pendant, and was rowed across to call on the Admiral, bearing with him his letter-books and details of the squadron. Stirling's first, and most unpleasant, job was to hand over to Popham a letter from Their Lordships.

Written on 28 July 1806, and signed by Admirals Markham, Pole and Neale, and counter-signed by B. Tucker, it was very short and very clear.

> Whereas we think fit that you shall forthwith return to England; you are hereby required to furnish Rear-Admiral Stirling (by whom you will receive this) with every information ... and having so done, take your passage to England accordingly in such ship as the Rear-Admiral shall appoint.

That first meeting set the tone for their relationship over the next four weeks: Stirling trying desperately to carry out his unpalatable task with delicacy and tact; Popham veering moment by moment from submissiveness to truculence, from obsequiousness to self-pity. The clash would be comic if it were not so sad, for it becomes increasingly clear that the Commodore—a Commodore no longer—is coming closer and closer to breaking-point.

Stirling's tact was manifested at once, for he invited Popham to re-hoist his pendant, irregular though that would be, as it would be more 'respectable' before the squadron he had commanded, the army he had co-operated with, and the enemy he had been fighting. Popham argues the irregularity, and turns the offer down: he is determined to drain the cup of humiliation to the dregs.

The situation was difficult for them both: Popham made it impossible. Touchy at the best of times, he was a mass of raw nerves, seeing slights where none was intended; Stirling, a bluff, outspoken man—'I often make mistakes when speaking too frankly'—trod as delicately as he knew how, but he had his instructions. He also had not only to take over the squadron, but plan future operations; he was a busy man. At the root of the matter was that directive in the Admiralty's letter, that he was to send Popham home 'in such ship as [he] should appoint'; and his decision that that ship should be the *Sampson*. Operational necessity, however, demanded that she should call at Cape Town, and then at St Helena, before finally heading for England and this incensed Popham beyond all reason.

In letter after letter—five in one day, on one occasion—he adduces a dozen reasons why such a voyage is unthinkable.[13] 'It is natural, Sir,' he wrote on 7 December, 'for me to feel mortified at the idea of having had any act of mine give their Lordships cause to supercede me'—and this was adding insult to injury. At Cape Town, and again at St Helena, if he goes ashore, his defeat and humiliation would 'draw those sort of remarks and gestures which will flow from jealous and vindictive minds'; while if he stays aboard, those same minds will know exactly why. These arguments, he continues, are not based on chagrin and disappointment, but simply on practical considerations: his private affairs will suffer; he has already been put on half-pay; it will prolong the separation from his wife and family '...endeared to me by every amiable quality, and who are already materially suffering in Health, and may still be worse from a conception that his disposition naturally unstable and subject to bilious attacks' may suffer a catastrophic attack.

Through the smokescreen of flimsy reasoning, the truth cannot be concealed: his pride has suffered a bitter knock, and the bruise is made infinitely more painful by being treated as little better than a malefactor. Moreover, though he does not say this in so many words, the sooner he gets home, the sooner he can justify his actions, 'if it should be necessary to enter upon such a subject'.

Stirling, while for a long time he remains polite and extraordinarily patient, also remains adamant. He has his orders, and as he cannot spare a ship specially to take Popham to England he must sail in *Sampson*. There is a brig sailing direct, but they have not room for passengers, so he had best go as arranged. Popham continues to refuse. 'For God's sake, Sir, take my meaning as it is intended, and do not let it be perverted. If you cannot consistent with the service allow me a ship to go direct, what can be more humble than my offering to go in a prize Brig...?'

By 10 December he is almost incoherent, invoking Montesquieu and the 29th Chapter of Magna Carta, muttering threats about seeking redress and threatening Stirling with the consequences, and ending his letter with savage sarcasm: 'I cannot return my farewell without offering my thanks for the interest you take in my having a speedy passage, and your sincere wish that I may long enjoy domestic felicity—I hope and trust by going direct it will not be long before I do enjoy that blessing.'

Stirling's only relief from this epistolary barrage was to write candidly and at length to Marsden. '...Sir Home Popham positively refuses to sail hence in the *Sampson*,' he wrote on the 10th, after this particular exchange, 'agreeable to my orders or letters or whatever else they may be termed ...'; and later retails an anecdote which perhaps most clearly encapsulates this tragi-comic affair.

'I had before this, begun to imagine that the Commodore wanted to frame some excuse for not going away [Popham had, at one point, offered to serve as his ADC] until some purpose, not evident to my senses, was answered, and that the moment one argument failed, another would be started, or something else be suggested...'.

So Stirling suggests that Popham puts his views and intentions in writing, 'and expressed my admiration of his fluency and style of writing...', at which Popham took offence, thinking he was being sneered at. 'I was distressed at having my motive so completely misunderstood when my desire [had been] to convey pleasure by bestowing praise, and apologised, as I always do, when I give pain without intending it.'

Although Stirling succeeds in keeping his temper with this extremely trying character, he makes no attempt to hide his feelings in his letters to Marsden.

This officer whose sense of public duty had induced him to carry such a high hand at the Cape of Good Hope that he expected people to insult him if he landed there... this officer... who had influence with Pitt, who (report asserts) has had the honour to associate with the family of my Sovereign... who had so much influence with Paul I that the latter refused to see him in case he was persuaded to change his mind...

This officer was not going to stop him doing what he thought to be right, whatever construction he chose to put on it. 'Sir Home calls himself in one of his letters, of an irritable disposition, and unfortunately I labour under the same misfortune.'

Stirling concludes his letter by mentioning a rumour that he is to be superceded. If true, 'I will retire without expressing a murmur. Should even Sir Home Popham succeed me, I will shew him my ideas of obedience. I will not throw one obstacle in his way, I will not say one word to hurt his feelings, or to interfere with the public business.' And if, conversely, Popham is to serve under him, he will comply without complaint.

For all the urgency of his pleading, Popham stayed on, hoping for letters, for a reprieve, to be sent on some 'other service'; hoping Stirling would relent and send him home in a man-of-war. But Stirling's patience has finally snapped. His replies become increasingly terse; and even when Popham finally elects to take passage in an American brig, the *Rolla*, as 'a private gentleman', Stirling is still not convinced that he is at last to be rid of him. Nor was he, quite. Just before Christmas, Popham asks him for four men from *Diadem*, his coxwain, signalman and two others, to sail with him in the *Rolla*. To which Stirling replied: 'I would with great pleasure direct four men to be sent to the *Rolla* for your personal convenience, if I was assured that you would actually proceed for England ...' It was their last exchange. On 27 December he was at last able to write to Marsden, '...The Commodore embarked on board the *Rolla*, and sailed last night without making any further application for men.'

Now, perhaps, he might be able to get on with the war.

NOTES ON CHAPTER XIV

1. Admiral Willaumez's squadron had, in fact, suffered gale damage and taken refuge in San Salvador before returning to France with many of the crew sick. Vice-Admiral

Sir John Duckworth destroyed Leiseignuis' five sail-of-the-line off Santo Domingo in a brisk action in February; and Linois was dealt with by Rear Admiral Sir Borlase Warren in the Indian Ocean.

2. Home Popham to William Marsden: 13 April 1806, enclosing Waine's letter. ADM1/58.

3. Lieut-General Sir David Baird, 1757-1829—'his figure was tall and symetrical,' according to Theodore Hook, his biographer, 'his countenance cheerful and animated'—had had an unusual career. In India he had been captured by Hyder Ali, father of the notorious Tipoo, at the grim battle of Perambaukam in 1780, and spent 3½ years in gaol in Seringapatam, most of the time in irons. After his release, he was twice passed over—to his disgust—in favour of Arthur Wellesley, but was given command of the expedition to Egypt in 1801, in which Wellesley would have served under him, if the latter had not fallen ill in Bombay with the 'Malabar Itch'. He and Home Popham first met in Jidda in May 1801 and hit it off from the start. Although Wilkie refers to him as 'a rough diamond', there was both a gentle and a generous side to his nature. Of Wellington, a few years later, he was to say: 'It is the highest pride in my life that anybody should ever have dreamed of my being put in the balance with him'. All three of them were to meet at Copenhagen in 1807. Baird lost an arm at Corunna two years later. For supporting Popham's South American adventure he was recalled, but not court-martialled.

4. General William Carr, Viscount Beresford (1768-1854). After the reconquest of Buenos Ayres, he and Col. Denis Pack escaped and joined the British forces then at Monte Video. Beresford went on to capture Madeira on behalf of Prince John of Portugal in December 1807, and later served with Wellington—who described him as 'the ablest man in the Army'—in the Peninsula, training the Portuguese Army. Creevey said of him that he was 'a low-looking ruffian with damned bad manners'. His portrait, by Sir Thomas Lawrence, is in Apsley House.

5. In a paper in the Royal Archives (RA Geo Mss 12/94-5) which summarises Popham's arguments, it is stated: 'Sir Home Popham seems to have acted according to his own discretion, but not from any momentary impulse as it is evident that he had this object in constant view from the moment of his sailing for the Cape.' And the writer suggests that he may have had a secret agreement with Miranda not to start the Buenos Ayres operation before April.

6. The Patriotic Fund had been established in 1803 at Lloyd's Coffee House, with the twin objects of helping the wounded and those bereaved by the war, and acknowledging outstanding military service.

7. The viper-tongued Lady Holland reported in her Journal (Vol. II): 'An instance of the money-getting spirit of Sir Home came to my knowledge recently. He wrote to the merchants of Manchester advising the exportation of certain goods, but to his own agent he bid him send him, upon speculation, a large quantity of silk stockings, with a hint that this order should not transpire. B. Frere assured me he was acquainted with the silk-stocking merchant who supplied the articles.'

8. Charles James Fox (1749-1806). His death, as the Whigs' 'one great man', was a blow to the Ministry of The Talents. Incompetent at either diplomacy or war, their uncertain touch undoubtedly increased Popham's problems: he could not have chosen a worse time for his venture.

9. Rear-Admiral Sir William Sidney Smith (1764-1840). His career included halting Bonaparte at Acre, secret service work, and (their only point of contact) involvement with Robert Fulton.

10. Liniers y Bremond, Santiago de (1753-1810). In June 1807 he had published a broadsheet

challenging *'las enormes falsedades y abultadas ficciones'* in Popham's despatches to the Admiralty (BL1565/178) After defeating Beresford and then Whitelock, he became Viceroy; but in 1809, having become identified with the Creole population, was deposed by the Spanish and executed.

11. Charles Grey (Lord Howick and 2nd Earl Grey) replaced Lord Barham as First Lord of the Admiralty in January 1806. Known for spending more time on his country estate than attending to government business. During a debate in the House of Commons on 21 December 1806, he spoke as follows: 'As to Sir Home Popham and Sir David Baird, I freely confess that I was one of those who advised their recall, and upon the ground that they did without orders, and upon their own judgement and responsibility undertake the expedition to South America. They did not leave a ship of the line at the Cape, and they diverted to their expedition a frigate bound for India with pay for the troops. Such conduct as this I consider highly reprehensible and a subversion of all discipline and good government.' Popham's 'circular letter to manufacturing towns' came in for special censure: 'What his motives for such conduct were I cannot say. Perhaps he wished to court some favour and protection against the censure which he must be conscious of deserving from government...'

That disapprobation was duly enshrined in a letter from the Admiralty of 25 September 1806; but the same letter went on: '... they [Their Lordships] are nevertheless pleased to express their entire approbation of the judicious, able and spirited conduct manifested by yourself, the officers, seaman and Marines ...' (Marsden to HP: ADM1/5378)

The truth was that Popham's enterprise had thrown government and country—particularly the mercantile community—into confusion. Although officially the government were compelled to come down hard on him, they could not afford to ingore the commercial opportunities which he had opened up. Wild schemes were launched for the conquest of Mexico and Chile—though on the news that Buenos Ayres had been recaptured by the Spaniards, the expeditions were all diverted to Rio de la Plata; and by the New year of 1807 there were more than thirty British merchant ships anchored in the river. But, as Fletcher Wilkie put it: 'The well-known commercial letter from the Commodore... that set every broken-down clerk and supercargo on the *qui vive*, emptied all the stores in Manchester and Liverpool, and sent us out as much long cloths, printed calicoes and sheetings, as would have reached across the Pampas to St. Jago— which all arrived a day after the fair.'

12. Impossible to verify, but conceivable. Certainly Barham, the architect of Trafalgar, was amiably disposed towards Popham. In a letter of 9 May 1806 he had written, with reference to Buenos Ayres: 'If I had continued in the Administration. I should have been disposed to have given full credit to your intentions ... it is said that Sir David Baird as well as yourself will be recalled, I trust however that you will succeed in your attempt before that happens.' Barham, though, was not called as a witness in the action between Home Popham and Capt. Ross Donnelly—which hinged on the former's exact status as a Commodore—in June 1807.

13. This bizarre correspondence can be found in full in the PRO in ADM1/58.

CHAPTER XV

'Whereas it is our intention... whereas we think proper'

1

THE *ROLLA* brig with Home Popham, his secretary Mr Hadden, and Captain King on board, reached Weymouth on Monday, 16 February 1807, fifty-three days from the Rio de la Plata. It was, said *The Times*, one of the quickest passages ever known. Popham immediately set off for 'his seat near Windsor'. He was home the following day – and what a tale he had to tell Elizabeth and the children! He had been away for eighteen months or more, and had touched extremes of both elation and despair.

Elizabeth, vicariously, had shared both. In one of the only two letters of hers that appear to have survived,[1] she wrote to Lord Melville in September 1806, '... in this sensation I experience a double gratification by the *receipt of a packet from Sir Home last night**... I confess the arrival of my letters last night and glorious termination of your Lordship's persecution, which reached me at the same time, excited such sensations as my feeble pen cannot describe.'[2]

The elation, of course, had already evaporated, and their reunion was brief. Her husband was faced with the most serious crisis of his career, and the following day he was in London. On that day their Lordships issued a warrant to John Cricket, Esq, Marshall of the High Court of Admiralty, for his arrest. 'Whereas it is our intention that Captain Sir Home Popham shall be tried by Court Martial ...; and whereas we think proper that you should take the said Sir Home Popham into your custody; but as it is not our intention that he should be put under greater inconvenience or confinement than is absolutely necessary, you are to take his honour for his appearance at the Court Martial...' The warrant was duly served and Popham arrested – in form if not in substance – on the 20th. Because he was still an MP, the House was duly informed. Trial was fixed for the 6 March on board HMS *Gladiator* in Portsmouth, so he had just over two weeks to put his defence in order.

He was to say at his trial that he had had no intimation that he was to be court-martialled until he reached England; but it is clear from his letters to Charles Stirling that he was well aware that he was going to have to justify his actions, if not in court at least before the Lords Commissioners. The eight weeks at sea in *Rolla*, though we have no record of his preoccupations, were unlikely to have been spent exclusively in admiring the view from the quarterdeck.

Now he set about drawing on those unfailing reserves of eloquence, that

* The words are underlined in her letter.

matchless power of self-exculpation, which Gillespie noted with irony and Tucker with bile; and when at 8.30 am on 6 March, the first gun was fired from *Gladiator* and the signal for a court martial was hoisted, and when, half an hour later, at the firing of the second gun, the members of the court went on board, the prisoner was ready—well, nearly ready—for the ordeal.³

2

Portsmouth was crowded, 'and much anxiety appears in the countenances and expressions of the numerous characters who have been awaiting the event of this most important trial', as *The Courier* reported leadenly. Home Popham himself arrived, with John Cricket carrying his sword, in his own barge, accompanied by Harrison, his counsel, Lawes his agent, and several friends. 'Sir Home Popham', *The Courier* continued—with a bit more verve—'appeared in perfect spirits; and as he came on deck, walked with his usual steady and undaunted air.' The Marine guard, which had presented arms for the members of the court, did not do so for him.

The President was William Young, Admiral of the Blue—that same 'pavement admiral' who had apologised to Popham for the state of *Antelope* three years before. Sitting with him were four Vice-Admirals: Gower, Holloway, Rowley and Stanhope; two Rear-Admirals: Vashon and Sir Richard Strachan; and five Captains: Graves, Scott, Linzee, Irwin and Boyle. The Judge Advocate was Moses Greatham, Esq., and the prosecution was conducted by a Mr Jervis. The occasion was one of considerable solemnity, for without any question what was at stake was the accused's reputation, and his future career in the Service.

As soon as the court was in session, the Admiralty order for which it had been summoned was read out. Essentially there were two charges: first that Popham had left the Cape in a defenceless state; secondly, that he had undertaken an expedition to the Rio de la Plata 'for which he had no direction or authority whatever.' 'And whereas it appears to us,' the indictment continued, 'that a due regard to the good of His Majesty's Service imperiously demands that so flagrant a breach of public duty should not go unpunished.' The court, then, was not called upon to decide whether Popham was guilty or innocent (his guilt was given) but to decide merely on his punishment—a point which he was quick to establish in his usual forceful terms.

The court was then sworn, and the various letters and instructions supporting the charges were read out. (They are already familiar from the two preceding chapters and there is no reason to repeat them.) However, Popham immediately asked for a postponement on the grounds that there were some that he had had no opportunity to study. This was refuted, but his request was granted then, and again next morning. So it was really not until 9am on Monday, 9 March that the trial finally got under way. Although reporters were allowed to be present, they were required to give up their notes at the end of each day, and give their word that nothing would appear in their newspapers until the trial was over. One refused, and was 'instantly ordered on shore'.[4]

3

It got under way with Popham's speech in his defence. As this ran to some 18,000 words and occupies more than 50 pages in the printed version—and deals with matters with which we, and indeed the Court, are and were familiar—it is only necessary to summarise the nub of his arguments. His opening remarks were characteristically combative. He had, he said, 'been brought before you upon a charge as extraordinary in its nature and unprecedented in the form and mode in which it is preferred as perhaps was ever submitted to the investigation of a Court Martial.'

This is good Home Popham rhetoric, containing—as ever—a proportion of truth within the inflated language. The truth was that he was presumed to be guilty: whether it was 'unprecedented' is open to question.[5] 'I am sent before you', he concluded his introduction, 'to receive not justice but punishment'.

After this opening broadside, he proceeded to a detailed justification of his actions. This was founded upon a number of points, some more convincing than others. To begin with, he maintained, since he had had no positive orders for the squadron's movements following the capture of the Cape, he could not have acted 'contrary to orders'. This was dangerous ground, for both he and Baird had had clear orders to send the troops on to India or, as amended, back to England. Not only did he admit this tacitly later in his defence, but during a debate in the House of Commons the previous December, Howick, the First Lord, accused them of having 'diverted to their expedition a frigate bound for India with pay for the troops'.

But what about acting *without* orders? There had been any number of well known instances of expedition commanders doing so, and with impunity. Admiral Rooke captured Gibraltar without orders; St Vincent sent Nelson off to capture Tenerife without orders (and it had been a failure); Admiral Hood had taken Toulon without orders, and subsequently lost it.[6] His own former captain Ned Thompson, Popham argued, had contravened his orders to remain in the West Indies by submitting to the pleas of the Barbados planters and escorting a convoy back to England. He had in fact been courtmartialled, but was honourably acquitted.

A commander on a distant station, he continued, must be allowed some discretion; and his conduct 'must in such cases be tried by the actual circumstances in which he was placed at the time, not by subsequent events or facts.' On his own past record—'his humble rank and limited services' as he put it—he should be trusted to make sound judgements in such circumstances. The argument was valid enough: captains and Flag officers were frequently having to act on their own initiative—and could expect to be courtmartialled if they did not. The question was whether it could be extended to justify this particular exercise.

Popham next went on to describe in some detail the background: the conversations with Miranda, Pitt and Melville; his own long paper on the subject; the political problem of Spain's allegiance to France, and England's hopes of breaking it. As this had still been a possibility in 1803/4, any such enterprises had been put in abeyance. In the meantime, he himself had heard that the Cape was only lightly held and restless under Dutch rule, and had suggested it as a possible objective. 'I sailed from England under the strongest conviction that I should, at some future period ... receive orders to strike a blow in South America.'

In February 1806, with the Cape Colony safely captured, he had heard not only that hostilities in India were over, so that the troops destined to go there* were no longer needed; but also that with Napoleon victorious in Europe, Spain was still under French hegemony and still technically at war with Britain.[7] In these circumstances, South America looked like a 'counter-balance'.

Popham turned next to the charge that he had left the Cape in a defenceless state. This was a tricky one, because after the squadron had left a French frigate *La Cannonière* had sailed into Table Bay, anchored, and sent a boat ashore. The boat and her crew were taken and the shore batteries opened up on the frigate. She was out of range, but weighed anchor in some haste and departed leaving her boat's crew behind. Fletcher Wilkie, who was still at the Cape, makes considerable play with this incident at Home Popham's expense: referring to the court-martial (his account was not published until thirty years later) he wrote: 'Sir Home boldly said, that ships of war would have been no use, and could not have gone out of Simond's Bay [with a leading wind]. He brought one of his petty officers [in fact, Thomas Browne, the Master Attendant at the Cape] forward, who spoke very learnedly about rock so-and-so on the starboard hand, and rock the other on the larboard; and made it quite evident to the court that it was impossible for a frigate to get out of Simond's Bay unless she had a contrary wind.'

The interrogation of Thomas Browne came later and was mainly concerned with the wind direction at various hours of the day; but it was all a bit academic in view of the fact the *La Cannonière* had in fact sailed in and sailed out again, and if she could do it presumably other ships could have done it too.

Popham was in rather smoother water when it came to the danger of a French squadron turning up, since none had; and as to leaving the Cape impetuously, that had been dictated by what he knew of weather conditions off the coast of South America and the state of the Rio de la Plata, later in the year.

But if, he went on, the Admiralty regarded the Cape as so important, was it not odd that the receipt of his despatches announcing its capture was acknowledged only in 'cold terms', whereas General Baird had been commended, and even Captain Donnelly had been warmly congratulated for 'the destruction of an insignificant French frigate' (this was less than fair to Ross Donnelly). Popham was conveniently ignoring the fact that the Admiralty had already expressed their extreme displeasure at his actions after hoisting his flag as Commodore; though, as he rightly said.

* So Popham and Baird *did* have orders!

after the capture of Buenos Ayres—for which he was being tried—he *was* congratulated, even if he had gone, as he neatly put it, 'beyond the exact limits of unrestricted instructions'.

Popham then touched on the subject of his supercession. 'I was left to take my passage to England in a small prize brig'—and that was punishment enough, surely? If any members of the court had read Stirling's letters to Marsden recounting the struggles of the last month in the Plate, they must have chuckled to themselves.

The government, he continued, had thought fit to send 3,000 men under Auchmuty as reinforcements: clear evidence that they approved of the idea of obtaining a foothold in South America. He had been able to wish Stirling every success 'because the more brilliant your [his] success is, the more it must bring to the recollection of my country the sound principles upon which I presumed to act.'

It was a variation on the standard Home Popham dialectic of *ex-post facto* justification, as well as scouting round the fact that by exciting the appetites of the mercantile community he had made it difficult for the government *not* to send reinforcements.

Next he dealt with the imputations that he had been actuated by 'sordid, instead of honourable, motives'. To refute them, he had only to mention the 180 vessels captured in the Plate and returned to their owners without penalty; the three million dollars of 'quicksilver and bark in small and very convenient packages' which he did not remove; and the 20-gun vessel *Neptune* which he had recommended should be *presented* to the government.

Advisedly, he did not mention the prize money, which alone might have been considered inducement enough; he had, after all, specifically mentioned the possibility of good pickings to Robert Fernyhough before they left Cape Town.

Nearing the end of his defence now, he returned to the question of a commander's discretion, and the importance of being allowed it, 'because an officer will be deterred by the reflection, that for venturing to attack or annoy the enemies of his country without positive instructions, his conduct may be prejudged by a superior authority at home, and ... be stigmatised "as a flagrant breach of public duty that should not go unpunished".'

He rounded off what was unquestionably a masterly performance with a summary of his actions, and the motives behind them. 'I consider myself as an humble individual, standing before you on a charge deeply affecting my character, but more deeply affecting the future interest of the Navy.' And he asked for an 'honourable acquittal'.

4

The rest of the third and the whole of the fourth day were wholly taken up with the interrogation of witnesses. Because he had not had adequate warning of the court-martial, Popham said, he had been unable to summon all the witnesses he would have liked. Nevertheless, he had secured several, first and most important, Henry Dundas, First Lord Melville, the former Minister for War and First Lord, and Popham's steady patron for a decade. Melville confirmed Popham's statements about the various meetings with Miranda in the autumn of 1804 and the plans for a South American adventure, aimed probably at Trinidad, remarking in a letter to Popham that December that 'he [Miranda] is not more importunate with you than he is with me'. He also agreed that *Diadem*'s original destination had indeed been South America.

At that point Admiral Young intervened. 'Was Sir Home Popham', he asked, 'appointed by your Lordship to any command authorising him to attack any part of South America?'

'Certainly not,' Melville replied, 'in the proper sense of those words.' Though he was prepared to agree that he had always considered Buenos Ayres 'the most important position for the interest of Great Britain upon that side of South America.'

This was as close as Popham was to get to establishing his authority to attack the River Plate. Such an expedition, somewhere, had been mooted, discussed, even planned:—but it had never actually been authorised; and when Miranda did finally land in Venezuela in 1806, he had only had, as Lord Grenville put it, the 'complicity' of the British government (and subsequently, the unauthorised help of Admiral Cochrane, for which he was reprimanded).

The other witnesses whom Popham called by and large confirmed his various contentions, which was after all why he had called them. William Sturges Bourne, one of the Treasury secretaries, testified that Popham had indeed suggested the expedition to Cape Colony; and William Huskisson in his wordy and circumlocutory way, was prepared to admit that 'A step was taken with a view to prepare and facilitate the execution of any attempt which might be made on Buenos Ayres, to which by their signature the Lords of the Admiralty were accessory ...' But he did not say what the 'step' actually was: obviously it fell far short of being an instruction to go ahead.

That concluded the third day's proceedings. When the court assembled once more on Thursday morning, Popham called William Marsden, who added nothing of consequence; and Thomas Wilson, the London merchant whom Popham had quoted before he left Cape Colony. He agreed now that, in conversation with Popham in June 1805, he had suggested 'the great consequence the trade of that country [South America] would be to this country.' After him came Thomas Browne, whose evidence regarding the winds in Table Bay has already been mentioned. He staunchly supported Home Popham's arguments, which was the important thing.

The last witness for the defence, and the most forthright, was King, the lieutenant whom Popham had promoted to post captain after the squadron had left Madeira. Much of his evidence again concerned the security of the colony in the squadron's absence, a situation with which Baird had been completely satisfied. This was because the captured brig *Rolla* (which later brought Popham home from the Plate) had had on board French mail, including a letter from Admiral Linois to Governor Jansens saying that he intended to visit Cape Town in the course of his intended search for two homeward bound Indiamen. It was this letter which had put the squadron on the alert in February and March; and when the French ships failed to appear, and then *La Volontaire* was captured in early March with half her crew down with scurvy, and supporting evidence that another French squadron—that of Admiral Willaumez—had abandoned her South Atlantic cruise, Home Popham felt it was safe to leave, and Baird had agreed.

King's crisp, straightforward evidence more than balanced the unfortunate escape of *La Cannonière*. Admiral Young's final question to him was: 'You have said, you did not hear of any capture being made by the enemy, in the vicinity of the Cape, after the sailing of Sir Home Popham, and his squadron?' To which King agreed.

'After some few more questions and observations,' the published account continues, 'at six o'clock the Court adjourned until nine o'clock tomorrow morning.'

5

Next day, the fifth and last of the trial, Popham was asked if he wished to call any more witnesses. He mentioned three whom he had intended to call, 'but they chiefly go to corroborate the evidence of Captain King, I do not therefore now mean to call them; but that it may not go abroad that I had no witnesses to support me, I beg that their names may be entered upon the minutes...' This was allowed; but various additional papers 'respecting the proceedings in Buenos Ayres' were ruled to be wholly irrelevant. The President added that 'any reflection which may have been made in the House of Commons, or elsewhere, upon your conduct, can have no influence whatever upon our minds.'

Home Popham still had a couple of shots left in his locker. The first was a somewhat tepid testimonial from Lord Howick to the effect that 'the greatest confidence had been placed in [him] by the Emperor of Russia'—who, incidentally, had been assassinated six years before. The second was Popham's closing speech, and it deserves quoting. Having 'thrown himself entirely upon the justice and wisdom of the court', he went on:

> I have suffered much in my feelings and character; but I do trust and hope your judgment will relieve the one and rescue the other. If, in my zeal for the service I have exceeded the limits of due discretion, I trust it will appear, that I was solely actuated by an anxious desire to promote the interests, the honor, and the glory of my country. Aided by my brave followers, and under the protection of Divine Providence, I was put into the possession of two capital cities, in two different quarters of the globe. Upon a close examination of my defence, I trust it will be found that the very head and front of my offending, hath this extent, no more.. I retire, trusting in your wisdom and justice, for my honourable acquittal.

It was 11 o'clock on Wednesday, 11 March. Popham and his friends withdrew, the court was cleared, and the members retired to begin their deliberations. They took four hours to reach their verdict. Home Popham was recalled and took his place at the foot of the table, 'the Members being covered', and the Judge Advocate read out the sentence.

Briefly, Sir Home Popham was found guilty on both counts, and for these his conduct was considered to be 'highly censurable'; '... but', he continued, 'in consideration of circumstances, the Court doth adjudge him to be only SEVERELY REPRIMANDED... And he is accordingly hereby severely reprimanded.'

There was one last, small, significant ceremony to be performed. 'The Provost Marshall then proceeded to the President, and presented the sword of Sir Home Popham to him, when he was ordered to return it. The Provost Marshall returned to the bottom of the table, and with a respectful salutation, returned the sword to Sir Home Popham, and the Court was dissolved.'

6

The Trial of Sir Home Popham was a cause célèbre, there is no doubt about that. It was reported at length—once it was over—and to the populace at large the result was taken to be, in effect, an acquittal. As such, it was extremely popular.

> Upon Sir Home Popham getting out of the ship and into the boat [*The Courier* reported] he was cheered by acclamation from a vast number of boats, which waited the issue of the trial, and also an immense multitude assembled upon the beach. As soon as Sir Home had landed the acclamation was repeated, and the horses were taken from his carriage that waited to convey him to his lodgings; which Sir Home perceiving, he declined to enter the carriage, and, after thanking the people for their attention, exhorted them to disperse... But the people continued to follow him until he reached the house of Captain Madden, expressing as they went along the strongest interest in his fate...

So much so that they 'immediately set the bells ringing in compliment to him; in fact the town is filled with a mixture of sorrow and joy.' And the same account noted that 'Sir Home seemed to feel his spirits renewed by their enthusiasm; he smiled and frequently pulled off his hat, and, as it were, instinctively waved it in the air when the people cheered him.' They had not forgotten that only six months before the *Narcissus* had arrived from the Plate, and the 'specie' had been drawn through the town by thirty sailors with the Marine Band playing martial tunes.

Beyond the borders of Portsmouth, however, opinion was by no means unanimous. *The Times* orated 'that the expedition was undertaken, not only without orders, but rashly, inconsiderately, and with every probability of injury to the public service'; and that it was rash and ill-judged. It summed up by saying: 'The whole result of the expedition appears to be, that the officers who planned it have made their private fortunes by it, that the troops they carried thither are all prisoners of war, and that we now have a much more difficult task to perform in South America than we had previous to this short-lived capture.'

The *Morning Post*, by contrast, considered that it was not a court-martial offence and was only treated as one out of vindictiveness, part of 'the marked hostility towards Sir Home Popham by a part of the present Administration before they came into office... It is obvious that his merits have been undervalued, and that his offences may have been enforced beyond what can be reconciled with liberal policy.' The result was far from disgracing him.

In the course of a long leader, the writer turned round a quotation from *Tristram Shandy*: 'Your honour knows I had no orders,' said Corporal Trim. 'True,' said my Uncle Toby, 'you acted very properly as a soldier, but very badly as a man,' and concluded that, though Home Popham may have acted improperly as a soldier, 'no person of honest principles can, for a moment, doubt his having acted properly as a man.'

For the most part, the other papers tended to agree and the City of London, seeing the expedition as a brave attempt to open up new markets, went so far as to present him with a sword of honour. Only *The Times* remained implacable. A week after the trial was over, Popham, his solicitor and Captain King went to pay their respects to 'The Merchants and Underwriters of Lloyd's Coffee House', who had voted, six months before, to present Popham and Beresford with 'vases of £200 each' out of the Patriotic Fund. They were warmly welcomed in the Subscription Room, which was 'unusually crowded'. *The Times* produced, not a straight report of the event—at which Home Popham made a brief speech which was received with three cheers and loud acclamation—but a savage satire. Taking as its refrain the catch-line 'Maldonado is safe', it raked over all the old scandals in the guise of a spoof speech by Popham himself: his absence from any battles ('the blood I have lost, the wounds I have received...'); the Romney affair ('my feats in the Red Sea... display a peculiar nicety of making out bills, and swelling accounts, for the good of the naval service'); Ostend (... what was the consequence of that expedition? 'Tis well-known, we knocked down a sluice and lost half the army'). 'At Buenos Ayres, however, it was contrived with no common management, to take the town, ship off the dollars, and lose *all* the army. But... Maldonado is safe.' This amiable exercise in character assassination concludes:
'If I should be raised to the peerage on account of my future prowess, for my professional skill, for my adherence to discipline, and my commercial zeal, I wish to be granted the title "Baron Maldonado".'
'The Committee were mute with wonder, and the hero retired to mingle with the unconscious crowd in the street below.'

Except that it was rather too witty, it could have been written by Benjamin Tucker.

Meanwhile, and unknown to Home Popham or anybody else in England, General Auchmuty had been busy. On 3 February he had captured Monte Video after a seige lasting a fortnight; and on the same day as the court-martial started he wrote to the War Office to tell them of the arrival of Beresford and Colonel Pack after their escape, and the information which they had brought with them.[8] This was to the effect that the Spanish authorities were at odds with the local population: the former determined to maintain Spanish suzerainty, the latter determined to get rid of it. It may have been news to Auchmuty, but Popham had recognised it months before. In any case the responsibility would not be his for very much longer, for on 24 February Lt-General John Whitelocke was appointed as his successor, with orders for 'the reduction of the Spanish settlements at Buenos Ayres. 'How the Devil such a man as this could have been appointed to such a command,' General Lord Paget wrote, 'has been the subject of amazement to the whole Army, for, independent of his manners which are coarse and brutal to the most insupportable degree, he is notoriously known to have the greatest antipathy to the smell of gunpowder.' Within six months he had fully justified this dubious military reputation.

Henry Brougham may have considered that Sir Home Popham should have been shot, rather than reprimanded, for his part in this unfortunate enterprise; and the historian of the Army Sir J. W. Fortescue, declared roundly that the verdict of the court was 'utterly wrong, he should have been dismissed the Navy.' The Lords Commissioners of the Admiralty thought differently. Less than four weeks later, the following announcement appeared: 'The Lords of the Admiralty have appointed Sir Home Popham to the command of a small squadron to cruise off the Continent, in the Rivers, etc with a Roving Commission.'

'Baron Maldonado' was too valuable to be thus drummed out of the Navy.

NOTES ON CHAPTER XV

1. The two letters from Lady Popham, both to Lord Melville, are among the Melville Papers in the William L. Clements Library.

2. Melville's impeachment, on a trumped-up charge of misappropriation of funds, by the Naval Paymaster ten years earlier, was initiated by a vote of censure in the House of Commons in April 1805. He was exonerated in September 1806, just as the news of the capture of Buenos Ayres reached England.

3. At least two verbatim versions of the court-martial were rushed out in the summer. The fuller of the two (British Library, G19449) has a fulsome preface by an anonymous admirer of Popham, and an Appendix which includes a number of the letters quoted during the trial. This is the copy with notes by 'B. T. Esq., Late Secretary to the Admiralty', i.e. Benjamin Tucker. They are not flattering. The other edition is BL 1132.d.31

4. Reporting restrictions were normal in court-martials.

5. As to Home Popham's claim that the wording was 'unprecedented', it was certainly unusual. The normal form of words was 'to hear and examine', 'to inquire into', 'to examine', 'to enquire into the Conduct and Proceedings of...'; and 'to try him for the same'. No instance has been found in which this form of words *followed* the accusation that the officer concerned was guilty, which was the case with Home Popham. It is worth noting that the court's verdict, in his trial, included the statement that he had

been found guilty of the charges.

6. Admiral Sir George Rooke captured Gibraltar in 1704; Toulon surrendered to Lord Hood in 1793; Nelson's forlorn assault on Tenerife took place in July 1797, and cost him his right arm.

7. Spain had formally declared war on Britain in December 1804, and remained unhappily under French occupation until the Battle of Vittoria in 1813.

8. Beresford was still in South America. He and Col. Pack had 'absconded' from captivity up-country and reached Monte Video at the end of February.

CHAPTER XVI

Return to
the Continent
1807-9

1

HOME POPHAM'S problems dwindle almost to vanishing point when seen in the context of the war as it stood in 1807; and in order to understand what he was involved in that summer, it is necessary to glance briefly at events in Europe. Napoleon's ambitions, after the disaster of Trafalgar and the consequent loss of his command of the sea, grew if anything more grandiose and ruthless. In October 1806 he had knocked out the Prussians at the Battle of Jena; in November he had issued the Berlin Decrees, imposing a total blockade on England; then he turned eastwards. Defeated, for the first time, in a gory battle with the Russians at Preuss Eylau—which turned both Russia and Prussia once again towards England, he responded by conscripting another 300,000 of his long-suffering countrymen, marched east again in the spring of 1807, and annihilated the Russians at the battle of Friedland in June.

This defeat quenched Russian hopes of a new alliance against him, and two weeks afterwards Tsar Alexander signed the Treaty of Tilsit, which formally allied his country with France. Once more, it seemed, the Baltic was to be closed to British ships and naval stores, and the powerful Danish fleet—eighteen ships-of-the-line, fifteen frigates and thirty other vessels—was going to be forcibly at Napoleon's disposal. For Britain the situation was one of considerable danger.

On a quite different issue, that of limited emancipation for the Irish Catholics, the Ministry of All the Talents had been dismissed by the King at the end of March, to be replaced by the Tories—'All Mr Pitt's friends without Pitt'—under the elderly Duke of Portland. On the Irish question they did, and wished to do, nothing: but on the threat in the Baltic they acted with a speed and resolution almost equal to that of their arch-enemy. The Danes were 'invited' to hand over their fleet to Britain for safe-keeping; and in the likely event of their refusing to do so, Admiral Gambier was ordered to sail with seventeen ships-of-the-line, seven frigates, and sixteen sloops and gun-brigs, and transports carrying 18,000 troops, with all expedition to the Kattegat. The ultimatum was rejected; and on 26 July the fleet left Yarmouth Roads.

The man appointed First Captain, or Captain of the Fleet, in Gambier's flagship *Prince of Wales* was Sir Home Popham; and Gambier's orders stated firmly 'that the orders of Sir Home Popham... issued under my direction, are to have the same force as if issued by myself.'

2

The immediate result was a vehement protest within the Service. On the very day Gambier issued his orders, three of his captains, Samuel Hood, Richard Keats and Robert Stopford, wrote to him expressing 'the extreme sorrow and concern with which as senior captains in the Navy we are penetrated in seeing ourselves placed in situations which in any degree subject us to an inferiority to Captain Sir Home Popham'. Admiral Sir C. Pole, writing to Captain Byam Martin who had been removed from the *Prince of Wales* to make way for Popham referred to the disgust of the Service at this 'injudicious and disgraceful appointment', and went on, 'I fear Gambier hath been the dupe on this occasion, and instead of proposing a first captain, the Duke of York or some other person of this description hath named Sir Home Popham'. It was not merely his lack of seniority which they objected to, he said, but his character.

In view of the fact that the three captains had nineteen, eighteen and seventeen years' seniority respectively as against Popham's twelve, and all had fine records, their indignation would have had some justification under any circumstances: being made subject to a more junior captain who had, only four months before, been court-martialled and severely reprimanded—'hitherto found a bar almost insuperable to advancement in the navy'[1]—and who had never commanded a ship in action, was intolerable.

On all these counts they had a case. But so had the 'Duke of York or some other person of this description' for appointing him. The operation on which the fleet was bound was not a naval battle—most of the Danish ships were 'in ordinary', i.e. laid up—but an amphibious assault on the the island of Zealand and the Danish capital; and if there was one branch of warfare in which Popham was the acknowledged expert, it was combined operations.[2] The appointment was certainly tactless, 'a serious administrative blunder' one naval historian calls it, but those who made it had valid reasons which did not necessarily involve favouritism.

In any case the captains' protest came too late, and being the good naval officers that they were, they suppressed their indignation and the expedition went ahead as planned. In the event, while Popham remained a captain, if the senior one, both Hood and Keats had command of independent squadrons throughout the operation, and were addressed by Gambier as 'Commodore'.

3

The operation lasted a bare six weeks, was entirely successful, and does not merit more than a cursory description here. Once into the Kattegat, the fleet divided. Keats, with four sail-of-the-line, three frigates and ten smaller vessels, fiddled his way through the shoals and currents of the Great Belt on the west side of Zealand in order to cut the island off from the Danish mainland, and thus the chance of its receiving reinforcements. At the same time Popham took the transports through the Ore Sound on the east side, ready to put the troops ashore at Vedboeck, twelve miles north of Copenhagen. A fresh demand that the Danes should surrender their fleet and join an alliance with Britain was rejected by the francophile Crown Prince; and on 16 August the first British troops, under the overall command of Lord Cathcart, were put ashore unopposed, and covered by the guns of the fleet. Within a couple of weeks the British under Major-General Sir Arthur Wellesley had defeated the defenders—mostly militia 'weak in body and muddled in mind... and inclined to down arms when fired at'—at Kjoge, and invested Copenhagen. The most persistent opposition came from a squadron of praams and gunboats, for which the British gunboats were no match; but they were eventually silenced by the batteries which the invaders established ashore. Thereafter, it was only a matter of time.

There are only glimpses of the Captain of the Fleet during this period; but with all the coming and going of craft of every kind from ship to ship and from ship to shore, he was undoubtedly kept busy. Several times Gambier sent him 'to communicate my sentiments to his Lordship [Cathcart] in regard to the co-operation of the naval force'; and his hand is clear in the drafting of the cipher for the use of the commanders. In his final Dispatch Gambier wrote, 'I feel it my duty to make a peculiar acknowledgement of the aid I have derived from Sir Home Popham, Captain of the Fleet, whose prompt resources, and complete knowledge of his profession, especially of that branch which is connected with the operations of an army, qualify him in a particular manner for the arduous and various duties with which he has been charged.' And Popham said, rather smugly, in a letter to Lord Melville, 'I wish you could hear Admiral Gambier's opinion of me now. I think and I am vain enough to think, he would astonish you.'

Certainly this, taken in conjunction with Cathcart's tribute to the 'perfect cordiality' that existed between Army and Navy suggests that Popham's appointment was justified: he was always better liked by soldiers than by his fellow senior officers.[3]

On 1 September the city was called upon to surrender: the governor refused, and the following evening the bombardment began and was carried out with spectacular thoroughness, if only with reluctance. 'Many rockets were thrown,' Gambier wrote, 'and in a short time a considerable fire was seen in the town, and not long after a second fire broke out, and both burnt for many hours. Two thousand shells were fired that night.' And, two days later, a vivid touch: 'About 4 the spire of the largest church took fire and fell'. The bombardment continued off and on for three days, and on the fifth the Governor proposed an armistice for settling the terms of a capitulation. Not only had a great deal of damage been done, the British had cut off virtually all the water supplies to the city of Copenhagen. The ironic truth was that we really had no quarrel with the Danes; all we wanted was to keep their fleet out of French hands.

That evening Gambier noted, 'At 6 I went onshore to consider with Lord Cathcart the terms of capitulation for the city, with which Major-General Sir Arthur Wellesley, Sir Home Popham and Colonel Murray were charged and sent in.' And,

Cathcart added, 'those officers have insisted on proceeding immediately to business. The capitulation was drawn up in the night between the 6th and 7th.'

'It is a proud day for England,' Home Popham wrote to Melville in the letter already quoted, 'to take the fleet of a Naval Power and say I will put [it] in your own dockyard, and, when I have done I will take away all your surplus stores. Such is comprehended in the first of the two Articles of the Capitulation which I wrote (the 3rd and 4th) and on which there was much discussion and I would not cede one iota.' Apart from those two clauses, which summed up the purpose of the operation, the terms were lenient, and included the departure of all British troops as soon as those two had been fulfilled. It was this that angered Canning, the Foreign Secretary: it was what happened when you left these things to the military instead of the politicians.

4

As soon as the terms had been accepted, the work of fitting out the Danish fleet ready for sea was put in hand. In July, just before hostilities began, Captain Bearman of the *Procris* had reconnoitred the dockyards and found the ships 'in the most perfect state of repair and could be at sea within six weeks... and the dockyard itself well supplied with much timber and every kind of stores'. In the event, the first convoy was ready to leave within a fortnight, while Home Popham and his merry men set about stripping the yards. 'The service at the Arsenal continues to be carried on with a degree of zeal and alacrity', Gambier reported, 'that reflected the highest credit on all concerned'—or, as was said in the House of Commons later, 'Sir Home Popham was packing up everything that could be carried away, and collecting every old hammer he could find.'[4] Even vessels on the stocks were dismantled and shipped out, to be reassembled in England. By the time the work was complete the wretched Danes would be lucky if they could build and launch so much as a gig.

The operation had achieved its purpose; but there were a great many people at home who thought that purpose, as Windham put it, no better than 'a war of plunder'. The matter was given a thorough airing early the following year when the Motion for a Vote of Thanks to those concerned, including Home Popham, was put in the House of Lords by Hawkesbury, seconded by Moira, and opposed by Holland and Grey, the last-named observing that 'the object of the expedition to the Baltic was neither of sufficient magnitude, nor attended with sufficient difficulty, to entitle those engaged in it to the thanks of the House.' They got it, nevertheless, and Home Popham duly appeared on 1 February and acknowledged the tribute with a gracious, and mercifully short, speech of thanks.

Necessary it may have been, but for various reasons it left an unpleasant taste. In Popham's case, it comes out in his letter to Melville, which continued:

> This is the fourth [he surely meant the third] capitulation I have made in twenty months in three-quarters of the Globe, has any man in the Kingdom done

so much in such distant quarters, and all I ask of the present Administration and of my country, is to give me a patent Place not less than £1,000 a year, I am sure few dispassionate men could be found would think my request extravagant; but I am so unlucky a dog that I never expect anything to succeed for myself.

There is an echo here of those final, dire days in the River Plate, and a glimpse of the unhealed scars left by his court-martial: the least sympathetic side of his complex and insecure personality. But that letter has an added interest, for he sent it to Elizabeth for forwarding, which she did with a covering letter of her own, one of the few that have survived. For that reason alone it would be worth quoting in full; but it contains deeper tones. It is dated September 18th, from Wimpole Street.[5]

'My Lord',
        I enclose you a letter from Popham, as he heard you had quitted London and did not know where to address you. I hope this fresh instance of his genius and exertions will arouse a little liberality towards him from the present Ministers, I believe you know he planned this expedition, the world must know how material a share he had in the detail and execution of it. He has been deprived of the one flattering circumstance, doubly so to him under every consideration, and another person sent home with the dispatches and himself kept as a slave; nay, my Lord I know facto (?) that it will be difficult to convey to the world, & I just understand that Admiral Stanhope has either written home, or declared that he was so anxious upon publick grounds that Sir Home Popham should be sent to England to explain everything, and that the Admiral after resisting by general argument made use of this expression, 'I have seen so much of the extraordinary talent of Sir H.P. and his readiness on every occasion of difficulty, that if I were to send him home I should consider it an injustice to the country and I never could sleep a wink.' After this, my Lord, have I not a right to ask for my husband to be kept with his family, & not to be in a situation to contend with the Enemies of his country and his Political Enemies any longer. I wish all these circumstances could be conveyed to our good King, I really think he would step out of the common course to do something for a man who has capitulated with three Capitals in Europe, Africa and America. I beg your Lordship's pardon for pressing you so long & I trust you will believe me with great esteem
                            very faithfully yours
                            E M Popham

My best compliments to Lady Melville.

5

For the next year and a half Home Popham was ashore and, as Elizabeth had hoped, was at last able to spend some time with her and the family at Titness Park.[6] With the formation of the Ministry of all the Talents, a coalition in fact, after Pitt's death in 1806, Popham had been elected MP for Shaftesbury; and with the fall of that administration a year later and the return of the Tories under Lord Portland, for Ipswich, a seat he was to hold until 1812. As far as is known, he never went near either of his constituencies.[7]

There are oblique references in several of his letters, especially to Lord Melville, to what the latter calls 'the routine of political intrigue... which has appeared in the most disgusting and mischievous shape', with MPs plotting and angling for office; but no appointments came Popham's way, and his contributions to parliamentary business were largely confined to his own affairs. And, as usual, in Parliament or out of it, the past continued to plague him.

In June 1807, a month before he sailed for Copenhagen, Captain Ross Donnelly, who had taken some useful prizes with the *Narcissus* off the Cape in 1806, brought an action against him claiming that Popham had wrongly taken a Flag officer's share of the prize money as a 'commodore with a captain under him', when in fact he was only a 'ten-shilling commodore' with no such privilege. Donnelly won, and Popham had to pay back £2,000. Less than a year later, and in the very month in which he was being thanked by the House of Commons for his part in the taking of the Danish fleet, a fat dossier of 'Papers Respecting the Ship *L'Etrusco*' was laid before the House.

The origins of this interminable case were described in Chapter IV, and the process of trying to reverse the original decision of the Admiralty Court had dragged on ever since. De Rebeque had eventually succeeded in establishing his claim to one-third of the cargo's value and received just over £12,000; a Cantonese merchant with the pleasing name of Skeykinkwa, who makes his first and only appearance at this point, got £16,000; and Georgi, the 'captain of convenience', a bare £1,035 14s 11d. By 1803 ship and cargo had been sold, the former at the knockdown price of £7,050; and there was £38,953 3s 1d left—'falling far short of the original value of the property', as Popham pointed out. In addition, of course, he had lost freight charges of £27,000.

The crux of the matter was that he had infringed the East India Company's monopoly, and his defence that he had carried on his trading 'with the knowledge, and under the *apparent sanction* of the Servants of the East India Company' carried no weight with the court. This argument of tacit approbation, which he had also used during his court-martial, was subject to the test of success; and in both cases, 'unlucky dog' that he was, he had failed.

Nevertheless—and it is significant that these things tended to happen when his Tory friends were in power—in September 1805 Mark Robinson, now a captain, was awarded £2,450 for 'the general expenses incurred by his obtaining condemnation of the said ship and cargo'; and his victim got whatever was left, less legal expenses. Which is to say that Popham received £10,000 on account that year, a further £8,000 a few months later, and finally, in May 1808, the balance of about £7,000. £25,000, less his legal expenses which must have been formidable, was not a very good return, after fifteen years, on his original investment in the good ship *L'Etrusco* and her cargo of blue china bowls and powdered sugar candy, Souchong Tea and Gum Benjamin.

But even this belated reparation did not pass unchallenged. No sooner were the papers laid before the House than Mr S. Lushington (Yarmouth), raising the question of how the Droits of Admiralty were distributed, launched a savage attack on Home Popham, accusing him of smuggling, and of absconding when a process of Court was served upon him. To this Popham responded characteristically by citing the services which he had carried out for the East India Company, and categorically denied the charges of smuggling. Sheridan, speaking next, and in his usual sardonic style, started smoothly as if he were going to support Popham, and then added, 'but how the Hon. Captain could increase his professional knowledge by landing teas at Dungeness...'–to be smartly checked by Eldon, the Chancellor.

The matter was finally closed by an adroit speech by the Advocate-General in which he justified the grant by admitting that perhaps Home Popham had committed an offence, though 'it was perfectly well known to the Indian Government that he was there, and it was the policy at that time to encourage exportation from India in foreign vessels'. All the same, by trading from Canton without a licence he had broken the law–but was the *captain's property* a fit forfeiture for the Crown to take advantage of? The Advocate-General, by a channel of legal sophistry too subtle for the lay mind to follow, thought that it was not, and that therefore his share should be returned to him. It was a conclusion at last, but Home Popham would never be allowed to forget it.

6

In November 1807 he had been appointed, with Captains Thomas Hurd and Edward Columbine, to the newly formed Admiralty Chart Committee. Their brief was to help Alexander Dalrymple, the Hydrographer (he was the first, and had been appointed ten years earlier) to select the best charts from the thousand which had been published in England for issue to HM ships. Dalrymple had already done a great deal of work on the project, but had published very little, and resented any' interference. He was a proud and obstinate old man with too much to do, for he was also Hydrographer to the East India Company; and when the Chart Committee turned their attention to the organisation and proper function of the Hydrographic Department, relations with him became strained. In February 1808 the Committee submitted their report, and it was, by implication, critical of Dalrymple's effectiveness in his job. But it contained important recommendations. Most importantly, they recognized 'the necessity of establishing a system which may enable the Government to offer to the British Marine, as well commercial as military, a collection of correct charts adapted to the general purposes of navigation in every quarter of the globe'; and suggested the sale of charts to pay for the outlay.

Present opinion of Dalrymple's work during his ten years as Hydrographer varies, but he was a sick man and it is clear that his time was up. Although he was over seventy, however, he refused to resign. 'I will never agree to be superannuated', he said; so he had to be dismissed, and died three weeks later. It was a sad end for a man who, whatever his shortcomings, had done much of the groundwork; and the Chart Committee in their final report were able to set out the guidelines which ensured the future and enduring reputation of the Admiralty Hydrographic Service.

7

On 4 June 1809 Home Popham was summoned to the Admiralty by the First Lord, the Earl of Mulgrave, to give his advice on a planned expedition to Walcheren and the estuary of the River Scheldt. The French had eight sail-of-the-line and a number of frigates and gunboats based in the river, as well as a busy dockyard at Antwerp, and the intention was to go in and destroy both. Popham jotted down his thoughts on the matter, and a week later saw the Earl of Chatham, C-in-C designate of the land forces, and the Secretary for War, Viscount Castlereagh.

In a highly tendentious account of what became known as the Scheldt Expedition, John Barrow, the Second Secretary to the Admiralty at the time, described the birth of the operation in the following words:

> The contriver of this scheme was said to be—as indeed it turned out—Sir Home Popham, who, by his insinuating and plausible address, had prevailed on Lord Castlereagh... to undertake it; and no doubt the more readily, being assured by the projector of the certainty of success: and to Popham, of course, were entrusted the arrangements for the landing and debarkation of the forces...
>
> ...this great naval armament was placed under the command of Sir Richard Strachan, and the military force (to the astonishment of all) under the Earl of Chatham.

Popham was called in partly because of his reputation as a master of combined operations, and partly because he had been briefly in Antwerp during the Flanders campaign fifteen years before. But Barrow was wrong as well as uncharitable: the idea for the expedition came not from Popham but from George Canning, the Foreign Secretary, and was inspired by the need to create a diversion, a 'second front', to help Austria whose army had given Napoleon a bloody nose at the Battle of Aspern-Essling on 22 May. Once involved, however, Popham became—who could doubt it?—a powerful advocate, though with one vital proviso which Barrow does not mention: the expedition must sail before the end of June, or, as he said later, 'we were liable, if we remained behind that time, to have to encounter the greatest of difficulties in Expeditions, the Elements.'[8]

Apart from the importance of not leaving it too late in the season, as at Den Helder ten years earlier, success depended on speed and surprise: speed in securing the Wielingen Channel into the Western Scheldt by silencing the batteries on Walcheren to the north and on Kadzand to the south; surprise in getting ships and men up the river to Antwerp before the French could bring up reinforcements. But, given that the Commander-in-Chief was, as Arthur Bryant remarks, 'notorious, even in the society of 18th century London, for his leisurely ways and epicurean habits', speed was unlikely[9]; and surprise had already been partially compromised by the presence of British frigates reconnoitering off the coast, as well as by intelligence from Napoleon's spies.

'I had frequent communication with Lord Chatham before I left London', Popham said; and John Barrow wrote:

A day or two previous to the fleet getting under way, Sir Home Popham called at the Admiralty, and pledged himself, in the most solemn manner, without hesitation or admission of a doubt, to Wellesley Pole (First Naval Lord) and me, that from his knowledge of the Scheldt, and every part thereof,[10] he was perfectly prepared to conduct the forces up that river to Sandvliet, where the troops would be immediately landed, and would reach Antwerp after a short march...

As it happens, Popham would have done exactly that if there had been any forces to conduct, but that was hardly his fault.

8

Those forces, mustered not by the end of June but a month later, were certainly adequate: nearly 40,000 men, 400 transports, and among over 200 men-of-war, 37 ships of the line—though some of them had had their lower guns removed so that they could carry horses. This impressive display of naval and military might left the Downs, before an equally impressive throng of spectators,[11] on 25 July and bowled across the North Sea with a leading wind. Home Popham was 'Captain of a Private Ship in the fleet' HMS *Venerable*, with special responsibilities for landing the troops and for navigation in the river.[12] Ironically, the Austrians whom the operation was designed to help had been knocked out of the war at the Battle of Wagram five days before the fleet sailed. It was not a good omen.

By the 28th they were off the Dutch coast and the favourable wind had turned into a gale, which meant they were on a lee shore and in deadly danger. Popham shifted into a smaller vessel, the *Sabrina*, and with great skill piloted the armada into the comparative shelter of the Roompot, between North Beveland and Schouwen, where they anchored. (The name translates as 'Creampot', a felicity of which Barrow makes great play.) The whole of that stretch of the coast is encumbered with shoals, and one only has to picture the scene as it might have been painted by, say, Turner[13]—the great lumbering ships plunging under reduced sail off that low-lying, inhospitable coast, struggling for an offing—to realise what a superb feat of navigation and ship-management Popham achieved in shepherding them all to safety. His skill in doing so was readily acknowledged by Sir Richard Strachan in his dispatches. The expedition was saved, but at a cost which was never to be recovered.

Ships and men were on the wrong side of Walcheren, and to reach Flushing, which guarded the northern side of the Wielingen, the troops would have to subdue three garrisons while they marched the dozen miles across the island. Delay in achieving the initial objectives was now inevitable; and the situation was to be quickly made worse by the fact that the landing intended for Kadzand was also frustrated by the seas breaking on the beach, as well as by the fact that the garrison had been reinforced at Breskens, the fort which dominated the southern side of the entrance.

By the 30th the gale had blown itself out and disembarkation was able to start. The first strongpoint, Ten Haak, was quickly dealt with, and Popham sent some of the gunboats into the Veere Gat separating Walcheren from North Beveland to bombard the next one, Veere. That surrendered the following day; meanwhile the troops were on their way across the island, took Middelburg, and were outside Flushing by the 1st of August. And there for the next four weeks they remained. Others were more energetic. Lieut-General Hope had landed with 8,000 men on South Beveland and marched east, mopping up enemy troops as he went, to Batz at the far end, where he waited for the arrival of Chatham and the main army and the fleet.

The French were busy transferring reinforcements across the Wielingen Channel to Flushing, and Strachan ordered Popham to bring the gunboats through from the East to the West Scheldt to put a stop to it. This was rather more easily ordered than obeyed, for the channel was narrow, beset by mudbanks, and with the wind, which had freshened again from the south-west, blowing straight down it. The only way to get sailing vessels through was by warping, an appallingly slow and laborious business of laying out an anchor by pulling-boat and heaving the ship up to it on her windlass—over and over again. 'Early the next morning,' Popham wrote on the 5th, after seeing Chatham at his headquarters at Middelburg, '... I returned to the flotilla, and succeeded (though the weather was extremely bad) in getting many of the gunboats round the Calor Sand into the West Scheldt, and anchored them before Flushing, just clear of gunshot.'

The situation at that point was this. The island of Walcheren was in British hands apart from Flushing, and the passage between Walcheren and South Beveland (the back door, as it were, into the West Scheldt) was impeded only by the hazards of getting through it, for the whole of South Beveland had been cleared of the enemy by Hope. But the main channel into the West Scheldt, the Wielingen, was still dominated by the two forts on either side of it. As early as the 4th both Chatham, from his headquarters at Middelburg, and Hope at Batz, were urging

Strachan to force his way through with the battleships, while Strachan was lying off waiting for Chatham to take Flushing; and Chatham was settling down for a good old-fashioned siege. This was to become the subject of bitter recrimination afterwards, and of an epigram which summed it up:

> Lord Chatham, with his sword undrawn,
> Stood waiting for Sir Richard Strachan;
> Sir Richard, longing to be at 'em,
> Stood waiting for the Earl of Chatham.

Who was at fault? Officially both were exonerated: unofficially, one may consider Strachan too timid, and Chatham too leisurely; but whereas the latter had only his native indolence to contend with, the former had the weather, which was terrible, a succession of sou'westerly gales followed—'provokingly', as Strachan put it—by a south-easterly wind blowing straight down the river. Nevertheless, while Popham had been busy sounding and buoying the channel and getting gunboats up to Batz,—'I sailed up the river at night,' he was to recall, 'with a foul wind, without any buoys in the river, and depending for the safe passage of my division, upon my personal recollection of the state of the channel, having 16 sail of sloops of war and 50 gun-brigs and gun-boats under my command'—Lord William Stuart, Captain of the *Lavinia*, took ten frigates through between the forts for the loss of twenty killed and wounded.

'The cannonading was tremendous,' wrote Robert Fernyhough, who was in one of them, 'about 600 pieces of ordnance firing at the same time, which, added to the bursting of shells over us, was a magnificent, yet an awful sight... The frigates could only be distinguished at intervals, emerging from the smoke ...'

But the expedition was already falling apart. While the Navy was gradually mustering its forces at the junction of the East and West Scheldt in preparation for forcing a passage up to Antwerp, and more troops were joining Hope's at Batz, ready to cross from South Beveland to the mainland for the attack by land, Chatham, his preparations for the siege of Flushing almost complete, was receiving regular intelligence of massive French reinforcements pouring into Antwerp, of defences being strengthened and the land being inundated. On Walcheren itself the great sea dyke had been cut, on Napoleon's direct order, and the water level in the dykes and ditches—and in the besieger's trenches—was inexorably rising.

The siege of Flushing finally opened on 13 August with a colossal bombardment by rockets and artillery by land and mortars and cannon from the vessels offshore, the sloops and gun-brigs 'tacking backwards and forwards to cover us, and the bomb-ships keeping up a constant fire of shells.' The battleships should have been there too, but as Chatham's journal notes drily, 'The fleet cleared for action but could not get under way'—that 'provoking' south easterly wind again. Next day they added their metal to the rest, and with the town devastated and burning, Monnet, the French Governor, sent out a flag of truce. Terms were agreed and the final capitulation took place on the 16th. After rather over two weeks the preliminary objective had been achieved and, as Keats reported to Strachan, 'the navigation of the West Scheldt is now open.' And he went on, with regard to the river above Batz, 'Sir Home Popham is examining the channels. Although we are now master of the navigation to Lillo [the fort on the right bank which dominated the final passage up to Antwerp]... it is in the enemy's power by sending a superior naval force to deprive us of it, as far as Batz, before some larger ships ascend.'

To those who were not in possession of the facts, it appeared as if the operation was at last going as planned. 'We are up the Scheldt, a short distance from Antwerp,' Robert Fernyhough wrote from the frigate *Statira*, 'the enemy's fleet lying there, of which we hope to be in possession before many days are past. A strong chain or boom, runs across the river, from one battery to another, which must be forced before we can reach the enemy.'

To anyone in possession of the facts, matters had a very different colour. There was not merely the question of the lateness of the season, nor of the reinforcements, now reputed to be 40,000, which the French were rushing into Antwerp: another, even more threatening, foe had begun to make its appearance—Walcheren fever. This devastating sickness, an unholy combination of malaria, typhoid, dysentery and cholera, was a regular feature of the island in the autumn months, but was made infinitely worse on this occasion by an exceptionally wet and stormy August, and by the flooded dykes and ditches. It started in the third week ashore: 1,564 men down with it by the 20th; 3,000 by the 25th; 4,000 by the 28th; 8,000 on 1 September. Nor did it only strike those ashore. 'We have lost many men by sickness,' Fernyhough wrote on the 21st; 'Sixteen officers died in the fleet in one night; and we also committed to the deep the bodies of fourteen men; indeed the Walcheren fever is making dreadful ravages'.

9

Chatham shifted his headquarters to Goes on South Beveland on 21 August, still apparently determined to press ahead; and four days later Home Popham, General Brownrigg the Quartermaster-General and the Adjutant-General Howard Douglas went ashore to look at the beach near Sandvliet as a possible landing place for the troops—and were observed by 'a Picquet of Cavalry' which suddenly appeared on the dyke. They were a long way from their boat, and the fact that they were not cut off and taken prisoner suggested to them that, perhaps, the surface was not as firm as it looked. Not that it mattered, for Chatham had already called in his commanders to consider the military situation. On the 27th Strachan and Keats were summoned as well. Strachan himself had no doubts at all: they had missed their chance of taking Antwerp; they could not take the outlying forts—Sandvliet, Lillo, and Doel on the opposite bank—without the co-operation of the Army, and since the only reason for taking them was to clear the way for the attack on Antwerp, and that had been abandoned, there was no point in taking them in the first place.

Chatham had to agree, and the following day he announced that since 'no further military operations can be attempted with any prospect of success', South Beveland would be evacuated and any troops not required for the defence of Walcheren—which was to be retained—would be sent home. The following day the Journal noted, 'Sickness continued to spread rapidly, and… it was feared that suitable ships and medical aid might not be available' for the numbers of invalids. And that, too, was to be proved hideously true.

A week later the first troops left for England, 11,000 of them sick; and soon, of the 18,000 left on Walcheren to defend it, half were down with the dreaded miasmatic fever. Chatham departed in *Venerable*[14] in mid-September, and Strachan, who was ill, a week later; but the decision as to whether to hold on to Walcheren or not was still being postponed. Popham, back in London in early November, wrote to Lord Melville: 'The Government is now complete, and some say Mr Perceval [the Prime Minister] thinks it is perfect. Nothing has been decided about Walcheren, at least I believe not; they have been so inconsistent, and so unsteady, that I really believe they are disposed to evacuate it.'

In fact the decision had already been taken. Captain Crawford noted on 30 October, '…we suppose it is settled not to keep the island, for soon after [the departure of the Earl of Dalhousie and Sir Eyre Coote] our people on shore began to dismantle the batteries of their copper and brass guns'; and three weeks later, 'a hundred men from each line-of-battle ship are employed on shore daily in dismantling the batteries and putting the guns and mortars on board the transports… some are employed in breaking up the piers of the new harbour, and filling it up with rubbish to prevent the enemy's ships from entering in and lying up in the winter (to be clear of the ice coming down the Scheldt).'[15]

The last troops were embarked on 9 December, and the last ships sailed just before Christmas. The expedition which had left the Downs in such high feather five months before had cost the country the best part of £1m, 4,000 lives (only 106 in action) and 12,000 sick, many of whom died later while others never fully recovered their health. When General Brownrigg referred to it, as early as 29 August, as 'this extensive calamity' he could have had only an inkling of the unmitigated disaster that lay ahead.

10

An inquiry was announced to be instituted in the House of Commons into the conduct of the leaders of the expedition, [John Barrow wrote in his flippantly malicious way] and Sir Home Popham, being previously asked by the Secretary of the Admiralty what defence he meant to set up in the House of Commons?—said, 'Don't be alarmed: depend on it, when I get up to speak I shall be so intensely listened to that you may hear a pin drop.' He got up, carried the expedition triumphantly till it met with a gale of wind—and 'Sir, without loss or damage of a single ship, I anchored the whole securely in the Room-pot.' The security of men-of-war in the Cream-pot raised such a general shout of laughter, that poor Sir Home's speech shared very much the fate of the luckless expedition.

It has to be said that there is no evidence for this mirthful scene, either during the endless debates on the expedition nor during the Committee's hearings. If it happened at all, it must have been outside the Chamber: more likely it was Barrow's merry invention.

The main subject of contention centred on the disagreement between Chatham and Strachan; and this was triggered off by the discovery that, on his return, Chatham had submitted a private account of the expedition to the King without informing the House of Commons that he had done so. 'I could not possibly suspect that Lord Chatham to the irregularity of presenting immediately to His Majesty such a Paper as that which I have received, had added the impropriety (to use no stronger term) of endeavouring to exculpate himself by private insinuations against the conduct of others.' Strachan's letter to Croker at the Admiralty suggests the general tone of the aftermath of what, by any standards, was a dreadful waste of lives.

As for Home Popham, he was—not unusually for him—in an ambiguous position. Blamed for being at least partly responsible, praised for his skill and judgement during it, the confidante of the C-in-C yet no more, officially, than 'the captain of a private ship', it was difficult to know quite where he stood or how he came out of it. Although at the end of the long debate in the house of Commons both ministers and commanders-in-chief escaped censure by a narrow majority, perhaps it was as well for him that, in the Scheldt itself, he simply had a difficult job of seamanship to do, and did it supremely well.

NOTES ON CHAPTER XVI

1. 'A Discourse on our Late proceedings in the Baltic': pamphlet quoted in the *Naval Chronicle*, Vol. XIX, p68. Popham's appointment as Captain of the Fleet was, of course, picked up by the newspapers. Some, such as the *Sun* and the *Courier*, justified it; others, notably the *Morning Chronicle*, were merciless: 'as a Naval Officer [he] ranks very low indeed... nobody ever heard of him, but in his own vapouring dispatches... an empty, prating, forward person... he is employed much out of his turn in services where he has praised himself very much...etc.'

2. In a letter to J. W. Croker from *Venerable* in July 1812, Popham wrote, 'There are two points on which I hold myself impudently high—Navigation and combined operations.' Both skills have been readily acknowledged by naval historians ever since, as has his contribution to signalling.

3. One has only to compare the prolonged and acrimonious arguments between the Earl of Chatham and Admiral Richard Strachan after the Scheldt fiasco two years later to see that 'perfect cordiality' was by no means the rule. (See below, concerning Walcheren.)

4. This explains Fletcher Wilkie's earlier remark about his 'being able to plunder an enemy's dockyard in the most complete and scientific manner.' The remark here was made by the Irish MP George Tierney during the debates after the expedition.

5. William L. Clements Library. Prize money for captains after Copenhagen amounted to £736 17s 6d each—'which falls short of their expectations.'

6. Titness Park, described in the Victoria County History of Berkshire as a small manor house in the Gothic style set in its own park. Its boundary ran close to the northern end of Virginia Water. The house has since been demolished.

7. By entering Parliament, Halevy says in *A History of the English People*, 'Naval Officers were thus enabled to make the nation witness to their quarrels.'

8. Apart from the C-in-C's Dispatches, the Earl of Chatham's Journal, etc. the Scheldt Expedition was debated at length in the House of Commons in January 1810 and again in March; and the Inquiry conducted by the Committee of the Whole House is in three volumes of Commons Papers, 1810: VI, VII, VIII.

9. 'His very name was almost proverbial for enervation and indolence,' said the *Annual Register*.

10. *But* on arrival 'The signal was now made for all Captains to repair on board the Admiral... and we were assembled on the Quarter Deck, under the instructions of Sir Home Popham, who handed each of us a good-sized card on which was a plan of the estuary. We were to guide our motions by it. Sir Home entered into some details relating to the Frigates' proceedings. Some of them were not sufficiently clear... [and I] requested his instructions... He candidly admitted that he could not give me any... as he had never been there. This made its impression upon the other Captains, who let out a few remarks.' Letters of Sir Byam Martin. NRS, Vol. II.

11. 'Among the visitors of the fleet... was Sir William Curtis, who was wafted to the Downs in a yacht... beautifully painted, adorned with a streamer bearing devices prognosticating victory and glory, and carrying delicate refreshments of all kinds to the military and naval commanders and the principal officers.'

12. Enter Peter Finnerty, 'the libeller and seditionist, who had been already in the pillory in Ireland... involved Popham... in most glaring indiscretion (only equalled by the vanity which prompted it) in connecting himself with such a *polisson*. Finnerty, it seems, declared... that Sir Home had written a letter of invitation to go over with him to Walcheren... and write the history of the expedition, in which no doubt Popham expected honourable mention. The Secretary of State (not Lord Castlereagh) ordered him to be sent back...' Robert Plumer Ward: Memoirs...

   Finnerty, an Irish journalist, had been, according to Plumer Ward, Popham's shorthand writer on his court-martial, and this had been the start of their acquaintanceship. Finnerty was Parliamentary reporter for the strongly Whig *Morning Chronicle*, and his association with Popham was to have repercussions later on. (See Chapter XVII, 3.)

13. For example Turner's 'Wreck of a Transport', painted at about this time.

14. Popham was posted back to *Venerable* the following August, but he nearly did not have a ship to go to. As Crawford reported: 'One of these nights [of NW'ly gales] we heard guns of distress from the seaward, but the weather was so stormy we could send them no assistance. When daylight appeared we saw *Venerable* coming in before the wind nearly waterlogged, with her main and mizzen-masts gone... she soon drove on a bank, threw some of her guns overboard, and struck on them, which damaged her bottom. We towed her into the new harbour...' at Flushing. She was repaired and returned to England with 'thrummed sails under her bottom' to reduce her leaks. Her Master was court-martialled and dismissed the Service. *Venerable* was only one of many ships which were wrecked or damaged during the operation.

15. Captain Crawford reported on 9 October: 'Received from the *Berwick* cutter six copper submarine carcasses...', goes on to describe how they were intended to be used, and continues: 'Johnstone the smuggler laid one down near the gates of the new harbour before Flushing surrendered, but we never heard of any damage being done by it. As for our part we never tried them—indeed, our Admiral said it was not a fair proceeding.' And Popham himself had minuted, before the expedition sailed, 'Mr Congreve should be directed to examine the submarine locks as fast as possible and see that they are in perfect order; to prepare 40 copper carcasses that will contain from 2 to 3 barrels, 20 that will contain 5 barrels, and 10 to contain 10 barrels.'

The legacy of 'Mr Francis' and his infernal machines persisted: this re-emergence stirred up fresh controversy in the *Naval Chronicle*.

CHAPTER XVII

'Here lay the beauty of naval operations' 1810-12

1

WHEN SIR Home Popham was despatched to Corunna in *Venerable* in August 1810 with orders to co-ordinate the operations of the Royal Navy and the Spanish regular and irregular forces along the northern coast of Spain, the Peninsular War was in its third year. The Duke of Wellington,[1] taking care to conserve his army, was retreating into Portugal, luring Massena's 70,000 Frenchmen to misery and starvation before the impregnable Lines of Torres Vedras. Apart from this enclave—nearly thirty miles of natural and artificial fortifications defending Lisbon—the British Army held no other territory in the Peninsula that autumn; but French control of Spain and Portugal was apparent rather than real. There were still Spanish armies—of a sort—in the field, and roaming guerrilla bands, the *partidas*, ready to descend from the mountains like wolves and harass the forces of occupation.

These fluid, irregular forces under 'Chieftains' of varying competence and ferocity but of a shared, unswerving purpose, had come into being spontaneously after the 'Second of May'—*Dos de Mayo*—in 1808, when Murat suppressed with appalling savagery a national uprising in Madrid. That, reported indelibly by Goya, followed by Napoleon's devious imposition of his brother Joseph as King of Spain a week later, ensured for the French the implacable hatred of the Spanish people. With the genius of Wellington to lead them, a massive British army to support them, and the Royal Navy in control of the seas, the Spaniards and the Portuguese would eventually bring to an ignominious end Napoelon's Iberian adventure. To this débâcle the guerrillas made a vital contribution.

In Andalucia, in Catalonia, Leon, Galicia, Navarra and notably along the northern seaboard from Corunna to the French frontier, they kept thousands of French troops, and often an entire army, engaged in holding strongholds and seaports, and in protecting supply convoys struggling along the 'great road' from Bayonne. Under the two Mina's, nephew and uncle, Francisco Longa, Porlier, El Pastor (whom the British called Don Gaspar), Renovales, Mendizabel and others, a thousand—sometimes more, sometimes fewer—would materialise out of the misty hills to harry and slaughter any French unit they could surprise, and vanish with their spoils back into their mountain hideouts: the quintessence of irregular warfare. By 1810 the British government had begun to realise their potential value, and Captain Mends in the *Arethusa* was already operating off the northern coast when Popham arrived early in September.

2

Popham's orders were 'to confer with the Junta on the best mode of carrying on operations against the enemy on the coast of the northern provinces, with a view to divert their attention, and draw off their forces from other parts of Spain; or, if practicable, to drive them out of those provinces altogether.' This referred to the units of the regular Spanish Army, whose commander-in-chief in Galicia was Captain-General Francisco Castanos. But Popham was also to investigate ways of giving assistance 'to the patriots' in their efforts against the enemy; he was to gather as much information as he could about the Spaniards—their wishes, the numbers they could raise, and what ports should be attacked and held, both as rallying points for the guerrillas and as bases for a British squadron. He was, in sum—and the phrase precisely encapsulates the purpose of it all—to suggest the best ways of 'carrying on *a desultory and distracting kind of warfare* against the French upon the coast'. (Author's italics.)

Within a week of his arrival at Corunna Popham had met and conferred with the members of the Junta and written his report. In it he suggested that San Sebastian, close to the road from France, would be the most effective base; given that, northern Spain would provide 'a great field for enterprise', but three regiments, artillery, and two engineers would be needed to exploit the advantages properly. From intercepted despatches he had learnt that the French lived in terror of 'the Brigands who harass the troops most actively' and who, they feared, might be reinforced, leading to a general insurrection in Navarre. 'The possible effect and operations of this *levy en masse* is also to be calculated on as no small advantage, if merely as a demonstration to Lord Wellington's Army...'; and Popham notes that the guerrillas are short of arms, ammunition and food. He himself, he concludes, is eager to undertake the service in *Venerable* as soon as he has, in accordance with his order, returned to Spithead. In the meantime, Captain Mends and his small squadron would co-operate with one of the groups of 'brigands' commanded by Renovales.[2]

On her way home *Venerable* ran into fog off the Cornish coast: when it suddenly cleared, she was close aboard a vessel which turned out to be the *L'Alexandre*, 'Ketch Privateer from St Maloes'. She was promptly captured.

A few days after their return Admiral Gambier, commanding the Channel Fleet, ordered *Venerable* to relieve *Valiant* in Basque Roads: and for the remainder of 1810 she and her company were engaged in that bleakest and most tedious of naval duties, keeping watch off the French coast, reporting ship and troop movements from Ushant south to Belle Ile. They spent a lot of the time anchored in the lee of the offshore islands of Houat and Hoëdic, and only got home once, in early October. Popham's request, submitted at the end of November, to be allowed to return to attend Parliament was granted in principle, but was only to be granted in practice on *Venerable*'s return. Relieved by the *Gibraltar*, she was back in Plymouth 'to replenish her stores and provisions' early in the New year, and he was granted six weeks leave.

3

Why he requested leave 'to attend parliament' is not clear, since he appears to have taken no part in the debates during 1811; but he was certainly in the House early in the year, for Plumer Ward noted in his Diary : 'During one of the debates of the last week in the Lords, Sir Home Popham came up to me behind the Woolsack.' And Ward continues:

> He had lately complained to me of being not only ill-treated, but insulted, by the Admiralty; in being sent on a special mission to the coast of Spain, but immediately recalled, and the command given to Captn. Mends who had failed. Popham always added, that if *he* had continued he would *not* have failed; he was much affronted at being reduced to act as a private Captn. of his ship, the *Venerable*, in the Channel Service. I thought him always a gallant and skilful officer, and so far had lent myself to his complaints; but...

But—who should reappear at this inconvenient moment but that egregious fellow Irishman, 'eccentric, extremely quick, ready and hot-headed', Peter Finnerty. He, having been hauled back from Walcheren and believing it to have been on the orders of Castlereagh, had written an article in which he accused the latter of having authorised atrocities in Ireland in 1798. This had brought a libel prosecution, and on 7 February 1811 he had been sentenced to eighteen months in Lincoln Gaol. It was Popham's association with this '*polisson*' that incensed Plumer Ward; and Popham's explanation, he said, 'made things in my mind very little better; and that he would find my impressions upon the matter not at all singular, for all his friends thought of it in the same way. He looked vexed, and said with some bitterness, he wondered how it should have that effect.'[3]

Although it is impossible to connect Popham's indiscretion in associating with Peter Finnerty directly with his not being employed in Spain until two years later, his conversation with Plumer Ward strongly implies it. It is a measure of Popham's curious naivety that he should have been surprised: in Tory eyes, Finnerty was a blackguard, and anyone who mixed with him was damned.

So Popham remained all that year in *Venerable*, and most of his letters were written on board, sometimes in Cawsand Bay, sometimes in Portsmouth, sometimes off the French coast. In August, for instance, he was in Quiberon Bay, and writing to Croker on the subject of his son, Mr William Popham, who had been ordered 'to act as Lieutenant of the Pompee. It is from the general impression of the liberality of my Lords Commissioners of the Admiralty to the Sons of the Officers, that I have been induced from the feelings of a Father to enclose this order, instead of allowing it to be sent by Mr Popham.'[4]

But his main preoccupation was with the revised edition of his *Signal Book*, for which, at last, he had full Admiralty backing, and on 9 May he wrote: 'I hope the additional experiment we shall make on the present cruise will enable me to announce that I am ready for publication, under their Lordships' Approbation,

Sanction, and Authority.' Ten days later he wrote to John Barrow at the Admiralty that the job was complete. So it might have been: nevertheless, it continued to keep him busy off and on throughout the year, and did not finally appear until 1813. (See Chapter XII.)

The improvement of communication, between ship and ship, ship and shore, and on land as well, is one of the unifying strands which runs, like a coloured yarn, through the last twenty years of Popham's life and ties in with his abounding mental energy. This manifested itself most vividly in his enthusiasm for Fulton's contraptions, but bobs up again and again in a dozen different contexts and always with the merits of the case enthusiastically and forcefully argued. Theories about blockade or the advantages of replacing transports with converted men-of-war jostle with recommendations for improved ships' guns, 'an apparatus for extracting foul air from ships' holds', a new kind of pump which he has seen demonstrated at Battersea, or an improved compass and binnacle which he has devised for *Venerable* and which the ship's Master, J. Noble, approved in every respect. He even invented a 'two-tiered' oared vessel which is mentioned, though not described, by Sir William Dillon. It followed that anyone with some revolutionary idea—for capturing the French fleet, say, like Baron D'Imbert, or destroying it, like a Stephen Parsons who wrote to him in 1812—tended to regard Home Popham as a likely supporter. Others, relying on his 'general benevolence and good character... and well-known goodness'[5] simply wanted him to put in a plea for their sons.

The other strand that runs through his life, of course, is litigation. The *L'Etrusco* business continued spasmodically from 1793 to 1809; an action for debt against him and John McArthur, arising out of his first ship the *Stadt van Weenen*, brought in 1789, was heard in the Court of King's Bench in 1808; and the question of his powers as a Commodore on the expedition to Cape Colony in 1805-6 were challenged by Captain Ross Donnelly in 1807, and Captain King in 1812 in a *Memorial presented... to His Majesty in Council*. What with legal fees, and the expense of producing successive editions of the *Marine Vocabulary*, it is hardly surprising that money is a subject that recurs regularly in his letters.

In March 1812 he made one of his rare speeches in the House of Commons, on a proposal to build a breakwater in Plymouth Sound. He had produced a report on the subject, he said, seven years earlier; and the engineer John Rennie had prepared a survey; but controversy had arisen over how many ships would be able to anchor inside it: was it fifty, or thirty six, or thirty, or only twenty? As a result, nothing was done. Now, however, a resolution calling for £80,000 for the work was before the House, and Popham supported it, citing in its favour the effectiveness of the breakwater at Cherbourg, which he had been able to observe during his patrols on the French coast.

It was his last appearance as a Member of Parliament, for at the end of May he received his orders for Spain, and he set off from London to rejoin his old ship in Portsmouth. No one had told him that she had shifted down-channel and was back in Cawsand Bay, and he had to hire four horses to get himself there. His claim for £43 expenses was rejected!

4

Biscay and the north coast of Spain came under the jurisdiction of the Admiral in command of the Channel Fleet, now Lord Keith who had replaced Gambier the previous year. Keith is described as 'steady, persevering and cautious', and this comes out clearly both in his instructions to Popham, which he sent him at the end of May 1812, and in his later correspondence. He was not, therefore, the ideal commander for someone as independent, imaginative, impulsive and energetic as Home Popham.[6]

The latter's orders, briefly, were to blockade the coast from Gijon to the French frontier and intercept the enemy's supplies and communications; and to capture a seaport which would provide a safe anchorage for the squadron, and enable him to 'hold frequent and uninterrupted intercourse' with the guerrillas, with a view to assisting His Majesty's Spanish Allies and 'annoying the enemy'. Once he had his base—and Keith was unable to say positively which it should be—he was to carry out his orders subject 'to a sound discretion in choosing his points of attack'. He is absolutely forbidden to endanger the safety of either the ships or the troops, and he is to take particular care when landing the latter in heavy surf or in the face of superior numbers. There was to be no improper use of liquor; and if the troops were to be ashore for two or more days, they were to be issued with only one day's *mixed* spirits. 'I rely,' Keith wrote, 'with the fullest confidence on your exercising the soundest discretion... and on your applying the zeal, experience and professional skill for which you are distinguished...'

In essence, Keith's orders followed closely the recommendations which Popham himself had made two years before, and on those put forward by the British Commissioner in Corunna, General Sir Howard Douglas.[7] He had been sent to Spain by Lord Liverpool the previous year and on his arrival in September had immediately gone to see Wellington, who fully supported the idea of independent action along the north coast. Sea power was being put to similar use in the Mediterranean.

Popham's squadron consisted initially of his own ship, *Venerable*, and *Magnificent*, both ships-of-the-line, five frigates and two sloops; over the months both the number of ships and the type varied. *Surveillante*, which was already on the coast, was to come under his orders as well.[8] On board were two battalions of Royal Marines, and a stock of muskets and munitions for the guerrillas. They sailed at the beginning of June, and on the 9th *Venerable*, having parted company with the rest, reached Corunna. There Popham met Douglas and Castanos,—and together they worked out plans for the coming months.

Much depended on Wellington's movements. In January the Anglo-Portuguese Army had taken Ciudad Rodrigo, and in March, with fearsome casualties, Badajoz. Wellington had now succeeded in securing the two gateways into Spain from the west; and having in May separated the armies of Marmont, who was west of Madrid, and Soult to the southwest, on 13 June began his advance towards Salamanca and Burgos and, it seemed possible, the very lair of the Corsican tyrant himself—though at that moment that individual was away and marching towards Moscow. But there was still another French force in Spain to be reckoned with, the Army of the North under Caffarelli, which could be called upon to reinforce Marmont unless it could be kept busy elsewhere.

This was where the guerrillas, aided and sustained by the squadron, had vital work to do; and four days after Wellington crossed the Agueda on the road to Salamanca, Popham, with Howard Douglas on board, rendezvoused with the rest of the squadron off Cape Machichaco. On 19 June, just as the battle of Salamanca was beginning, he made his first contact with the guerrillas, 'marching forward with great spirit' at Lequeitio, between Bilbao and San Sebastian.

The French had strengthened the fort and fortified the convent—having, presumably, first removed the nuns. For two days the squadron battered by a gale, could only stand offshore under double-reefed topsails; and Popham, afraid 'that if any accident happened to them [the guerrillas] in the first instance, there would have been an end to all future confidence in the squadron, dared not risk a landing. On the 20th the weather moderated, and *Venerable* ran in to 'within a small half-mile' of the beach and set about bombarding the shore installations. But the ships' guns would not elevate sufficiently, and it was decided to try and land a 24-pounder on an island facing the town and heave it to the top. Ashore, Don Gaspar's patriots were ready for the assault.

Once the gun was ashore—landed despite 'a very heavy surf beating against the rocks'—the problem remained of getting it to the summit. 'A hawser was attached to the trunnions... and the seamen drew it through the surf, and looped it to the horns of the oxen, when the guerrillas lent their aid, the sailors again gave their strong arms, and the united force ran it up hill.' Perhaps 'ran' is a slight hyperbole: it took 100 seaman, 400 guerrillas and 20 draft oxen to drag it there, and as Popham wrote to Keith, 'I do not believe there was a man or officer in the Squadron was not astonished at the sight of a Gun dragged up such a hill.'

The French garrison was suitably astonished, too. Once ranged, it quickly breached the fort, and although the garrison put up a staunch fight and drove off the guerrillas' first assault, the latter rallied 'and dashed on with cheers, disappearing in the dense smoke, which rose in clouds, and enveloped the breach. An instant more decided the struggle, and the air rang with cries as they put the defenders to the sword.'

Next they turned to the convent. This surrendered the following day, and the sailors blew it up: 290 prisoners were taken without British loss, and were shipped to England in *Magnificent*. This was a heartening start, and exactly the kind of operation the squadron was there for. News of it alarmed the French throughout Guipuzcoa as much as it encouraged the *partidas*, and a French relieving force rushed over from Bilbao arrived too late. 'From a neighbouring height', Fulton writes, 'they saw the squadron sail away with the captured garrison, while the guerrillas vanished, leaving them uncertain where they would appear next.'

'Here' Charles Oman summed up, 'lay the beauty of naval operations.'

5

Napoleon himself, observing that the secret of the guerrillas' strength depended largely on the presence of the Royal Navy, had decreed that 'all churches, convents, and strong houses, situated near the mouths of the creeks and rivers between Santander and San Sebastien' should be entrenched. And because the guerrillas, nourished by the squadron, were such a continuing threat to his communications, 'he desired, if necessary, the whole Army of the North should be employed to scour the lines of communication.' Since Caffarelli's army amounted to 120,000 men, the importance of preventing them from joining Marmont's Army of the Centre cannot be exaggerated. This is precisely what they achieved.

From Lequeitio the squadron sailed west, their first target the fort of Bermeo. They anchored and landed a company of Marines, but the garrison had already left. In the convent they found a quantity of French provisions which, Popham reported, 'were instantly distributed to the poor': they then blew up both it and the guardhouse and immobilised the guns, either by spiking the touch-holes or knocking off the trunnions. And while they were there they watered the ships.

There was a whole chain of these little coastal forts to east and west of Cape Machichaco, right round to the mouth of the Rio Nervion below Bilbao, and one by one they were given the same rough treatment.

'We landed parties', young Robert Deans wrote in his journal,[9] 'and destroyed all their batteries, spiked the guns and blew up the guardhouses.' Sometimes, as at Portugalete where the French were in some force, they were only able to 'annoy' them; and the French returned the compliment, for it was here, according to Deans, that 'a large shot from their battery went right through one of the boats, pulling, with about twenty men in her, and did not touch one of them.'

Popham, always eager to see things for himself, went ashore with Douglas along the estuary to reconnoitre, but had to retreat in a hurry 'before it was too dark, for fear of being surprised in a country which was particularly calculated for such a purpose'. Often one or other of the ships was detached, either to maintain contact with the guerrillas or to carry out a spot of individual demolition; and on 25 June, following up information from Longa (one of the most active guerrillero leaders) Popham ordered 'Line of Battle', and *Venerable* and *Surveillante* sailed boldly into the entrance to Bilbao and opened up with 'spherical case shot' on the French garrison in the fortress of Algorta. Whereupon the latter prudently removed themselves into a nearby wood.

The speed and unpredictability of the squadron's movements, matched by the elusiveness of the *partidas*, combined to drive the French forces to distraction. No sooner had they set off over rough country and appalling roads to relieve one of their beleaguered little garrisons than they received reports of an attack on another somewhere else; and, inevitably, the strength of the squadron's complement of sailors and Marines became exaggerated.

'The march of the French', Popham reported to Keith, 'in such force in different directions is the strongest and most unequivocal proof of the great advantage which the squadron has proved to be of, to the common cause. Our object is to distract the enemy by rapid movements, followed by strong demonstrations.' There were some unpleasant intimations of the enemy's reactions. At Algorta the French General threatened to hang two Spaniards who had been in touch with the British, to which Popham replied that if he did so as a reprisal for the bombardment, he—Popham —'will instantly kill two Frenchmen till he has gone through the whole of the ninety-five' prisoners he had on board. No more is heard of this grim exchange; but as, by 24 June, they had already destroyed thirty guns and magazines, the French command had some grounds for being rendered, as Popham quaintly put it, 'outrageous'. One bunch of French soldiers the squadron picked up had cut off fingers or a thumb as a way of avoiding further service.

At the end of the month Francisco Longa wrote to Home Popham from Orduna, thirty miles south of Bilbao, to say that he had 5,000 men, but was being threatened by 9,000 of the enemy from Vitoria. Nevertheless, '...be assured, Sir, the whole of my attention has been directed to your glorious expedition from the first moment I heard of it...' and he promises his full co-operation. And that co-operation was to produce its first solid achievement a few days later.

In the meantime the squadron turned east to assault Guetaria. Only a dozen miles from San Sebastian, and close to the main route into Spain from France, its capture would be a major triumph. They landed a number of guns in expectation of support from the guerrillas; but when this failed to materialise and a French flying column was reported approaching instead, they had to re-embark the guns and leave in a hurry. Guetaria, like Santona to the west, was to tantalise and frustrate them for as long as they remained on the coast.

Longa, however, having evaded the Vitoria force, arranged to join forces with Popham in an attack on Castro Urdiales, west of Bilbao. They met there on 6 July; the squadron anchored off and two guns and the Marines were landed. A French force arrived to relieve the beleaguered town, but was sent packing, and the Governor surrendered with his garrison of 150 men and twenty guns. 'The Castle of Castro', Deans wrote, 'is immensely strong, built after the very old plan of Forts—on a high projecting rock'; the walls of the magazine were nine feet thick. Castro was not the sheltered harbour that Popham was looking for, but it was a useful foothold, and when he sailed to work with Renovales on a proposed attack on Bilbao, he left some of his Marines to garrison it.

A westerly gale kept the squadron at sea, a French flying column kept Renovales at bay on land, and Popham continued east to make another attempt on Guetaria.

This time he had the support of both Mina ('we are on the best of terms,' Popham wrote to Keith, 'in consequence of my attentions to him when he was wounded') and the *partidas* under Jauregui from Guipuzcoa, and the operation started well. The squadron got their heavy guns ashore and began a bombardment, while the guerrillas blockaded it on the landward side. However, news of the attack had reached d'Aussenac in Bayonne, and he hurried over with 3,000 men and drove off Jauregui. Once more the British sailors had to leave in a hurry, but this time without thirty men and two of the guns.

On the face of it, it was a reverse; but as Popham wrote to Keith on 19 July: '...the primary object of all our attentions... is to assist Lord Wellington...; and no operation has so completely met this principle as the one at Guetaria, which diverted the Baron Aussenac's division from a junction with Marmont, weakened it by all the numbers he lost on the 17th under a heavy fire of Grape from the *Lyra* and *Goldfinch*...'

This letter included a desperate plea for more arms (they had already landed 1,500 muskets, ammunition and other stores for Longa) 'to hold together the many thousand volunteers' who were ready to join the guerrillas. If he could have given Don Gaspar arms, he says, he would have had 3,000 men and he might have destroyed d'Aussenac. General Mina, he goes on, is the most powerful and independent of the chiefs, and 'is only to be gained not ordered'. Give him arms, and he would join with Gaspar and be of the greatest use to Lord Wellington.

Three days after Popham wrote this letter, on 22 July 1812, Wellington met Marmont at Salamanca and won his greatest victory up to that date. In that victory, the absence of virtually all of Caffarelli's Army of the North played an important part, as Wellington clearly recognised. On 28 July, in a letter to General Lord William Bentinck, he remarked, '...I find that Sir Home Popham, with a few hundred marines and guerrillas of the north has succeeded in preventing Caffarelli from despatching anything to Marmont's assistance, except cavalry...' And to Popham himself, a few days later, 'I beg leave to congratulate you upon the success of your operations... I trust, therefore, that you will not discontinue them.' That trust was not misplaced: indeed, the squadron had just brought off its greatest coup.

6

From Guetaria they sailed westward once more and on 22 July were off the harbour of Santander, thirty-five miles beyond Bilbao. Porlier and his brigands were already investing the town, but were hampered, as the *partidas* invariably were, by the lack of siege artillery. The entrance was guarded by the Castello de Ano on the headland; a little way offshore was the Isla de Mouro, and on it Popham landed a battery to bombard the fort. He then went ashore to confer with Porlier. Between them he and Longa had 4,000 men, and a concerted plan was worked out. With the guardian castle under bombardment, Popham landed the Marines in Sardinero Bay to the north, while the Spaniards launched an attack on the town itself. Popham then transferred to *Surveillante* and led the frigates boldly past the headland and into the harbour.

About 2pm [he wrote in his despatch] I made the signal for the ships to lead in; the *Lyra* and *Insolent* ran ahead to sound, and then *Surveillante*, *Medusa* and *Rhin* bore up, in close order, engaging the Castle, the Island Battery firing at the same time with great effect. Not a man was hurt in running in, although an incessant fire of musquetry was kept up from the Castle in addition to its guns. The moment we rounded the point and anchored in the Harbour, the enemy evacuated the Castle.

This was only the beginning, however. The French continued to defend the town, and an assault by Spanish and British forces on the 27th failed with twenty-seven of the latter killed and thirty-one wounded, among them Captain Sir George Collier of *Surveillante*, and Captain Lake. Robert Deans was involved in what he describes as 'a sharp action', and was forced to retreat to the Castello de Ano, where he spent a miserable night in the rain. Next day they blew it up, leaving 'nothing to be seen but a heap of stones'.

For a time the situation remained unchanged, with the British in possession of the fort and harbour, and the French in possession of the town; but help, in the shape of a third guerrilla force under Mendizabel—who was nominally in command of all the local guerrilla bands—arrived, bringing captured dispatches revealing that the French were planning to evacuate the town. With Caffarelli and part of the Army of the North to cover them, the Governor and his garrison of 1,600 slipped out during the night of 2-3 August, leaving eighteen spiked guns behind, and the British and Spanish moved in. Life quickly returned to normal it seems, 'A pretty town,' Deans confided to his journal, 'and a great deal of pleasant company. Amused ourselves strolling about for a few days...' and before the week was out balls were being held.

It was, as a modern fighting man would say, all right for some. For others, for Home Popham in particular, there was work to be done. The capture of Santander was not merely a notable achievement: it appeared to fit the need for a secure anchorage, and he immediately set three of the ships' Masters to survey it with that in view. They reported that two or three ships-of-the-line, six frigates and almost any number of smaller vessels might lie to their own anchors within its shelter; and more large ships if moorings were laid. The holding was poor between the entrance and the town, but better farther up. It was a great relief for, as Popham reported, 'upon this coast there is so heavy a sea that ships materially suffer by it'; and Sir Charles Oman states quite unequivocally that its capture 'was the most important event that had happened on the North Coast of Spain since 1809'. The importance, moreover, would increase during the following twelve months.

With his usual thoroughness and breadth of vision, Popham had already begun to consider Wellington's needs, and he closely interrogated Porlier and his staff on the state of the roads between the port and Burgos, which he predicted would be the next target, now that Salamanca was won. Six or eight heavy guns, he reckoned, would be needed for the siege, and it should be possible to have them hauled there by oxen.

The shrewdness of this estimate was to be demonstrated six weeks later, but for the moment Wellington's intentions lay elsewhere. A week after the capture of Santander he was marching not on Burgos but on Madrid, and he entered the capital on 12 August. When he did finally take up Popham's offer of siege artillery, it was too late.

7

At the precise moment at which Home Popham and the guerrillas were securing the vital base which had been one of Keith's original instructions, the Commander-in-Chief of the Channel Fleet was writing him an angry letter, threatening to have him relieved. Keith never came nearer to this southern frontier of his command than Douarnenez Bay, and it was from his flagship *San Josef*, either there or 'off Ushant' and very occasionally from Cawsand, that he kept watch on the Atlantic coast and despatched his letters of instruction, anxiety or reproof to his ingenious subordinate.

The reasons for the outburst were relatively trivial: Popham, he said, had not been in touch with him for a month; he had sent ships direct to England instead of via him; and he had not detached *Magnificent* and *Insolent* when ordered. At the same time Keith was writing to Croker at the Admiralty: 'Their Lordships are not uninformed of the little disposition that has been shown throughout the late operations on the North Coast of Spain to pay proper attention and respect to the Commander-in-Chief or his orders... but it is hoped that the animadversions that have been made will have a proper effect...'

Popham wrote a suitably humble reply, giving his reasons: a breakdown in signals, the need to send Collier and Lake and the French prisoners home, and so forth. It was all a bit bureaucratic when contrasted with what Popham was actually achieving, and it is difficult to believe that Keith was as put out as he pretended, or meant the threat of supercession seriously, for only three days before his letter to Croker, just quoted, he had written: 'Sir Home appears to have maintained a perfect cordiality with the Spanish chieftains, and to have inspired them with much zeal, and the meritorious exertions manifested by him and the officers, seamen and marines serving under him are such as cannot fail to recommend them to the notice of their Lordships and to the favour of their country.'

One wonders if the tedium of blockading the French coast had not disturbed Keith's judgement, for he also told Croker that Popham had never been authorised to issue provisions and arms to the guerrillas, and had turned down a request by Popham for 'some dollars and arms'. Yet what else could 'assisting the partisans' mean? Howard Douglas certainly considered that supplying them with military stores was essential, and indeed arranged to do so from the base at Corunna.[10]

The whole affair quickly blew over; but once again it revealed the problems of a Commander on detached service, and those of the C-in-C who, even over the comparatively short distances involved here, could not always be in full possession of the facts. Perhaps Home Popham had been remiss in not submitting regular returns of provisions and so forth—one of Keith's complaints—but that he was doing splendidly the job he had been sent out for there could be no doubt whatever. Wellington, certainly, expressed himself 'fully satisfied of the use they [the squadron's operations] have been to his movements'—and Caffarelli, in the opposite sense, would doubtless have agreed.

Santander was in Allied hands, and in mid-August the squadron returned to

Bilbao[11] and took the strongpoint of Portugalete, downstream from the city. Mariano Renovales and Mendizabel threatened it on the land side, and after a half-hearted action the French Governor retired. The following day he had second thoughts and tried to win it back, but was held by Mendizabel. At which Caffarelli mustered every man he could lay his hands on, some 7,000, and at the end of the month recovered it.

This completely upset Popham's plans for trying once again to take Guetaria—as he was being urged to do by Wellington—for the various guerrilla forces had become dispersed, and the squadron retired disgruntled to Santander. Deans' comments are both savage and unfair: he wrote of the 'dismayed Spaniards' retreating as soon as a French force approached, 'for they are always ready to run'. He was, he said, 'quite disgusted with the behaviour of the Spaniards, and heartily tired of the expedition.'

Deans, who was only twenty, obviously had small idea of what the *partidas* were achieving in their own opportunist way, or of the problems that beset them, always on the alert for some overwhelming French force while living from hand to mouth in the rugged foothills of the Cordillera Cantabria. In addition, they were never too happy operating outside their own particular territories and Mendizabel had no real authority over them. If they did not always live up to the squadron's expectations, on many occasions they proved themselves doughty allies.

8

At the end of August Wellington left Madrid in the care of Lt-General Sir Rowland Hill, and headed north for Valladolid and his main objective, the heavily fortified town of Burgos. Early in September Popham sent Lieutenant Mcfarlane to meet him with letters and dispatches, and 'one of my signal books which he wished to use as a cypher' (and, despite his professed contempt for it, several of Wellington's letters to Popham thereafter are in code).

> The guerrillas in the north [he wrote to Popham a little later], and Mendizabel, should do everything in their power to harass the enemy, to prevent them from collecting magazines of provisions, and above all, from communicating with each other. Any town or village which should supply the enemy with anything, unless obliged by force of arms, should be destroyed. If the Spaniards [he went on, with characteristic acerbity], will not raise regular armies and fight like other people, we must make the whole population enter into the war if they choose to continue it.

He was still agitating for the capture of Guetaria, and during the first half of September Home Popham expended a great deal of energy trying to set up yet another assault on the place. To ensure success he needed not merely a substantial guerrilla force for the actual siege, but a covering force to fend off any interference by the French; and for this he needed Mendizabel and his men. After prodigious efforts, Popham succeeded in co-ordinating the movements of three of the bands—Gaspar's, Campillo's and Renovales'—but Mendizabel refused to move. In letter after letter Popham presented the most cogent arguments in favour of immediate action: Wellington's wishes, the lateness of the season, the importance of the target. And in letter after letter Mendizabel fully agreed but... First, Porlier had been ordered elsewhere by General Castanos, then Longa is missing, then Renovales, and so on and so on. Popham's patience becomes steadily more attenuated, and on 12 September he tried to force the issue. The Marines, he told Mendizabel, were embarked; ships were standing by to take on the Spanish vanguard, 'and my Barge will be on shore at 8 o'clock to have the honour of bringing Your Excellency on board.' But the barge stood by in vain, and Popham was forced to send the expedition on ahead while he continued to put pressure on the 'vacillating' General.

In all other respects the operation was under way. Captain the Hon. Pleydell-Bouverie in *Medusa* duly arrived off Guetaria, disembarked the Spaniards, a battalion of Marines, and a number of guns, and made contact with Don Gaspar and Campillo who had 2,300 men close to the town. The garrison consisted of a mere 220 men and a siege should have presented few problems, but exactly the situation which Popham had feared, and which Mendizabel should have been there to forestall, developed: 4,000 French had been called up to relieve the garrison and were reported approaching. Without Mendizabel to hold them off the British and Spanish were in jeopardy, and Popham was forced to cancel the operation. Troops and guns were re-embarked, the guerrilla bands melted away, and any idea of taking Guetaria was abandoned—in consequence', Popham wrote, 'of General Mendizabel's refusal about any sincere co-operation.'

'Although I most gratefully receive the information and advice of any good officer,' Popham wrote to him in a last taut, reproachful letter, 'yet it is almost an invariable practice with me to act for myself...'

A disappointment it undoubtedly was, and a particularly frustrating one; but, like all the squadron's operations, its benefits did not depend on its success. 'The threat alone', Brigadier-General W. P. Carroll wrote to Popham on 24 September, 'produced advantages in drawing troops there.' The combined efforts of the squadron and the 'insurgents' had kept Caffarelli and 14,000 men uselessly employed and prevented them joining the forces opposing Wellington. 'The arrangements for the expedition reflect great credit on you, Sir Home...'

Guetaria had evaded them, but there was still one more French stronghold, the formidable fortress of Santona, between Castro and Santander, which Caffarelli had been strengthening. Now it was reputed to have between 80 and 100 guns ranged along its battlements; but ships of the squadron were blockading it closely, and the garrison, according to the intelligence reaching Home Popham, were falling sick as well as growing increasingly hungry. General Castanos was in favour of the attempt: however, before anything could be planned Popham had other, and more urgent, calls on his attention.

9

Wellington was before the walls of Burgos on 19 September, and at once set about besieging it with the impatience which, uncharacteristically, seemed to overtake him when faced with a fortified town—witness Badajoz. He was short of siege artillery, dangerously so, as Howard Douglas pointed out.

'The enemy's guns are 24-lbers, my Lord; and we have only three 18-lbers and five 24-lb howitzers. The 18-lbers will not breach the wall, and our fire must be overpowered unless your Lordship brings up some more guns from the ships at Santander.'

'How would you do that?'

'With draft oxen as far as the mountains, and then drag them on by hand. We can employ the peasantry, and put a hundred men to a gun.'

'It would take too long.'[12]

The Army was also short of powder and shot. The soldiers were actually paid to collect spent French musket-balls, but there is no such commodity as used gunpowder, and on 29 September Popham received a request for forty barrels.

It was 'on shore in an hour,' Popham wrote in his dispatch, 'but it was seven hours before I could get the mules', and Wellington had it a week later. Considering that each barrel weighed ninety pounds and the distance was more than seventy miles, much of it through the mountains and all of it along dreadful roads, the response was commendably prompt. 'It is a pity', Charles Oman comments drily, 'that Wellington did not think of asking for heavy ships' guns at the same time.' His refusal to do so, or indeed to send for those lying idle in Madrid, continues to baffle historians of the campaign of 1812.[13] Not until 2 October, after a series of assaults against the main fortress had been driven back by the resourceful garrison commander General Jean Louis Dubreton, did he finally accept Popham's offer. Two 24-pounders were on the road by the 9th, and nine days later had been dragged the fifty backbreaking miles to Reynosa, more than halfway. A naval long 24-pounder weighed 2½ tons, the short version rather less: whichever the ones despatched, the task of heaving and hauling them up over the passes of the Cordillera must have strained men and beasts to the limit.

Nor can the men have been pleased when, on that same day, Wellington's final assault received the same rebuff as the earlier ones, and having decided to abandon the siege, he ordered the guns to be returned to Santander. The retreat began twelve days later. The siege had cost the Army more than 2,000 casualties against the defenders' 300, had achieved nothing, and had allowed the French time to muster their own armies in pursuit. The autumn rains, which had washed out the trenches before Burgos, fell relentlessly and turned the retreat into something resembling a rout. When the troops finally reached their winter quarters at Ciudad Rodrigo a month later, 18,000 of them were on the sick list.

Despite the anxieties and setbacks of the siege of Burgos, Wellington still found time to consider the position of the squadron, and on 17 October he wrote a long letter to Home Popham:

The possession of Santona is very important in every point of view, particularly if the possession should facilitate your remaining on the coast. You know best whether you can obtain the possession with the means in your power. If you cannot, and if you think that the attempt will draw towards you the enemy's operations, and that you may be obliged to withdraw from Santander, it is much better that the attempt should not be made. What I want is, that your squadron and marines should remain on the coast during the winter...If they should lose Santander, it is very obvious that they must go to Coruna or home; and either would be a misfortune under present circumstances...

I wish I could send you a better General than Mendizabel, and better troops than his are; but they are not to be found...

He had no doubts about the value of the squadron in keeping a large number of French troops occupied, and was worried that Lord Keith would insist on withdrawing it—something Keith had first mentioned as early as the first week in September, and permitted to be postponed only with reluctance. In an earlier letter, written on 12 October, Wellington's views are made doubly clear:

...the enemy, as well as the Spaniards, will be convinced that nothing is intended to be done, even though the Marines remain, if you should go away in the *Venerable*; and I apprehend that I shall have upon my hands in Castille more of the enemy than I can well manage.'

And he underlines the importance he attaches to the presence of Popham himself: 'If you were not known to be in that ship, possibly her removal from the coast would not be very important'. The frank and generous recognition of the part Popham's squadron was playing on the coast was not extended to events connected with the siege of Burgos. In what seems like a sour attempt to excuse his own shortcomings on that occasion, Wellington wrote to Lord Liverpool after it was all over:

In regard to means, there were ample means, both at Madrid and at Santander, for the siege of the strongest fortress. That which was wanting at both places was the means of transporting ordnance and military stores... Popham is a gentleman who picques himself on overcoming all difficulties. He knows the time it took to find transport even for about 100 barrels of powder and a few hundred thousand rounds of musket ammunition that he sent to me. As for the two guns that he endeavoured to send me, I was obliged to send my own cattle to draw them, and felt great inconvenience from the want of those cattle in subsequent movements of the Army.

That these allegations were untrue has already been shown, and Oman deals with them trenchantly. Calling them 'ungrateful', he goes on:

Popham got them [the guns] across the mountains from Santander by his own exertions, and would have sent them some weeks earlier but for Wellington's refusal to ask for them. And it was the ammunition sent by Popham [in double-quick time, it should be added] which alone enabled the siege to go on for as long as it did.

10

In a letter to Keith written from Santander on 26 October, Popham refers to 'the various extraordinary duties which the nature of the service has imposed upon me', and hopes that he has acted 'in a manner to meet your Lordship's aprobation.'Not the least extraordinary of those duties were those connected with the *partidas*. In an earlier letter, he had written, 'I have had eighteen officers at a time embarked at my table, and a proportion in the wardroom, and I am now receiving on board three Generals and their suite besides a number of other officers'. All this was costing him a lot of money, for which he should be reimbursed. On many of the operations that summer and autumn the squadron carried numbers of guerrillas to the scene of the action.

And there were more 'extraordinary duties' to come. With Guetaria impossible, Popham turned his attention to the only other French stronghold west of San Sebastian, the coastal fortress of Santona. Wellington gave orders to Mendizabel to support operations against it; but while Popham in his usual whirlwind fashion—reminiscent of his energetic disturbance of the Imperial Russian dockyards in St Petersburg thirteen years before—set about preparing for the siege, Mendizabel again showed no inclination to exert himself.

> I convened the Junta [Popham wrote to Wellington on 20 October] and all the civil and military authorities here, provided wood and iron and gave to the Provincial officer of the Artillery the complete supertintendance of the work, out of respect for the Spaniards, and with a view of betraying them into a little zeal and interest for the sake of the country...'

The work being the casting of mortar shells and shot. He took over the local ropewalk so that they could work under cover, set up forges and 'sawing-racks' for preparing mountings for the gun-batteries, and, as may be imagined, did succeed in instilling a bit of 'zeal' into everyone—except Mendizabel.

What made the latter's dilatoriness all the more infuriating was not only the deteriorating condition of the Santona garrison, but the apparent reason for his refusal to bestir himself: 'an influence', Popham tells Keith, 'more alluring than any military command', though 'when I found this assertion came from a lady, it was impossible to pursue it any farther.' When at the beginning of December the wretched General did at last consent to come and see Popham, he was an hour late and stayed only a few minutes before going off to Mass; then, making extravagant promises about ordering Mina to come down to Santona to cover them against any movement by the Army of the North, went off to the theatre! Popham's exasperation reached flashpoint. 'If the man had been an English general, I should have felt myself bound, to ask for an enquiry into his conduct.'

But in truth the squadron's usefulness was over for the year. The capture, and retention, of Santander had been its high point but now Wellington was miles away with a sick and disconsolate army. Caffarelli, leaving 20,000 men to guard the coast, had taken the Army of the North to join the Army of Portugal in the pursuit; and the guerrillas, supplied and armed and heartened by the British, would be able to make havoc with French garrisons and French communications during the winter months—and did so, in fact, so satisfactorily, that Caffarelli was forced to return.

Beyond the intense and curiously enclosed world of war in the Peninsula, the greater war was running its unpredictable course. Napoleon's march into Russia had first been halted and then turned into a terrible retreat at the same time as, but a thousand times worse than, Wellington's after Burgos. During the summer, while Popham's squadron was knocking the sea-forts of the Cantabrian coast about, the United States declared war on Britain. Neither of those events greatly affected the squadron, though the odd American ship which strayed into its path was captured, and in November orders were received to 'seize or destroy' all American ships.

But Lord Keith was becoming more and more uneasy about 'the large ships' remaining on the Spanish coast, and prospects of attacking Santona gradually faded as November slipped away. 'We all expected shortly to be seriously employed,' Robert Deans noted in his journal—for this final operation was not abandoned until 4 December—'when on the 13th to our great joy, the *Fairy* arrived, with orders for our return to England... we were all most heartily tired of co-operating with the Spanish, whom we found were a vile and treacherous set altogether.' Except for the girls in Santander, Deans had never had much time for them.

Venerable sailed on 21 December and was back in England on the 30th. Robert Deans was not the only one to be glad that that particular tour of duty, arduous and often frustrating, was over. On 5 December Popham had written to Keith: 'I am also equally sensible to the kindness of your feelings about Lady Popham's indisposition; she has indeed been suffering under the effects of rheumatic fever, considerably increased by my absence.'[14]

He had been away for six months, and the squadron's work had been enormously valuable; quite apart from keeping the French Army of the North busy, the setting-up of Santander as a port for the supply of the Allied Army, though of limited value in 1812, was to prove a major asset the following year when that army raced through to Vitoria and the Pyrenees. 'The recent Allied offensive,' a recent historian writes, 'coupled with Popham's raids and the incessant guerrilla attacks, had turned it [N. Spain] into a hotbed of rebellion that defied subjugation.'

Yet for this outstanding job of work Popham received no recognition, a slight of which he remained bitterly resentful.

NOTES ON CHAPTER XVII

1. Arthur Wellesley had been raised to the peerage as Viscount Wellington and Baron Douro after the Battle of Talavera the previous year.

2. Contrary to the statements by Oman and others, Popham did not take part in the two raids of October 1810 on Gijon and Santona, the second of which was frustrated by bad weather and followed by the loss of two Spanish ships, which dragged their anchors and were driven ashore with the loss of 600 lives: he was cruising off the French coast. Log of *Venerable*, ADM51; ADM1/144; and Plumer Ward, op.cit.

3. Finnerty's activities are described in DNB. See also *Gentleman's Magazine*, Vol XCII, Part 1, p644.

4. William Craddock Popham (1791-1864). This letter suggests that he was with his father at this time, but see below, Chapter XVIII, vi.

5. Letter from William Wetherell, Feb 1812. ADM1/2341.

6. Admiral Lord Keith, George Keith Elphinstone (1746-1823). Like Popham, he had as a young man made a voyage to China, but in an East India Company ship commanded by his brother. Unlike Popham, he had founded his fortune thereby. His second wife was the daughter of Dr Johnson's friend, Mrs Thrale, the little girl he called 'Queenie' and with whom he played games. For Popham's correspondence with him, ADM1/144-151; for that with the guerrilla leaders, papers in WLC.

7. General Sir Howard Douglas (1776-1861) was both a soldier and a scientist. Like Popham, he was an FRS; he wrote treatises on naval gunnery, on fortifications and on military bridges, the last, it was said, giving Telford the idea for the suspension bridge. He had been at Walcheren in 1809 as Assistant Quartermaster General, and he and Popham had met there. Douglas was not only a brilliant man, but seems to have possessed unusual charm and warmth. It was at least partly due to him that Home Popham was sent with the squadron to assist the guerrillas. (See S. W. Fullom, and Oman, op cit.) One of the first things he discovered on his arrival in Spain in 1811—and promptly forestalled—was that British arms supplied to the Spaniards were about to be shipped to South America to quell the rebellious colonials!

8. A number of writers, Oman and Bryant among them, refer to Popham as 'Commodore' during these operations, and Gates promotes him to Admiral; but nowhere in the Admiralty documents does it appear that he was instructed to hoist a Commodore's pendant—though it would have been reasonable if he had been so instructed—and Lord Keith addresses him as 'Captain'. Commodore, in this context, must be regarded as a courtesy title only. In a letter to Melville, April 1813, Popham said he declined the offer of a pendant in 1812.

9. Journal of Lt Robert Deans (later Rear-Admiral) (1792-1867). He was serving in *Venerable*, and recorded in his Journal, on their way from Corunna to Cape Machichaco, 'about this time *I got acquainted with Miss Popham, whom I found a very pleasant girl.*' Tantalisingly, there is no other mention of her. One can only assume that Sir Home had brought one of his daughters along with him, perhaps Caroline, who would have been sixteen, or Mary, who was a year younger.

10. Wellington's letter, 17 October, replying to a request by Popham of 17 July. It ends, in Wellington's driest vain: 'It has not been customary, I believe, to give shoes and greatcoats to guerrillas.' And see HP to Croker, 26 July.

11. Bilbao in current Spanish spelling, Bilboa in Popham's, Bilbo in Basque.

12. After the seige had been abandoned, Wellington was said to have exclaimed to his officers, 'Douglas was right; he was the only man who told me the truth.' He wasn't the only one: Popham had suggested it long before.

13. The most recent, Dr David Gates, refers harshly to Wellington's 'complacency and ineptitude' at Burgos.

14. Not long before he left for Spain, Popham had written in a private letter' '... I have a little girl who I have promised to attend to her school as Lady Popham is confined...' This is, admittedly, ambiguous: she may have been ill then, or she may have been giving birth to their last daughter, Harriet—date unknown.

CHAPTER XVIII

Missing the Action 1813-17

1

IN LETTERS written early in 1813 Popham makes it quite clear that he expected to return to Spain, just as he had in 1810, and felt justifiably aggrieved at not being given the appointment. 'I tried very hard to continue in *Venerable*,' he wrote to Keith on 23 January, 'but I was overpowered.' The ostensible reason was that *Venerable* was due for a major refit: the actual reasons—for he could have been found another ship—are more subtle and more difficult to clarify.

There is a hint in a letter from Keith to Melville, written in September of the previous year: 'I have private information that Popham and Mendizabel are not well together and it is not imagined that the latter will act heartily with the former. It is stated that none of the Regular Spanish Officers are inclined to Sir Home Popham consequent of some old misunderstanding at Buenos Ayres, but of which I am ignorant.'

On 5 January 1813 Popham himself wrote to Melville, hoping to see him, 'before I am practically superceded in the *Venerable*.' And he continued:

> I am aware from a variety of circumstances that the Service on which I have been employed, has not fully gratified the unnatural expectation which has been established about its issue; but the unqualified approbation of Lord Wellington so strongly recorded in my Favor and so personally marked, added to your Lordship's kind letters, are conclusive that this calculation is to be attributed to Causes very far removed from the stirling facts.

What those expectations were, and who entertained them, is not entirely clear, though Lord Bathurst, the Secretary of War, had written to the Secretary of the Admiralty while Popham was in Spain expressing his apprehension that 'the views of Lord Wellington were likely to be counteracted' by Popham's operations—which was patently untrue. At all events, he was still hopeful of being appointed if 'another little squadron' was going to be sent to Spain, not least because it 'would silence the suspicions of many, that I have not pleased my superiors, and check the reiterated question of Friends: "Why are you not employed?"'

As is clear from the Finnerty affair, Popham had a certain careless aptitude for making enemies; and instead of being given the Spanish squadron, he was appointed to the *Stirling Castle* for the humdrum task of taking Lord Moira,[1] the Governor General of India designate, to Calcutta. The round voyage was to take a year, during which Wellington was able, not least because of having a supply base in Santander, to drive the French out of Spain once and for all. By the time the *Stirling Castle* was back in Portsmouth, the Army of the Peninsula was over the Pyrenees and Napoleon was on his way to exile on the Isle of Elba. The war appeared to be over.

2

Perhaps it was partly as a result of his disappointment and frustration that he took one look at the ship's company he had inherited and sent off a bitter letter to Melville complaining that the ship was manned by 'a host of dwarfs', 157 men between 4ft 11in and 5ft 4in in height, totally incapable of working a 32-pounder which weighed three and a half tons. Not to mention '63 most miserable Marines', and a bunch of Americans who were 'a great pest'. In view of the fact that we were at war with America, and there was more than a possibility that the ship, which would be escorting a convoy to a position south of the Line, might fall in with one of their heavy frigates, he felt his anxiety was justified. But justification, as always, included self-justification.

'I have raised three of the best ship's companies that ever went to sea,' he continued in the same letter, 'and it is the absence of such men as I had in *Romney*, *Diadem* and *Venerable*, that has made me resort to every honourable and manly mode of obtaining relief... by holding in Fee every Constable and Peace Officer on each side of the water...'

With the support of the C-in-C Portsmouth, Sir Richard Bickerton, he managed to rid himself of some of the 'dwarfs' and most of the Americans, but was still short of a full complement when Moira, his family, his servants and his baggage arrived early in April; and they did not finally sail until the 20th. In company were the frigate *Indefatigable* and a mixed bag of merchantmen and East Indiamen bound variously for St Helena, 'The Brazils', the Cape and India. The Admiralty's instructions were clear and it all sounded perfectly straightforward; but it ended up, not for the first time, with Sir Home Popham incurring Their Lordships' 'marked dissatisfaction'.

The passage to Madeira was notable mainly for the slowness, but also for the squall of hurricane force which hit the convoy without warning when they were a week out. It 'burst upon us' Moira noted in his Journal, 'with a suddenness and violence like which nothing had ever been witnessed by any officer in the ship', and although it only lasted an hour, it left the ships with sails 'shivered into shreds', masts gone by the board, and one of them on her beam ends and presumed lost—though she turned up later under jury rig.

Moira and his family stayed ashore while Home Popham found himself beset by problems, which he described in a brief letter to the Admiralty: brief, he explained later, because 'whilst on the Coast of Spain it had been intimated to me, that my correspondence was then thought too prolix'! Three of the convoy, he said, had not come into Funchal, but had simply slipped past the island in the dark while four others 'have written to me to say they propose to sail immediately and keep company, as they are all armed ships and only wanted protection to Madeira'. Meanwhile he had detached *Indefatigable* and sent her ahead to Tenerife to organise wine (the best available, Popham said, speaking from experience) and beef for the voyage on.

From this Their Lordships got the impression that Popham had simply allowed the convoy to disperse without protection, and they were furious: as soon as he reached Calcutta, he was to explain his actions to the C-in-C, Sir Samuel Hood. Of the storm to come, of course, he was quite unaware as he set off with the remaining ships to rejoin *Indefatigable*, pick up the provisions at Tenerife, and proceed with the voyage. They called briefly at the Cape Verde Islands, fired 'great guns in honour of Old George's birthday' somewhere north of the Line on 4 June, and stopped at the 'Isle of France' in mid-August. They had been driven so far to the eastward, one member of the company wrote in his journal, 'we might almost get to Madras as soon as the Isle of France, but afraid to run the risk of our stock falling—then what would become of the ladies?'

Neither from this account, nor from Moira's, does one get any sense of what life was like on a man-of-war which was carrying such an important personage, as well as a number of young women among his retinue. '... I think we get on tolerably well with our passengers,' Popham wrote to Lord Melville in May; 'I wish I could say as much about the ship's company. I have done everything in my power to make him happy.' And, a month later, '...Lord Moira, I believe, continues to be much more content with the voyage than I am.'

The anonymous diarist, however, seems to have got on 'tolerably well' with the retinue, and when they finally reached Calcutta at the end of September he wrote, 'I parted from the girls with much regret. Indeed it was mutual...' And Moira himself took leave of the ship 'with great cordiality... thanking [the people] for their good conduct and attention...' So perhaps the dwarfs had proved more useful than their captain had feared, and the Americans had not been such a pest after all.

3

The *Stirling Castle* sailed for Madras and home on 22 November 1814 with dysentery on board, and within ten days seventy-five of the crew were down with it and 'ulcers'. Driven too far south by the northeast monsoon, Popham made for Pondicherry instead where, the diarist notes, 'we put 120 men ashore in three hours and fumigated the ship twice a day'. In spite of which he attended 'some balls and one concert' and approved of the girls; but 'Mrs M. and Sir Home, not having been introduced among them' (presumably the local bigwigs) 'by the neglect of Colonel Frazer, they received no invitations.' Frazer was the East India Company's Commandant and Governor; 'Mrs M' was a Mrs Maitland, presumably a passenger returning to England for later in the voyage the diarist notes that she 'is very attentive'—but to him, not to Sir Home!

They had to leave nearly a hundred of the crew behind, including one 'who hanged himself in a fit of derangement in Pondicherry Hospital'; and a further thirty-three died on board during the course of the voyage after that. Three were drowned, two fell to their deaths, one from the main yard and one into the hold; and 'a steward's mate 'was found tranquilly dead in his hammock'. In addition, eight men including a midshipman fell overboard, but were picked up. For their captain, who had always prided himself on running a taut and healthy ship, the entire voyage must have proved a sore trial. He was also desperately busy on the final revision of the *Signal Book*: as he wrote to Melville when he got home, 'It occupied... by far the greatest part of my time during the voyage'—and one suddenly has a glimpse of him in his stern cabin, attended by his assistant Mr Bond, poring over the files of manuscript sheets of his *Marine Vocabulary*. Under 'Table of Provisions and Stores', Pendant N, Numbers N67 to N98: 'C' N67 Cabbages, N68 Cables, N81 Carrots, N85 Cheese, N94 Compasses, azimuth. Or, a little later, N1D to N9D: N4D Flannel Drawers, N7D French Beans, N9D Frocks, duck. And so on and on, through the alphabet, fumigating lamps, glue, hand pumps, hats, hops, Lisbon wine, lime juice, machine for sweetening water, molasses, mutton, nails, needles, oakum, onions, opium, pease, pigs, port wine, potatoes and ND8 Putlock plates. Then the sentences: CF When will you be able?; and the Syllables, 'principally intended to spell the Names of Officers in the Army and Navy'; and the 'Telegraphic Examples', viz:

No. of Hoists	Symbols	Significations
Five	BOE	Your
	AC8	Sister
	852	married
	85F	to
	C87	a Lord of the Admiralty

Through the stern windows, past the 'carved work of the ship's stern' where, Lord Moira had noticed, a yellowhammer had found refuge from the squall on the way out, the deep blue of the Indian Ocean and the white wake rippling out in trails of foam and bubbles under the burning sun; and as they rounded Cape Agulhas, Bartholomew Diaz's 'Cape of Storms', in February, the ship doing 12 knots in the squalls. The carpenter had reported rot in two of the masts: would they hold till they got home? And the sickness on the messdecks: had the measures he had taken stopped it? Go back: N2D Fishes for masts, N1D Fish... Would it be completed in time? Would it ever be completed at all—after fifteen mortal years?

At St Helena the *Stirling Castle* picked up a convoy of seventeen sail, and on 10 May recaptured the *Joan of Bristol* which had been taken by an American privateer the *Little Adams*—so *that* war was still going on—and thirteen days later she was anchored at Spithead after a voyage which had lasted for thirteen months, one week and three days, to find the world turned upside down.

4

For while they had been rolling back from St Helena, the war in Europe had come to an abrupt end. Paris had fallen to the Russian and Prussian armies on the last day of March, Napoleon had abdicated a week later, and on 24th May 1814 Louis XVIII entered France. The House of Bourbon was restored, and Europe was at peace once again. This was in the wide world beyond the stern windows of the *Stirling Castle*, but the repercussions from those remarkable events would soon be affecting her too. Within a week of his return, Home Popham learnt that Tsar Alexander of Russia and King Frederick William of Prussia, attended by a vast retinue of princes and nobles and including Metternich and von Blücher, were to visit England, and that there was to be a naval review in their honour at Portsmouth. This was not something he intended to miss.

In the meantime, however, there were other matters to engage his attention. On 2 June he was instructed to prepare the ship for service as soon as possible, in spite of her rotten masts. On the 4th he received the news that he had been promoted to Flag rank and was now a Rear-Admiral of the White. On the 5th he applied for leave to 'attend to some family concerns', and was refused until the Admiralty received his explanations regarding the dispersal of the convoy twelve months before, for they were still dissatisfied with the reasons he had given. Whereupon he settled down and wrote a report, prolix even by his standards and thirty pages long. The gist of it was that the three ships that had failed to come into Funchal had slipped away during the night; and the masters of the four which had asked permission to proceed independently, and which he had refused to give them, simply departed without it, in the dark and 'with great adroitness'. And for detaching the *Indefatigable* to Tenerife, this had been purely so that the provisions should be ready for them on arrival and they would not be delayed.

'My whole life, Sir,' he declared to John Wilson Croker, the Admiralty Secretary, with a characteristic flourish, 'has been devoted to my country, and I will not allow that my zeal has ever been behind anyone in the Service of the Navy.' And to support this irrefutable statement he quotes his capture of the Cape and Buenos Ayres and his operations at Copenhagen, and on the north coast of Spain co-operating with Lord Wellington, 'whose liberal and flattering appreciation of my zeal and exertions have been transmitted to their Lordships and publicly recorded in the Despatches.' Then there are his Signals, highly approved by Sir Samuel Hood and dozens of other senior officers—all of whom are quoted among the *fourteen* enclosures that accompany the letter.

This extraordinary document was written on 8 June. Three days later the ship is ordered to Cherbourg to pick up a detachment of Russian troops and convey them to Kronstadt; and at some point Elizabeth and her daughters arrive and leave with them the following day. 'Sailed from Portsmouth,' our anonymous diarist recorded on the 12th, 'Lady Popham and girls on board'; and he goes on:

Our fleet consists of twelve sail of the English line, four Russian, and two

French, six or seven frigates, etc... Walked on shore with the Ladies [trust him]—'a dirty town, and ill-paved streets—the children and lower classes of inhabitants crowded round the English ladies, and I suppose we had no less than 100 people following us all the time we were on shore, as well as the windows of the houses crammed full, gazing at us, to our no small amusement.

Three days later he notes, 'We learn we are to be here some time'.

This however, turns out to be a false rumour, for, as *The Times* reported on the 22nd, 'Arrived from Cherbourg the *Ville de Paris* and eight other sail-of-the-line, including the *Stirling Castle*—without the Russian troops, though 8,000 of them marched into the town the moment the fleet was pulling away.' Why the change of plan? And why the sudden departure?

5

The answer, of course, was the Naval Review, which was scheduled to begin that very day. Before the *Stirling Castle* had been despatched to Cherbourg, Popham had written to Melville to say that he had already drafted a plan for it and given it to Admiral Bickerton; and on the subject of the Tsar:

> Your Lordship must be aware of the intimacy with which I was honored by the present Emperor of Russia* when I was employed on a mission in that country, and that his Imperial Majesty used to sail with me on the Neva; the Honourable mark of distinction which I wear emanates from him and I have a small Pension attached to it for saving his father's life. Under these circumstances I most certainly should like to be employed for the few days of the Review, without which I cannot appear for fear it should be considered by His Imperial Majesty that I was in disgrace.[2]

Whether, in the event, he was able to renew his acquaintance with the Tsar does not emerge from the many reports of the occasion, but if he failed to do so it was not for lack of trying, for two days after his letter to Melville he was writing to Colonel McMahon on the same subject, asking him to put in a word with the Prince of Wales on his behalf.[3]

In any case, personalities were quite swamped by reports of the turmoil and excitement of the Review itself. Portsmouth, *The Courier* reported on the 22nd, was jammed with sightseers, 300,000 of them at a guess 'and at Spithead upwards of thirty Sail of the Line, and frigates and other ships of war, which will make the whole amount to more than fifty sail. They are moored in proper order, and in the manner calculated to give the best possible effect to the grand spectacle which is about to take place.' The flags of seven admirals were flying from the

---

* In 1799 Alexander would have been twenty-two.

assembled ships, presumably that of Rear-Admiral Sir Home Popham among them; though on that same day he was in fact superceded in the *Stirling Castle*, and from then on his letters are headed simply Portsmouth. After all that, the Royal party failed to turn up.

They arrived the next day, however, and were led into the town, according to ancient custom, by the rope-makers of the Dockyard; and all admirals, captains and commanders were presented and kissed the Royal hand. Then the Imperial party accompanied by the Prince of Wales, boarded the Royal Barge and with the standard flying and the guns firing a salute, were rowed down the lines of ships. Yards were manned and they were given three hearty cheers. Next they went aboard HMS *Impregnable* and the ship was immediately surrounded by hundreds of rowing-boats 'to form a floating platform for several hundred yards'. The Tsar insisted on going down to the messdecks where he had a tot of rum with the tars. It was not 'neaters' but grog, six parts of water to one of spirit, and, said the Tsar, 'would be no worse for being stronger!' One is inevitably reminded of the scene with his father - at which he was probably present - on board the *Nile* fifteen years before, and one would like to think that Home Popham was present on this occasion also, but that cannot be substantiated. That night Portsmouth and Southsea 'were generally illuminated in the most splendid manner... and many transparencies were exhibited.'

On the following day the Royal party visited the Dockyard. The Tsar, who had been the toast of the town ever since he landed at Dover a fortnight before, was fascinated by the blockmaking machinery, and by the steam-engine.[4] They then went to watch the forty-odd ships 'perform various evolutions'. The firing of salutes was continuous and deafening, and it was noted that the Tsar's sister, the Duchess of Oldenburg, 'bore the shock of the firing with much fortitude'. They were at sea again on the next and final day—one more like October than June, it was said—when the whole fleet got under way once more and sailed out past St Helens for what was intended to be a 'regular naumachy'—a mimic sea-fight—but was cut short by the weather. Nevertheless it had been a rousing success from beginning to end.

It is impossible to be sure what part, if any, Home Popham played in the festivities. In his letter to McMahon he had remarked that when he asked Lord Melville to allow him to hoist his flag, 'Joe Yorke says he will do all to prevent it, that I am a *damned* cunning fellow [Popham's underlining] and that I shall monopolise all the credit to myself if anything is well done.' No doubt we should never have heard the last of it.

Meanwhile he was officially unemployed, and smarting under the judgement of the Lords Commissioners that his explanation of the convoy affair was 'very far from satisfactory', 'his reasons were inadequate', and they expressed 'their marked dissatisfaction of his proceedings... which, at the period when they occurred was a continuation of the war, exposed the trade of His Majesty's subjects to unnecessary risk and occasioned considerable anxiety not only to the public mind but in that also of their Lordships.[5] So one may say that almost his first communication from the

Admiralty since his promotion to Rear-Admiral was a rocket: this was quite in character.

Not that it discouraged him from one moment from badgering Melville for another appointment: a Colonelcy of Marines, perhaps? or supervising the embarkation of the cavalry at Boulogne? But nothing was to materialise until the following year.

6

His life on half-pay, however, was neither idle nor uneventful and he was at last able to spend some time with Elizabeth and their family at Titness. After all the years of sea-time, Elizabeth's plea was answered. Their fourth son, Edmund, had died suddenly in 1809, and William, the eldest, was now eighteen and a lieutenant. 'I ought not to be the Herald of my son,' Popham wrote to Melville at the end of June 1814, 'but I wish you to know that he was at the capture of the Cape, Buenos Ayres, Copenhagen and Walcheren, that he was a second time in South America and is now in North America, and he has been mentioned to the Admiralty for his conduct in action'. For the first two, of course, he had been with his father in *Diadem*. But Caroline, who was twenty, and Mary, a year younger, were probably still at home, as were the two youngest boys, Brunswick Lowther and Strachan Irving. There was one other daughter, Harriet.

On 3 January 1815 he was made Knight Commander of the Military Order of the Bath;[6] and on 25 March, on the news that Napoleon had escaped from Elba,

---

The relevant passage in Popham's letter to Col McMahon of 10 June 1814. Sir Joseph Yorke was one of the Lords of the Admiralty.

he wrote urgently to Melville suggesting that he should hoist his flag at Deal, ready to undertake any operations 'on the coast of Flanders or in the Scheldt where I have so long served'. His request was not granted—indeed, there would have been no call on his services: instead, on 19 May he was appointed to command in the Thames, and hoisted his flag, more prosaically, in HMS *Thisbe* at Greenwich on the 23rd. Soon afterwards he transferred to the *Iris* and she was to be his official headquarters for the next twelve months, though in fact he lived in a rented house ashore. The job was routine, and after the Battle of Waterloo a month later a peacetime one, of laying up ships 'in ordinary', of postings and courts-martial, requests for leave, and daily returns on 'ships fitting and dismantling' in the River, and were the Royal Yachts to be included in the monthly reports?

But there were still the final details of the *Signal Book* to be settled (in April 1816 he is ordered 'to attend their Lordships on Tuesday next at 1 o'clock' bringing them with him) until they were finally printed in an edition of 1,200 the following year. And his interest in novel weapons was still alive: early in the same year he reported on a certain John Bland's 'repeating firearm', which he considered 'too dangerous on board ship'—too dangerous, presumably, for the user.

His long self-imposed task of improving ship-to-ship and ship-to-shore communication by flag had not diminished his interest in the problems of communication in general, for a year earlier, in the same month in which he delivered his final draft of the *Signal Book*, he wrote to Melville on the subject of his 'improved shore telegraph'. 'Another mode has occurred to me of communicating the whole of my vocabulary by a Shore Telegraph, considerably more simple than the one which I have already submitted to your Lordship.'

No details of his original 'mode' have come to light; but the improved mode is well documented, was duly adopted, survived for nearly half a century and deserves attention.

7

The need to send messages rapidly was as important ashore as at sea, but nothing more satisfactory than beacon fires was evolved until the French inventor Claude Chappe produced his 'T-Type' telegraph in 1794. It consisted of a stout mast 18 feet high with a crossbeam pivoted in the centre at the top. At each end of this was a short arm which swivelled through 180°. Crossbeam and arms were thus all articulated, and used in conjunction could form 196 different signals. Between 1794 and 1800 chains of Chappe's telegraph connected Paris to Lille, to Strasbourg and to Brest. Others later included Boulogne, Lyons, and even Turin, Milan and Venice, keeping step with Napoleon's conquests. In addition the French had a coastal semaphore system based on a post and moveable arms like standard railway signals.[7] It was said a sentence could be transmitted by Chappe's system over a distance of 100 miles in five minutes in favourable conditions.

At the time England had nothing comparable. With the outbreak of war with

France and the possibility of invasion, the Admiralty recognised the need for it; and when details of Chappe's idea reached the Duke of York's headquarters in Flanders (it is tempting to think that Popham might have seen them there) and were passed on to Whitehall, their Lordship's acted swiftly. They did not copy Chappe's system, however, and Depillon's coastal semaphore had not yet been installed; instead, they adopted a quite different method, recommended by the Rev. John Gamble who had been the Duke of York's chaplain. The Admiralty Telegraph consisted of six shutters, three feet square and mounted in pairs in a frame like a guillotine. Each shutter, operated separately by ropes, had two positions, open or closed, and working them was likened to bell-ringing. By the end of 1796 a whole series of these machines had been built on suitable 'Telegraph Hills' and other eminences from the Admiralty building in Whitehall to Deal, Sheerness and Portsmouth. After the Peace of Amiens and the resumption of the war it was extended to Yarmouth, but the projected Plymouth line was never completed. In good weather a message could reach Portsmouth from the Admiralty in about a quarter of an hour.

The system worked well, and references to orders and information arriving 'by telegraph' occur frequently in letters; it was only allowed to fall into disuse after Napoleon's first abdication and the Peace of Paris in May 1814. Then came his escape, and the panic of the Hundred Days: if the war was to be renewed, the Admiralty would again need rapid communication with the main Naval ports, and it was decided to reinstate it, or something comparable.

There was no shortage of alternatives. According to Sir Francis Ronalds, who had submitted an electric telegraph of his own invention—which was rejected—'everyone knows that telegraphs have long been great bores at the Admiralty'; which is hardly surprising since 'a hundred plans of telegraphs have been sent to their Lordships'. Out of this *embarras de choix* they settled on Home Popham's, which he had been busy perfecting since writing to Melville in April when he said he had thought of trying it out in Windsor Park but decided it was too public.

By the end of June 1815 the war really was over, but the Admiralty decided to go ahead with the replacement system; and an Act of Parliament was passed 'for Establishing Signal and Telegraph Stations'.[8] Work started on a trial line; and in May 1816 *The Times* reported:

> The Telegraph frames [the original shutter type] at the top of the Admiralty are being removed, and the improved semaphore consisting of a hollow mast from which two arms project in various directions will be erected in their stead. The utility of this invention is to be tried, by way of experiment, in a few days from London to Sheerness, and the number of stations it is said, will not exceed nine. Several are erected.

In fact there would be thirteen between London and Deal and Dover, and fourteen between London and Portsmouth. In the trials it was found to be easier to read

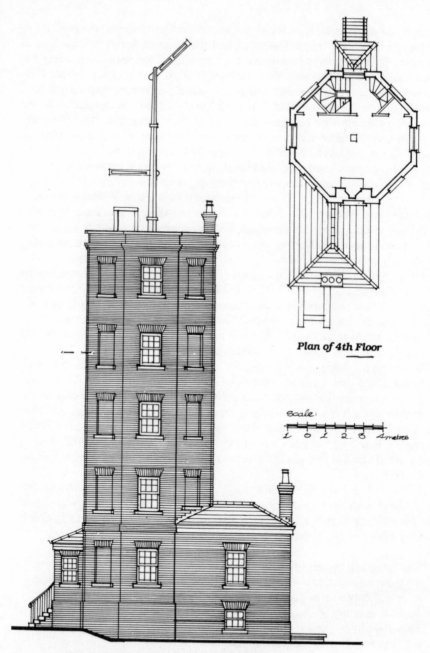

Plan of 4th Floor

Scale:

1 0 1 2 3 4 metres

CHATLEY HEATH TOWER
Aspect from the South West

than the shutters: work went ahead, and the line was working at the end of July. It was the only one to be completed in Popham's lifetime.

He submitted the design to the Society of Arts that same year, the working drawings were published in their *Transactions* and he was awarded their Gold Medal. The mast could be swivelled through 360°, and all the machinery, the rods and bevel wheels which controlled the arms, and the arms themselves when at rest, were housed inside it. The mechanism was made by the same Henry Maudslay who had been responsible for the block-making machinery in Portsmouth Dockyard, and very beautiful it was, a fine example of precision engineering. The movement of the arms was by winch handles, and two dials showed the position of each to the operator.*

* See back endpaper.

7

A month before the Sheerness trial, Popham wrote to Croker at the Admiralty, 'In considering the difficulty of displaying flags in a calm, it occurred to me that the powers of the new Telegraph Semaphore, might be so employed on the quarterdeck of a ship as, in a great measure to obviate the use of flags'. That, after having spent the previous sixteen years perfecting his flag signals! The idea had been approved, he said, by several flag officers and captains, and by 'some scientific men unconnected with the Navy'; and quite apart from anything else, 'upon the saving that must result from the diminished use of Buntin... I cannot think it necessary to dwell.'

He enclosed a drawing and instructions for the 'Sea Telegraph', and it was gradually introduced onto the quarterdecks of His Majesty's ships. As an extra refinement, Popham's 'Sea Semaphores' were mounted on wheeled trucks.

One of the multitude of hopeful telegraph-inventors was a Lt. Col. Charles Pasley[9] who produced his own 'polygrammatic Telegraph', a most elaborate affair which, in a later, much-simplified version, was not unlike Popham's; and when the Admiralty adopted the latter, Pasley accused him of plagiarism. Nothing happened then; but a few years after Popham's death Pasley's 'Universal Telegraph for Day and Night Signals' started to replace Popham's, which had not proved quite as successful as its inventor had predicted.

In its final and simplest form, 'Semaphore' became 'flag-wagging', one man with two hand-flags, which was still being taught to ratings up to the Second World War—and perhaps still is—with the Morse Code and the signal lamp at night when

Opposite: Chatley Heath Signal Tower, near Cobham, Surrey, one of fourteen Semaphore Stations linking the Admiralty with Portsmouth and only completed after Popham's death. The tower is over 60ft high and was semi-derelict when, in 1965, it was taken over by Surrey County Council and restored. It contains some of the original machinery (see back endpaper), and is open to the public at weekends in summer.

radio silence forbade the use of Wireless Telegrapy.

In October of that year, 1816, Home Popham replied to a letter from the Admiralty in which he had been directed 'to state what personal expenses I may have incurred in preparing the Signal Books and Semaphores'. This letter gives a clear answer to what one writer on signals guessed had 'probably... been of some pecuniary expense to him'. In the early days, Popham says, he had kept no accounts, 'for I never imagined the system of communication, could have been brought to its present state of utility'. He then describes the various stages of its development from its beginnings in 1799 to his second edition in 1803 'which was very generally used almost immediately... and copies were transmitted to Lord Nelson and many other officers...', though they were not issued officially until 1805.

'From that period I have been almost unceasingly engaged in making improvements', culminating in his being told to revise the Admiralty Signals in 1812. Through a Mr Lethbridge, who had handled his affairs since 1804, he estimates that the work had cost him on average £150 a year, 'independantly of about £300 which the two Editions alluded to, cost me in printing.' He goes on to say that 'without the constant assistance of one person, and frequently more, I could never have brought this object to the satisfactory conclusion which I trust I have, for independantly of the employment of Mr Robertson who was with me five years previously to Mr Lethbridge, I have had for nearly the last six years the constant services of Mr Bond, who in addition to a small pecuniary allowance has latterly lived at my expense...' As for his work on the Semaphores, that had only involved 'travelling charges going to and from Chatham and other places several times' and could not have cost him more than £30.

Scribbled across the second page of the letter is a minute for the Navy Board in Croker's hand: 'Direct the Navy Board to pay Sir Home Popham the sum of £2,000 in full for his expenses and disbursements of all kinds... Tell Sir H. Popham that their Ldships consider this as final settlements of his claims on these points... and he is not to incur any further expenses without the previous sanction of the Board.' The letter authorising payment, headed 'Admiralty Office. 23 Dec 1816', includes before the word 'expenses' the word 'trouble'.

It is usually stated that Home Popham was paid this sum for his land semaphore; but it is clear that, far from being a reward for that, it was a (somewhat grudging) reimbursement for work done voluntarily over many years, by which the Navy was the regular and enduring beneficiary. Popham's Semaphore[10] continued to be the Admiralty's only fast method of communicating with· its main naval bases at Portsmouth, Chatham, Deal and Dover until 31 December 1847, when the 'electric telegraph', unsusceptible to fog and darkness, replaced it—much to the dismay of *The Times*. Not only would it throw out of work the ageing officers, many of them war veterans and some of them partially disabled, who manned the stations, but everyone knew 'the proneness to derangement of the electric mode of communication'; and how easy it would be for 'any ill-disposed person to cut the wires'. But there was no stopping Progress. Not even at sea where, despite the adoption of new-fangled ideas such as steam, Popham's flag signals and his *Marine Vocabulary* continued, modified but essentially unchanged, until the end of the century.

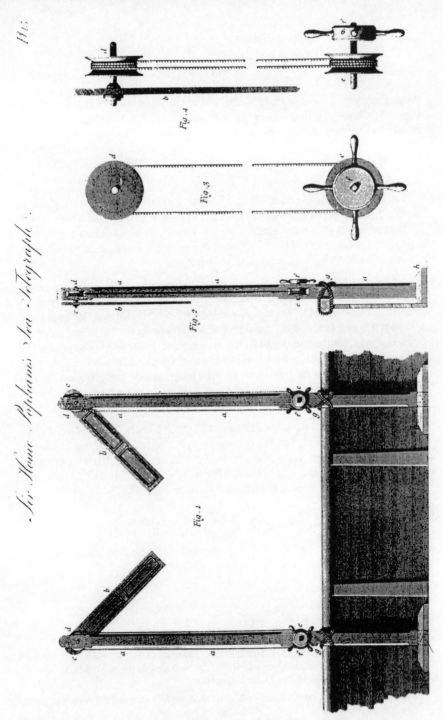

Sir Home Popham's Sea Telegraph.

Fig. 4

Fig. 3

Fig. 2

Fig. 1

Popham's Sea Telegraph, introduced on board HM Ships during his last years but later replaced by Lt.Col. Charles Pasley's 'Universal Telegraph'.

9

As a postscript to the year 1816, the following letter from Lord Keith, Home Popham's C-in-C when he was on the coast of Spain, to N. Vansittart the Chancellor of the Exchequer, requires no comment.

London, 21st June 1816.

Sir,

I have just received from Sir Home Popham, an Officer of very considerable merit, a Letter... by which it appears that he feels himself in some degree hurt at a part of a letter attached to the Memorial which I had the honour to present on behalf of the Navy, not having been accompanied by one from Lord Wellington, which he now transmits.

I confess that it would have been much better if Lord Wellington's Letter had been attached, because it would, if possible, have substantiated the co-operation more fully: but my only reason for not introducing that and many other Letters establishing the merit of Sir Home on the service alluded to, was to prevent the Memorial from being too much swelled with documents, and rather to establish the express orders of Government upon the subject, than the distinguished services of Sir Home, which were known by His Majesty's Ministers to have been most important to Lord Wellington's operations.

From the favourable consideration that has already been given to the Memorial, I am not, I hope, asking too much in requesting you to take an opportunity of mentioning the circumstance in the House, in order to satisfy the mind of an active and zealous Officer, whose merit is well known, and to whom I have, very unintentionally, given cause for complaint.

> I have the honour to be,
> Sir,
> Your most obedient humble servant,
> (Signed) KEITH,
> Admiral.

NOTES ON CHAPTER XVIII

1. Francis Rawdon Hastings (1754-1826), First Marquis of Hastings and Second Earl of Moira. His Journal of the voyage to India, not included in the published volume of his Indian journal, is in MS in Duke University.

2. This letter in WLC contains the only reference to HP's saving Paul's life that has been found.

3. RA GEO MSS: Library, Windsor Castle. In the same letter Popham mentions that he

has 'a most beautiful ivory box' for Princess Charlotte from the Moiras, 'two beautiful spotted deer from the interior of Asia' which he suggests giving to the Prince Regent, and a curious collection of birds'. One is reminded of Ned Thompson's death on the coast of Guinea.

4. The blockmaking machinery was invented by Marc Brunel, Isambard's father, and built by the great engineer Henry Maudslay. L.T.C. Rolt describes it as 'perhaps the first example of fully mechanised production in the world'. The Tsar was so impressed he tried to persuade Marc Brunel to accompany him back to St Petersburgh. (See L.T.C. Rolt: *Isambard Kingdom Brunel*, pp 10-14.)

5. The Admiralty had a case: in October 1813 the British Consul in Madeira, Mr Veitch, had written to them of the dangers to the trade there, 'a place of rendezvous' but 'not a place of safety' as privateers, especially American, could prey on ships coming and going. A frigate should be stationed there permanently. The story that Popham had dispersed the convoy was repeated by Lloyd's, and he threatened Mr Bennett, the Secretary of Lloyd's Coffee House, with 'a prosecution for libel'. Bennett apologised, saying he had been misinformed.

6. The Most Honorable Order of the Bath, founded 1725; enlarged 1815 into two divisions, Civil and Military. Popham's investiture was on 12 April 1815. Over 200 naval and military men received it that year.

7. I am indebted to *The Old Telegraphs* by Geoffrey Wilson for much of the historical detail on signalling systems in this chapter.

8. 55 Geo III. C.128. 29 June 1815. It is difficult to conceive why the Admiralty decided to abandon the old system in the first place, or why they imagined they did not need such a method of communication.

9. Lt-Colonel Sir Charles William Pasley, RE, KCB, 1780-1861. He was severely wounded at the siege of Flushing in 1809, and it was there that he (and Popham?) saw the French coastal signalling system.

10. Popham's Semaphore was adopted in America in 1837; and 'During the siege of Lucknow (1857) Martin Gubbins, Financial Commissioner of the Residency, turned up particulars of the construction... in the *Penny Cyclopedia*. A machine of the Popham type was made and erected...' to make contact with the relieving force at Alambagh, 3½ miles away. Wilson, p199. op.cit.

CHAPTER XIX

Friend of the
Black King
1818-20

1

IN OCTOBER 1816 Home Popham wrote to the Admiralty asking for twelve months' leave of absence 'to go to Paris and other parts of France'. He gave no reasons, and none have come to light; it has not even been possible to discover where he went or what he did or whether Elizabeth or any of the family went with him. Perhaps he felt like a holiday. If so, it was an ideal opportunity. He was unemployed, the war was over, his Land Telegraph was under construction, and his claim for expenses had been agreed; and it may simply have been that, in common with hundreds of his contemporaries, he was curious to see something of the country which had dominated Englishmen's thoughts and actions for over twenty years.

Whatever the reason, there is no doubt that he was in France for at least part of the next twelve months. Across his application is scrawled the one word 'Grant'; and in September 1817 he was writing to Earl Grey from Paris: 'On the arrangements for the relief of the biennial command, Lord Melville has proposed Jamaica to me, which I have accepted, and shall take my leave of Paris next week.' The rest is a tantalising blank.

That he had kept in touch with naval affairs during his absence is clear. In his letter to Grey he discusses the difficulties of introducing 'young gentlemen to the Service' presumably in the light of the rundown after the war; and back in London in November he was writing to the Admiralty on the subject of the binnacles and compasses made to his design, which the Navy Board had rejected as not being enough of an improvement as to justify the expense. 'I have ever thought, that too little attention has been paid to the improvement of compasses. Our ultimate reliance must be on them—the responsibility of men's lives and the fate of ships rest on their correctness. No expense is spared for Sextants and Timepieces, where hundreds of pounds are considered nothing...' And he points out that in forty-eight hours of thick weather, with an 8 knot wind, an error in the compass of 1° 'would throw the ship out upward of thirty miles'.[1]

In the meantime there were all the preparations to be made for departure, not, this time, for a solitary life in the stern cabin of a ship of war, but ashore in the Admiral's house in Kingston and with the company of Elizabeth, his son Home, and at least one of his daughters. Moreover, their eldest son William was out there already, in command of HMS *Tyrian* of the Jamaica squadron. Yet, what must have appeared in prospect as promising a pleasant change from the years at sea, united with his wife and family, was to be, in many ways, one of the most bitter periods of his life: the irony of it all underlined by the fact that, during his first year in Jamaica, he received yet another honour, being created a Knight Commander of the Order of Guelphs.[2]

2

They sailed in HMS *Andromache* towards the end of the year, and Popham took over his command on 26 January 1818. Jamaica had been in British hands since 1655 and had remained at the centre of Caribbean affairs ever since, headquarters of the buccaneers, a naval base, and through its sugar plantations a source of wealth and influence back home. The prosperity engendered by sugar and, to a lesser extent, by cotton, had suffered as a result of events outside the colonists' control: American independence, wars, Napoleon's blockade of European ports, competition from, particularly, Cuba and Hispaniola, and the abolition of the slave trade. Many plantations lay derelict, and as one writer put it, 'stagnation and decay set in'.

Yet the island also had a vigorous entrepot trade in manufactured goods from England with Cuba and the ports of Central and South America, and in bullion from them, notably Vera Cruz, and was still, as one writer put it with more truth than elegance, 'in the very belly of all commerce'. It also possessed a jealously independent House of Assembly, and a merchant class both plaintive and vociferous. At the same time the Caribbean swarmed with latter-day buccaneers: pirates and privateers sailing under a variety of flags and alert to pounce on any ship they could take and plunder. Within two months of his arrival, Home Popham mentioned in his Intelligence Report to the Admiralty that there were 'two insurgent privateer schooners', a large schooner under Mexican colours, a ship under Haitian colours 'commanded by a Pirate called Pinel', and a 'long low ship cruising under a Buenos Ayres flag ... with an English-American crew and looking for the *Iphigenia* Spanish frigate with $3-4 million on board'[3], all somewhere between the Antilles and the Mosquito Gulf. In order to pacify the Kingston merchants he was compelled to institute a convoy system, as in wartime. One of the causes for their complaints had been that the ships of the squadron were being employed to carry specie from Vera Cruz and other ports on the Spanish Main, a job which suited their captains as they were paid freight for the work.

There were a number of complicating factors, in an area which was in a state of constant political upheaval. On the mainland of South America various insurgent forces were at work driving out the Spaniards. Miranda, Popham's old associate, had died two years before; but Simon Bolivar working from New Granada (now Colombia) was about to establish, once and for all, the independence of Venezuela. Argentina, liberated but divided, was loosely linked with Chile, where Jose de San Martin and Bernardo O'Higgins, with the assistance of Admiral Thomas Cochrane, were working towards the same end. And in the original Spanish colony of Hispaniola a tripartite division had emerged: Santo Domingo, still Spanish, occupying the eastern half of the island, and the two, mutually inimical, parts of Haiti the western. In the northern half was Christophe, King Henry I, still undisputed master of his black fiefdom; in the southern, the mulatto republic of President Pétion.

> The northern section, [Popham wrote to Melville in April]... is governed by an arbitrary savage, aiming at absolute Monarchy, cruel in the extreme, universally hated. The southern part has been governed by a man who is anxious to establish a Republican government. [And he continued] It will be said, I know, that an Empire of Blacks so near this important island is pregnant with danger... but the independence of San Domingo is an advantage...

An advantage not least, because the restored French monarchy under Louis XVIII had already made one attempt to reimpose French sovereignty over Haiti—and had been rudely rebuffed; an advantage also because the chaos there during the previous twenty years had destroyed the island's predominance as a sugar producer. At the same time, a land no more than 120 miles away where slavery had been abolished represented a kind of exemplary threat in an island whose economy depended on slave labour and where the effects of the abolition of the slave trade were starting to bite.

More will be heard later of that 'arbitrary savage'; but the month before Popham wrote that letter Alexander Pétion had died, and was succeeded by Jean-Pierre Boyer. No one quite knew what the result would be in that incorrigibly volatile island, and Popham sent HMS *Primrose* to report. They found the island calm, and both Boyer and Christophe well disposed towards the British. Nevertheless the merchants were uneasy. 'As all changes of Government in that country since the French Revolution', one firm wrote to Popham, 'have hitherto been marked by scenes of carnage and by destruction of property ... the merchants living there were anxious for protection.' Since that property, in Port-au-Prince and the other ports in the Republic, amounted to £1 million they had reason to be worried.

Slavery, inevitably, was the most intransigent issue besetting not merely Jamaica and the West Indies as a whole, but the entire Western Hemisphere, for the great West Africa–West Indies–Britain triangle of trade had been built upon it and now the very foundations were crumbling. While Wilberforce and Clarkson[4] had been at work in England, agitating for the abolition first of the trade and finally of the institution of slavery itself, Revolutionary France had cut through the whole process in five dramatic years. Representation by the free mulattoes of San Domingo, granted by the Directory in 1791, led in turn to the doomed mulatto rising against their white overlords, and the slave rebellion in the same year which resulted in the death of 2,000 whites and 10,000 blacks, and the destruction of 1,000 plantations.

'Brown equality' had led to a demand for 'Black freedom'; and in 1794 the slaves, in an extraordinary alliance with the local French Revolutionary forces and led by the former slave Toussaint L'Ouverture, drove out first the British who had occupied Port-au-Prince, and then, three years later, the French. In 1801 Toussaint occupied the eastern half of the island as well, freed the slaves, declared himself Governor-General of the whole island, and published his own constitution.

Such independence incensed Bonaparte, who despatched a major expedition to restore the colony to France and the blacks to slavery, thus wiping out everything the Revolution had granted them. The ensuing campaign was stained by the most appalling cruelty by the French under Le Clerc: Toussaint was taken by treachery, shipped to France, and left to die in an icy cell in the Jura; but it was to no avail. Yellow fever did its deadly work among the French forces; and with the resumption of the war after the Peace of Amiens, Bonaparte was unable to reinforce them. In 1804 the French remnant was evacuated, as prisoners of war, by the British and the brutal Dessalines became the ruler of Haiti. After his assassination in 1806, San Domingo was returned to Spain and Pétion took over the southern half of Haiti, Christophe the northern. And, as a result of French duplicity and savagery, as well as the abolition of the slave trade by Britain in 1807, the latter came to be regarded as the true guardian of Haitian independence. This was the troubled and divided principality which Rear-Admiral Sir Home Popham set out to visit in HMS *Iphigenia* in May 1819.

3

On the way the Squadron first visited Campeche, then Vera Cruz—where certain matters concerning the free passage of British ships had to be resolved with the Governor,—and Havana, to which certain British ships were, illicitly, still trading in slaves. They arrived at Cap Henry, Christophe's capital, in the middle of the month, wondering what they would find there, and little realising that they were about to witness the most astonishing kingdom in history.

Henri Christophe, King Henry I, had been born a slave in Grenada in 1767, had served for a time as a steward in one of D'Estaing's ships, and had fought outstandingly in the campaigns that ousted the French. On his election as President of the State of Haiti (as opposed to the Republic in the south) in 1807, he had set out with demonic energy to achieve two main goals. The first was to ensure that the French never returned as colonists. The second was to demonstrate to the world that black people were just as capable as white of creating a humane, educated and civilised society.

A man of massive presence, to begin with unable to read or write but with a formidable intellect, he set about the task of shaping to his design the amorphous society which was the legacy of servitude. In the ten years preceding Popham's visit he had introduced a legal system, the Code Henry, complete with courts and procedures and a judiciary; employed an English doctor to create a comprehensive medical and hospital service, and English teachers to establish a first-class educational system on 'Lancastrian' principles.[5] On assuming royal status as Sa Majesté Henry, Roi d'Hayti, in 1811, he created an entire *Ordre de la Noblesse* with his son, Jacques Victor, as Prince, his delightfully named daughters Francoise Amethyste and Anne-Athenaire as Princesses Royal, and his Queen Marie Louise — a baker's daughter and 'a very amiable and charitable woman, quite destitute of the affectation, which generally accompanies so extraordinary a rise as hers' — as Reine d'Hayti. Below them came a hierarchy of Dukes, Counts, Barons and Chevaliers, prominent among them the Duc de Marmalade and the Duc de Limonade, place names bequeathed by the French occupation but sounding somewhat frivolous to our ears.[6] Despite the French titles, English was to become the official language, the Catholic religion and morality were to be strictly enforced, and the land system reformed.

Christophe's model was Frederick the Great, and when he came to build his main palace near Cap Henry (now Cap Haitien) on the north coast, he called it *Sans Souci*. He built other palaces elsewhere; and 2,500 feet up at La Ferrière in the mountains behind *Sans Souci* an impregnable fortress, Citadel Henry, his final bastion against the possible return of the French.

Home Popham left no record of his visits to this truly strange and wonderful place, but one of his lieutenants of *Iphigenia*, signing himself simply GWC, wrote a long and fascinating account of it in a letter to a friend, which was published in Blackwood's Edinburgh magazine.

> The Admiral landed at six in the morning of May 16... Sir Home Popham was received at the landing-place by a guard of honour, where carriages were waiting to convey the party [eight of them all told, including two captains, the surgeon of the Port Royal hospital, and the writer] to the house allotted for our reception...uncommonly clean, well-furnished, and provided with a library and plenty of servants.

There was a guard which turned out every time Popham left or returned, and sentries at the door and, oddly, at the head of the staircase. Christophe himself was away at the frontier, but the party was warmly welcomed by Baron Dupuy, 'said to have greater influence than any other man'. The lieutenant continues,

> The Admiral then waited on the Duke of Marmalade, governor of Cape Henry; after which we sat down to breakfast, and found a most sumptuous entertainment provided...Sixteen places were provided for whatever guests Sir Home Popham thought proper to invite. Carriages and horses were kept constantly in readiness.

The lieutenant goes on to describe very shrewdly the country's recent history, the fear and loathing of the French and yet, at the same time, the wish to have their independence acknowledged by France and guaranteed by England, 'for without Great Britain as a third party, such is their opinion of French perfidy they will not even enter into a negotiation with them'. He discusses the Code Henry, the strict morality often enforced personally by Christophe, the 'magnificent palace of *Sans Souci*' with its superb local workmanship, the discipline of the Army, and the schools. 'The Admiral', he says, 'visited these institutions, and was much pleased with their order and regularity, and with the proficiency of the boys, several of whom were examined for his satisfaction.'

The picture which this little scene creates is irresistible: the English Admiral Home Popham who, one feels, was good with children, at his most genial; the solemn rows of black faces; the English dominie, Gulliver or Sanders, hovering round and quizzing them, and beyond the windows, the mountains shimmering through the heat under the billowing trade wind clouds. Was it all too neat, too orderly, too perfect, to last?

Although Christophe was still away, the party was entertained every evening

with balls, given for our amusement by the order, and at the expense of the King. The colours of the company varied from the black to the white. Some of the Creoles were uncommonly pretty, and agreeable; and the extraordinary good manners of the generality of the company (whether black, brown, or white) were truly admirable... We danced quadrilles (in the Creole style) and now and then an English country dance...

On Thursday the 19th, the Governor gave a grand entertainment in honour of the Admiral. We sat down, about fifty, to dinner. The entertainment was excellent, and conducted in very good style.. As soon as dinner was over, the Duke of Marmalade, in a long speech proposed the 'health of the King of Great Britain, and perpetual amity with the great nation over which he reigns.' This was drunk with great applause. Sir Home Popham then, in a complimentary speech, gave 'the Health of the Good King Henry.' The Haytians appeared to devour every word he uttered, and *received the toast with more enthusiasm than I ever witnessed...* A band of music attended, and struck up a tune to every toast.

Late that night Christophe returned to his capital, and at ten o'clock the following morning King and Admiral met for the first time.

The entrance to the palace is both handsome and convenient. In the halls are the prints of distinguished British statesman, soldiers and sailors, together with several military and naval victories. We were conducted, through two lines of officers to a large and splendidly furnished room, rendered delightfully cool by artificial means. The Court-uniform of the officers is dark green, with crimson facings, and a profusion of embroidery; their pantaloons of white satin, embroidered with gold... In a few minutes the King and his son, the Prince Royal, entered the room... The ease and dignified elegance of his deportment did not fail to excite our admiration. He was dressed in a plain green coat, decorated with the grand cross of the Order of St Henry, white satin breeches, and crimson Morocco boots. Though covered upon his entrance, he took off his hat, and desired us to be seated. His hair is perfectly grey, his countenance very intelligent, and his whole person well-proportioned; his manners are particularly pleasing, without the slightest appearance of affectation or arrogance.

He first addressed himself to the Admiral, congratulating him on his arrival, and expressing his hope that he intended to make a long visit.. He then complimented him on his well-known abilities, said he was no stranger to the services he had done his country, mentioned the Popham code of signals now used in the navy and concluded by inviting us to his Palace of *Sans Souci*...

This invitation Home Popham had to refuse, for he had been away from his station already for far longer than he had intended.

The King then spoke to each of us, quite in a familiar manner; his whole conversation was highly flattering to England. The Prince Royal, only fifteen years old, is one of the fattest fellows I ever saw... and might easily pass for ten years older. His dress was as superb as gold, silver, and jewels could make it. In his hat he wore a large plume of ostrich feathers... I was told, he is a very good-natured boisterous lad.

After remaining half an hour, we retired, leaving the Admiral and the King *tête-a-tête*. Their conference lasted about two hours...

A conversation which, it seems clear, formed the basis for a respect and friendship which was natural and sincere. 'No man', the lieutenant wrote, 'could be better calculated to make a favourable impression than Sir Home Popham; his engaging manners, and enlightened understanding, made him popular with everyone.'

Back in Jamaica things were seen rather differently. Major-General Henry Conran, writing to Henry Goulburn, the Secretary at the Horse Guards, noted wryly in a private letter, '...we are much amused by the denunciations of the Jamaica politicians against Sir Home Popham for paying a visit to the Emperor of Hayti at Cape Francis: His Majesty played his part admirably, they say, and the Admiral is no bad actor himself. I should have enjoyed a peep.'

Of all the incidents in Popham's career, none—not even his captivation of Paul I—has quite the sheer delightful improbability of this genial meeting. There seems no doubt that they got on splendidly together; and as with Paul, and the Duke of York, and the Spanish guerrilleros, his openness and charm—which his enemies called plausibility—his obvious lack of prejudice and affectation, shine clear. But let our lieutenant have the last word. 'I never spent a more agreeable week than at Cape Henry,' he wrote, 'and I never met with so much kindness and hospitality... I could go on for ever, so pleasing are my recollections of our amiable Haytian friends.'

4

In the *Gentleman's Magazine* for 1819 there is the following brief note:

'March 31st. Miss Popham, daughter of Sir Home and Lady Popham, died.' No first name, no cause of death; but it was in the shadow of that loss that he had set out to visit the frontiers of his command. And there was worse to come. Yellow fever, which had destroyed whole armies in every West Indian war, and which had helped drive both the British and French out of Haiti, flared up with special virulence that year. The Pophams' daughter died before the epidemic reached its full force, at the start of the hurricane season of July to October, but when it did the effects were devastating, both in the ships of the squadron and, more drastically, in the barracks ashore.

Major-General Conran wrote to Goulburn of 'the sad visitation we have had here during the utmost violence of late malignant Yellow Fever... the dreadful effect of this hideous disease produced despair and consternation, and the moment a man was taken ill he gave himself up for lost.' And he went on to describe how, for eighty days, he helped in the Uppark Hospitals 'those in the greatest extremity, torrents of Black Vomit gushing out, and in the last delirium... Many of my friends and all my white servants perished.' The official return of deaths in the garrison between 1 June and 30 November tells the grim story: 689 officers and men, women and children. In the squadron matters were not much better: in one ship alone, the *Sybille*, there were at one point 159 cases—though the greater proportion did recover. Ships were being used as convalescent homes, and Popham recommended a sea voyage as an effective form of treatment: at least it took them out of the reach of the *Aëdes* mosquitoes which carried the virus.

But the remedy was unsuccessful as far as their son Home was concerned: at the end of November he died at Vera Cruz of 'a pulmonary affection' on board that same *Sybille*, in which he had sailed 'in the hope of deriving benefit from the voyage'. A pulmonary affection, however, does not sound like yellow fever.

Such personal griefs could not, of course, be allowed to interfere with the C-in-C's official duties. The waters round the island, and particularly the approaches to Port Royal and Kingston along the narrow arm of Palisadoes, seem never to have been accurately surveyed, and the Admiral addressed himself to the matter soon after taking command.[7] But by commandeering the yacht *Sea Breeze* for the work, he came up against—not for the first time—the Commissioner of the Navy at Port Royal, a Mr Woodriff. He had charge of the Dockyard, and for the whole period of Popham's tour of duty kept up an unending stream of complaints on the subject of stores, repairs, the behaviour—towards himself—of certain officers of the squadron, and so on and so forth. He comes across as one of those enduring types of petty bureaucrat, obstructive and self-important, after 'fifty-two years of maritime [sic] servitude, forty-four in the Royal Navy', as he wrote defiantly in one of his interminable letters to the long-suffering C-in-C.

'Be assured,' Popham wrote in reply at one point, 'that the Service will be carried on with more advantage to the Public, and certainly with more advantage to every individual, by conciliating any trifling difficulty or irregularity, than by acting under the impression of long lasting irritation.' But it made no difference: the letters, and the occasional exasperating meetings, continued without abatement.

Beyond the narrow world of the Dockyard, beyond Palisadoes, beyond the horizon, the turbulent life of the Caribbean churned on. Sometimes it touched the island, with the arrest of an illegal slave-trader or the hijacking of a schooner by its slave crew who made away with her to Haiti and freedom; in the presence of a suspected privateer off the north coast, or in the odd behaviour of a lieutenant who challenged a captain to a duel for calling him 'lubberly'; or in the engaging person of Sir Gregor MacGregor, His Highness Gregor, Cacique of Poyais, former Adjutant-General to Francisco Miranda and comrade in arms of Simon Bolivar; a soldier of fortune who turned up one day in March 1819 with 400 supporters with the expressed intention of 'recommencing operations against the Spaniards in the Main', his first target Porto Bello. Since Britain was taking some pains to keep out of the struggle for independence in the Spanish colonies, MacGregor, self-styled Captain General of the Forces, New Granada, was given short shrift.[8] Nevertheless, the spirit of independence which Home Popham had glimpsed, and tried to nourish, fifteen years before, had now become irresistible.

5

In Haiti in 1819 and early 1820 President Boyer and King Henry I were on the verge of war, and in February Boyer succeeded in clearing the latter's guerrillas out of the mountains in his half of the country. But Christophe wanted peace: peace which would give him time and opportunity to complete his grandiose plans. To this end he employed Clarkson to try and open negotiations with France for a commercial treaty—though only on condition that Haiti be recognised 'as a free, sovereign and independent state' and Home Popham to mediate between himself and Boyer. In April 1820 Popham visited them both, Boyer at Port-au-Prince first.

There was no eager lieutenant to record their exchanges, and perhaps that is just as well. Boyer proved adamant that he wanted no treaty with Christophe. 'In less than a year,' he said, 'his reign of terror will be ended, and the Haitians of the Artibonite and the North will be once more united with their brothers in the West and South. Christophe is reduced to complete impotence.'

The prediction was accurate. Over the fifty-two year old King—and indeed over the fifty-seven year old Admiral, too—the Furies were gathering. Popham had suffered a slight stroke earlier in the year, for which 'the Bath waters of St Thomas, often beneficial, had not helped him', and in the kingdom of Christophe discontent with his increasingly arbitrary and impatient rule was beginning to bubble ominously. After his abortive mission to Port-au-Prince, Popham spent five days at Cap Henry. Like Conran on the previous occasion, one 'would have enjoyed a peep', but the curtains at *Sans Souci* remain drawn. Popham, Cole says, 'had developed a great respect and admiration for him, a liking that Christophe returned, taking great pains over the entertainment that he provided for the admiral and paying marked attention to his advice.'

That advice was specifically to keep trying to reach an accommodation with Boyer; and on his return to Port Royal, Popham wrote a a stiff letter to Boyer, underlining Christophe's sincerity in wanting peace between them. It went unanswered; but in any event, for one of the protaganists immediately, and for another very soon, matters were no longer within their control.

6

On June 3 1820 Home Popham wrote to Croker at the Admiralty to say that he was forced to avail himself 'of the option of appointing a successor', owing to the state of his health.

> I should have returned to England in the *Iphigenia*, but that I am under severe medical treatment, and this is the first day that I have quitted my room.
>
> I have been in the habit all my life of using a great deal of exercise, which I have been prevented doing in this climate, and it has brought on a great determination of blood to the head and shows a considerable disposition to Paralysis; and as I have had two attacks within four months, they must be considered as premonitory of something more serious.

His three doctors agreed. In their medical report they referred to 'His known anxiety upon all points of business, his extreme feelings upon the severe visitation of sickness in this island during the last season; with the calamities by which his Family has been visited, and the marked predisposition which has been now shown to Paralysis...' It was essential, they said, that he should return home at once.

He was a sick man, and had been all that year, but it had not stopped him visiting Haiti nor, as he wrote in another letter to Croker on the same day as he resigned, cruising farther afield. In a search for 'suitable spar timber I took an early opportunity of examining the Cape Spiritu Santo and Charlotte Harbours in the northwest Coast of Florida, and the Coast of Texas.' And on 15 June, the day he and Elizabeth sailed for England, he sent a long report to the Admiralty on the subject of smuggling on the north coast of the island. His 'anxiety upon all points of business' persisted to the last day of his final command. Ironically, their ship was the *Sybille* in which their son had died: they arrived at Spithead on 26 July.

NOTES ON CHAPTER XIX

1. But according to Cdr WE. May, Popham's design was finally adopted in that year.
2. The Royal Guelphic Order, another creation of the Prince Regent's, in 1815, had Hanoverian connections, and appears either as KCH or, less correctly, as KCG. Few were awarded (only one other in 1818) and in 1837, on the accession of Queen Victoria and under the rules of the Salic Law, it became a purely Hanoverian Order.

3. The Spanish *Iphigenia* (confusingly, there was a British ship of the same name in the same waters) was wrecked, and Popham sent one of the squadron to her assistance.

4. Thomas Clarkson (1760-1846), founder with Granville Sharp of the Abolitionist Society, was a close friend and associate of Christophe.

5. The monitorial system of education established by Joseph Lancaster (1778-1838) and introduced into Haiti by the English teachers.

6. For much of the information on Haiti, and Popham's relations with Christophe I am indebted to *Christophe, King of Haiti* by Hubert Cole. There is a splendid evocation of Haitian society under Christophe in *The Traveller's Tree* by Patrick Leigh Fermor—though it was not Popham who rescued the Queen and Princesses on Christophe's downfall for he had left Jamaica three months before. Christophe himself suffered a near-mortal stroke during the rebellion against his rule and shot himself on 8 October. Within a few months everything he had created and striven for had disintegrated.

7. Various letters referring to survey work in Jamaican waters, instruments, etc, are in the Hydrographic Dept, MOD (N), at Taunton; and I am indebted to Lt. Cdr. Andrew David for drawing my attention to them.

8. MacGregor's dates are uncertain, but after his capture—and subsequent loss—of Porto Bello, he tried to start an Utopia on the Mosquito Coast. This also failed, and he finished up in Venezuela, honoured as one of the heroes of the struggle for independence. (DNB)

Epilogue
1820

WITHIN SEVEN weeks of his return to England, Home Popham was dead. He and Elizabeth had gone to Cheltenham, presumably on account of his health, and there, for a time, he seemed to be improving. Although he wrote to a friend in late August, 'I have been troubled with my pains in the head these last few days, and pulsation has been affected from 73 to 59,' his handwriting, his correspondent noted, was as firm and his style as clear as ever. A few days after writing that letter, however, on 11 September 1820, he suffered a third, and fatal, stroke. He was buried, with his sword, five days later, in the churchyard of St Michael and All Angels, Sunninghill, not far from his home; and there his memorial may still be seen today.[1]

No account of his funeral appeared in the papers, and the obituaries were, for the most part, brief, without warmth or distinction, and, curiously enough, identical. 'We are sorry to announce the death of that very active and meritorious Officer... few men have seen more service, or displayed more talent.. he rose entirely by his own merits...'etc; and nearly all of them ended in 1803 with the words: 'His public employment and service have since been on a larger scale, and, as a matter of history, are generally known.'[2]

Only the *Gentleman's Magazine*[3] went a little further, offering the, rather uncharitable, suggestion that his appointment as C-in-C, Jamaica was 'equal to a second acquittal in regard to the vast sums which he was accused of having embezzled, under charges for repairs and stores; that command has been generally bestowed for the purpose of repairing the indigence which enterprising commanders might have incurred in the course of long service.' Considering that he had been completely cleared of the accusations arising out of the *Romney* affair fifteen years before, and had done a great deal of notable work since, this was no more than gratuitous muck-raking, and shows how inexpungible the stain from that episode had proved. In parenthesis it is worth making the point that if he had embezzled so much, he would hardly have been indigent. However, when his will was proved on 23 September, his personal property came to rather less than £18,000: not by any means a fortune, though considerably more than it sounds in current terms.

The *Gentleman's Magazine* did have the grace to note that 'His telegraphic improvements were no less conspicuous for professional ability and excellence', and concluded, 'Perhaps Sir Home has not left one Officer behind of his own age who has seen more service, or been employed in more important affairs.' And that was that.

There was one notable exception to these reach-me-down epicedia. A gentleman signing himself simply 'D', and describing himself as a friend of forty-five years standing, supplied the *Morning Post* with a full column behind the ineffable rhetoric and banality of which there does emerge a warmth of affection and admiration which the others so noticeably lacked. In particular—though in a phrase that might have been improved—he extols the marriage of Home and Elizabeth: '...two bodies so perfectly animated with one spirit...', and quotes Popham as declaring, 'I have a wife that compensates me for all that is frail in friends and malignant in enemies'—though out of Elizabeth's hearing! A happy marriage and unswerving loyalty to his friends are the particular qualities the writer chose to emphasise in over a thousand words of the woolliest encomium; but at least he wrote from the heart.

The truth was that the exploits for which he might have been justly applauded had largely been achieved eight, ten, fifteen years before; and, as is the way of the world, were either forgotten or overshadowed by the scandals. Perhaps it is only surprising that none of his obituarists mentioned the smuggling of tea ashore at Dungeness. Now when he is remembered at all, it is more for his achievements than his indiscretions, with the exception of the Buenos Ayres adventure: his revolutionary work on signalling, his mastery of amphibious operations: and his interest in every aspect of seamanship, navigation and hydrography, and the tools of those trades, the sextant, the chronometer, the compass. In a time of wars when the ideal naval hero was a Nelson or a Hood, a Duncan or a Howe, it was his misfortune to have missed the famous battles and to have become instead a specialist in a rather unpopular discipline—for there was rarely much love lost between the Navy and the Army on the occasions when they were compelled to work together. At this distance, however, it is possible to view his achievements, as well as his attractive, vulnerable, impulsive character, more clearly. Certainly few of his contemporaries had careers more various or more intriguing: Sidney Smith and Thomas Cochrane come to mind as two of those sailors whose lives followed a comparably unconventional course, and their biographies have been written. Popham's has not, and it is time he was given his due.

Despite the lack of any of his letters to his family and friends, his personality emerges with all its complexity and contradictions: behind the insecurity, and indeed part of it, a keen sensitivity; behind the quick brain and the high professional ability, a dangerous over-enthusiasm; behind the charm, a deep humanity. All in all, a good man; as someone said of him, 'a pleasant man, but a *dasher*'.

There is one final irony. His epitaph, on the handsome memorial at Sunninghill which celebrates in symbols his signal book, his flags and his semaphore, and in words his main achievements, Copenhagen, Buenos Ayres, North Coast of Spain and Cape of Good Hope, has been totally erased by wind and weather.[5]

THE END

NOTES TO EPILOGUE

1. It lies to the north of the west door of the church, close to the new hall, and consists of a plinth with four panels, surmounted by a broken column topped by an urn and flames. Mr W. J. Franklin, the Churchwarden, says in a private letter to the author: 'During excavations for the new Hall... the side of the vault which is brick built was exposed, and while uncovered we got the builder to make good a small portion which had decayed. He told me that in the vault there are three lead coffins on top of each other, and with the aid of a torch they could see the Admiral's sword stood on end at the far end of the vault.' Mr Franklin goes on to say that a service was held by the grave on the centenary of his death, and adds: 'Would be rather nice to have the inscription recut on the Memorial!' I agree, and intend that it shall be done.

2. Obituaries appeared within a week in the *Morning Chronicle, Courier, Morning Herald, Globe, Bell's Weekly Messenger* and the *Gloucester Journal*, among others. Most of them were virtually word for word the same; but the last included all his decorations, and decided that he was 'gallant and distinguished'.

3. *The Naval Chronicle* had unfortunately stopped publication two years before.

4. Attributed to Mrs Nicholson Calvert, and quoted in *The History of Parliament: the House of Commons 1790-1820*, (1986).

5. In truth the missing epitaph is no loss; it went as follows: 'In memory of Rear-Admiral Sir Home Riggs Popham, KCB, KCG, KM, FRS, who died at Cheltenham September 11th 1820 aged 58 years. Affection's fondest terms are found too weak to state his conduct as husband or a father, and as a friend 'twere difficult to do him justice, yet memory retains what language fails t'express. His public services were great and various but those let history tell. This page posthumous has to record still nobler triumphs, these his great success excited envy and envy persecution but both were foil'd in their attempts upon his character, for Truth was supreme and Justice found the verdict while he added most feelingly this last, the best and strongest confirmation - forgiveness.'

   Just to round the story off: Elizabeth outlived her husband by 45 years, to die in Bath in 1866 at the age of 94. Hers is one of the lead coffins referred to above; in the third is interred, for some reason, their grand-daughter Catherine Mary, who died twelve years later. Two of their sons, William and Brunswick, became admirals, while their sister Caroline married John Packenham, who also became an admiral. Mary went her own way and married into the Royal Horse Artillery. (Details from *A West Country Family*: op.cit.)

ACKNOWLEDGEMENTS

Among the many people who have helped me during the research and writing of *A Damned Cunning Fellow,* I should like to thank especially Lt.Cdr. A C F David, formerly of the Admiralty Hydrographic Department, who guided me in my search for Home Popham's charts and, despite a formidable programme of work of his own, went out of his way to send me useful references; Mr Quentin Keynes for the loan of numerous books and Popham's and Thompson's Journals; Mrs Anne Maier for invaluable help in unravelling the activities of the 'Ostenders'; Professor Dorinda Evans of Emory University, Atlanta, Ga. for leading me to Mather Brown's portrait; and its owner, Mr Walter Impert, for photographing it and allowing me to reproduce it on the book's jacket. Mrs Jill Kinahan, Curator of Historical Archaeology at State Museum, Windhoek, has been generous with information on the Namibian survey voyage and related matters; and Mr Randolph Vigne kindly sent me his paper on the secret motive behind that expedition. Through Michael Popham I received not only enthusiastic encouragement but also introduction to Mr Boris Reford of Montreal who owns, and sent me the photograph of, the 'piece of plate'. Dr N A M Rodger put fresh heart into me at a time when Home Popham seemed likely to slip back into the obscurity from which I was trying to rescue him, as did Dr David Procter and Dr R J B Knight of the National Maritime Museum. Alan Popham, whose father produced *A West Country Family* continues to be most generous with information culled from that work's sources; and Phoebe Mason, who edited the manuscript, provided inestimable help and encouragement during the long months of research. There were many others who provided lesser, but still important, contributions, too many to name individually. My thanks to them all, and not least to those often nameless members of the staffs of the libraries and institutions, here and in America, that are listed in the bibliography. They were universally patient with my requests and prompt with help and advice. Finally, to my wife Mary, special thanks for all her practical help and enthusiasm. Without her support, it is unlikely that the book would ever have been published.

H.P.

SOURCES AND BIBLIOGRAPHY

Manuscript Sources

Public Record Office, Kew
Admiralty Records, notably the Letters from Flag Officers and commanding officers to the Secretary of the Admiralty in ADM 1, a veritable treasury of information. Captains' Logs, records of courts-martial, etc. are also at Kew.

Public Record Office, Chancery Lane
Joseph Popham's letters and appointments are in *Morocco FO 52*, Vol. 1 and *State Papers, Barbary States*, Vols 20, 21.

India House
The Minutes of the Secret Committee of the East India Company are in the India Office Library; as is the reference to the *Madona* (see Chapter IV), (Ch) L/MAR/Misc C125.

National Maritime Museum Library
Lieutenant's Logs and Journals are kept here, including the Anonymous Log (N/S/5) quoted in Chapter XVIII, and Robert Deans's Journal, JOD/43.

Letter Collections

Manuscript
Don Papers. BL Addl MSS 46702 (see Chapter V).
Grey, 1st Earl, Papers. University of Durham.
Melville, Henry Dundas, 1st Viscount, Papers. Scottish Record Office.
Wellesley, Arthur, Viscount Wellington, MSS. BL Addl MSS, 13756, 7, 8.

Other Journals

Captain Edward Thompson: Autograph Journal. BL Addl MSS 46120
Thomas Boulden Thompson, Home Riggs Popham: The Journals of these two young lieutenants, *Narrative of a Voyage performed in HMS Nautilus* and *Voyage to South Africa*, were kindly lent to the author by Quentin Keynes, Esq. Other copies of Thompson's Journal exist, one in the PRO, and a version of both his and Popham's is to be published by the State Museum, Windhoek, Namibia, with a commentary by the Curator, Historical Archaeology, Mrs Jill Kinahan.

Other Sources

There are more of Popham's letters, some of them duplicates of those in the PRO and elsewhere, in the following libraries:

William L. Clements Library, University of Michigan, Ann Arbor
The Huntington, San Marino, California
William R. Perkins Library, Duke University, Durham, N. Carolina
The National Library of Jamaica holds a Letter Book of Popham's.

Published Works (NRS: Navy Records Society)

Aitchison, C.U.: *Treaties, Engagements & Sunnuds*, Vol VIII. (Calcutta 1874)
Almanac Royal d'Hayti. 1816-20
Anon: *Memoirs of the Administration* (Benjamin Tucker). (1805)
Ardouin, Beaubrun: *Etudes sur l'Histoire d'Haiti*. (1853-60)
Barrow, Sir John: *An Autobiographical Memoir*. (London 1847)
Blackwood's Edinburgh Magazine, Vols 9, 10
Brougham, Henry: Life and Times of, (1871)
Bryant, Arthur: *The Years of Endurance*. (London 1942, 1975)
        The Years of Victory.   (London 1944, 1975)
        The Age of Elegance.   (London 1950)
Cambridge History of India, Vol V.
Castlereagh, Lord: Memoirs & Correspondence, Vol VII. (1850-53)
Cobbett, William: *Political Register*. (1804)
               Parliamentary Reports.
Cole, Hubert: *Christophe, King of Hayti*. (1967)
Commons' Journals: *Passim*
Crawford, Capt. A.: *Reminiscences of a Naval Officer*. (1857)
Creevey, Thomas: *The Creevey Papers*. (1963)
Croker, J. W.: *The Croker Papers*. (1884)
de Madariaga, Salvador: *The Fall of the Spanish American Empire*. (1947)
de Rougement, H.: *History of Lloyd's Patriotic Fund*. (1914)
Dictionary of National Biography (DNB). *passim*
Dillon, Sir William: *Narrative of Professional Adventures*, 1790-1839. (NRS 971)
Dropmore: Report on the Manuscripts of J. B. Fortescue Esq preserved at Dropmore.
    (Historical MSS Commission)
Evans, Dorinda: *Mather Brown*. (Wesleyan University Press 1982)
Fast, Howard: Term Reports of Cases in the Court of King's Bench, 1801-14
Fernyhough, Lt Robert: *Military Memoirs of Four Brothers, by the Survivor*. (1829)
Forbes, Vernon S.: *Pioneer Travellers of South Africa*. 1750-1800
Fortescue, Sir J. W.: *History of the British Army*. (1899-1912)
Fox, Henry, Baron Holland: *Further Memoirs*. (1905)
Fullom, S. W.: *Life of General Sir Howard Douglas*. (1863)
Fulton, Robert: *Torpedo War and Undersea Explosion*. (USA 1810, London 1908)
        'Torpedo War', (*Magazine of History* 1914)
Furber, Holden: *The John Company at Work*. (Harvard 1948)
Gardner, Cdr. James Anthony: *Recollections*. (NRS 31)
Gates, Dr David: *The Spanish Ulcer*. (1986)
Gentleman's magazine, passim
Gillespie, Major Alexander, RM: *Gleanings and Remarks collected during Many Months*
    Resident in Buenos Ayres. (1818)
Hickey, William: *Memoirs*. Vol III 1782-90.) (1913-25)
High Court of Admiralty: Cases determined in Prize Cases. (1905)
History of Parliament: (1986)
Hook, Theodore: *Life of Sir David Baird*. (1832)
Howard, D. and Agers, J.: *China for the West*. (London and NY 1978)
Hutcheon, Wallace S.: *Robert Fulton, Pioneer of Undersea Warfare*. (Naval
    Institute Press, Annapolis, 1981)
Keegan, John: *The Price of Admiralty*. (1988)
Keith Papers: Letters and Papers of Admiral Viscount Keith. (NRS 62, 90, 96)
Lewis, Michael: *The Navy of Britain*. (1949)
London Gazette. passim

246

London Gazette. passim
Longford, Elizabeth: *Wellington: the Years of the Sword.* (1969)
Macpherson, P.: *History of European Commerce in India.* (1812)
Martin, Admiral of the Fleet Sir Thomas Byam: *Journals and Letters, 1773-1854.* (NRS 12)
Mead, Commander H.P.: 'The Story of the Semaphore'. (*Mariner's Mirror,* Vol 20, 1934)
Naval Chronicle. passim
Oman, Carola: *Nelson.* (1947)
Oman, Sir Charles: *History of the Peninsular War.* (7 Vols, 1902-30)
Parkinson, C. Northcote: *Trade in the Eastern Seas.* (1937, 1966)
    War in the Eastern Seas, 1793-1815. (1954)

Parliamentary Debates. *passim*
Parliamentary Papers (Misc) Vol. X '...respecting the Ship L'Etrusco' (1808)
Perrin, W. G.: The Second Capture of the Cape of Good Hope. (Naval Miscellany, Vol III. NRS 63)
Philips, Sir Cyril H.: *The East India Company.* (1961)
    David Scott, Director of the E.I.Co. (Camden 3rd Series, 1951)
Phillips, John G: *China Trade Porcelain.* (1956)
Piratical States of Barbary, The: A Complete History. 'A Gentleman' (1750)
Popham, F. W.: *A West Country Family: The Pophams since 1150.* (Privately printed, 1976)
Popham, Rear-Admiral Sir Home Riggs: *A Concise Statement...* (1805)
    A Description of Prince of Wales Island... (1791, & with charts 1799)
    Telegraphic Signals or Marine Vocabulary. (1803-12)
Richardson, William: *A Mariner of England.* (1908)
Rolt, L. T. R.: *Isambard Kingdom Brunel.* (1957)
St Vincent, Earl: *Life and Correspondence,* ed. EP Brenton. (1838)
Shaw, William A.: *The Knights of England.* Vol I (1906)
Spencer, George, 2nd Earl: Private Papers. (NRS 46, 48, 58)
Trial at Large between Captain Ross Donnelly and Sir Home Popham. (1807)
Trial of Sir Home Popham:
    Verbatim Report with Preface by 'Aeschylus (heavily annotated by Benjamin Tucker.)
        BLG 19449
    Ditto. BL 1132.d.31.
Ustinov, Peter: *Dear Me.* (1977)
Vassall, Elizabeth, Baroness Holland: *Journal.* (1908)
Ward, Robert Plumer: *Memoirs of the Political Life of,* (1850)
Wellington, 1st Duke of: *Despatches,* ed. Col. Gurwood. 12 Vols (1834-9)
    Supplementary Despatches and Memoranda. 15 Vols (1859-72)
Wheeler and Broadley: *Napoleon and the Invasion of England.* (1908)
Wilkie, Lt. Col. Fletcher: 'Recollections of the British Army in the Late Revolutionary Wars.' (*United Services Journal,* Vols 1-4, 1836)
Wilson, Geoffrey: *The Old Telegraphs.* (1976)
Wilson, Timothy: *Flags at Sea.* (HMSO, 1986)
Windham, William: *Diary, 1784-1810.* (1866)
Wright, Iona S. and Nekhorn, Lisa M: *Historical Diary of Argentina.* (New Jersey and London, 1978)

INDEX

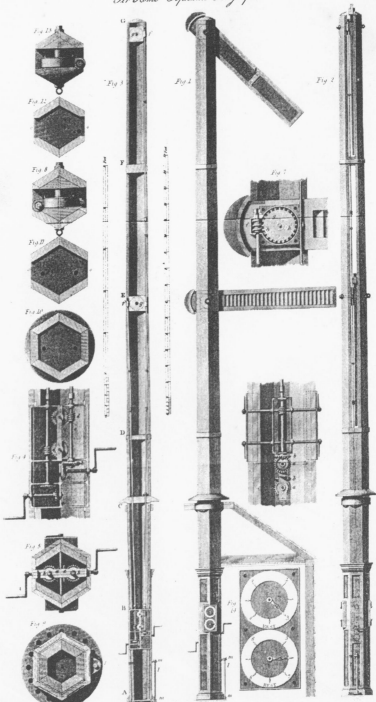

Fig 13.

Fig 12.

Fig 8.

Fig 11.

Fig 10.

Fig 4.

Fig 5.

Fig 6.

Fig 3.

Fig 1.

Fig 2.

Fig 7.

Fig 14.

REST

REST

Drawn by J. Clement

Engraved by J. Bow